Australian Critical Decisio

The 1980s was a time of significant social, political and cultural change. In Australia, the law was pivotal to these changes. The two High Court cases that this book explores – *Koowarta v Bjelke-Petersen* (1982) and the *Commonwealth v Tasmania* (1983) – are famous legally as they marked a decisive reckoning by the Court with both international law and federal constitutionalism. Yet these cases also offer a significant marker of Australia in the 1980s: a shift to a different form of political engagement, nationally and internationally, on complex questions about race and the environment. This book brings these cases together for the first time. It does so to explore not only the legal legacy and relationship between *Koowarta* and *Tasmanian Dam*, but also to reflect on how Australians experience their law in time and place, and why those experiences might require more than the usual legal records. The authors include significant figures in Australian public life, some of whom were key participants in the cases, as well as established and respected scholars of law, history and Indigenous studies. This collection offers a combination of personal recollections of the cases, as well as a consideration of their ongoing significance in Australian life.

This book was originally published as two special issues of the *Griffith Law Review*.

Ann Genovese is an Associate Professor at Melbourne Law School, Australia, and an historian of modern Australian jurisprudence. Her projects aim to bring to life stories of how Australians have practised and experienced their law since 1950. Recent publications include *Sovereignty: Frontiers of Possibility* (2013) and *Rights and Redemption: History, Law, Indigenous People* (2008).

Australian Critical Decisions

Remembering the *Koowarta* and *Tasmanian Dam* cases

Edited by
Ann Genovese

Routledge
Taylor & Francis Group
LONDON AND NEW YORK

First published 2017
by Routledge

2 Park Square, Milton Park, Abingdon, Oxfordshire OX14 4RN
52 Vanderbilt Avenue, New York, NY 10017

Routledge is an imprint of the Taylor & Francis Group, an informa business

First issued in paperback 2018

British Library Cataloguing in Publication Data
A catalogue record for this book is available from the British Library

ISBN 13: 978-1-138-69205-3 (hbk)
ISBN 13: 978-0-367-07706-8 (pbk)

Typeset in Times New Roman
by RefineCatch Limited, Bungay, Suffolk

Publisher's Note
The publisher accepts responsibility for any inconsistencies that may have arisen during the conversion of this book from journal articles to book chapters, namely the possible inclusion of journal terminology.

Disclaimer
Every effort has been made to contact copyright holders for their permission to reprint material in this book. The publishers would be grateful to hear from any copyright holder who is not here acknowledged and will undertake to rectify any errors or omissions in future editions of this book.

Contents

Citation Information

The chapters in this book were originally published in the *Griffith Law Review*. When citing this material, please use the original volume, issue information and page numbering for each article, as follows:

Chapter 1
Koowarta: A Warrior for Justice: A Brief History of Queensland's Racially Discriminatory Legislation and the Aboriginal Litigants Who Fought It
M. Langton
Griffith Law Review, volume 23, issue 1 (March 2014), pp. 16–34

Chapter 2
Internal and external affairs: the Koowarta *case in context*
Hilary Charlesworth
Griffith Law Review, volume 23, issue 1 (March 2014), pp. 35–43

Chapter 3
Justice in whose eyes? Why lawyers should read black Australian literature
Nicole Watson
Griffith Law Review, volume 23, issue 1 (March 2014), pp. 44–60

Chapter 4
Recovering the foundations of Koowarta: *the struggle of the Aboriginal Land Fund Commission to purchase land in Queensland*
Alexander Reilly
Griffith Law Review, volume 23, issue 1 (March 2014), pp. 61–78

Chapter 5
Koowarta*: constitutional landmark, transition point or missed opportunity?*
Sean Brennan and Megan Davis
Griffith Law Review, volume 23, issue 1 (March 2014), pp. 79–91

Chapter 6
Practising law and politics in 1980s' Australia: the liberating effect of Koowarta v Bjelke-Petersen
Maureen Tehan
Griffith Law Review, volume 23, issue 1 (March 2014), pp. 92–109

Chapter 7
Koowarta *and the rival Indigenous international: our place as Indigenous peoples in the international*
Mark McMillan
Griffith Law Review, volume 23, issue 1 (March 2014), pp. 110–126

Chapter 8
Koowarta: a vital turning point for Aboriginal rights and Australia
Summing up the symposium
The Hon Michael Kirby AC CMG
Griffith Law Review, volume 23, issue 1 (March 2014), pp. 127–144

Chapter 9
Reflections on legal issues in the Tasmanian Dams Case
The Hon Sir Anthony Mason AC KBE GBM
Griffith Law Review, volume 24, issue 1 (March 2015), pp. 16–21

Chapter 10
The Tasmanian Dam Case*: an advocate's memoir*
The Hon Michael Black AC QC
Griffith Law Review, volume 24, issue 1 (March 2015), pp. 22–40

Chapter 11
Limitlessness in Australian Constitutional Legal Narrative: The memory of Black's Address in the Tasmanian Dam Case
Rebecca LaForgia
Griffith Law Review, volume 24, issue 1 (March 2015), pp. 41–57

Chapter 12
Experiences of coming to law: An Interview with Bob Brown on the Tasmanian wilderness society as client in the Tasmanian Dam Case
Martin Clark
Griffith Law Review, volume 24, issue 1 (March 2015), pp. 58–67

Chapter 13
Nineteen eighty three: A jurisographic report on Commonwealth v Tasmania
Ann Genovese and Shaun McVeigh
Griffith Law Review, volume 24, issue 1 (March 2015), pp. 68–88

Chapter 14
Tasmanian Dams *and Australia's Relationship with International Law*
Madelaine Chiam
Griffith Law Review, volume 24, issue 1 (March 2015), pp. 89–105

Chapter 15

Making sense of indigeneity, aboriginality and identity: race as a Constitutional conundrum since 1983
Mark McMillan and Martin Clark
Griffith Law Review, volume 24, issue 1 (March 2015), pp. 106–126

Chapter 16

Law and the practices of 'damming': Tasmanian Dams Case *as a turning point*
Lee Godden
Griffith Law Review, volume 24, issue 1 (March 2015), pp. 127–146

Acknowledgements

There are many people to thank for their help in bringing this book to life. First, I would like to thank all of the contributors, who generously committed themselves to the project. It has been a pleasure and honour to work with all of them. Second, I would like to thank my colleagues at Melbourne Law School who helped organize the 2012 and 2013 Turning Point Symposia, where these papers were first heard and discussed. In particular, I thank the then directors of the three centres at Melbourne Law School who supported the project: Professor Adrienne Stone (Centre for Comparative Constitutional Studies); Professor Lee Godden (Centre for Resources, Energy and Environmental Law); and Professor Di Otto (Institute International Law and the Humanities). At Melbourne Law School, the Dean Professor Carolyn Evans, Emeritus Professor Cheryl Saunders, and the Michael D Kirby Chair of International Law Professor Anne Orford also gave important institutional and personal support to the project, for which I thank them. Robin Gardner and her team at the Melbourne Law School Research Service: Louise Ellis, Fiona MacDowall, Cate Read, Tom Wood, Dan Wiseman, Andrew Butler and Skye Chapman have all been wonderful to work with. They all gave a great deal of time and energy to the publication of the essays after the symposia, for which I will always be grateful. Most importantly, I thank Vesna Stefanovski, who was in all ways a joint convener of the 1982 and 1983 Turning Points symposia. Third, at *Griffith Law Review* I thank Managing Editors Tim Peters and Edward Mussawir for their recognition that 1982 and 1983 raised important jurisprudential questions and histories that would resonate with the journal's readership. I also thank them for the great deal of hard work, and good humour, in bringing the journal editions to press, and for their institutional assistance with the reissue of the journals with Routledge. At Routledge, Peter Gane, Emily Ross, Reanna Young, Jess Harrison and Rhona Carroll have made the reissue possible, and done so with warmth and care.

Lastly, on a personal note, I thank my friends: Ann Curthoys, Julie Evans, Lee Godden, Mark McMillan, Shaun McVeigh, Peter Rush, Maureen Tehan. Our conversations are threaded through this book, and your commitment to work together on things that matter makes that work a pleasure.

INTRODUCTION
Australian Critical Decisions: Remembering the *Koowarta* and *Tasmanian Dam* cases

Ann Genovese

Introduction

This book began its life at symposia to mark the thirtieth anniversaries of the 1982 High Court decision *Koowarta v Bjelke Petersen,* and the 1983 High Court decision *Commonwealth v Tasmania.*[1] All anniversaries are of course occasions to reflect upon events. They offer a form of ceremony that includes the opportunity for participants and witnesses, and inheritors and custodians of the event's legacies, to tell stories to a gathered audience. The purpose of staging a ceremony to commemorate these significant Australian constitutional cases was to understand them better as judgments. It was also to consider them as contested hearings that shaped, and were shaped by, the relationships between a *polis* and its law – as public trials. Gathering together to show a decision as a public trial involves two activities, as I describe in the Introductions to the special editions of the journal *Griffith Law Review,* where the essays in this book were previously published.[2] The first activity is about record keeping. The essays you are about to read collect records of *Koowarta* and *Tasmanian Dam* as events of public law and public participation, some of which were available at the time and open to review, and others created for the symposia, available only as a consequence of distance and reflection. By drawing these different sets of records of *Tasmanian Dam* and *Koowarta* together, this book gives form and meaning to the events of 1982 and 1983 as a projects of the 1980s. In doing so, 'Critical Decisions' also acts as a record of our own time, and understands its purpose is to review, refresh, and publicise these judgments as of critical importance to accounts of Australia since the 1980s, and to make the law and its institutions central to those accounts.

This combined task of record and review is a conventional practice for historians, and yet remains a tentative activity in the legal academy, particularly in the writing of modern Australian (and also international and transnational) legal history. It is however a task that is necessary to allow the formation and experience of jurisprudence that remains close to the present to be known and made available to the widest possible

---

[1] *Koowarta v Bjelke-Petersen* (1982) 153 CLR 168 (hereafter 'Koowarta'); *Commonwealth v Tasmania* (1983) 158 CLR 1 (hereafter 'Tasmanian Dam case' or 'Tasmanian Dam'). The symposia were called 'Turning Point 1982: Remembering Koowarta', and 'Turning Point: 1983: Remembering Commonwealth v Tasmania'.

[2] This book consolidates the following volumes: Special Issue: Critical Decisions: *Commonwealth v Tasmania* 1983 (2015) 24(1) *Griffith Law Review;* Special Issue: Critical Decisions: *Koowarta v Bjelke-Petersen* 1982 (2014) 23(1) *Griffith Law Review*. Genovese (2014a) pp 1–15; Genovese (2015a), pp 1–15.

audience.[3] Undertaking this jurisprudential task, and demonstrating that it is a collective activity, is the primary consideration, and contribution, of this book.

The conditions of viewing: the contributors

The papers on *Koowarta*, in Section One, are by Marcia Langton, Hilary Charlesworth, Nicole Watson, Alexander Reilly, Megan Davis, Sean Brennan, Maureen Tehan, Mark McMillan and former High Court Justice His Honour Michael Kirby AC.[4] All of them have taken up important duties in Australian public life. All of them have also taken up different personae in relation to *Koowarta:* as actors in its original performance, as inheritors and teachers of its jurisprudence, as official scribes of its legacies. (Sometimes of course they have played more than one of those parts in their own lives, as I will explain below). The papers on *Tasmanian Dams,* in Section Two, are by former High Court Chief Justice His Honour Sir Anthony Mason AC KBE GBM, (in 1982 and 1983, part of the Majority in both *Koowarta* and *Dam*), former Federal Court Chief Justice His Honour Michael Black AC QC, (in 1983 advocate for the Tasmanian Wilderness Society [TWS], who appeared as amicus curiae in the case), and former Australian Senator and Leader and Founder of the Australian Greens Party, Dr Bob Brown (in 1983 leader of TWS). All three consider not only what the case meant as a major event of Australia in the 1980s, but also reflect on the duties they took up as judge, advocate, and client in 1983, at the High Court. The other contributors in Section Two are legal scholars: Rebecca La Forgia, Mark McMillan and Martin Clark, Lee Godden, Madeline Chiam, Shaun McVeigh and myself. We explain the significance of the case over the past thirty years to the development of areas and categories of law in which we hold expertise. But we also seek to demonstrate in our writing how other experiences of living with law in Australia join our doctrinal exegesis, and shape our address to the case. This is as teachers in Australian law schools, but also as indigenous men of law (McMillan), collaborators (McVeigh and Genovese, McMillan and Clark,) interlocutors (Clark), and as practitioners of philosophy, geography, literary theory and Australian history (McVeigh, Godden, La Forgia, Genovese, and Chiam).[5]

All the contributors to this book, in their stories, show the movements between what a community considers orthodox and heterodox about the experiences of law in life; and the political, moral or theoretical motivations for why those movements occur. This includes understanding how one record or telling of an event of law enables a retelling or a review of another, in a different idiom and by different actors, for a different experience of the present. These considerations are of general importance for what Shaun McVeigh and I call *jurisography*, or the practices that join the writing of history and the conduct of jurisprudence.[6] Understanding the relationship and diversity of records of lawful experience includes making plain what the cases decided, and how the matters came before the High Court. As such, it is part of my task in this introduction to set the scene for readers unfamiliar with *Koowarta and Tasmanian Dam* as High Court decisions, as well as to recall the events of 1982 and 1983 for readers who are already familiar with the cases.

---

[3] Compare for example: Lee and Winterton (2003); Crotty and Roberts (2008), and a forthcoming special collection on *Tasmanian Dams* by Coper and Stellios. Our project here is to join these kinds of accounts together, and ask additional questions about the nature of jurisprudence as integral to both forms of history writing.

[4] (2014) 23(1) *Griffith Law Review*.

[5] (2015) 24(1) *Griffith Law Review.*

[6] Genovese (2014b), p 444; Genovese and McVeigh (2015a), pp 69–70; Genovese (2014a), p 2.

The practices of recording: the cases

In *Koowarta*, the High Court was asked to determine whether the *Racial Discrimination Act 1975* (Cth) was valid. That question carried relevant facts. John Koowarta, of the Winychanam /Wik people of Cape York, had made an application on behalf of his people for financial support from a Commonwealth statutory body, the Aboriginal Land Fund Commission (ALFC). The funds were to assist the purchase of the Archer River Pastoral Holdings, a lease that lay over Wik country. The ALFC had been established in 1974. It was a direct result of the 1967 Referendum, which had removed the constitutional barriers of the Federal Parliament to make laws for the Aboriginal peoples of Australia.[7] The ALFC's purpose was to assist Aboriginal peoples who lacked other financial means to purchase the leases that lay over traditional lands (if available) and to transfer that title to newly formed Indigenous Corporations who would have responsibility for the land. (Reilly, in his essay, explains how this occurred). In Koowarta's case, the ALFC made a decision in his favour. The Archer River Holdings, however, were subject to conditions for sale or transfer, conditions that were lawfully enacted under the *Land Act 1962* (Qld)[8]. The main condition was that any property transaction that concerned the lease was subject to the veto of the Minister for Lands of the State of Queensland. Relying on these powers, the Minister refused permission to the AFLC to purchase the lease for Koowarta. In Australia then, (and now, as Kirby forcefully critiques in this volume)[9] there was no common law right to the reasons for administrative decisions. That reasons were given in this case by the Minister (again, as Kirby notes) was a matter of politics, not of law. These reasons relied on the executive policy, that "[t]he Queensland Government does not view favourably proposals to acquire large areas of additional freehold or leasehold land for development by Aborigines or Aboriginal groups in isolation."[10] In Queensland at this time there was an absence of authority capable of refuting or rendering unlawful that state policy on the basis of Indigenous land entitlement. Instead, Koowarta, assisted by his legal team, made an application to the High Court arguing that Queensland Government, led by the Premier Joh Bjelke-Petersen, discriminated against them on the basis of their status as Aboriginal people. They argued that this was unlawful, as it was contrary to the *Racial Discrimination Act 1975* (Cth).[11] The Queensland Government, in response, argued that the Act itself was invalid – that the Federal Parliament lacked jurisdiction, and that Queensland state law, and authority, would prevail in the absence of any relevant federal law. Koowarta's legal team countered that the *Racial Discrimination Act* should be read as valid under the race power (s 51 (xxvi)), which after the constitutional amendments in 1967 enabled the Federal Parliament to make special laws for the people of any one race, and that this included protection from discrimination based on being a member of the Aboriginal race. Alternatively, they argued that the external affairs power (s 51 (xxix)) was

---

[7] These complexities have been considered in *Kartinyeri v The Commonwealth* (1998) 195 CLR 337, and as Kirby, Tehan, Brennan and Davis note in this volume, remain complex and unresolved legally and politically.

[8] *Land Act 1962* (Qld) s 4(2).

[9] Kirby been arguing this judicially also for some time, see *Osmond v Public Service Board of NSW* [1984] 3 NSWLR 447, reversed in *Public Service Board of NSW v Osmond* (1986) 159 CLR 656.

[10] *Koowarta* (1982) 153 CLR 168 at 20, per Gibbs CJ.

[11] As per the *Racial Discrimination Act 1975* (Cth) ss 9 and 12. Note this is a truncated procedural history: there were other measures built into for resolution of the AFLC decision making processes: see Kirby and Reilly in this volume.

capable of an interpretation that would validate Australia's commitment to international treaties, and conventions, if written into domestic law (in this case, the United Nations Convention on the Elimination of all Forms of Racial Discrimination (CERD)). The judgment held that the *Racial Discrimination Act* was valid, by virtue of the High Court's recognition that the obligations of international law could be carried in national constitutional jurisdiction, via the external affairs power. The State of Queensland could not lawfully make a decision contrary to the protections offered by the *Racial Discrimination Act*. Mr Koowarta, in legal terms, won his case.[12]

The immediate legal issue before the High Court the following year, in 1983, was straightforward, and uncontroversial: whether the *World Heritage Protection Conservation Act* (1983) Cth and accompanying regulations were constitutionally valid. What was controversial were the reasons why the legislation and regulations had been passed in the first place. In 1982 the Tasmanian Government had enacted legislation that authorised the Hydro Electric Commission of Tasmania (HEC) to construct a power station on the Gordon below Franklin River, in South-West Tasmania. The project was intended to generate low cost electricity, as well as provide employment and infrastructure for the State. The HEC had successfully undertaken similar projects throughout the twentieth century, in the course of which rivers and lakes had been dammed, and surrounding wilderness flooded. Over time, local activists argued in increasingly vocal terms, and in increasingly organised political demonstrations, that the natural wilderness required protection. These campaigns were without success. In 1972, for example Lake Pedder had been flooded, despite significant opposition. The destruction of Lake Pedder however gave a sense of urgency and renewed purpose to environmental activists, and aided them to consider different forms, and a different scale of opposition, to the building of the Franklin Dam when it became public knowledge in 1976.[13] Significantly, the formation of the Tasmanian Wilderness Society (TWS) to contest the building of the Franklin Dam, and the energy and political acumen of its spokesman, Dr Bob Brown, drew the nation into recognition of what was environmentally at stake in the Tasmanian Wilderness. Through their considered operation of blockades, non violent protest, savvy engagement with media, the TWS communicated to Australia and the world knowledge that the Gordon below Franklin was an area of immense beauty, and one of the last remaining temperate rainforests, with trees and botanical species at least 3000 years old. In addition, in 1981, through the activities of TWS it became public knowledge, and not only indigenous knowledge, that the area housed significant indigenous sites with evidence of human habitation over 20,000 years old and that these sites (the Deena Reena and Kutakina caves) were in danger of permanent destruction of being flooded if the HEC scheme was to proceed. It was this knowledge that contributed to the successful inclusion of the South-West Tasmania Wilderness as a UNESCO World Heritage site in 1982, an Executive act of the Fraser Coalition Government made possible by Australia's status as signatory to the World Heritage Convention.[14]

---

[12] See Charlesworth, Kirby, and Brennan and Davis this volume for a detailed analysis of the decision.

[13] See McQueen (1983), pp 15–17 for one account.

[14] The Liberal-National Fraser Government had continued the important work of the Labor Whitlam Government, in protecting the natural heritage of Australia throughout the 1970s. In 1974, Australia became a signatory to the World Heritage Convention (adopted by UNESCO in 1972), had hosted the UNESCO Convention in 1981, and had nominated and had listed five sites (including the Great Barrier Reef), by December 1982. See Toyne (1994), pp 35–37. For a more fulsome and nuanced history of environmental protection and the State see Hutton and Connors (1999) pp 128–164.

By early 1983, through the leadership of the TWS and diverse participation by many concerned citizens across Tasmania and the mainland, the dispute over the value and meaning of the South-West of Tasmania had become much more than a state politico-economic issue.[15] It had become a heated debate about the responsibilities a nation and its people owed literally to their country, as a place of natural beauty and of historical and global significance. In these terms, the issue of whether, and how, a Federal Government could stop the HEC building a dam, and countermand authorising State legislation, had become a point of policy differentiation between the major parties. In the lead up to the March 1983 Federal election, despite the Fraser Government's commitment to environmental protection, the Coalition remained committed as a party to a policy of intervening as little as possible in the authority of states. The Australian Labor party (ALP), however, chose former Australian Council of Trade Unions (ACTU) leader Bob Hawke as their Prime Ministerial candidate in a dramatic leadership challenge just weeks before the election. This was in no small part because the 'No Dams' campaign (as it became known) had resonance within the electorate, because 'the world was watching,'[16] and because Hawke articulated a robust conviction that a Federal Government had a role to play in preventing Tasmania and the HEC from building the Dam. As has been described by many commentators, the Save the Franklin campaign, which started outside of traditional political divides, was instrumental in the ALP's victory in March 1983, as attested to by the many ballot papers scrawled with the slogan: 'No Dams!'[17]

After the election, and before the first sitting of the new Parliament, the Hawke Government had enacted regulations that operated to prevent the Franklin project from going ahead.[18] These regulations were mirrored in accompanying legislation, debated with great heat and conviction, in both houses of Federal parliament, yet passed by ALP majorities on 23 April 1983.[19] Almost immediately, and as indication of the urgency of the economic and political questions at stake, the Tasmanian Government made application to the High Court to contest the constitutional validity of the Act and Regulations. Their legal argument was in essence about the scope and constitutional interpretation of Federalism. They argued that the Franklin project was authorised by valid State law, and that there was no source of power for the Federal parliament to make *World Heritage Properties Conservation Act* (1983) Cth to stop the project proceeding.[20] The State of Tasmania, unsurprisingly, were joined by the other States. The Commonwealth, on the other hand, argued that The Act and regulations were valid under four sources of constitutional power: section 51 (xx) (on the status of HEC as a trading corporation), section 51 (xxvi) (on protection of the indigenous sites as of benefit to one race), the 'Nationhood' Power, and most significantly, S 51 (xxix), the External Affairs power. *Koowarta v Bjelke Petersen*, had of course established only the year before that S 51 (xxix) was wide enough to vest

---

[15] See Connolly (1981) for one account of the complex politics of the dispute in Tasmania.

[16] Pybus and Flanagan (1990).

[17] See for examples of accounts on the 1983 election, in different genres, Harper (2008), and Brown (2012/2013).

[18] Regulations were issued under s 69 of the *National Parks and Wildlife Conservation Act* 1975 (Cth).

[19] Commonwealth, *Parliamentary Debates*, House of Representatives, 23 April 1983, No 131, p. 45–55.

[20] In addition, the State of Tasmania argued that the Commonwealth's action would result in Federal acquisition of state property without 'just terms' (s 51 (xxxi)), and that it offended s 100, the implied restriction on the Commonwealth cannot threaten the existence of the states. For a classically delineated, and now classic, summary of all legal arguments, and judgments, see Coper (1983), pp 1–26.

jurisdiction in the Commonwealth Parliament to make valid domestic laws that gave effect to treaties and Conventions to which Australia was a signatory (and where the subject-matter was international in character).[21] This was precedent on which the Commonwealth felt they could rely, and they argued that because Australia was signatory to *World Heritage Convention* 1975, and Australia had been successful in listing South West Tasmania on that register in 1982, the Act was supported by power given in s 51 (xxix). The States and Tasmania, on this central point, countered that 51 (xxix) could not be interpreted so widely, as the mere existence of a treaty did not make the subject matter of domestic legislation 'international in character', and, moreover, would enable the Commonwealth to infringe on States' power to legislate in many areas. The Court not only heard the matter very quickly, but also wrote their judgments in almost record time. The decision was handed down on 1 July 1983, in Brisbane. In legal terms, the Commonwealth legislation was upheld as valid, by a majority of 4:3.[22] In political terms, the result was that there would be, as the media announced it, 'NO DAM!'[23]

Reading *Koowarta* and *Tasmanian Dam* as public trials

The authors in this edition all rightly take these stories, from the legal record, as the starting point for their reflections on the *Koowarta*, and *Tasmanian Dam* decisions. They all explain how *Koowarta* is understood as a turning point in Australian law, because the legal record (judgment and citation) signified the moment when the High Court engaged in a different way with both international law and federalism, and re-shaped the future legal relations of Australia (between States and Commonwealth, between nation states, and between people). *Koowarta* carried that jurisprudence and it was upheld by the High Court 1983, in *Tasmanian Dam*.[24] In offering the orthodox legal records and stories of both cases it is perhaps obvious to observe that no judgment is inevitable; and what is clear, as a matter of jurisprudence and historiography and comparison, is that since 1983 *Dam* has been seen as more than a legal record, in ways that *Koowarta* has not. Although deeply significant for many people – especially the Wik peoples of Arukun – for the majority of Australians in the 1980s *Koowarta* did not register as a major political contest, where a High Court hearing became a forum for staging public argument. Exploring this difference between the decisions, and showing how they join together in complex ways as public trials, is of course part of the shared project of this book.

For example, *Tasmanian Dam*, despite its continued public recognition, is a surprising judgment on which to reflect as legal scholars because of what we assume it represents, and what, in fact, it does not. *Tasmanian Dam* was not, as the premise of this collection makes plain and as all contributors remind in their papers, the first case to widen interpretation of the external affairs power, as it followed and applied the decision of *Koowarta*. *Tasmanian Dam* was not the first case to be heard by a Superior Court in Australia that had facts emerging from environmental disputes (as Michael Black and Lee Godden

---

[21] See for full discussion see Charlesworth this volume.

[22] See Coper (1983) for a full analysis; noting that despite the Majority finding of validity, the Acts and Regulations in part needed to be redrafted, as they were not wholly supported by the power.

[23] *The Examiner*, 2 July 1983; *The Canberra Times*, 2 July 1983 headline read, in contrast, 'Federal Victory'.

[24] *Commonwealth v Tasmania* (1983) 158 CLR 1.

remind us in their contributions). Further, and despite having the dubious honour of taking up an entire volume of the *Commonwealth Law Reports*, it was not a decision that departed from the *Engineers*[25] doctrine on the Constitutional interpretation of Federalism, again as Sir Anthony Mason and Michael Black reiterate in their essays. In other versions, the accounts of the event written by historians of political or social history, it is important to note that *Tasmanian Dam* dispute was also not responsible for the sudden birth of an environmental movement in Australia, nor was it the only significant political protest that focused on protection of the built and natural environment through public participation in the 1970s and 1980s.[26]

What makes *Tasmanian Dam* a public trial, and a critical decision, is how law was called, and how it answered. The public commitment to the facts leading the matter go to the High Court (that Australian country is unique and worthy of protection), the speed with which the High Court heard the application, and the speed of their decision, means that the case is understood as public and political in ways that *Koowarta* (which concerned, at heart, the claim to lawful country by Indigenous Australians) was not. As many contributors to this edition note, *Tasmanian Dam* was the first occasion on which the Chief Justice of the High Court, Gibbs CJ, released a public statement to explain to the people of Australia why the Court decided the case as it did.[27] This is extremely significant: it is an understanding by the Court that although all Australians live with the law, the language and forums of law are alien to many. It really mattered in this case to explain that the duty of the High Court is to uphold and decide law, not to engage in moral or political judgment. This reminds us that constitutional hearings are never only official stories told by Courts; and shows us that in 1983 this mattered to the public, and was recognised by the Court for the first time.

Robert Cover, the late American jurisprudent, has famously written about US constitutional hearings in these terms, describing the political and moral narratives that communities bring to court as *jurisgenerative*.[28] Cover wrote in the 1980s, contemporaneous with the events of *Tasmanian Dam* and *Koowarta*. He argues in 'Folktales of Justice' (first published in 1985), for example, that law (and its judgments) offer a bridge for communities to understand the commitments with which they live, the means by which those commitments can be publicly contested, and a form by which alternative futures can be imagined. Jurisprudentially, Cover is calling down the promise of law, for people who participate in a world that conditions and imagines its environs, and creates the conditions of its just (and unjust) relationships.[29] As a means of practice, the consideration and insistence that 'law shares its dignity' and official account with other versions and experiences of coming to law,[30] and living with what Court's decide, is the forms by which those accounts are made available as story, or narrative. This is historical,[31] yet is an articulation in another register of the need for judges, lawyers and university jurists to

[25] *Amalgamated Society of Engineers v Adelaide Steamship Company* (1920) 28 CLR 129.
[26] See Hutton and Connors (1999); Burgman and Burgman (1998); Wright (1994a); and Wright (1999b).
[27] *Tasmanian Dam* (1983) 158 CLR 1 at 60.
[28] Cover (1995), pp 95–172 and 103–111.
[29] Cover (1995), pp 173–201.
[30] Cover (1995), p 177.
[31] A point that is central to Cover's work: (1995), at p 96. For example, Cover directly references historiographer Hayden White's essay 'Narrative and the Representation of Reality', in articulating how narrative is a form of and for jurisprudence.

record and publicise the law they teach, practice and decide. Cover's work is drawn upon in this edition, in Section Two, by Rebecca La Forgia, and by Shaun McVeigh and myself, and in doing so we all show how Cover has been inherited in Australian juristic thinking, and has contributed to the purpose of the telling of our own stories and shared projects. What we take from Cover, and what is offered here, is that what is brought to law, and by whom, in 1982 and 1983, is a story about how law is experienced in the life of a community, as much as a permissible narrative about the common law, and that this requires many forms of jurisprudential address.

Section one: *Koowarta*

It is salient, then, to explain in more detail why it is *Koowarta* has not been the focus of collective jurisprudential consideration in Australian scholarship before now,[32] in order to make the innovation, and contribution, of the papers in Section One very clear, and to enable them to be read in relationship to the papers in Section Two

To begin, there is an empirical reason why *Koowarta* may not be as visible to legal scholarship as *Dams*, and that is because of Mr Koowarta's success, in legal terms, in the High Court. The judgment in Koowarta's favour was highly significant politically for Indigenous Australians. It was, and is, an important moment and symbol, a 'beacon' as Marcia Langton explains, of the history of Indigenous peoples' address to law through courts in an ongoing struggle for recognition and justice. Yet the Queensland Government, as a response to the ruling, legislated under State law to make the Archer River Holdings a National Park. This action prevented Mr Koowarta and the people of Aurukun from living in, on and with their land. The hand back of the land has still not occurred in full;[33] and this is rarely told as part of the description of the case in legal forums (although it features prominently in the accounts given by the authors in this book). In 1982, and since, however, the polity's vision of the case may well have been clouded by the High Court's validation of the *Racial Discrimination Act* – the ruling may have obscured the reality of law on the ground in the aftermath of the decision. It was not easy for most Anglo-Australians to see what Indigenous Australians lived as matter of course: that *Koowarta* was both a story of courage, and yet also an event that asked other questions of us a community, that were not necessarily redeemed by the judgment. These were, and remain, questions about how we might confront the legal creation of 'race' and its denials of human experience in our history; or how we might live honourably with the conduct of and between laws, in time and place and memory. Such questions are directly considered by all the contributors in Section One. For Langton, Davis, Watson and McMillan, as Indigenous leaders, scholars of law and anthropology, and as public figures, they are addressed as both a politico-legal and a lived encounter. For Tehan, they are questions shaped by her experience as a legal practitioner for the Pitjantjatjara community in the 1980s, and also shaped, as they are for Brennan and Reilly, as a scholar and researcher who has worked alongside Aboriginal peoples since then. For Charlesworth, they are questions shaped by her experience as an Associate to Justice Stephen in the High Court when this case was decided, and subsequently in her commitments to bring Australia's international and domestic obligations into a just relationship and pattern of recognition. And for Michael Kirby, as a former Justice of the High

---

[32] There are some exceptions to this point, notably Woodley (1998); and Evans (2008).

[33] See for coverage of this event ABC Television (2012).

Court of Australia, these are questions of personal commitment that have shaped the writing and realisation of Australian law as an Australian jurisprudence. That these remain significant questions at the time of writing[34] only reminds how urgent it is to make visible the rival records of Australian jurisprudence that *Koowarta* carries, and these contributors tell as lived experiences of law.

The empirical problem of visibility in 1982 suggests additional, interrelated reasons why *Koowarta* has not always been addressed as it might. These reasons inform the method and content of the papers in Section One. First, the decision and its records are artefacts of the need to invent and recognise methodological practices adequate to their time. *Koowarta* is a 1982 event of law. Yet there is reluctance by many historians (and other scholars) to write about the very recent past as history. As the American historian Tony Judt has argued, this is pervasive, and has consequences:

> The 20th Century is hardly behind us, but already its quarrels and its dogmas, its ideals and its fears, are slipping into the obscurity of mis-memory. Incessantly invoked as 'lessons', they are in reality ignored and untaught. This is hardly unsurprising. The recent past is the hardest to know and understand.[35]

This reluctance has had implications for our understanding of jurisprudence as situated. Without overstating the case, this reluctance is exacerbated if the past is too localised; it is harder to see, unless a writer is committed to recognising that domestic politics is also a history of the experience of life lived in and with law. For example, writing about *Koowarta* as a story of a life lived as an Indigenous person under the infamously punitive Bjelke-Petersen Government, and bearing the weight of decades of colonial, then state, legal violence, has not been done – until now. It is this story, and the relationships formed through shared personal experience, that Marcia Langton offers us here. Her powerful account of meeting John Koowarta, as a man of law, opens a way for her to explore the broader history of how Aboriginal peoples have encountered Anglo-Australian law, before and after 1982. What she records is a lived history of the encounter between laws; and through telling it, she invites reflection on what the life of Koowarta, and of Langton herself, might mean for a public recognition of land justice as the expression of lawful relations. Another example of the reluctance to address the recent, and local, past has been the under-exploration of the ramifications of the Commonwealth responsibilities for indigenous peoples after 1967, especially in the 1970s and 1980s. Nicole Watson in her paper makes it very clear that this has had profound effects on the practices of living with law outside of the courtroom, for Koowarta, and many others. She brings to life the personal experience of political action as a response to law; and cautions that the accounts of grassroots political struggles of and written by Aboriginal peoples, need to be re-joined to the dominant script of litigation. Her contention is that it is only in doing so that the Australian public are offered a counter, and a more immediate, way to see and commit as a community to Indigenous peoples' experiences of jurisprudence. As Watson notes, this is a project of humanity and justice, and requires forms of engagement by us all. Alexander Reilly, in his paper, performs his commitment to excavate the *Koowarta* judgment in different ways for the present by reanimating its facts. He too returns us to the early 1970s, to show that the practices of the

[34] I refer here to debates about the proposed repeal of s 18C of the *Racial Discrimination Act 1975* (Cth) by the Abbott Government in 2014.
[35] Judt (2008), p 4.

practices of the Aboriginal Land Fund Commission, and struggles on the ground, were not as polarised as we might imagine from a reading of the judgment. His paper suggests that in *Koowarta* as legal record, we fail to see how other forms of commitment to land justice were argued; and as such miss an opportunity to think carefully about the complexity of the relationships between state, law, and everyday administration. In this way, he reminds that quiet battles often stand in the wings of the dramas played at trial, and in court.

As Watson, Langton, and Reilly show, making visible the recent and local past is about more than telling it as the end point of history, of telling how it came to be, or marking it only as political. Making visible these, and other, records of *Koowarta* is about looking forward, to explain how living history is the present experience of lawful relations, be it in Aurukun, Queensland, the office of the ALFC, the High Court in Canberra, the Tent Embassy, or in Australia as a nation state. These papers also indicate that the citation of *Koowarta* may be the prominent record precisely because it has been understood too well as a lesson in Judt's terms, spoken in the language of law. The result, as Reilly makes clear, is that what the legal facts carry can be mis-remembered. In addition, the dominance of the institutional story as much as its recent provenance does not easily invite those untrained in the techniques of law to contemplate the judgement differently. Yet the fact that John Koowarta had the courage to come to law in a certain time and place, as is already demonstrated, can of course be told in other modes, styles, or traditions. This shows us *Koowarta* may not have come into view as a public trial before now because scholarly practices capable of telling its manifold stories were also realised in the 1980s. Coterminous with this judgment was the emergence of the forms and styles of telling Aboriginal histories as part of national histories, (a practice exemplified and led by Aboriginal writers, as Nicole Watson argues in her paper). Critical legal scholarship that considered relationships with other disciplines to make sense of obligations to law and justice to indigenous peoples also emerged at this time. The methods by which legal and historical accounts of indigenous and settler colonial relationships are written (and understood as not written), and by whom, have taken thirty years to be joined to each other, and to mature in ways responsive to the Australian conditions of law lived on the ground.[36] We see these methods practised here, and should take them as training in how to tell these stories well so that the widest possible audience can see, hear or read them. They are represented as poetry (in Watson and Kirby), as new constitutional history (Davis and Brennan, Charlesworth), as history of encounter (Tehan, Reilly, Watson, Langton), as memoir (Watson, Charlesworth, Tehan), as critical race theory (Watson). Significantly, and of no surprise because the contributors were invited to consider their own relationship with this case, we can also now record *Koowarta* as different genres of biography, or legal life writing. This includes writing from the perspective of the personal, community and family (in McMillan, Watson, Langton); but also as official and institutional, of how lawyers and judges make their decisions (Kirby, Charlesworth, Tehan). These different activities of animating the events and stories of the past, and writing them in different ways in the present, communicate what was understood to be urgent and relevant in the legal questions then, in 1982. And, as noted, by doing so these contributors make very plain that there are differences in how law, and whose law, has been experienced in official and unofficial lives, in the thirty years since.

---

[36] The scholars and writers who have contributed to this development are too numerous to mention here. For a broad assessment of how these forms of scholarship have come into relation see generally Curthoys, Genovese and Reilly (2008); and Watson's account of the work of specific Indigenous scholars and writers in this volume.

Another reason that *Koowarta* has not until now been in view as a public trial (and not only a judgment) is that Australian jurisprudence has itself matured since 1982. Although the judgment (and citation as representation of that judgment) is 'about' the *Racial Discrimination Act*, and whether it would be valid under either the race power (it was not) or the External Affairs powers (as it was), the very question of race is muted in its transposition to a narrative of High Court commitment to a new federalism, and a new internationalism. The contributors remind us that this is a problem only if *Koowarta* is read as a lesson, or a ratio, of a particular and limited kind. In her paper, for example, Hilary Charlesworth gives a unique perspective on how, and if, *Koowarta* should be considered a turning point of law. As noted, she was Justice Stephen's Associate, and 'a real time observer' of what was an 'uncharacteristic' 'passion and charge' in the conduct of a High Court decision.[37] As she puts it, all the legal actors in the case understood they were witnesses to a significant event. In carefully explaining the way the decision was taken by different members of the Court in this context, she lets us inside what it meant for the institutions of law to think about how Australia was changing as a nation in the 1980s; and that one of its signal legacies was that it opened space for proper debate about the relationships between international, national and local spheres of lawful concerns. In making that point, Charlesworth standing on the other side of her relationship to this case, as an International Law Professor, notes that the Court in *Koowarta* elided how Australia might meet its human rights obligations, and that this remains the case. With Michael Kirby, and Megan Davis and Sean Brennan in their papers, Charlesworth also reminds us that re-viewing the legal record of *Koowarta* reveals the entrenchment of structural and material practices of race, and how that has occurred in Australia because of the exertion of law's authority, and its specific, settler colonial form. The minority, they all argue, talk a great deal about internal legal histories – constitutional precedent, and States' rights. But as Hilary Charlesworth wrote with Andrew Byrne in 1985[38], and notes again here, if this case was about States' rights, it was about the right of Queensland Government to racially discriminate, deny Aboriginal peoples their land. That the rights of States remained, despite the threat to federalism the case provoked in some commentators at the time, can be seen clearly in the savage legislative response of the Queensland Government to exclude land rights through creation of State Reserves as National Park, and the lingering and still unfulfilled promise of hand back.

Importantly, in their paper, Sean Brennan and Megan Davis also address 'the race question' as a proper matter for constitutional law. They return to the judgment, and carefully explain how members of the Court considered the races power, as Koowarta's legal team had invited them to do; and how it came to be that the *Racial Discrimination Act*, as a redress of barriers to equality based on race, was validated through the external affairs power alone. Brennan and Davis show us the precariousness of not only the process of judgment, but of the implications of constitutional interpretation for Indigenous peoples. They remind that *Koowarta* exemplifies the hazards, complexity and stress of constitutional litigation, and that it was, in many respects, a missed opportunity to clarify the form and content of the race power. At the same time, by drawing attention to the current demands for constitutional recognition of Aboriginal and Torres Strait Islander peoples, they show why review of a decision like *Koowarta* is essential for continual public debate

[37] Charlesworth, this volume pp 43–51.
[38] Byrnes and Charlesworth (1985).

about 'our country's intractable problems with race'.[39] In this way, Brennan and Davis, and Charlesworth, join the arguments and experiences offered by Langton, Watson and Reilly. Despite the complex stories embedded in the judgments about the move from separate colonial states to a sovereign nation that looks outwards, these contributors show us that the jurisdiction of States to legislate over Indigenous peoples remained; and could be exercised in different ways than that promised by the *Racial Discrimination Act*. This story of legislative and executive force in Australian history is distinct and distinctive, and long, which is Langton and Watson's point. Different stories and records are told in the interstices of making and administering these state, and it must be noted, federal laws.

It is this point that Maureen Tehan also considers in her paper. She makes a compelling case for the reconsideration of *Koowarta* as having the greatest influence on municipal law. This is easily overlooked in the excitement about the international, that *Dams* carried forward, and where very different questions were asked. As Tehan argues, *Koowarta*'s immediate impact was to open 'both legal and political possibilities for Indigenous peoples', and, she importantly adds, for 'those working with them'.[40] What Tehan then tells is her recollection what it was like to be a lawyer, working with Indigenous communities, in the immediate aftermath of the decision. This was a 'double edged sword'.[41] On one hand the validity of the *Racial Discrimination Act* liberated practitioners to use different avenues and techniques of law to progress land rights and use; on the other, it created impediments to jurisprudence and the practise of negotiation as the *Racial Discrimination Act* was built on the foundations of a formal equality of all peoples before the law. She documents the legacies and ramifications of *Koowarta* through the life of the *Racial Discrimination Act* since then, in *Gerhardy v Brown* (1985), *Mabo v The State of Queensland (no 2)* (1992) ('*Mabo*'), and the recent decision of *Maloney v R* (2013).[42] In doing so, Tehan shows that in the everyday activities of law, the obligation of the Anglo-Australian lawyer is to pay close attention to the techniques, traditions, duties and practices of their own law. Anglo-Australian lawyers are then better equipped to work with their Indigenous clients, and to recognise the law as 'the foundation for creative and ambitious political action to advance [Indigenous clients'] rights and entitlements.'[43]

Mark McMillan's contribution to this collection is in many ways in conversation with that of Tehan, and others. He responds to her call for practitioners of Anglo-Australian law to take their obligations seriously, by arguing that jurisdiction as a technique is not only central to legal practice, but also central to an Indigenous experience and retelling of *Koowarta*. McMillan contends that *Koowarta* shows what it meant to take part in an 'Indigenous International'. McMillan, in using this term, is reminding that Indigenous peoples' relationship to their land – as matter of law and life – has always involved the exercise of jurisdictional activity that is inter-national, as well as transnational. In this way, McMillan recasts *Koowarta* as an event of law that opened up a place for more than two rival jurisdictions to meet. In four different stories, McMillan explores the ways in which we can think about *Koowarta* as part of this 'Indigenous International', which has a past, present and future that moves and is shaped by the agency and commitment of Indigenous

[39] Brennan and Davis, this volume.
[40] Tehan, this volume p 100.
[41] Tehan, this volume p 101.
[42] *Gerhardy v Brown* (1985) 159 CLR 70; *Mabo v Queensland [No. 2]* (1992) 175 CLR 1 (hereafter '*Mabo*'); *Maloney v the Queen* (2013) 298 ALR 308.
[43] *Gerhardy v Brown* (1985) 159 CLR 70; *Mabo; Maloney v the Queen* (2013) 298 ALR 308.

jurisprudence. He does this, importantly, by contributing to this edition his own account of how techniques of laws are predicated upon the transmission of the experiences and stories of lawful relationships, and that the forms of sharing and telling those stories is an inseparable part of his own practice of Wiradjuri jurisprudence.

Finally, it must be stated that another reason *Koowarta* has not been clearly in view as a form of jurisprudential address, as McMillan and others suggest it can be, is that the jurisprudence of Australia has taken time to accept that it must take some responsibility for 'our intractable problem with race'.[44] In *Koowarta*, in the majority judgments, it could be argued that the jurisprudential gesture toward redress by law to Indigenous people is constitutional, and political. This is most obvious in Justice Murphy's judgment; where he includes, unusually, a bibliography for his reasoning that the *Racial Discrimination Act* is a valid expression of Australia's obligations to international conventions on the elimination of racial discrimination. Importantly, alongside the work of Anglo-Australian writers committed to making visible the injustice of laws of Aboriginal peoples (such as Charles Rowley), Murphy J cites works by the indigenous writer and activist Kevin Gilbert. By writing Gilbert into the *Commonwealth Law Reports*, Murphy J lets us see him as a jurisprudent, someone whose work tells an account of dispossession as a lived experience of law in Australia that requires redress. (The importance of Gilbert's life and work is discussed in this volume by Nicole Watson).[45] By 1992, ten years later in *Mabo,* the question had changed. It had become one of the moral reckoning of Australian common law.[46] As has been well documented, it is *Mabo* as public trial that makes visible the modern Australian consciousness of the violence of terra nullius. The central legal question in *Mabo* is the lawfulness by which Indigenous Australians were dispossessed of their land; and how and by what means Australian law might think with Indigenous peoples assertion that their land was their law and life. John Koowarta and Eddie Mabo carry the same question to the Court, in different facts. But *Mabo* is possible because of *Koowarta.* This is an extremely significant point, made volubly in most contributions to this volume, and cannot be restated strongly enough. When *Koowarta* was decided, there was still an optimism amongst Indigenous activists and their supporters that the Australian state, through legislative means, was capable of recognising Indigenous peoples' assertion of their law and status. *Koowarta* is after all a case about claiming protection of that status through the *Racial Discrimination Act.* But as Noel Pearson has argued elsewhere, throughout the 1980s the 'well spring of goodwill' that suggested the State could meet its responsibilities had evaporated.[47] This is evident in the circumstances of the Queensland Government's response to *Koowarta*; and is made clear by Tehan in her essay on the implications of the decision for a proposed national land rights scheme in the 1980s. In the face of failure by the State, Indigenous people – through the exemplar of *Mabo* – turned to the Courts directly, to force the common law to account. *Koowarta* – as an experience of the conduct of a case – prepared the institutions and officials of law for how to think with a different history of Australia, and how to think about our relationship to each other as a proper question for domestic and international law. It is no accident that Ron Castan QC, for example,

---

[44] Brennan and Davis, as above, this volume.

[45] Murphy J cites Gilbert's *Because a White Man'll Never Do It* (1973), and *Living Black* (1977): *Koowarta* (1982) 153 CLR 168 at 242–243.

[46] *Mabo* (1992) 175 CLR 1 at 44, per Brennan CJ. For an oft-quoted discussion of this judgment in terms of a 'jurisprudence of regret' see Webber (1995).

[47] This is a point Pearson has made on many occasions; see for example Pearson (2011), p 37.

as Kirby reminds in his essay, appeared for both John Koowarta and Eddie Mabo in the High Court. It is axiomatic that without a jurisprudential experience of *Koowarta* in any sense, *Mabo* could not be seen as a great Australian public trial, in which the Australian common law came of age, and the conduct of lawful relations in Australia between Indigenous and non-Indigenous Australians could be open to re-imagination. This re-imagination of *Mabo* has not of course been without its expressions and experiences of regret and misjudgement and pain since 1992. But it is a story told in manifold ways, and in multiple and rival records,[48] exemplified in these stories of *Koowarta* as part of its origins. These are stories of and about Land Rights, the *Native Title Act 1993* (Cth) and the need to create new understandings about land (Langton, Reilly, Tehan); obligations to the international community (Davis and Brennan, Charlesworth, McMillan, Kirby); the practices of municipal law and the ongoing significance of the *Racial Discrimination Act* (Reilly, Tehan, Davis and Brennan, Kirby); the arguing and deciding and dissents of cases like *Wik Peoples v Queensland* (1996) and *Wurridjal v The Cth* (2009)(Kirby),[49] and the teaching of law as an encounter, in the academy and outside (Watson, Reilly, Langton Tehan). All these contributors have, it must also be noted, participated in the re-imagination of *Mabo* as a public trial in Australia, in their practices of native title and international law, constitutional law and legal theory, law and politics; and we are fortunate to be offered that experience in these papers.

Michael Kirby's paper draws these records and reviews of *Koowarta* together.[50] He summarises the forms and content, and significance, of what it means to write about and create different accounts of *Koowarta* in our own time. Kirby reminds that although *Koowarta* stands as a turning point, where the majority valorises the nation as outward looking and engaged, as committed to the hopes and legal recognitions of the post 1945 global world order, the ways in which this international trajectory has unfolded remain complex and unfinished for Australia. By returning to the individual judgments of 1982, the judgments and activities of Courts that followed *Koowarta*, and the other contributors' papers, Kirby invites us to view, and review, the decision not only for what was said, and done. He also reminds us to look at the points of juridical contention, as to how Anglo-Australian law might take responsibility for the creation and perpetuation of 'race' occurring in tandem with the assertion of international law, and with the political quest for land justice lived and experienced by Indigenous people in everyday life. Kirby's long career in bringing these duties together in a meaningful way in his own office as a judge of the High Court of Australia, gives particular urgency and relevance to this hope that the law and state understands the nature of consultation, of the conduct of meeting between Indigenous and non Indigenous Australians, as 'an absolute prerequisite' for justice as lived.

---

[48] There was for example great publicity attracting the twentieth anniversary of the *Mabo* decision, including statements read in Parliament, coverage on all news services, a commemorative ABC television drama of the life of Eddie Mabo, and a conference on *Mabo* at the University of Queensland on 31 May 2012. See also many of the publications that surrounded this anniversary and reflected on the ongoing consideration by scholars and writers of *Mabo* as a signal event of law for the Australian community, for example Bauman, Glick and AIATSIS (2012); and Keon-Cohen (2013). This consideration has been of long duration, see for example Sharp (1996), and Attwood (ed) (1996).

[49] *Wik Peoples v Queensland* (1996) 187 CLR 1; *Wurridjal v The Commonwealth* (2009) 237 CLR 309.

[50] At the symposium, Michael Kirby was invited to act as a commentator for the proceedings at their conclusion, and his paper also performs this task of synthesis and reflection.

Section two: *Tasmanian Dam*

The papers on *Tasmanian Dam*,[51] in Section Two, begin with other reflections on the duties of judicial and legal office. This includes how such duties inform the ways the case was argued and decided in 1983, as well as how they shape the forms of record and review today. Sir Anthony Mason, for example, in his paper reminds us that the proper conduct of courts, and the duties of judges in Australia, is to decide law, according to doctrine, precedent, and the Constitution. 'For my part', he notes, 'I have no hesitation in rejecting the suggestion that my decision reflected or was motivated by any view of the undesirability or otherwise of constructing the Dam. And I have no doubt that this was the position of my colleagues. We were concerned solely with legal issues."[52] This statement of Sir Anthony's makes clear the central adherence of the Court to legalism, which has importantly shaped and given meaning to the rule of law in Australia for a very long time. Yet it also shows us how legalism is in itself a form of proper conduct, and a way for a Justice of the High Court to discharge their duties of office (an observation also made in my paper with Shaun McVeigh). In taking up his responsibilities as an eminent Australian jurist, Sir Anthony makes two important points in refreshing the record of *Tasmanian Dam*, that are clear in the doctrinal reasoning of the High Court. The first is about constitutional law as national law: that the reserved powers doctrine that Tasmania relied on in argument 'probably served Australia well in the early years of Federation before state-based communities were transformed into a nation (with a sense of 'national identity and national economy', as Sir Anthony describes), but that this had changed, and was recognised by the Court as having changed, at least by the Payroll Tax case of 1971.[53] This reminds us that there is an historical meaning to nation in constitutional law that is aligned with changing ideas about national political organisation. The second point is about the interrelationship between Australian and international law, and how Australia is understood as a state actor in international terms. In both *Koowarta* and *Tasmanian Dam* a key legal question is of course whether the ratification and implementation of a treaty conferred legislative power on the Commonwealth. In his review of the majority and minority judgments, Sir Anthony Mason is clear that Australia, as a state, had obligations by 1983: that it was proper for the Court to consider that 'Australia's relations with other countries would . . . be affected by whatever Australia did or did not do internally'.[54] The expansion in the range of matters dealt with by international treaties since 1900 (including the elimination of racial discrimination, and the preservation of heritage) is simply the consequence of increased and expanded international activity in which Australia played a part. What we are reminded of here then is that the relationship between the legislative and executive arms of government (with the world, and with the concerns of the Australian people in the formation of legislation) had changed by 1983, and that treaties formed the bridge between these relationships. In these terms, the *Tasmanian Dam* judgment was simply the proper conduct of the High Court's

---

[51] Other papers were also presented at the 1983 symposium: Libby Connors and Drew Hutton offered activist and historian's perspectives on the legacy of the *Tasmanian Dam* dispute for current environmentalist projects; and Darren Parker argued for a lawful recognition of Palawa law and its care of the River, in order that Anglo-Australian jurisprudence might reconceptualise 'heritage and culture' as an encounter of laws.

[52] Mason this book p 153.

[53] Mason this book p 154, *Victoria v The Commonwealth* (1971) 122 CLR 353.

[54] Mason this book p 156.

obligations to maintain the Constitution according to decided principles and doctrine, and with accepted interpretative conventions.

In his paper, by way of conclusion, Sir Anthony Mason also turns his attention to the way that *Tasmanian Dam* was argued and presented. This is an important point that joins the reflections on both *Tasmanian Dam* and *Koowarta*. Reading the essays together, in one volume, it becomes possible to understand these cases as critical decisions of their time. It is perhaps obvious, but worth repeating, that a judgment is not confined by the boundaries of the *Commonwealth Law Reports*. As the contributors in Section One ably demonstrate, how we understand a trial or hearing as an experience of living with law in time and place includes recording how parties decide to pursue a case, how they are advised and represented, how arguments are conducted and formed on their behalf, and who attends in the public galleries to witness their hearings. It is worth remembering, then, that although the Tasmanian Wilderness Society were the protagonists and instigators of the contest over Heritage values in the political realm, they were not parties to the legal issues before the High Court. Instead, they were given an opportunity to argue that they should be heard as *amicus curiae*, as a friend of the court, despite their lack of standing, or legal interest, in the matter of Constitutional validity of the Commonwealth legislation. Michael Black in his paper explains how the amicus brief was brought to life, argued, and heard by the High Court. Black was the leading counsel for the TWS, part of a team, as he notes, that also included Pierre Slicer in Hobart, and Bryan Keon Cohen, as his Junior in the High Court. Importantly for the aims of the symposium and this collection, Black, although a previous Chief Justice of the Federal Court and a senior custodian of Australian law, does not write in the same genre as Sir Anthony. He writes instead a memoir of an advocate, and offers personal insight into the culture of practice during the *Tasmanian Dam* dispute in 1983. In doing so, he shows what the articulation of a consciously Australian advocacy might mean in the development of Australian law. Although memoirs as a form of writing are personal, and often reveal something private about the writer and their past, a legal memoir of an advocate belongs to a longer genre of judicial and legal life writing, and has different obligations. Black understands (as he notes in a foot note at the start of his paper) that there are restraints in writing about a case in which he appeared as counsel, and that these are matter of propriety and professional duty (toward both court and client). But he is cognizant that it is only because of the distance between the 1980s and the present that those restraints can be relaxed. As an account of living with law as an advocate, Michael Black shares thoughts, anecdotes and fragments of a time, and tells us a great deal about what it meant to conduct oneself as a counsel in 1983. This is an important contribution not only to the record of the case, but highlights the necessity of gathering of stories of the recent past as inherent and integral to the collective biographies of Australia legal life as we understand it now. In his story, and its form, there are three things in particular that resonate. The first is about institutions, about what it meant as a member of the Constitutional Bar in the 1980s to come to the newly opened High Court in Canberra, and how the Court and its official (and unofficial) ceremonies were understood as national and Australian in very material and literal terms. The second is about relationships, between clients and their counsel, as well as camaraderie of the Bar. For Black, the style, technique, and form of exchange in any hearing, inside and outside the courtroom, is formative to how we contemplate the significance of the conduct and outcome of the case. Finally, and Black argues that this should not be underestimated, a record of a case like *Tasmanian Dam* is a matter of context, both legal and historical, and that these contexts should be joined together to make our own past intelligible and meaningful as experiences of Australian law that can declare itself in those terms.[55]

By writing about *Tasmanian Dam* as memoir, Michael Black also shows us that the fragility of the personal experience and exchange in the institutions of Australia law needs recording, from multiple standpoints. Sir Anthony Mason in his paper reflects in conclusion on Black's appearance before the Court in June 1983, and although praising its brevity, and acumen, cautions that Black's submission was not decisive in the outcome of the case. He suggests that to address it in those terms, and by implication without connection to the other submissions and arguments presented to the Court in June and July 1983, would be an error or historical revision. (This is a conclusion with which Black, in his careful exposition, and refusal to individualise a collaborative experience of life at the Bar in 1983, would agree). But in thinking about 'what happened' during an important constitutional decision, and returning to transcript to do so, other contributors who were not present in the High Court in 1983, and have learned and inherited the lessons of 1983 as matters of law and juridical scholarship, bring other standpoints and perspectives to the consideration of what forms of argumentation mean as questions of law and as matters of shared memory.

In her contribution, Rebecca La Forgia considers how the interpretative practices of the High Court create stories by which Australians come to inhabit their law. An Australian scholar of constitutional and international law, with expertise in literary and cultural theory, La Forgia undertakes an in-depth textual analysis of the transcript of Michael Black's amicus submission, and his exchanges with the bench. (It is important to note that as a consequence of La Forgia's desire to examine Black's rhetoric for her paper at the symposium in 2013, the High Court placed the *Tasmanian Dam* transcript on Austlii for public scrutiny and legal analysis for the first time). La Forgia's contention is that memory of law, of 1983, and what might be considered of relevance and significance to juridical life and argument, must always go beyond the judgment of the Court. With reference to Avishai Margalit's *The Ethics of Memory* (2004), as well as Cover, La Forgia is concerned not only to reveal what is hidden or lost in written records of constitutional courts, but to examine what those records evoke.[56] Through close reading of Michael Black's submission, La Forgia shows us how advocacy is both rhetoric and record and has audience and readership. In doing so, she reminds us that it is in the poetry and beauty of a place, represented in the submissions and representations in a constitutional matter before the High Court of Australia, that we can glimpse how law is not limited by its institutional settings, but is capable of being imagined and reimagined in changed local and global conditions. Black's very brief submission on behalf of the TWS lasts, she argues, not simply because he spoke of beauty, because his rhetoric was 'imbued with commitment to make the audience part of the poetic'.[57] It is in Black's invitation to the Court in 1983 to witness, and experience, the issues of *Tasmanian Dam* as 'a relation between self and nature,' as well as matter of doctrine, that opens his address as constitutional story capable of reanimating the meaning of the case for audiences today.

We hear the story of the TWS experience in Court from another different perspective in an interview with Dr Bob Brown, conducted by Martin Clark. Clark is a young scholar of

---

[55] *Mabo* (1992) 175 CLR 1 (Brennan J).
[56] Margalit (2004).
[57] LaForgia (2014), p 55.

public international law and theory who also collaborated on a paper for this collection with Mark McMillan.[58] Bob Brown's recollections are primarily about the experience of *Tasmanian Dam* as political event, and he offers important memories about what it felt like to see the culmination of a long battle on the river conclude in the public institutions of Australian law. In conversation with Clark, Brown also reflects on his experience as *amicus curiae*, and how the TWS chose to 'come to law.' We publish the interview here in transcript form. Brown's account of 1983 is unselfconscious, as he has spoken many times on the record about the *Tasmanian Dam* political campaign, and is a professional and experienced interview subject. Clearly, however, an interview as an oral history offers a unique record of a past event, as both the interviewer and their subject have experienced that event differently. In his brief commentary on these interviews, Clark steps back from his role as Brown's interlocutor, and offers insight into why Brown's interview for this collection is a particular story of law. Clark gives an analysis of the public law question of standing, from the standpoint of the public law scholar. What Clark draws out for us to consider, when reading Brown's reflections on his motivations and experiences about coming to law, are the changing forms of relationship between matters of public law and political concerns. He reminds us of something very simple but easy to overlook if legally trained: that the opportunity to be heard before Australian courts can be entirely different from perspective of clients, witnesses, and amicus curiae, and that forms of address to law have a legal, as well as a personal and political, history. As noted in relation to the papers in Section One on *Koowarta*, this story is central to the developments of Australian public law in the 1980s, and is in many ways yet to be written and told, although of course we begin to do so collectively in this book.

Together, it is important to note that Mason, Black, Brown and La Forgia do not seek to claim the *Tasmanian Dam* decision as a redemptive moment or turning point that remains fixed in Australian law. Rather, it is their different experiences of the case that help scholars, and a wider readership, remember what we once wanted from law, and how that carries a range of meaning into our own time. This includes being clear that the ways in which we conduct our practices as lawyers, judges, and jurisprudents today, and what we might take for granted as part of those practices, were yet to come in 1983. Most importantly, for example, place, race and environment were joined together legally and factually in both *Tasmanian Dam* and *Koowarta*, through the subject matter of the treaties tested and relied on in dispute, and over the interpretation of the races power in s 51 (as McMillan and Clark make very clear in their paper). But it was not yet possible to consider how lawful claims of Indigenous peoples might be connected to matters of environmental protection, nationally and internationally, and that this might shape an Australian jurisprudence that cared for country, and relations on country.

The significance of joining together *Tasmanian Dam* and *Koowarta* for us today relies, then, on how we publicise what is a matter of doctrine and jurisprudence. As already discussed, after (and because of) the 1992 decision of the High Court in *Mabo* we have obligations to understand Australian jurisprudence as Australian, and this informs how we

[58] Clark (2013) undertook the important task at the Melbourne Law School symposium in July 2013 of interviewing judge, advocate, and client (Mason, Black and Brown) on their recollections and perceptions of the Tasmanian Dam case for the Melbourne Law School High Court Blog. I invited Martin to revisit, and extend his interview with Bob Brown for the special edition of Griffith Law Review on the case, and we reprint this interview here.

understand the conduct of lawful relations between peoples. Reviewing *Tasmanian Dam* in this way – in terms of not only what it was, but also what it was yet to become as a conduct of jurisprudence – is the direct question posed, and explored, by Shaun McVeigh and I in our paper. To reflect on that question, we stand to the side of the review of the events of 1983 as constitutional decision, and present the jurisprudence of *Dam* and 1983 in terms of incidents of legal thinking in the conduct of the office of the jurisprudent. Our report provides a brief chronicle and record of the patchwork of law projects and engagements that pattern the events of *Tasmanian Dam* into the scholarly work of jurists in Australian universities. We suggest that in 1983 juristic writing about *Tasmanian Dam*, and alongside it, noted how law was conducted in Australia. Yet we contend that this writing was not yet cast as a jurisprudence that considered itself to be distinctly Australian in its concerns, and its forms of address, to peoples and land, in time and place. Our point is that understanding *Tasmanian Dam* as a matter of record in and of 1983 enables us to explore, think and reflect upon the writing of jurisprudence in our own time.

The question of the relationship between *Tasmanian Dam* as judgment of 1983 and jurisprudence yet to come is also discussed by Chiam, McMillan and Clark, and Godden, although each raises that question differently. Madelaine Chiam in her paper, for example, analyses why it is that *Tasmanian Dam*, despite its limited doctrinal innovation, retains its status as the touchstone judgment for debate over Australia's relationship with international law. Chiam is a public international lawyer with a long standing concern to interrogate the contours and effect of international law in Australia. Chiam (with others) has described this municipal effect as a 'deep anxiety', in which international law is understood (by the Australian community, and their legislators and Executive) as 'an intrusion from "outside" into our self-contained and carefully bounded legal system'.[59] Chiam returns to this trope in her essay here. She argues that the controversies and dilemmas of 1983 indelibly drew Australia's 'deep anxiety' about international law into relation with the promise of what international law might hold, for state and citizens alike. In three distinct temporal frames (1983, 1994/5, and the present), Chiam demonstrates that the core public (and political) tension posed by *Tasmanian Dam* about the arrival of the international has continued to be experienced as both a debilitating threat to national autonomy, and as a cosmopolitan desire for the nation, through its law, to take its place as an international actor. Chiam undertakes her analysis by bringing the operation of state-craft into conversation with legal doctrine, emphasizing questions of treaty negotiation, and treaty recognition in domestic law. Importantly, she also asks how Australian legal scholarship has described, and responded to, *Tasmanian Dam* as part of that conversation.[60] She argues that it was ultimately the public commitments of international legal scholars, with a shared jurisprudential concern for Australia, and Australians, to 'not just participate in but lead the broadening fields of international law'[61] (in particular, human rights and international environmental law), that offered a disruption to the narratives that coloured the political furore of 1983. Despite celebrating these scholarly commitments, and noting their significant ongoing legacies, Chiam is careful to document the ways in which deep-seated ambivalence to an Australian experience of international law has continued. As she explains, the Australian state struggles with the content of rights claims,

[59] Charlesworth, Chaim, Hovell and Williams (2003), p 424.
[60] Chiam (2015), pp 89–105.
[61] Chiam (2015), p 97.

and struggles, at times, with the idea that some matters – including those of environmental protection – are an international concern. Chiam ultimately recommends that such ambivalence is unproductive for Australia, and her people. Nevertheless, her essay reminds us that Constitutional hearings like *Tasmanian Dam* are important precisely because they enable complex stories of Australia's place in the world to take hold in our shared imaginations, and our national histories, and this holds potential for shaping how Australia might conduct her sovereign and lawful responsibilities today.

While Chiam joins *Tasmanian Dam* to the international, Mark McMillan and Martin Clark join it to political debate on the national stage. They invite us to read their paper in particular way: as witnesses to a conversation between them as Western trained Wiradjuri jurist and an Anglo-Australian public law scholar. In doing so, they explicitly consider how race, as a lived experience of law, and as a constitutional matter, is able to be discussed as an activity of collective jurisprudence in Australia. In their paper, they offer a reflection on Brennan and Davis' arguments in Section One, and continue a careful exposition of High Court interpretation on s 51(xxvi) from 1983 onwards. They read this against an historical reckoning of race classification by the state, which has demanded much from Indigenous peoples. McMillan and Clark argue that these two forms of legal histories are still not properly joined together in Australian law, with the consequence that there is a continuing juridical obfuscation about what 'race' signifies, and for whom. For both McMillan and Clark, returning to other stories that High Court decisions carry – the stories of how Indigenous peoples have mobilized and politically understood constitutional engagement – is an essential prerequisite for a shared national conversation about the conduct of relations between peoples and laws on the question of race, and more importantly, its distinction from indigeneity. In particular, McMillan and Clark return to the themes raised by Langton and Watson in Section One, and assert the political centrality of the 1967 Constitutional referendum for Indigenous peoples in these stories. They argue that the promise of inclusion that the referendum carried continues to offer possibilities for renewing techniques of constitutional practice and decision-making, and that these techniques are necessary to redress the limits of participation imposed by the classification of race in the legislative record. Although McMillan and Clark are careful to remind that Constitutional interpretation, because of its reliance on text and doctrine, remains limited in its ability to incorporate the significance of social movements or changes in political worldviews, they nevertheless insist that different techniques in constitutional practice can make a difference. It is their own engagement in the activity of constitutional conversation and jurisprudential collaboration – what they offer from their own traditions, and how these meet – that suggest ways of reinscribing the interpretative commitments of constitutional law for all Australian peoples.

Finally, Lee Godden draws direct attention to place in her address to *Tasmanian Dam*, by accounting for the relationship between people, law, and their environment. Godden is Australia's senior legal scholar on the theory and management of water, and a senior administrator and advisor on the relations between native title law and environmental management. In her work, as is demonstrated in her contribution here, she practices between the disciplines of environmental law, history and geography, and joins these together to offer an account of how we ought to take care of the natural world. Godden begins by showing that the centre piece of the events of 1983 – the contention over the building of a dam – already carried jurisprudential, legal and long historical meaning about how people frame their relationships to rivers. For Godden, then, the Franklin Dam is not only a matter of political fact for the High Court, and the Hawke Government, but a 'technological, social and legal artefact, with attendant biophysical impacts.[62] Godden argues that management of environmental risks have always been 'major motivating mythologies in the nation building narratives that have supported dam construction across much of Australia's post colonisation history'.[63] But it is after 1983, and after the failure to dam the Franklin River, that different forms for imagining and managing the relationship between people and rivers within the Australian continent, and in conversation with international law, became possible, and necessary. Through her analysis of these different forms of regulation and legal practice, Godden reminds us that water remains both a source of life and a site of contest in a nation such as Australia. Significantly for this collection of papers, she also reminds that how we mediate our relationship to natural resources, thirty years after *Tasmanian Dam*, is incomplete without proper recognition of Indigenous legal thought and practice on the care for rivers as a care for place.

Conclusion

In conclusion, the contributors to this edition collectively remind that the cases of *Koowarta* and *Tasmanian Dam* are not definitive turning points, judgments caught in amber, but are juridical events that show Australian law unfolding in ways that do not only interrupt the permissible narratives of precedent. This is evidenced not only in the papers that follow, but in the activity of gathering together at the Melbourne Law School to remember and reflect on the cases. At the symposia in June 2013 to commemorate the *Tasmanian Dam* decision of 1983, and in May 2012 to commemorate the *Koowarta* decsison of 1982, we began with an acknowledgement: that our meeting took place on Indigenous country, the country of the Wurundjeri peoples of the Kulin nation, a place of and in their law, taken care of by their honoured custodians past and present.[64] Acknowledgment of country is an important convention and practice of our own times. It is a recognition that the experience and conduct of life in Australian institutions resides in a place that is indelibly shaped by encounters between people, that must be honoured, although those encounters have not always been honorable. What is implicit in an acknowledgment of country taking place in an Institution of Anglo-Australian law is that such acknowledgment is not only a political convention, but also an expression of jurisprudence. This means that for those of us who practice and teach law in Australia, honouring traditional custodians of land is now part of an acknowledgment that we are responsible for the care of our own law, and the conduct of lawful relations with Indigenous peoples in the place we live. That this has become possible, in the ways that it is has since the 1980s, is because of critical decisions like *Tasmanian Dam* and *Koowarta*. The following essays serve to remind how such critical decisions carry many public, juridical and personal stories, and that together, these stories call to account the experience, and promise, of Australian law.

References

Secondary Sources

ABC Television 7.30 Report (2012) 'Cape York Land Agreement Makes History', 22 May, http://www.abc.net.au/7.30/content/2012/s3508700.htm.

Bain Attwood (ed) *In the Age of Mabo: History, Aborigines and Australia*, Allen and Unwin.

[62] Godden (2015), p 129.

[63] Godden (2015), p 143.

[64] Mark McMillan conducted acknowledgment of country at both Symposia.

Toni Bauman, Lydia Glick and Australian Institute of Aboriginal and Torres Strait Islander Studies (2012) *The Limits of Change: Mabo and Native Tittle 20 Years On*, AIATSIS Research Publications.

CF Black (2010) *The Land is the Source of the Law: A Dialogic Encounter with Indigenous Jurisprudence*, Routledge.

Hon Michael Black AC QC (2015) 'The *Tasmanian Dam Case*: An Advocate's Memoir' 24(1) *Griffith Law Review* 22.

Bob Brown (2012/2013) 'Environmental Flows' (Dec/Jan) *The Monthly*, p 20.

Sean Brennan and Megan Davis (2014) '*Koowarta*: Constitutional Landmark, Transition Point or Missed Opportunity?' 23(1) *Griffith Law Review* 79.

Meredith Burgman and Verity Burgman (1998) *Green Bans, Red Union: Environmental activism and the New South Wales Builders' Labourers Federation*, UNSW Press.

Andrew Byrnes and Hilary Charlesworth (1985) 'Federalism and the International Legal Order: Recent Developments in Australia. Implementing Treaties in Australia' 79(3) *American Journal of International Law* 622.

Hilary Charlesworth (2014) 'Internal and External Affairs: The *Koowarta* Case in Context' 23(1) *Griffith Law Review* 35.

Hilary Charlesworth, Madelaine Chiam, Devika Hovell and George Williams (2003) 'Deep Anxieties: Australia and the International Legal Order' 25 *Sydney Law Review* 424.

Madelaine Chiam (2015) '*Tasmanian Dams* and Australia's Relationship with International Law' 24(1) *Griffith Law Review* 89.

Martin Clark (2015) 'Experiences of Coming to Law: An Interview with Bob Brown on the Tasmanian Wilderness Society as Client in the *Tasmanian Dam Case*' 24(1) *Griffith Law Review* 58.

Martin Clark (2013) 'Remembering the Tasmanian Dam Case' http://blogs.unimelb.edu.au/opinionsonhigh/2013/07/24/clark-tasmanian-dam/.

Bob Connolly (1981) *The Fight For the Franklin: The Story of Australia's Last Wild River*, Cassell Australia.

Michael Coper (1983) *The Franklin Dam Case: Commentary and Full Text of the Decision in Commonwealth of Australia v State of Tasmania*, Butterworths.

Robert Cover (1995) 'Nomos and Narrative' in M Minnow, M Ryan, A Sarat (eds) *Narrative, Violence and the Law: The Essays of Robert Cover*, University of Michigan Press.

Martin Crotty and David Andrew Roberts (eds) (2008) *Turning Points in Australian History*, University of NSW Press.

Ann Curthoys, Ann Genovese and Alexander Reilly (2008) *Rights and Redemption: History, Law and Indigenous People*, UNSW Press.

Shaunnagh Dorsett and Shaun McVeigh (2012) *Jurisdiction*, Routledge.

Raymond Evans (2007) *A History Of Queensland*, Cambridge University Press.

Ann Genovese (2014a) 'Critical Decision, 1982: Koowarta v Bjelke-Petersen' 23(1) *Griffith Law Review* 1.

Ann Genovese (2014b) 'On Australian Feminist Tradition: Three Notes on Conduct, Inheritance, and the Relations of Historiography and Jurisprudence' 38(4) *Journal of Australian Studies* 430.

Ann Genovese (2015a) 'Critical Decision, 1983: Commonwealth v Tasmania' 24(1) *Griffith Law Review* 1.

Ann Genovese and Shaun McVeigh (2015b) 'Nineteen Eighty Three: A Jurisographic Report on Commonwealth v Tasmania' *Griffith Law Review* 68

Kevin Gilbert (1973) *Because A White Man'll Never Do It*, Angus and Robertson.

Kevin Gilbert (1977) *Living Black: Blacks talk to Kevin Gilbert*, Penguin Press.

Lee Godden (2015) 'Law and the Practices of 'Damming': *Tasmanian Dams Case* as a Turning Point' 24(1) *Griffith Law Review* 127.

Melissa Harper (2008) '1 July 1983 Saving The Franklin River: The Environment Takes Centre Stage' in Martin Crotty and David Andrew Roberts (eds) *Turning Points in Australian History*, University of NSW Press.

Alice Hungerford (2013) *UpRiver: Untold Stories of the Franklin River Activists*, UpRiver Mob.

Drew Hutton and Libby Connors (1999) *A History of the Australian Environment Movement*, Cambridge University Press.

Tony Judt (2008) *Reappraisals: Reflections on the Forgotten Twentieth Century*, Penguin Press.

Bryan Keon-Cohen (2013) *A Mabo Memoir: Islan Kustom to Native Title*, 2nd edn, Zemvic Press.

Hon Michael Kirby AC CMG (2014) '*Koowarta*: A Vital Turning Point for Aboriginal Rights and Australia Summing Up the Symposium' 23(1) *Griffith Law Review* 127.
Rebecca LaForgia (2015) 'Limitlessness in Australian Constitutional Legal Narrative: The Memory of Black's Address in the *Tasmanian Dam Case*' 24(1) *Griffith Law Review* 41.
M. Langton (2014) 'Koowarta: A Warrior for Justice: A Brief History of Queensland's Racially Discriminatory Legislation and the Aboriginal Litigants Who Fought It' 23(1) *Griffith Law Review* 16.
HP Lee and George Winterton (eds) (2003) *Australian Constitutional Landmarks*, Cambridge University Press.
Avishai Margalit (2004) *The Ethics of Memory*, Harvard University Press.
Hon Sir Anthony Mason (2015) 'Reflections on Legal Issues in the Tasmanian Dams Case' 24(1) *Griffith Law Review* 16.
Mark McMillan (2014) '*Koowarta* and the Rival Indigenous International: Our Place as Indigenous Peoples in the International' 23(1) *Griffith Law Review* 110.
Mark McMillan and Martin Clark (2015) 'Making Sense of Indigeneity, Aboriginality and Identity: Race as a Constitutional Conundrum since 1983' 24(1) *Griffith Law Review* 106.
James McQueen (1983) *The Franklin – Not Just A River*, Penguin Books.
Noel Pearson (2011) *Up from the Mission: Selected Writings*, 2nd edn, Black Inc.
Cassandra Pybus and Richard Flanagan (eds) (1990) *The Rest of The World is Watching*, Pan Macmillan.
Alexander Reilly (2014) 'Recovering the Foundations of *Koowarta*: The Struggle of the Aboriginal Land Fund Commission to Purchase Land in Queensland' 23(1) *Griffith Law Review* 61.
Nonie Sharp (1996) *No Ordinary Judgment: Mabo, the Murray Islanders' Land Case*, Aboriginal Studies Press.
WEH Stanner (1969) *The Boyer Lectures 1968: After the Dreaming*, Australian Broadcasting Commission.
Maureen Tehan (2014) 'Practising Law and Politics in 1980s Australia: The Liberating Effect of *Koowarta v Bjelke-Petersen*' 23(1) *Griffith Law Review* 92.
Phillip Toyne (1994) *The Reluctant Nation: Environment, Law and Politics in Australia*, ABC Books.
Nicole Watson (2014) 'Justice in Whose Eyes? Why Lawyers Should Read Black Australian Literature' 23(1) *Griffith Law Review* 44.
Jeremy Webber (1995) 'The Jurisprudence of Regret', 17 (5) *Sydney Law Review* 5.
John Woodley (1998) 'John Koowarta: Mabo of the Mainland' 17 *Social Alternatives* 26.
Judith Wright (1994a) *Collected Poems: 1942–1985*, Angus & Robertson.
Judith Wright (1999b) *Half a Lifetime* (ed Patricia Clark), Text Publishing.

Cases

Amalgamated Society of Engineers v Adelaide Steamship Company (1920) 28 CLR 129.
Commonwealth v Tasmania (1983) 158 CLR 1.
Gerhardy v Brown (1985) 159 CLR 70.
Koowarta v Bjelke-Petersen (1982) 153 CLR 168.
Mabo v Queensland [No. 2] (1992) 175 CLR 1.
Maloney v the Queen (2013) 298 ALR 308.
Osmond v Public Service Board of NSW [1984] 3 NSWLR 447.
Public Service Board of NSW v Osmond (1986) 159 CLR 656.
Victoria v The Commonwealth (1971) 122 CLR 353.
Wurridjal v The Commonwealth (2009) 237 CLR 309.
Wik Peoples v Queensland (1996) 187 CLR 1.

Legislation

Land Act 1962 (Qld).
National Parks and Wildlife Conservation Act 1975 (Cth).
Racial Discrimination Act 1975 (Cth).

Koowarta: A Warrior for Justice
A Brief History of Queensland's Racially Discriminatory Legislation and the Aboriginal Litigants Who Fought It

M. Langton

Centre for Health and Society, Melbourne School of Population and Global Health, University of Melbourne, Australia

The Koowarta case was one of several that began in the 1970s when indigenous people took action against racial discrimination and denial of rights to land by the Queensland government. The granting of mining leases over Aboriginal reserves instigated further litigation, including the Peinkinna and Wik cases. To understand the decision by the Queensland cabinet to deprive Koowarta of the land transfer of the pastoral lease purchased by the Aboriginal Land Commission, and the events that followed his case, this article details the history of 'native' administration in that state. Late in the history of this 'protectorate', the mining industry (and its generous treatment by the Queensland government) led to abuses of the Aboriginal peoples of the western region of Cape York Peninsula. The Koowarta case laid the ground for the recognition of native title in pastoral leases, a matter which John Koowarta's neighbours, the Wik, Thaayorre and Alngith peoples, pursued with the same determination.

I first met John Koowarta in Aurukun in 1990. He was short, slight, but ruggedly tough, with a glint in his eyes that telegraphed his determination. I met him again in 1990 in Brisbane when Noel Pearson brought a delegation of elders from Cape York to talk to then Premier Wayne Goss about the need for land rights. In 1995, after Koowarta's death, I worked with Dr Peter Sutton to document the traditional ownership of his land for the purposes of documenting a case for his claim, this time under the Native Title Act 1993 *(Cth). We travelled across his country with his widow, children and other family members. I learnt that he had, for many years, been a mechanic and welder. He did not know his country at all well, which is why our fellow travellers Koppa and Dugal were asked by him to come along. They had been nomads in their time. From his homeland up in the ranges, the noise and mayhem of Aurukun was far away. One of his witty kinfolk referred to Aurukun as 'little Beirut'. His name 'Koowarta' was an important one. It refers to sacred narratives of his country: ku' = dog + waat = promiscuous one (larrikin). This is a reference to the Leech (Ularrk) totem of John's patriclan. 'Dog' is not a reference to Dingo (which was one of his totems) but to the fact that a man of this clan would have a dog called Waat. One day, as we drove across his land, one of the white men who worked for the pastoral lease drew his rifle and pointed at a dingo. Every woman in the vehicle dived across to the front to grab his rifle – this dingo was a sign that Koowarta's spirit was present. He was one of several warriors for justice in Queensland that I detail here who were fighting against Queensland state apartheid.*

Introduction

In several legal cases in Queensland that began in the 1970s, indigenous men and women began to cut the Gordian knot of hateful laws that denied their humanity. In doing so, they followed their brothers and sisters elsewhere who had blazed the trail. Aboriginal and Torres Islander peoples living in Queensland in the 1960s were entitled to feel outrage at their situation. In the south, in the cities of Melbourne, Sydney and Canberra, enlightened politicians and campaigners for equal rights were overturning the old system of separatist exclusion of Aboriginal people, yet in Queensland the state intensified its draconian racialist grip on their lives. As in the Northern Territory, where hard won rights were recognised much earlier, it was in response to the granting of mining leases over Aboriginal reserves that Aboriginal action in Queensland was instigated, including litigation, and then, in turn, repressive measures by governments and retrograde court decisions.

This is the Queensland in which the decision to deprive John Koowarta of his land was made, and that the High Court ruled upon. To understand this decision by the Queensland cabinet and the events that followed the High Court case, it is necessary to traverse the history of 'native' administration in that state, the repressive legislation that separated Aborigines into Crown reserves in deprived circumstances and, in particular, the deprivation of both civil rights and the right to live freely as Aborigines, which led to a series of cases, of which Koowarta was only one. Late in the history of this 'protectorate', the mining industry, and its generous treatment by the Queensland government, led to abuses designed to strike terror into the hearts of the Aboriginal peoples of the western region of Cape York Peninsula. The Peinkinna[1] and the Wik cases[2] ('the pastoral leases case') can also be understood in the context of this history. Koowarta's case expressed his unwillingness, and that of his people, to continue to suffer the injustice of racism and the deprivation of their rights to their traditional land, and it laid the ground for the recognition of native title in pastoral leases, a matter which his neighbours, the Wik, Thaayorre and Alngith peoples, pursued with the same determination.

The 1897 Act and Subsequent Legislation

The seeds of repressive laws against Aboriginal people had been sown early in Queensland. The *Aboriginals Protection and Restriction of the Sale of Opium Act 1897* (Qld) (1897 Act) came into force on 1 January 1898. Its purpose was to separate Aborigines from the growing white population. It was drafted during the final colonial push for control of all the land in the state of Queensland, a move that required the removal and 'pacification' of its indigenous inhabitants. This widespread removal of Aboriginal people from their traditional territories was

[1] *Peinkinna & Ors v Director of Aboriginal and Islander Advancement* (1978) 17 ALR 129.
[2] *Wik Peoples v Queensland* (1996) 187 CLR 1.

justified partly because of the devastating impact of opium supplied by Chinese immigrants who had come to try their chances on the north Queensland goldfields. The removals were also a deliberate population control method, and resulted in what Charles Rowley later called a 'gulag archipelago'.[3] There were divergent approaches to Aboriginal populations according to their proximity to the larger white settlements.[4] Two newly established 'protectors of Aborigines' directed this administrative regime, relying on police as agents of the colonial state to remove Aborigines from areas where the colonists were taking up blocks of land to graze their stock. In time, district protectors were drawn from police ranks to streamline an increasingly methodical pattern of removal. If female, old and infirm, or young and weak, the Aboriginal detainees were confined in the administered settlements of the reserves where they were subject to the whim of superintendents appointed under the Act. If male and fit, they were usually contracted as unfree – and unpaid – labourers to the new settlers.[5]

At the time of the 1897 Act, a few large reserves existed in Cape York Peninsula at Yarrabah in North Queensland, and several smaller ones operated in southern Queensland, such as at Cherbourg, near Kingaroy, and around Brisbane. Others that had been operating in the 1870s had already been sacrificed to colonial expansion. The reserves became restricted areas, accessible only by permit under s 11 of the 1897 Act. The administrative machinery of this regime depended on a 'network of protectors' who, as Kidd explains, invoked relocation provisions to incarcerate thousands of Aboriginal people.[6] The protectors were capable of extraordinarily arbitrary decisions, and yet they dutifully wrote down in their 'removals registers' an ever-growing number of reasons for their verdicts on the fate of each person they selected for removal: being born of Aboriginal parents; of mixed parentage and under the age of 16 or associating with 'full-blood' Aborigines; being a female of mixed parentage; refusing to work where directed; failing to 'support' one's family; being defined as a neglected child; being described as promiscuous; using alcohol or opium (a legal drug until 1905), to name a few. Any of these categories was grounds for removal from family and country, and confinement on the reserves.[7]

The Act's provisions enabling these assignments were unequivocal. Section 9 stated:

> It shall be lawful for the Minister to cause every aboriginal within any District, not being an aboriginal excepted from the provisions of this section, to be removed to, and kept within the limits of, any reserve situated within such District, in such manner, and subject to such conditions, as may be prescribed. The Minister may, subject to the said conditions, cause any aboriginal to be removed from one reserve to another.[8]

The large-scale movement of Aboriginal people from locations throughout the state to detention in Aboriginal reserves must have contributed significantly to the

[3]Rowley (1970).

[4]Kidd (1997), pp 46–47.

[5]Meston (1896); Kidd (1997), p 4; Kidd (1998); Kidd (2000).

[6]Kidd (1998), p 1.

[7]Kidd (1998), p 1.

[8]*Aboriginals Protection and Restriction of the Sale of Opium Act 1897* (Qld), s 9.

decline of the Queensland Aboriginal population. Whereas in 1881 the Aboriginal population was estimated at 20,585, by 1921 the estimate was 12,614. Even without taking into account the factor of natural population growth, more than a third of the Aboriginal population had disappeared in 40 years, except for 'about 1,400 wild and wandering natives in the northern and western fringes of the State'.[9]

With the new legislation and regime in place by 1898, the colony was able to institute forced removals of both individuals and groups, and their incarceration in administered reserve settlements.[10] By the turn of the century, many of these groups had been displaced into refugee camps around the larger settlement areas, or had set up camp in remote inaccessible places. Even so, sometimes they were eliminated by ruthless settlers, or recruited as labourers on the hundreds of luggers then plying the coasts.

The rationale for the Act lay in protecting the Aboriginal race from vice and improving the welfare of a group relegated to extinction. However, it was implemented to expedite the separation, control and exploitation of thousands of Aboriginal and Torres Strait Islander peoples. Both in the reserves, and throughout the rural areas where they were forced into labour, and at some of the reserve settlements, such as Yarrabah and Palm Island, the inmates suffered starvation, illness and debilitating discriminatory measures designed to ensure that they could not escape an administrative regime which, by the 1960s, the state had honed to a superb mechanism of apartheid and oppression.

Indeed, by 1960, the overwhelming majority of Aborigines and Torres Strait Islanders in Queensland had been moved to reserves under a series of statutes that originated in the 1897 Act. It was superseded by the *Aboriginals Preservation and Protection Act 1939* (Qld) and the *Torres Strait Islander Act 1939* (Qld), which provided that most Aborigines and Torres Strait Islanders living in Queensland were effectively wards of the state.[11] This followed a 1937 gathering of Queensland Ministers in Canberra who came, at the invitation of the Commonwealth, to discuss the 'problem' of the growing 'coloured population'. The result of this meeting was incremental changes to the legal regime governing Aborigines to more assimilationist policies.

Under the *Aboriginals Preservation and Protection Act 1939* (Qld), the Director of Native Affairs was the 'legal guardian of every aboriginal child under 21'.[12] The Director also had wide powers of control over a defined category of 'aboriginals', but his powers did not apply to 'a half-blood child living with and supported by a parent of such child who is not subject to this Act',[13] in other words, those children who had been taken into white households as child labour or, as was sometimes the case, fostered or adopted. By the time this Act was repealed and replaced by the *Aboriginal and Torres Strait Islander Act 1965* (Qld) the Director of Aboriginal and Islander Affairs (who replaced the role of Director of Native Affairs) was no longer the legal guardian of indigenous children. However, these niceties were often lost on

[9]Australian Bureau of Statistics (1924).

[10]Rowley (1970); Loos (1982); Kidd (1997), p 5.

[11]This Act remained operative until 1965 when it was repealed by the *Aboriginal and Torres Strait Islander Affairs Act 1965* (Qld); the 1965 Act was repealed by the *Aborigines Act 1971* (Qld) and *Torres Strait Islander Act 1971* (Qld).

[12]*Aboriginals Preservation and Protection Act 1939* (Qld), s 18(1).

[13]*Aboriginals Preservation and Protection Act 1939* (Qld), s 22.

the officers who implemented the terms of the legislation in far-flung and remote Aboriginal reserves, pastoral leases and rural townships.

Reserve Life

For the tens of thousands incarcerated on the reserves up until the 1960s, life changed little. Their lives were administered by superintendents who controlled such rights as movement, association and residence. Men and women residing on reserves could not leave unless they had formal documentation, which required that they report to police at their destination. If they were employed at all, they were paid 'training' wages which were often garnisheed or confiscated by the Chief Protector, and sometimes by local police, amounting to endemic fraudulent accounting often sanctioned by the state. Dormitories were maintained for the incarceration of children, while 'trouble makers' and the severely ill were separated from their families and removed to remote reserves.[14]

The poverty on the reserves was dire, resulting in chronic and epidemic health problems. Reserve residents were denied the right to vote, to marry without the permission of the superintendent, to travel and, in most cases, to attend school beyond primary level.[15]

Some Aborigines and Islanders, if they had left the reserves, could obtain an exemption from the status of controlled ward by proving their commitment to 'live like the white man'. But most could not achieve this goal, prevented at every turn by discrimination and race hate. To rent a house was sometimes possible, but to buy a home was impossible. To get a job was sometimes possible, but to be paid equal wages was not. Some Aboriginal people 'passed' as people from other ethnicities, living a lie, claiming to be Māori or Hawai'ian. Even in the suburbs of Brisbane, the regime had agents who would report on the people exempted from some of the conditions of the Acts and, in such circumstances, if too many relatives came to visit, or the garden was untidy, a window broken, or music played too loudly, a report would be made to the Director of Aboriginal Affairs, Dr Pat Killoran. They would be promptly arrested and returned to a reserve chosen by Killoran. Some families managed to evade the scrutiny of the departmental agents, but they were a wily minority.[16]

This situation continued until the late 1960s, after which some Aboriginal people worked as free agents, being able to leave the administered reserve settlements when the legislation curtailing labour movements was repealed.[17] In 1966, amendments to electoral laws granted indigenous Australians the right to vote in state elections and, in the same year, the department abolished taxes and deductions that had been withheld from Aboriginal employees for almost 50 years.[18] The Queensland government

[14]See Rowley (1970); Loos (1982); McGinness (1991); Briscoe (1996); Langton and Loos (2008).

[15]See Rowley (1970); Loos (1982); McGinness (1991); Briscoe (1996); Langton and Loos (2008).

[16]See Rowley (1970); Loos (1982); McGinness (1991); Briscoe (1996); Langton and Loos (2008).

[17]Kidd (1997), p 12.

[18]Kidd (1998), pp 12–13.

retained control in other ways, however, as Kidd points out: '[a]s other statutory controls over Aboriginal lives were removed, social monitoring was redefined from the police to the secular, under area managers'.[19] There were some welcome reforms, but much too late for the families impoverished and marginalised by the previous regimes:

> In 1966, the department ceased nearly 50 years of multiple levies and deductions from Aboriginal earnings. For the first time, account holders gained access to their bank passbooks and control of their savings. On Aboriginal communities, Aboriginal councils, courts and police were formalized to increase social participation. The abolition of compulsory work contracts and discounted wages endorsed the atmosphere of 'liberalisation'.[20]

As Kidd has observed, it was no coincidence that electoral and wage laws were repealed almost simultaneously, since, by creating a constituency through enfranchisement, governments could no longer deny Aboriginal peoples a place within the Australian polity. As Kidd demonstrates so meticulously, under the reserve system in Queensland, indigenous communities were construed by both the Queensland and Commonwealth governments as economic and civic burdens throughout the 20th century. The priority of both tiers of government had been to minimise this burden rather than to provide governance. Even before the 1897 Act legislated for the relocation of Aboriginal people, the state of Queensland shirked responsibility for Aboriginal peoples. For the duration of the reserve era, it sought to prop up an unviable system, firstly through missions, then through the appropriation of indigenous peoples' wages and, finally, through Commonwealth subsidies. Indeed, without the financial support of churches and the voluntary work of missionaries, the reserve system would have collapsed.[21]

The Queensland government also relied on the misappropriation of indigenous wages held in trust accounts to fund an administrative regime which, ironically, was purported to be for the benefit of people diminished to the point of requiring state welfare. Kidd describes this as a persistent tactic:

> Analysis of internal documents held by the department reveals a complex web of negligence, fraud and misappropriation in the official handling of income generated by Aboriginal workers. Financial abuses occurred at several points: non or under-payment of wages and 'pocket money', fraud by police protectors, unofficial departmental appropriations, and official government confiscation.[22]

The government's appropriation and mismanagement of Aboriginal wages was most acute during John Bleakley's term as Chief Protector – an appointment that began in 1914 and lasted almost 30 years – in which he progressively increased the use of Aboriginal employees' and military servicemen's wages on services and goods that should have been funded by the government.[23] He did so by means of levies charged on Aboriginal wages, as well as by more underhanded means, such as

[19]Kidd (1998), p 12.

[20]Kidd (1998), p 12.

[21]Kidd (1997), pp 61–62.

[22]Kidd (1997), p 130.

[23]Kidd (1997), p 69.

depositing unclaimed moneys into a government account.[24] Bleakley shrewdly increased minimum wages from 1914 to counter war-time funding cuts. This decision benefitted the government rather than indigenous employees, whose money was constantly skimmed off by the Chief Protector.

The extent of the gross misuse of Aboriginal funds was revealed in a 1922 public service inquiry into the Aboriginal subdepartment. It was reported again in a 1932 public service inspection which revealed an entrenched practice amongst police of pilfering from Aboriginal savings, often through doctored receipts.[25] Happily for Bleakley, this justified the centralisation of the greater proportion of Aboriginal wage funds into a government account. This fund provided the general maintenance levies for Aboriginal management, as well as being invested to produce income for the government and dipped into to prop up other government funds in deficit.[26] When, in 1935, William Forgan Smith's Labor government challenged the previous coalition's financial operations, Bleakley and his Minister, Hanlon, falsely denied the appropriation of Aboriginal trust funds. Hanlon did acknowledge the use of funds in savings accounts, but insisted, again falsely, that these were used only for the benefit of Aboriginal people and not for departmental purposes.[27]

The end of the war brought a new chapter for missions, with the realisation that state and federal governments had not shouldered their responsibility for Aboriginal welfare in Australia, instead relying on the mission system to provide Christian charity.[28] With the financial strains of the war, the Queensland government lobbied hard for financial assistance in Aboriginal affairs from the Commonwealth. While the Commonwealth influence over the state governance of Aboriginal affairs was apparent at least since the 1920s, and certainly during the 1940s, it had, beyond a handful of welfare provisions, largely shirked financial and political responsibility for indigenous Australians.[29]

Mining and the Queensland State

Almost a century after the 1897 Act, indeed as late as 1984, the intent of this system of removing and controlling the state's Aboriginal population in administered reserve settlements continued under the terms of the *Aborigines Act 1971* (Qld) and the *Torres Strait Islanders Act 1971* (Qld).[30] Two exceptions were made in 1978

---

[24]Kidd (1997), p 131.

[25]Kidd (1997), p 132.

[26]Kidd (1997), p 133.

[27]Kidd (1997), p 134.

[28]Loos (2007), pp 97–99.

[29]Kidd (1997), p 153.

[30]See Brennan (1992), p 29 for an important reference to information about the progress towards this Act. He cites Reid's (1988) unpublished PhD thesis, *History of Philanthropic Movements Towards Protection of Aboriginals in Queensland in the Nineteenth Century*. Rev Duncan McNab, a Catholic missionary and a member of the Aborigines Commission, applied on 24 July 1876, on behalf of Aborigines, for selection of homestead blocks of land in the Logan district under the *Crown Lands Alienation Act 1868*. They were refused. The calendar is published by the Western Cape College. A copy can be viewed at www.westerncapecollege.eq.edu.au/aurukun_cultural_calendar_2007.pdf.

under Premier Bjelke-Petersen's government: Aurukun and Mornington Island were the subject of an extraordinary takeover executed under the terms of a new statute, the *Local Government (Aboriginal Lands) Act 1978* (Qld). The statute was designed to allow a bauxite mining project at Weipa proceed without the inconvenience of any Aboriginal rights in land. It also had the effect of neutering and removing the Uniting Church which had, until then, managed the two reserves.

This followed the discovery by mining company Comalco of bauxite in western Cape York in the 1950s. In 1957, the Queensland parliament passed the *Commonwealth Aluminium Corporation Pty Limited Agreement Act 1957* (Qld) ('the Comalco Act') and the government issued mining leases to the company. Nearly 8000 square kilometres were excised from the mission reserve. Said to be the world's richest deposits, further exploration established that the ore body extended from north of Weipa where the Presbyterian mission Mapoon had been established in 1891, to the south of the Embley River where another Presbyterian mission, Aurukun, lay.

Both missions were operated as closed communities under the supervision of the missionaries. By 1907, Mapoon was operating as an industrial school under the *Industrial and Reformatory Schools Act 1865* (Qld) with dormitories filled with forcibly removed children from all over the Cape. In 1946, conditions at Mapoon had been described as 'nauseating'.[31] There were dormitories for children at Aurukun too, where their lives were strictly regulated. In the *Cape York Justice Study Report*, the excruciating details of these extraordinary events are recounted.

> With only 45 houses for 280 people, in 1951, the housing stock was officially condemned. There were severe food shortages and contaminated water. At Aurukun, people were eating the cash crop of coconuts to survive, while almost £30,500 of their confiscated earnings were held in trust, which the Department refused to permit to be used for any purpose other than 'development'. In 1953, 12 delegates from Mapoon lobbied Director of Native Affairs Cornelius O'Leary on Thursday Island, complaining of stalled improvements and a succession of untrained superintendents. They had also learned, although it was supposedly secret, of plans to relocate Mapoon to Bamaga at the tip of Cape York. Aurukun was also in revolt at this time, several stock workers learning that they were being worked on the mission for a pittance. O'Leary visited but was given a hostile reception, and seven 'agitators' were removed to Palm Island.[32]

'Palm Island', or Great Palm Island, was another Aboriginal reserve off the coast near Townsville, controlled by the department itself rather than a mission, and used as a penal settlement.[33] Hundreds of 'troublemakers' from the reserves and missions

---

[31]Kidd (1997), p 171.

[32]Fitzgerald (2001), Draft history chapter for Cape York Justice Study, copy with author.

[33]Great Palm Island was gazetted as a 'reserve for the use of the Aboriginal people of the State' on 20 June 1914. All but two of the remaining islands of the Palm Islands Group were added to the reserve in later years. Palm Island was intended to be used for the resettlement of Aborigines brought from remote parts of Queensland. The Queensland Chief Protector of Aboriginals was intended, under the provisions of the *Aboriginals Protection and Restriction of the Sale of Opium Act 1897* (Qld), to use the Palm Islands to intern people who had been removed from the northern regions of Queensland. It remains a restricted area under government regulation. The Manbarra people are the traditional owners, many of whom remain living on the island among the descendants of Aboriginal people incarcerated on the island when it served as a penal settlement. These latter call themselves the Bwgcolman people.

around Queensland were sent there. By the 1960s, the abuses of Aboriginal people on Palm Island had been begun to be exposed by Joe McGinness. A pastor of the mission severely flogged a young man who had been caught 'consorting' with his girlfriend and ordered the young man to be removed from Palm Island. After a long and intense campaign against the pastor's actions, which gained unprecedented publicity, Queensland's Minister for Native Affairs, Dr Noble, continued to condone the punishment, describing it as 'part of the tribal way of living'.[34] Eventually, the persistence of McGinness and others eventually forced the government to hold an inquiry into the incident, which found that the pastor's behaviour was 'inexcusable'.[35] This single example of success gave heart to those elsewhere who sought civil rights and an end to the widespread practice of racist abuses.

Starvation among the populations of these Aboriginal internment settlements was widespread, and reports emanating from the reserves acknowledged this. Enforced population removals, such as that which had occurred at Cape Bedford and Cape Melville in Cape York, continued elsewhere in the state.[36] The people at Mapoon were not spared this fate: the Queensland government, motivated by Comalco's enthusiasm to proceed with this lucrative project, decided to forcibly remove the residents from the Mapoon mission, with the Queensland police being tasked with the operation. The mission announced its closure, and residents were told to go elsewhere, many of whom refused to go. On the morning of 15 November 1963, residents woke to find a contingent of police burning their houses and church, and shooting their dogs. They were rounded up by the police and relocated to the Northern Peninsula, to an area at the tip of Cape York Peninsula named 'New Mapoon' by the Queensland government. One of the residents removed in this raid was Rachel Peter who described the events for a Uniting Church publication:

> We're the ones that were moved out by police, by gunpoint, [on] that boat they sent for us ... sneaked in on us in the night ... they came from Thursday Island. We were really sad, but we just had to go because they told us we were going for questioning. At the Bamaga wharf they told us there were seven houses waiting for us to walk in and light the stoves. And when we arrived in Bamaga there were no homes. We were just standing out in the streets like a mob of cattle with nowhere to go.[37]

She added:

> This is what they do, but the world doesn't know. People don't know how we were treated. They destroyed the homes, burnt them down you know. And I seen all the burning down of the homes, the church ... it was destroying our culture, our lives. [38]

The Mapoon mission area was never used for mining, but, regardless of the disruption to the lives of the residents, the Queensland government refused to allow them to return. Alcan was issued with mining leases over large tracts of land in the

---

[34]Ah Kit (2003).

[35]Ah Kit (2003).

[36]Fitzgerald (2001), Draft history chapter for Cape York Justice Study, copy with author.

[37]Rachel Peter, as quoted by Collings (1997), p 6.

[38]Rachel Peter, cited in Roberts and McLean (1976), p 10.

vicinity. Further to the south, at Weipa, Comalco was given mining leases over 587,802 hectares of Aboriginal reserve land. Later, Comalco set aside 125 hectares of this for Aboriginal use, thus reducing the size of the reserve by 347,831 hectares.

On 21 November 1975, the Queensland government approved draft legislation for the start of a $100 million bauxite mining and alumina refining scheme at Aurukun, a decision that prompted a legal challenge by local Wik people. From 27 November 1925, William and Geraldine MacKenzie, the former a graduate in theology from Ormond College in Melbourne, had ruled the mission with fierce regard for 'Christian' propriety, and had been the subject of several complaints about their treatment of their Aboriginal charges. Until 1937, there was no wireless communication with the outside world and the MacKenzies' only contact with other missions was by lugger.[39] The mission staff patrolled the reserve on horseback. Nevertheless, the mission was visited by a few hardy individuals who had the courage to make formal complaints about the abuses they witnessed. One was anthropologist Ursula McConnell, who exposed a culture of abuse and punitive control – disobedience was met with whippings, residents were threatened with guns, chained to trees and imprisoned without food or water.[40] Although McConnell's report on Aurukun corroborated a letter of complaint Chief Protector Bleakley had received from the residents themselves, he failed to intervene, justifying the MacKenzies' behaviour as extreme but necessary in order to maintain order.[41] Anthropologist and naturalist Donald Thomson also witnessed instances of cruel and sadistic treatment, which he photographed and later published in southern newspapers.[42] One instance saw William MacKenzie shackle together three men and two women and march them at gunpoint 380 kilometres to Laura before they were transported to Palm Island. Kidd describes this as a regular occurrence, citing a similar incident a year earlier in which residents 'were beaten by police before they left Aurukun, flogged several times along the way including one woman who was six months pregnant, and the women were sexually assaulted'.[43]

The Referendum, and the Power of the Commonwealth to Legislate

Such racism of the Queensland government towards its Aboriginal citizens was not without opposition from the Commonwealth. Within Canberra, there was a widespread view that the states were failing Aboriginal people and that action needed to be taken. State neglect was at least one reason for Commonwealth support for a constitutional referendum. As George Williams writes:

> The obvious discrimination against Aboriginal people on the face of the Australian constitution was one factor in the emergence of moves to amend it. Another factor was a concern that Aboriginal issues were not being dealt with appropriately at the state

[39]Mackenzie (1981).

[40]Kidd (1997), pp 118–120.

[41]Kidd (1997), pp 119–120.

[42]Kidd (1997), pp 120–121.

[43]Kidd (1997), p 121.

level and that the federal parliament ought to be given primary responsibility for their welfare.[44]

Few constitutional referendums have succeeded in Australia, yet the 1967 referendum was passed by almost 90 per cent of Australian voters, easily the highest 'yes' vote ever. It signalled, Neil Westbury argues, the end of the first phase of the development of indigenous policies in Australia which had commenced with the development of the Australian Constitution.[45] Prior to the referendum, the Commonwealth government had jurisdiction only to determine matters in relation to indigenous peoples in the Northern Territory and the Australian Capital Territory. As such, responsibility for indigenous affairs fell within the Department of the Interior. Post referendum, the new Gorton government installed the first 'Minister in Charge of Aboriginal Affairs under the Prime Minister', responsible for the management of the Office of Aboriginal Affairs (OAA) and a Council of Aboriginal Affairs (CAA) which, when constituted, consisted of three non-indigenous men – HC Coombs, Barrie Dexter and William Stanner.

Land Rights and the Whitlam Government

The ascension of Gough Whitlam to power saw the beginning of an era of significant change in indigenous affairs. The Department of Aboriginal Affairs was established in 1973, replacing both the OAA and the CAA. The Whitlam government announced a policy of 'self-determination', leading to 'two early experiments in the creation of government sponsored Aboriginal representative structures, the National Aboriginal Consultative Committee (NACC) 1973–77 and the National Aboriginal Conference (NAC) 1977–85'.[46] The earliest of these, the NACC, was the first federal government body to be elected by indigenous people. However, as advisory bodies only, 'they suffered greatly from the criticism that they did not go far enough in giving decision making power in aboriginal affairs to Aborigines'.[47] Both the NACC and the NAC, according to the late Charles Perkins who was the Secretary of the Department of Aboriginal Affairs between 1981 and 1990, often came into contact with the states. These bodies, he said, fundamentally altered the nature of federal/state relations in respect of indigenous policy, laying 'the foundations for genuine new direction in Aboriginal affairs; the beginning of the establishment of the now 2000 Aboriginal controlled organisations throughout Australia'.[48]

The other significant Act of the Whitlam government was the introduction of the *Racial Discrimination Act 1975* (Cth) (RDA). The effect of this Act on the later development of the doctrine of native title is significant. Without it, native title might have been extinguished everywhere by federal and state extinguishing Acts, such as the Queensland legislation that purported to extinguish native title, which was later

[44]Williams (2000), p 652.
[45]Westbury (2005), p 26.
[46]Sanders (1993), p 475.
[47]Sanders (1993), p 475.
[48]Perkins (1992), p 224.

ruled inconsistent with the RDA and thus invalid by the High Court.[49] In Western Australia, similar legislation had been enacted to that overruled in the first Mabo judgment; however, it too was overruled in the High Court based on its inconsistency with provisions in the RDA.[50]

However, whilst the RDA has proved important in protecting Aboriginal people from racial abuse by the states, it does not provide protection from the exercise of racially discriminatory legislation by the Commonwealth, as George Williams has observed:

> Even the Racial Discrimination Act has proved a fragile shield. Few people realise that it has been overridden twice in the past decade. On both occasions, in 1998 in regard to native title and in 2007 for the Northern Territory intervention, a federal law provided that if it was racially discriminatory it was to operate despite the Racial Discrimination Act. [51]

Peinkinna's Case and the Fraser Government

In 1976, Prime Minister Malcolm Fraser inherited a remarkable legislative agenda from his predecessor Gough Whitlam. His government quickly asserted a commitment to Aboriginal self-management, passing a number of significant pieces of legislation which significantly worked to alter the state of affairs for indigenous people in Queensland and the Northern Territory. Undoubtedly the most significant of these was the *Aboriginal Land Rights (Northern Territory) Act 1976* (Cth) – drafted by the Whitlam government – which established a Territory-wide scheme for the granting of freehold title to indigenous groups with claims to areas of land. In addition, the *Aboriginal Councils and Associations Act 1976* (Cth), which established the Office of the Registrar of Aboriginal Corporations, was also soon to pass.

By the 1970s too, a new breed of missionaries had replaced the old regime of the MacKenzies at Aurukun. The new guard were concerned just as much for the rights of their Aboriginal friends as for their souls, and they assisted by ensuring that Aurukun residents had sound legal advice regarding the proposed mine. The residents' decision was to litigate and Donald Peinkinna was named as the applicant on the court documents. In 1978, he brought a case to the courts that challenged an agreement by the Queensland Director of Aboriginal and Islanders Advancement consenting to bauxite mining under which profits would be paid to him on behalf of Aborigines. The case was initially won in the Supreme Court of Queensland, which found the agreement constituted a breach of trust; however, the Queensland government successfully appealed this decision to the Privy Council which found against Donald Peinkinna in March 1978.[52]

Around the same time, the Fraser government attempted to override the Queensland government's racism by providing a federal statute to give Aboriginal people the right of self-management: the *Aboriginal and Torres Strait Islanders*

---

[49] *Mabo v Queensland (No. 1)* (1988) 166 CLR 186.

[50] *WA v Commonwealth* (1995) 183 CLR 373.

[51] Williams (2008).

[52] *Peinkinna & Ors v Director of Aboriginal and Islander Advancement* (1978) 17 ALR 129.

(Queensland Reserves and Communities Self-management) Act 1978 (Cth). Queensland immediately countered by legislating to preserve its system of racist exclusion by revoking the reserve status of the reserve lands of the Aurukun and Mornington Island communities in May 1978. The *Local Government (Aboriginal Lands) Act 1978* (Qld) provided instead for 50 year leases to the residents of Aurukun and Mornington Island, and switched the status of the land from 'Reserve' to 'Crown', which meant that the Queensland government was virtually taking it out of the reach of the Commonwealth. In addition, it meant that the Uniting Church in Australia, which had managed the communities and had vigorously supported them, was sacked.

The Peinkinna case, and the several that followed, all brought by Wik people to prevent the loss of their rights by government decree, are still celebrated at Aurukun where the school publishes a calendar, which, along with cultural and seasonal information, recalls the leaders who defended their rights and land. Peinkinna and others are often cited as the inspiration for several generations of Aboriginal leaders from western Cape York who inspired others to pursue their rights through the courts, and who also brought the parlous state of affairs for indigenous people in Queensland to the attention of successive Commonwealth governments. Premier Bjelke-Petersen would not acquiesce, however.

Koowarta's Case

Successive Queensland state governments, from the early 1970s to the 1990s, used environmental conservation legislation and instruments to prevent Aboriginal groups from acquiring and using land.[53] The most notorious of such actions was that taken against the late John Koowarta of the Winychanam group of Cape York. He was sometimes resident at Aurukun and also at settlements further inland following his attempted purchase, with the assistance of the Aboriginal Land Fund Commission, of the Archer River Pastoral Holding, located on his traditional territory in central Cape York. In February 1976, Koowarta and the Aboriginal Land Commission entered into a written contract with the lessees for the purchase of the lease, as well as the cattle and horses on the lease. However, the sale and transfer of the lease was subject to approval by the Minister for Lands of the State of Queensland, who used his authority to refuse the transfer. According to Collings, Queensland government policy explicitly opposed 'proposals to acquire large areas of additional freehold land or leasehold land for development by Aborigines or Aboriginal groups in isolation'.[54] The government gazetted a number of national parks over the pastoral properties that Aboriginal peoples had expressed interest in buying, with the intent to prevent them from purchasing the land.

On approximately 8 December 1976, the Minister for Lands stated the reasons for refusing to grant approval or permission for such transfer, including that:

> The question of the proposed acquisition of Archer River Pastoral Holding comes within the ambit of declared Government policy expressed in Cabinet decision of September 1972, which stated: 'The Queensland Government does not view favourably

[53]See, for example, Rigsby (2006).

[54]Hanks (1990), p 6 as quoted by Collings (1997), p 7.

proposals to acquire large areas of additional freehold or leasehold land for development by Aborigines or Aboriginal groups in isolation'. [55]

In the light of this policy, the recent development whereby the Aboriginal Land Fund Commission sought to acquire by transfer Archer River Pastoral Holding was reported in detail to state cabinet, whereupon cabinet said in June 1976:

> That Cabinet's policy regarding Aboriginal reserve lands, as approved in Decision No. 17541 of 4 September 1972 remain unchanged ... That in accordance with such policy and as it is considered that sufficient land in Queensland is already reserved and available for use and benefit of Aborigines, no consent be given to the transfer of Archer River Pastoral Holding No. 4785 to the Aboriginal Land Fund Commission. [56]

Koowarta appealed this decision to the High Court, citing the RDA: he argued that the Queensland government had breached this Act by refusing to grant a lease to the Aboriginal Land Fund Commission. The High Court agreed and, in 1982, overruled the Queensland government. It also upheld the Commonwealth's right to legislate for racial discrimination which, it said, came about when the Commonwealth had signed the International Convention on the Elimination of All Forms of Racial Discrimination pursuant to the external affairs power of the Australian Constitution.[57]

In a cruel twist, Koowarta and the Winychanam group were never able to acquire title to their beloved country as the Queensland government had gazetted the lease area as a national park. They had, however, successfully opposed the racist intransigence of Bjelke-Petersen's government and scored a very real victory in opposing racial discrimination. Indeed, the Koowarta case is the first example of the Commonwealth using the external affairs power as the basis for legislation able to directly limit the actions of state governments.

A Labor government was in power in Canberra under Prime Minister Robert Hawke when the *Land Act (Aboriginal and Islander Land Grants) Amendment Act 1982* (Qld) established the 'deed of grant in trust' ('DOGIT') land-holding scheme for Aboriginal communities. Brennan recounts that DOGITs were granted to Aboriginal and Islander communities throughout Queensland,[58] and that the *Community Services (Aborigines) Act 1984* and *Community Services (Torres Strait Islanders) Act 1984* provided for local government administration on all the reserves, renamed communities.[59] These Acts allowed for local councils with powers to make and administer by-laws to be elected in all the communities.

---

[55]*Koowarta v Bjelke-Petersen* (1982) 153 CLR 168 at para 2 (Gibbs CJ); Lauterpacht (1985), p 185.

[56]*Koowarta v Bjelke-Petersen* (1982) 153 CLR 168 at para 2 (Gibbs CJ).

[57]*Koowarta v Bjelke-Petersen* (1982) 153 CLR 168.

[58]Brennan (1992), pp 84–86.

[59]Brennan (1992), pp 63–64. As Brennan (1992), pp 91–92 noted, the *Land Act (Aboriginal and Islander Land Grants) Amendment Act 1982* (Qld) resulted in specific amendments to the *Land Act 1962* in order to effect exclusions from deeds of grant (s 334F). Section 45 of the *Forestry Act 1959* was amended in order to ensure that timber rights were excluded from deeds of grant and s 22 of the new Act provided that no mining tenement within the meaning of the *Mining Act 1968* shall exist or be approved on land granted in trust for Aborigines or Islanders without approval of Governor-in-Council.

Mabo's Case and Queensland Land Rights

On 22 May 1991, almost a decade after John Koowarta successfully appealed to the High Court, Queensland land rights, in the form of the *Aboriginal Land Act 1991* (Qld) and the *Torres Strait Islander Land Act 1991* (Qld), were passed into law. The timing was deliberate: it was a direct response to the case brought by Eddie Koiki Mabo who was seeking to establish his ownership of land on Mer Island in the Torres Strait. The intention of the Queensland government, then led by Labor Premier Wayne Goss, was to safeguard against the effects of the as yet undetermined case in the High Court of Australia, which was anxiously awaited by indigenous people throughout the country.

The provisions of these Acts enabled 20,000 square kilometres of vacant Crown land (1.16 per cent of the state) to be added to 34,000 square kilometres of land currently held by Aboriginals and Torres Strait Islanders.[60] The Acts transferred all existing DOGIT reserve lands, including the Aurukun and Mornington Island shire leases, to Aboriginal Trust ownership. They also established a land tribunal to hear claims for vacant Crown land (except in towns and cities), which was gazetted as claimable land. Unlike the *New South Wales Aboriginal Land Rights Act 1983* (NSW), no land acquisition fund was established in Queensland, as a result of the vehement opposition of Premier Wayne Goss to the recognition of Aboriginal rights. His control of the cabinet on this matter, and refusal to bring the legislation up to the standard of other jurisdictions, was met with violent protests and outrage throughout Queensland's indigenous communities.

The *Aboriginal Land Act 1991* (Qld) provided that claims in Queensland must be based on traditional affiliation or historical association with the specific land to be transferred in fee simple tenure, if the Minister agreed with the recommendations of the tribunal. The Act also provided for claims to be made on cultural or economic viability criteria when a leasehold tenure could be granted, but again only if the Minister agreed with the recommendations of the tribunal. Few grants have been made. National parks are claimable under specified criteria if the grantees agree to lease the land back to the Crown in perpetuity and the land is jointly managed. Again, in only one case has there been a grant of this kind made by the Queensland government. Further, hunting and gathering rights are limited to the traditional owners of the particular national park. Pastoral leases, stock routes and excisions from pastoral leases for 'living areas' are not claimable.

Following the passage of this procedurally difficult and ineffective legislation in Queensland, only Western Australia, Tasmania and South Australia did not have any statutory procedures for Aboriginal land claims. Thus, more than 30 years after the referendum which gave the Commonwealth power to make laws relating to Aboriginal people, there were signs that the Queensland government was finally acquiescing to Commonwealth pressure to bring its legislation and political treatment of indigenous people into line with modern standards, albeit reluctantly.

Mabo's case was decided soon after. The High Court declared in May 1992 that the Meriam people were holders of native title, rejecting the doctrine of *terra nullius*, and leaving open the possibility that native title might apply elsewhere where

---

[60]Brennan (1992), p 30.

Aborigines who could demonstrate a continuity of traditions in relation to their land that could be traced back to annexation. The court found that native title was extinguished wherever there was an inconsistent legal title, such as a freehold and certain types of freehold. The question of whether national park or pastoral leases impaired native title was not answered, and many other matters were left for future courts to decide.[61]

The reaction of vested interests against the indigenous inheritors of native title was hysterical and vindictive. While the Murray Islanders celebrated, pastoralists and miners expressed increasingly wild theories and fears for the future of the Australian land tenure system, and anxiety over impending Aboriginal compensation claims. Without certainty for their titles, investment would dry up, they asserted. Tim Fisher, later the Deputy Prime Minister in the Howard government, called the High Court judges 'piss ants'.[62]

The Wik Case and the *Native Title Act*

At Redfern Park in Sydney on 10 December 1992, Prime Minister Paul Keating delivered the 'Redfern speech' at the launch of Australia's celebration of the 1993 United Nations International Year of the World's Indigenous People. Among other things, he addressed himself to the very recent High Court decision, and explicitly recognised Aboriginal native title that had survived the British declaration of sovereignty:

> By doing away with the bizarre conceit that this continent had no owners prior to the settlement of Europeans, Mabo establishes a fundamental truth and lays the basis for justice. It will be much easier to work from that basis than has ever been the case in the past. [63]

His support for the Mabo case was a beacon for Aboriginal leaders who hoped that the judgment might deliver justice at last. Keating called state premiers and industry representative bodies to Canberra to resolve the mounting national debate that pitted the farmers and miners against indigenous people in a vicious debate based on fear and bald lies. Aboriginal leaders – including Noel Pearson who headed the Cape York Land Council, Mick Dodson, who had campaigned at the UN in Geneva and New York for recognition of indigenous rights, David Ross from the Central Land Council and Peter Yu from the Kimberley Land Council, the late Charles Perkins, former head of the federal Department of Aboriginal Affairs, among many others – convened in Canberra to fight back.

Meanwhile, on 30 June 1993, the Wik people of western Cape York lodged a native title claim over their territories, excluding the mining leases, in the Federal Court of Australia. Their long held grievance against the Queensland government would soon become another *cause célèbre* in the long struggle for the recognition of

---

[61]*Mabo v Queensland (No 2)* (1992) 175 CLR 1.

[62]Cited in Perkins and Nowra (2008), p 244.

[63]Keating (1992).

Aboriginal rights. The case was more complex than any before it. The claim covered 35,000 square kilometres of land, including an unused 100 year bauxite mining lease granted in 1958 and held by Comalco, 10 pastoral leases, a 50 year lease and DOGIT granted to local Aborigines, and two national parks located on western Cape York Peninsula. The case had 155 Wik applicants who represented 1000 people in the community, and respondents including Comalco and the Queensland government, the federal government, the Aboriginal and Islander Affairs Corporation, Aluminium Pechiney Holdings Pty Ltd, the Council of the Shire of Aurukun, Napranum Aboriginal Council, Pormpuraaw Aboriginal Council and Eddie Holroyd (an elder of the Pormpuraaw community). Among other things, the plaintiffs contended that the Queensland government had breached its fiduciary duty as trustee to the Wik in making the land grants, including a pastoral lease, mining leases and other titles, and that the grants were therefore invalid. The Goss Queensland government sought to rescue Comalco (now 67 per cent owned by the multinational CRA Ltd) from the native title claimants and demanded that the Commonwealth legislate to prevent the claim. Prime Minister Paul Keating was not amenable to Goss' demands, and the case proceeded.

The *Native Title Act 1993* (Cth), negotiated by Aboriginal leaders who met regularly with Keating and other parliamentarians, was passed by the senate on 23 December 1993. It established a regime of compromise for the hundreds of native title claims to follow in line with Aboriginal leaders' appeal to parliament for compromise and wisdom. The senate debate on the Bill, which ran to hundreds of pages, was the longest in the history of Australia.

Conclusion

The judgment of the High Court in the Wik case, handed down in December 1996, found in favour of the plaintiffs' arguments and established the principle of co-existence, which, in tandem with the growing and powerful movement for reconciliation with Aboriginal people, fundamentally changed the relationship between settler and indigenous Australia.[64] By 2001, the spirit of reconciliation had influenced even the mining companies and a settlement with substantial financial benefits was negotiated with the Wik people.[65] It was Koowarta's determination, and especially his case challenging the racial discrimination of the Queensland government, that paved the way for these welcome changes in the way that Aboriginal property and rights were treated at law.

Acknowledgements

I gratefully acknowledge the assistance of Dr Peter Sutton in ensuring that my recollections of these events and the people involved are accurately recorded. Many thanks also to Lily O'Neill and Emille Boulot of the University of Melbourne for their research assistance with this article.

[64]*The Wik Peoples v The State of Queensland & Ors* (1996) 187 CLR 1.
[65]Crooke et al (2006), pp 95–114.

References

Primary Legal Sources

Aborigines Act 1971 (Qld).
Aboriginal and Torres Strait Islander Affairs Act 1965 (Qld).
Aboriginal and Torres Strait Islanders (Queensland Reserves and Communities Self-management) Act 1978 (Cth).
Australian Constitution.
Aboriginal Councils and Associations Act 1976 (Cth).
Aboriginal Land Act 1991 (Qld).
Aboriginal Land Rights (Northern Territory) Act 1976 (Cth).
Aboriginals Preservation and Protection Act 1939 (Qld).
Aboriginals Protection and Restriction of the Sale of Opium Act 1897 (Qld).
Commonwealth Aluminium Corporation Pty Limited Agreement Act 1957 (Qld).
Community Services (Aborigines) Act 1984 (Qld).
Community Services (Torres Strait Islanders) Act 1984 (Qld).
Crown Lands Alienation Act 1868 (Qld) (repealed).
Forestry Act 1959 (Qld).
Industrial and Reformatory Schools Act 1865 (Qld).
Koowarta v Bjelke-Petersen (1982) 153 CLR 168.
Land Act 1962 (Qld) (repealed).
Land Act (Aboriginal and Islander Land Grants) Amendment Act 1982 (Qld).
Local Government (Aboriginal Lands) Act 1978 (Qld).
Mabo v Queensland (No. 1) (1988) 166 CLR 186.
Mabo v Queensland (No 2) (1992) 175 CLR 1.
Mining Act 1968 (Qld) (repealed).
Native Title Act 1993 (Cth).
New South Wales Aboriginal Land Rights Act 1983 (NSW).
Peinkinna & Ors v Director of Aboriginal and Islander Advancement (1978) 17 ALR 129.
Racial Discrimination Act 1975 (Cth).
Torres Strait Islander Act 1939 (Qld).
Torres Strait Islander Act 1971 (Qld).
Torres Strait Islander Land Act 1991 (Qld).
WA v Commonwealth (1995) 183 CLR 373.
Wik Peoples v The State of Queensland & Ors (1996) 187 CLR 1.

Secondary Sources

Australian Bureau of Statistics (1924), *Year Book Australia 1924*, www.abs.gov.au, 10 February 2014.
Frank Brennan (1992) *Land Rights Queensland Style: The Struggle for Aboriginal Self-management*, University of Queensland Press.
Gordon Briscoe (1996) *Disease, Health and Healing: Aspects of Indigenous Health in Western Australia and Queensland, 1900–1940*, unpublished PhD thesis, Australian National University.
Neva Collings (1997) 'The Wik: A History of Their 400 Year Struggle', 4 *Indigenous Law Bulletin* 4.
Peter Crooke, Bruce Harvey and Marcia Langton (2006) 'Implementing and Monitoring Indigenous Land Use Agreements in the Minerals Industry: The Western Cape Communities Co-existence Agreement' in Marcia Langton et al (eds) *Settling with Indigenous People: Modern Treaty and Agreement-making*, Federation Press.
Tony Fitzgerald (2001) *Cape York Justice Study*, Queensland Department of Premier and Cabinet.
PJ Hanks (1990) *Australian Constitutional Law: Materials and Commentary*, 4th edition, Butterworths.
Paul Keating (1992) 'Redfern Speech (Year for the World's Indigenous Peoples)', delivered in Redfern Park, 10 December 1992.

Rosalind Kidd (1997) *The Way We Civilise: Aboriginal Affairs – The Untold Story*, University of Queensland Press.

Rosalind Kidd (1998) 'Deficits of the Past or Deceits of the Present?: Defining Aboriginal Disadvantage' 31 *Southern Review* 11.

Rosalind Kidd (2000) *Black Lives, Government Lies*, UNSW Press.

John Ah Kit (2003) Debates: Ninth Assembly of the Northern Territory, First Session, 12 August 2003, Parliamentary Record No. 14.

Marcia Langton and Noel Loos (2008) 'The Dawn is at Hand', in Rachel Perkins and Louis Nowra (eds) *First Australians*, Melbourne University Publishing.

Hersch Lauterpacht (1985) *International Law Reports*, Butterworths.

Noel Loos (1982) *Invasion and Resistance: Aboriginal–European Relations on the North Queensland Frontier 1861–1897*, Australian National University Press.

Noel Loos (2007) *White Christ Black Cross: The Emergence of a Black Church*, Aboriginal Studies Press.

Geraldine Mackenzie (1981) *Aurukun Diary*, Aldersgate Press.

Joe McGinness (1991) *Son of Alyandabu: My Fight for Aboriginal Rights*, University of Queensland Press.

Archibald Meston (1896) *Working Conditions of the Various Mission Stations and Various Other Stations Where Food is Supplied to the Aboriginals by the Government*, State of Queensland.

Charles Perkins (1992) 'Aboriginal Australia and Public Administration', 51 *Australian Journal of Public Administration* 223. doi:10.1111/j.1467-8500.1992.tb00241.x

Rachel Perkins and Louis Nowra (2008) *First Australians*, Melbourne University Publishing.

Gordon S Reid (1988) *History of Philanthropic Movements Towards Protection of Aboriginals in Queensland in the Nineteenth Century*, unpublished PhD thesis, Australian National University.

Bruce Rigsby (2006) 'Custom and Tradition: Innovation and Invention', 6 *Macquarie Law Journal* 113.

Janine Roberts (ed.) (1976) *Mapoon Story*, International Development Action.

Charles Rowley (1970) *The Destruction of Aboriginal Society*, Australian National University Press.

William Sanders (1993) 'Reconciling Public Accountability and Aboriginal Self-determination/ Self-management: Is ATSIC Succeeding?' *CAEPR Discussion Paper 51*, ANU Press.

Neil Westbury (2005) 'Shifting our Thinking – The Future of Engagement Between Governments and Indigenous Australia Post ATSIC' 4 *Public Administration Today* 26.

George Williams (2000) 'Race and the Australian Constitution: From Federation to Reconciliation' 38 *Osgoode Hall Law Journal* 643.

George Williams (2008) *The Next Step: A Treaty and Facism-free Law*, Online Opinion, www.onlineopinion.com.au/view.asp?article=7037, 29 June 2014.

Internal and external affairs: the *Koowarta* case in context

Hilary Charlesworth

Regulatory Institutions Network, College of Asia and the Pacific, Australian National University, Canberra, Australia

This article is partly based on observation of the High Court deliberations on the *Koowarta* case in 1982 and partly on reflection on its significance in defining the relationship between the Australian legal system and international law. It also contrasts the broad approach of the majority to the external affairs power with its analysis of the races power. The article suggests that the intense legal debates about the proper spheres of international, national and state law contained in the judgments are reflected in political debates today.

Introduction

Three decades on, the intense controversy generated by the *Koowarta* case[1] has faded. It has become a footnote in constitutional law texts, largely overtaken in legal significance, at least with respect to the Australian Constitution's external affairs power, by the *Tasmanian Dam* case, decided a year later.[2] This paper seeks to recover some of the contention surrounding the case in 1982. It starts with my memories of the case as an observer, and then turns to the *Koowarta* judgment.

John Koowarta, a Winychanam (Wik-Mungkan) man acting on behalf of his community, requested the Aboriginal Land Fund Commission to purchase a pastoral lease over their traditional lands on the Archer River on Cape York in 1976. The Queensland Minister for Lands refused permission for the transfer of the lease on the basis of a policy adopted by the Queensland government in 1972. This policy prevented acquisition of large tracts of land for development by Aboriginal people in isolation 'as it is considered that sufficient land in Queensland is already reserved and available for use and benefit of Aborigines'.[3] Mr Koowarta contended that Queensland's refusal to allow the transfer of the Archer River lease breached the *Racial Discrimination Act 1975* (Cth) (RDA) and brought a claim for damages against Queensland Premier Joh Bjelke-Petersen and other government members. In response, Queensland sought a declaration in the High Court that the Act was invalid as outside the Commonwealth's legislative power. It was supported in this action by Victoria and Western Australia, while the Commonwealth intervened on behalf of John Koowarta.

---

[1] *Koowarta v Bjelke-Petersen* (1982) 153 CLR 168.

[2] *Commonwealth v Tasmania* (1983) 158 CLR 1.

[3] *Koowarta v Bjelke-Petersen* (1982) 153 CLR 168 at 177.

The RDA implemented the 1965 *International Convention on the Elimination of All Forms of Racial Discrimination*, to which Australia had become a party in 1975. The relevant sections of RDA were ss 9 and 12. Section 9 (based on the language of Article 1.1 of the Convention, which defines the term 'racial discrimination') provides that:

> It is unlawful for a person to do any act involving a distinction, exclusion, restriction or preference based on race, colour, descent or ethnic origin which has the purpose or effect of nullifying or impairing the recognition, enjoyment or exercise, on an equal footing, of any human right or fundamental freedom in the political, economic, social, cultural or any other field of public life.

Section 12 of the Act, among other things, prohibits racially discriminatory refusals to transfer land.

The High Court approached the case as one of competition between the legislative powers of the federal and state governments. Although the Commonwealth government had the explicit constitutional power to legislate with respect to 'external affairs' (s 51[xxix]), and thus in principle the power to implement international treaties, Queensland argued that the operation of a treaty prohibiting racial discrimination was primarily within Australia and thus not properly considered an 'external affair.' The Commonwealth also relied on s 51(xxvi) of the Constitution, the power to make laws with respect to any race, as a basis for the legislation.

In 1982, I was an Associate to Justice Ninian Stephen in the High Court. This was a wonderful vantage point from which to observe the court in action, at that stage still adjusting itself to its cavernous concrete new building in Canberra. The duties of Associates included research work and clerical duties, such as proof-reading. After reading accounts of the influence of judicial clerks in United States courts, I had rather grandiosely imagined that I might have a chance to contribute sentences, perhaps even paragraphs, to Sir Ninian's draft judgments. In fact, he was entirely self-contained in judgment-writing and my involvement was only as a sounding board for his ideas, and a checker of citations. I was always struck by Sir Ninian's broad reading, his urbanity and his marvellous sense of humour. He radiated a sense that life was much larger than the law, unlike many of the lawyers I had encountered until that time.

My law studies in the 1970s had left me with an impression of the High Court being riven by contention, as if ideological groups had formed which were in a fierce competitive relationship with one another. I remember being surprised by the civility of the atmosphere in the High Court, the collegiality of the judges and the sense of common purpose that transcended majorities and minorities on particular issues.

As an Associate, I had the opportunity to observe the *Koowarta* case being argued and decided. This was the last High Court decision in which Sir Ninian participated as he left the High Court in preparation to become Governor-General of Australia the day after the judgment was delivered. Sir Ninian had a particular interest in international law, having studied it at the University of Melbourne under Professor Wolfgang Friedmann, a brilliant German academic who went on to teach at Columbia Law School. As is evident in his judgment in *Koowarta*, Sir Ninian was familiar with international legal materials and less inclined to regard international law as a subversive import.

The *Koowarta* case had a large impact on me as it was quite unlike other cases I had encountered in my work at the court. Typically, the individual lives at the heart of High Court litigation were obscured by technical legal issues, and we had little sense of the identities or personalities of litigants beyond their surname. In this case, the unabashed discrimination by the Queensland government against the group led by John Koowarta seemed to encapsulate the plight of Indigenous Australians more generally. Inside the High Court, there was considerable build up to the case, and a lot of media attention.

I watched the argument in the main courtroom, crowded with barristers. It was uncharacteristically charged and passionate. I recall, in particular, Ron Castan's arguments on behalf of John Koowarta, this slight, intense man speaking with barely concealed emotion. According to the advocates, the choice was between eviscerating the powers of the Australian states on the one hand and maintaining the capacity for Australia to participate in the international community on the other.

There was much discussion among the Associates about how the case would be resolved; we all felt that we were witnesses to a significant event. As was common in that era in major constitutional cases, all members of the High Court wrote a separate opinion, with the exception of Aickin J who agreed with the Chief Justice's reasoning. At one point, six judges had circulated their draft decisions and the court was evenly split. Three judges (Gibbs CJ, Aickin and Wilson JJ) accepted Queensland's arguments that the RDA was outside Commonwealth legislative power. Three judges (Stephen, Brennan and Murphy JJ) found the RDA was valid as an exercise of the external affairs power; Murphy J also found it valid under the races power. We all realised that the judgment of Mason J would decide the case and were keenly awaiting it.

One day, Justice Mason's Associate, Alec Leopold, appeared in our chambers to distribute the judgment. It was one sentence long – along the lines of 'I have read the reasons for judgment of the Chief Justice and I agree with them and have nothing further to add'. I took the judgment in to Sir Ninian with a heavy heart. He looked at it with surprise and then puffed wistfully on his pipe for some moments. He never expressed any emotion about the final outcome of a case, but this time he appeared rather subdued. Suddenly, Sir Ninian threw his head back and started laughing: he had noticed that the date on his desk calendar was 1 April.

In the end, Mason J decided that the RDA came within the external affairs power, creating a narrow (4:3) majority for its validity. Although their emphases differed, the majority judges held that the notion of 'external affairs' included not only matters physically external to Australia but also matters that had a primarily domestic impact, such as the prohibition of racial discrimination. They regarded the founding of the United Nations in 1945 and the development of international human rights law as critical to the transformation of the power.

The majority acknowledged that its interpretation of the external affairs power would encroach to some extent on state legislative powers, but it was concerned that to hold otherwise would fetter Australia's capacity to act internationally. Murphy J described this fear most vividly when he repeated a concern he had expressed first in *NSW v Commonwealth* ('*Seas and Submerged Lands*') that a more limited view of the power in the manner urged by the states would make

Australia 'an international cripple unable to participate fully in the emerging world order'.[4] Thus, for the majority, the allocation of legislative competence between Commonwealth and states set out in s 51 of the Constitution would not in itself limit the scope of the external affairs power.

By contrast the three judges in the minority sought to exclude from the external affairs power a category of matters 'that are purely domestic and in themselves involve no relationship with other countries or their inhabitants'.[5] For them, racial discrimination fell into this category, even if there were international concern on the topic. The Convention, while an international agreement, had no intrinsically 'external' or 'international' element; racial discrimination, 'if it were to occur at all, would take place in the ordinary day-to-day intercourse of persons in Australia'.[6]

The minority saw the external affairs power as a potential Trojan horse, undermining the federal compact enshrined in the Australian Constitution. Their judgments suggest that they regarded themselves as gatekeepers against a fundamental breach of the Australian political system. This anxiety is captured in the warning by the Chief Justice that the outcome of the case, were the category of 'external affairs' read too broadly, could lead to the 'complete ... obliterat[ion]' of the Constitution's distribution of powers: 'there would be no field of power which the Commonwealth could not invade, and the federal balance achieved by the Constitution could be entirely destroyed'.[7] In similar vein, Wilson J predicted that:

> [I]f ss. 9 and 12 of the Act are valid exercise of the power to enact laws with respect to external affairs, it would be difficult to deny a power to implement any international obligation. Certainly the entire field of human rights and fundamental freedoms would come within the reach of paramount Commonwealth legislative power ... It is no exaggeration to say that what is emerging is a sophisticated network of international arrangements directed to the personal, economic, social and cultural development of all human beings. The effect of investing the Parliament with power through s. 51(xxix) in all these areas would be to transfer to the Commonwealth virtually unlimited power in almost every conceivable aspect of life in Australia, including health and hospitals, the workplace, law and order, the economy, education, and recreational and cultural activity ... So broad a power, if exercised, may leave the existence of the States as constitutional units intact but it would deny to them any significant legislative role in the federation.[8]

The manifestations of racial discrimination at issue in *Koowarta* are sublimated in the High Court's abstract discussion about the legislative powers of the Commonwealth. The major notes of passion appear in the minority judgments, quoted above, expressing concern about the future of Australian federalism. Gibbs CJ considered the Queensland policy of denying land transfers to Aboriginal groups briefly, but only to suggest that it was rather trivial. He observed that 'the act of discrimination

[4]*NSW v Commonwealth* (1975) 135 CLR 337 at 503.
[5]*Koowarta v Bjelke-Petersen* (1982) 153 CLR 168 at 192.
[6]*Koowarta v Bjelke-Petersen* (1982) 153 CLR 168 at 247.
[7]*Koowarta v Bjelke-Petersen* (1982) 153 CLR 168 at 198.
[8]*Koowarta v Bjelke-Petersen* (1982) 153 CLR 168 at 251–252.

alleged in the present case ... stands on an entirely different plane [to acts of genocide, torture, imprisonment without trial and wholesale deprivations of the right to vote, to work or to be educated]'.[9] He also doubted whether the RDA would even apply to the Queensland policy.[10]

The distinction between the majority and minority approaches in *Koowarta* depends on understandings of the elasticity of the international sphere. For the majority, the category of external affairs would inevitably increase over time. The majority judges accepted that behaviour within states has become a matter of international concern and thus an aspect of external affairs for Australia. The minority took a more literal view of the power: external affairs implicate a direct relationship with other countries or with persons or things outside Australia.[11] While the content of external affairs may well change over time, the requirement of externality provided some type of protection for the legislative dominion of the Australian states. On this analysis, racial discrimination had no international aspect. Contemporary commentary emphasised this fear. For example, John Finnis interpreted *Koowarta* as a dangerously centralist decision.[12] He saw it as proof that Australia should insist on the insertion of 'federal state' clauses in treaties which would make implementation of treaty obligations subject to federal divisions of power.

The majority judgments in *Koowarta* are often categorised on a spectrum of scepticism about the role of international instruments. Justices Mason, Murphy and Brennan are typically placed at one end of this spectrum because of their accounts of the scope of the external affairs power as including legislation implementing any treaty to which Australia is a party, subject to the requirement that the treaty not be 'colourable' or some type of ruse to expand Commonwealth legislative power.[13] The three judges in the minority, who insisted that the external affairs power only extended to implementing a limited class of treaties that had an unambiguously international element, are placed at the other end. Most commentators on the *Koowarta* case read the judgment of Stephen J as propounding a distinct view. He is placed sitting between the majority and the minority on the scope of the power through suggesting that a treaty in itself does not create an external affair, and that there is a further requirement that the treaty be on a topic of 'international concern'.[14] Indeed, John Finnis suggested that Stephen J in fact formed a majority with the dissenters on this point.[15] And, in the *Tasmanian Dam* case, the minority

---

[9]*Koowarta v Bjelke-Petersen* (1982) 153 CLR 168 at 206.

[10]*Koowarta v Bjelke-Petersen* (1982) 153 CLR 168 at 184.

[11]*Koowarta v Bjelke-Petersen* (1982) 153 CLR 168 at 201.

[12]Finnis (1983), pp 126–129.

[13]*Koowarta v Bjelke-Petersen* (1982) 153 CLR 168 at 231 (Mason J), at 240 (Murphy J), at 260 (Brennan J). Brennan J also read the power as extending to legislation dealing with other 'international persons', including the United Nations and its agencies (at 258).

[14]Zines (2008), pp 380–381.

[15]Finnis (1983), p 127. Sir Anthony Mason (2007, p 22), by contrast, considered that 'unfortunately, Sir Ninian's reasoning [in *Koowarta*] placed him in a position midway between the reasoning of the majority and that of the minority so that the decision lacked a ratio'.

judges invoked Stephen J's judgment to suggest that the World Heritage Treaty was not truly a matter of international concern.[16]

At the time, however, I think that Stephen J saw himself as taking the same approach as the majority on this point. While he contemplated the theoretical possibility of a bilateral treaty, 'whether or not the result of a collusive relationship', that was not on a matter of international concern,[17] he emphasised that it was 'difficult indeed to identify subject-matters which are of their nature not of international but only of domestic concern.'[18] He defined the quality of international concern that brought areas within the external affairs power as 'possess[ing] the capacity to affect a country's relations with other nations'.[19] The scope of the external affairs power, then, was not determined by the executive; rather it was 'in the hands of the community of nations of which Australia forms a part'.[20] This is effectively the same approach as that of Mason, Murphy and Brennan JJ. Stephen J also regarded the protection of human rights as so quintessentially a matter of international concern that this subject matter would fall within the power even if there were no relevant treaty. Thus, the external affairs power encompassed the implementation of principles of customary international law.[21]

The High Court's broad approach to the external affairs power contrasts with its restrictive account of the power in s 51(xxvi) which enables the Commonwealth to legislate with respect to 'the people of any race, for whom it is deemed necessary to enact special laws'. The court rejected the races power as a basis for the RDA because the legislation dealt with racial discrimination generally, rather than being directed to a particular race. Members of the court invoked the original intention of the constitutional drafters as the basis for this interpretation, without considering the significance of the 1967 constitutional amendment that had deleted the words 'other that the aboriginal race in any State' from s 51(xxvi). The sole judge who accepted that the RDA fell within the races power, Murphy J, offered a rather slight justification, stating simply that the word 'for' in s 51(xxvi) must be read as meaning 'for the benefit of'.[22] Many years later, Kirby J's dissent in *Kartinyeri v Commonwealth* analysed the races power in a way that is more consistent with *Koowarta*'s appreciation of the significance of developments in international human rights law in the context of the external affairs power. He argued that, in cases of textual ambiguity in the Constitution, 'this Court should adopt that meaning which

[16] *Commonwealth v Tasmania* (1983) 158 CLR 1 at 98–99 (Gibbs CJ), at 186–187 (Wilson J), at 305–307 (Dawson J). The High Court firmly rejected such an approach in *Victoria v Commonwealth* ('*Industrial Relations Act*' case), arguing that the majority in the *Tasmanian Dam* case had, in any event, decided that 'the intrusion of Commonwealth law into a field that has hitherto been the preserve of State law is not a reason to deny validity to the Commonwealth law provided it is, in truth, a law with respect to external affairs.' (*Victoria v Commonwealth* (1996) 187 CLR 416 at 484–485 [Brennan CJ, Toohey, Gaudron, McHugh and Gummow JJ]).

[17] *Koowarta v Bjelke-Petersen* (1982) 153 CLR 168 at 217.

[18] *Koowarta v Bjelke-Petersen* (1982) 153 CLR 168 at 217.

[19] *Koowarta v Bjelke-Petersen* (1982) 153 CLR 168 at 217.

[20] *Koowarta v Bjelke-Petersen* (1982) 153 CLR 168 at 218.

[21] *Koowarta v Bjelke-Petersen* (1982) 153 CLR 168 at 220, see also Mason J (at 234).

[22] *Koowarta v Bjelke-Petersen* (1982) 153 CLR 168 at 242.

conforms to the principles of universal and fundamental rights rather than an interpretation which would involve a departure from such rights'.[23] The majority's restrictive approach to the races power in *Koowarta* remains, however, influential.

Conclusion

Scholars have debated the jurisprudential significance of the *Koowarta* case with respect to the ambit of the Commonwealth's legislative power on matters of external affairs. For example, Geoffrey Sawer considered whether *Koowarta* had done anything more than confirm the High Court's decision in *R v Burgess*, ex parte *Henry*,[24] a 1936 case dealing with Commonwealth power to legislate to implement the *Paris Convention for the Regulation of Aerial Navigation*.[25] However, the external aspects of regulating air navigation are more obvious and literal than the prohibition of racial discrimination or the protection of human rights generally. *Koowarta* elaborated a capacious and mutable account of external affairs that has since secured Commonwealth legislation on topics from the protection of the environment[26] to the extraterritorial prohibition of child sex tourism.[27] It rejected a competitive account of the relationship between the international and the domestic spheres, presenting it rather as organic and symbiotic.

While the constitutional debate about the scope of s 51(xxix) is now muted, the relationship between Australian and international law remains controversial in the political realm. This can be seen in the way that successive Australian governments have responded to the views of United Nations human rights treaty bodies. Australia has accepted a variety of procedures that allow individuals within Australian jurisdiction to bring complaints of violations of human rights to the attention of the expert committees charged with monitoring international human rights treaties.[28] Access to these procedures is available only after all possible domestic remedies have been exhausted. On many occasions the treaty bodies have identified violations of human rights guarantees by Australian governments, but the standard response has been to reject the findings.[29] In the case of the *International Covenant on Civil and Political Rights* (ICCPR), for example, there have been 23 cases in which the United Nations Human Rights Committee has identified human rights violations by Australia. Australia has acted in accordance with the committee's views to remedy the violations in only two of these cases.

Koowarta illustrated the potency of federalism in debates over the protection of human rights in Australia. Despite the High Court's confirmation of the

[23]*Kartinyeri v Commonwealth* (1998) 195 CLR 337 at 417.

[24]*R v Burgess*, ex parte *Henry* (1936) 55 CLR 608.

[25]Sawer (1983–1984), p 199.

[26]*Commonwealth v Tasmania* (1983) 158 CLR 1.

[27]*XYZ v Commonwealth* (2006) 227 CLR 532.

[28]For example, the Optional Protocol to the *International Covenant on Civil and Political Rights 1966*.

[29]See United Nations Human Rights, Office of the High Commissioner for Human Rights, http://tbinternet.ohchr.org/_layouts/treatybodyexternal/TBSearch.aspx?Lang=en&CountryID=9&TreatyID=8&DocTypeCategoryID=6, accessed 25 May 2014.

Commonwealth's power to legislate to implement human rights treaties, Australia has not withdrawn federal declarations attached to such agreements before the *Koowarta* decision. For example, in relation to the ICCPR, Australia's instrument of ratification, deposited in 1980, states that 'the implementation of those provisions of the Covenant over whose subject matter the authorities of the [Australian] States exercise legislative, executive and judicial jurisdiction will be a matter for those authorities'.[30] Indeed, Australia has continued using similar declarations since the *Koowarta* case, for example in ratifying the *International Convention on the Elimination of All Forms of Discrimination Against Women* in 1983.[31]

The *Koowarta* case also illustrates the pyrrhic nature of many legal victories for the human beings involved. John Koowarta died destitute in 1991. He never gained possession of the Archer River lease (which was converted into a national park by the Queensland government in 1988 to avoid the impact of the High Court's decision) nor received compensation for Queensland's breach of the RDA. It was not until 2012 that the Queensland government finally returned part of the land to its original owners, the Wik-Mungkana people.

Acknowledgements

Thanks to Dr Ann Genovese for her invitation to participate in the *Koowarta* symposium in May 2012 and her helpful comments on the paper. Thanks also to the valuable suggestions of the anonymous referees.

References

Primary sources

Commonwealth v Tasmania (1983) 158 CLR 1
Kartinyeri v Commonwealth (1998) 195 CLR 337
Koowarta v Bjelke-Petersen (1982) 153 CLR 168
NSW v Commonwealth (1975) 135 CLR 337
R v Burgess, ex parte *Henry* (1936) 55 CLR 608
Victoria v Commonwealth (1996) 187 CLR 416
XYZ v Commonwealth (2006) 227 CLR 532

Legislation

Racial Discrimination Act 1975 (Cth)

International instruments

International Convention on the Elimination of All Forms of Discrimination Against Women 1979
International Convention on the Elimination of All Forms of Racial Discrimination 1965
International Covenant on Civil and Political Rights 1966

[30]United Nations, Treaty Collection, Chapter IV – Human Rights, International Covenant on Civil and Political Rights, Declarations and Reservations, https://treaties.un.org/Pages/ViewDetails.aspx?src=TREATY&mtdsg_no=IV-4&chapter=4&lang=en, accessed 25 May 2014.

[31]United Nations, Treaty Collection, Chapter IV – Human Rights, Convention on the Elimination of All Forms of Discrimination Against Women, Declarations and Reservations, https://treaties.un.org/Pages/ViewDetails.aspx?src=TREATY&mtdsg_no=IV-8&chapter=4&lang=en, accessed 25 May 2014.

Secondary sources

John Finnis (1983) 'Power to Enforce Treaties in Australia – The High Court Goes Centralist?' 3 *Oxford Journal of Legal Studies* 126.
Anthony Mason (2007) 'Justice of the High Court' in Timothy LH McCormack and Cheryl Saunders (eds) *Sir Ninian Stephen: A Tribute*, Miegunyah Press.
Geoffrey Sawer (1983–1984) 'The External Affairs Power' 14 *Federal Law Review* 197.
Leslie Zines (2008) *The High Court and the Constitution*, 5th edition, Federation Press.

Justice in whose eyes? Why lawyers should read black Australian literature

Nicole Watson

Jumbunna Indigenous House of Learning, University of Technology, Sydney, Australia

This article presents a challenge to legal scholars to engage with Indigenous literature. Because such literature is closely aligned to Indigenous movements, it is a rich source of information in relation to what Indigenous people believe is necessary for them to receive redress for the injuries of colonisation. Such engagement grounds the conclusion that litigation is rarely an end in itself, but rather one part of an enduring struggle for the transformation of relationships between Indigenous people and the state. Platforms written by Indigenous people are holistic and, in spite of diversity over time, they usually include at least three elements – the realisation of self-determination, the creation of a land base, and compensation for dispossession. Critical race theory provides a theoretical foundation for the incorporation of such platforms into legal scholarship. By engaging with Indigenous literature, legal scholars will be exposed to the shortcomings of the native title recognition process, and devise new frameworks that will support Indigenous self-determination.

Introduction

Most Australian lawyers are familiar with the name Koowarta. For the majority, it is a distant memory of the study of constitutional law, and the elucidation of the boundaries of s 51(xxix) of the Constitution. The *Koowarta* decision established that the Commonwealth could legislate to give effect to an international agreement, provided that some conditions were met. The agreement had to be *bona fide* and made with respect to a matter of substantial international concern. Furthermore, the legislation had to be substantially aligned with the terms of the international agreement, and not inconsistent with the Constitution.[1]

In spite of the decision's significance, little is known of the factual circumstances that preceded it. One casenote recounts that Mr Koowarta approached the federal Aboriginal Land Commission with a view to purchasing land in North Queensland for use by himself and members of his community.[2] The Commission entered into a contract to purchase the lease, but the agreement was stymied by the Minister for Lands, who refused to approve the transfer. The Minister acted on the basis that the Queensland government did not 'view favourably' attempts to purchase large tracts of land for 'development by Aborigines or Aboriginal groups in isolation'.[3] The

[1]Sawer (1984).

[2]Martin (1983).

[3]Martin (1983).

plaintiff argued that the Minister's actions were contrary to the *Racial Discrimination Act 1975* (Cth); ultimately succeeding in the High Court.

At face value, the *Koowarta* decision was a significant step forward for Indigenous rights. In reality, however, the victory was pyrrhic. John Koowarta's ancestral lands were dedicated as national park; and would be kept from his grasp for the rest of his life. Twenty-one years after John Koowarta's death, Premier Newman apologised for the wrong and stewarded over the partial revocation of the dedication of the Mungkan Kandju National Park.[4] All of which begs the question – did John Koowarta believe that he received justice?

The only record of Koowarta's sentiments, which the writer was able to locate, is in the brief dedication in Frank Brennan's book, *Land Rights Queensland Style*.[5] Brennan described a chance meeting with Mr Koowarta in Aurukun, a week after the High Court handed down its decision. According to Brennan, Koowarta 'knew nothing of the detail'.[6] But he glowingly described himself as the first man to 'break the seal'[7] of the Queensland government. It is understandable that Koowarta felt pride in his achievement, but such gratification is not necessarily the same as justice.

The apparent dearth of academic interest in Koowarta's own personal aspirations provides a window to a broader question rarely pondered in the legal academy – how do Indigenous people view justice? This article will argue that legal scholars can gain an understanding of Indigenous conceptions of justice by engaging with Indigenous literature. Such engagement grounds the conclusion that litigation is rarely an end in itself, but rather one part of an enduring struggle for the transformation of relationships between Indigenous people and the state.

Platforms written by Indigenous people have consistently made a body of demands and, in spite of diversity over time, they usually include at least three elements – the realisation of self-determination, the creation of a land base, and compensation for dispossession. Legal processes concerned with the recognition of property rights, such as native title, represent the colonisation, rather than an accommodation, of such platforms.

This article will be divided into three parts. Part 1 will examine Indigenous platforms from the nineteenth century to the era of the *Koowarta* and *Mabo* decisions. Part 2 will argue that critical race theory (CRT) provides a theoretical foundation for the incorporation of Indigenous literature into legal scholarship. Part 3 will provide examples of how such narratives can enrich legal scholarship.

Part 1: Indigenous conceptions of justice

Adam Shoemaker has argued that black Australian writing is bound to events that unfold in the sociopolitical milieu.[8] Political developments do not necessarily dictate the content of such writing. Rather, Indigenous literature is, 'so proximate to reality and to social events that these must be surveyed prior to a consideration of the works

[4]Michael (2012).

[5]Brennan (1992), p 1.

[6]Brennan (1992), p 1.

[7]Brennan (1992), p 1.

[8]Shoemaker (1989).

themselves, if they are to be fully understood and appreciated'.[9] This article takes the position that, because of this nexus between Indigenous literature and Indigenous movements, such writing is a rich source of information in relation to how Indigenous people view justice. Justice is defined in this context as the steps necessary in order for Indigenous people to begin to recover from the legacies of colonisation and attain genuine equality with other Australians.

Early petitions

Indigenous literature had its beginnings in letters and petitions to colonial authorities in the nineteenth century. Indigenous people had observed the power that emanated from the written word, and hoped that their claims would be taken seriously when documented. They also aspired to use writing as a means of reinforcing their own values and social order.[10]

Among the most prolific petitioners was the community of Coranderrk in Victoria. Established as an Aboriginal Reserve in 1863, Coranderrk was a safe haven for those who had been dispossessed.[11] Under the management of the progressive young preacher, John Green, Coranderrk became a prosperous farming community. In spite of such success, the Board for the Protection of Aborigines pressured Green into resigning, and eventually sold the land. For many years, the people of Coranderrk lobbied, by way of letters and petitions, for Green's reinstatement and security of tenure.[12]

Richard Broome has argued that some of the correspondence from Coranderrk represented attempts to elicit 'right behaviour' and, in particular, reciprocity, from the colonists.[13] The Kulin's moral code dictated that those who profited from the land had an obligation to support the original owners who had been dispossessed. A letter by one resident provides examples of transgressions of this moral code by Green's successors, which included a lack of neighbourliness, miserly rations and poor management.[14]

Early Indigenous political associations also reduced their claims to writing. The first such group was the Australian Aboriginal Progressive Association (AAPA),[15] which was based in New South Wales. Formed under the leadership of Fred Maynard in 1924, the AAPA fought for land rights, civil rights, and an end to the Aborigines Protection Board, which had gained notoriety for removing Aboriginal children from their families.[16] In 1927 the AAPA presented a petition to Premier Lang in which the following 'privileges of citizenship' were sought:

---

[9] Shoemaker (1989), p 8.
[10] Van Toorn (1999).
[11] Van Toorn (2006).
[12] Van Toorn (2006), p 133.
[13] Broome (2006).
[14] Broome (2006), p 43.11.
[15] Maynard (2003).
[16] Maynard (2003).

> That all capable aboriginals shall be given in fee simple, sufficient, good land to maintain a family;
> That the family life of the aboriginal people shall be held sacred and free from invasion and that the children shall be left in the control of their parents;
> That the incapables of the Aboriginal Community (the direct liability of the Government consequent upon neglect in the past) be properly cared for in suitable homes on reserves, the full expense of such establishments to be borne by the Government;
> That the supervision of all such aboriginal Homes, Hostels or Reserves be entrusted to the educated aboriginals possessing the requisite ability for such management;
> That the control of aboriginal affairs, apart from common law rights, shall be vested in a board of management comprised of capable, educated aboriginals under a chairman to be appointed by the Government.[17]

The AAPA never achieved freedom and equality for Indigenous people, many of whom would continue to live under 'protection'. However, its platform highlights the reality that the land rights movement has always been about so much more than the recognition of proprietary rights. While such narratives do indeed assert rights to land, they also demand the devolution of decision-making power to Indigenous people, and the means to achieve self-reliance.

The emergence of Black Power and community controlled organisations in the 1970s

It was not until 1964 that the first book written by an Aboriginal person was published. Kath Walker, later known as Oodgeroo Noonuccal, wrote her first volume of poetry called *We Are Going*.[18] Together with her contemporary, Kevin Gilbert, Noonuccal would gravitate towards the forefront of the Indigenous political struggle. Consequently, the work of both writers is revealing of what many Indigenous people of this era believed was owed to them as a matter of justice.

Noonuccal's poems were often strident calls for Indigenous people to be empowered to master their own destinies, such as 'Aboriginal Charter of Rights'.[19] In 1973, Gilbert became the first Indigenous person to publish a political text. In *Because a White Man'll Never Do It*,[20] he laid out a blueprint for Indigenous people's recovery which comprised the creation of a land base, the payment of compensation and self-determination. The latter was crucial in order to heal the psychological damage inflicted by colonisation:

> If there is to be a regeneration of blacks, it must come through self-determination, however hesitant the first steps. The only thing that years of white administration have proved to us is that it doesn't work, it can't work.[21]

[17]Attwood and Markus (1999), p 67.

[18]Walker (1964).

[19]Noonuccal (1962).

[20]Gilbert (2013).

[21]Gilbert (2013), p 168.

Self-determination, however, was impossible in the absence of compensation and a land base, both of which would equip Indigenous people with the means to live free of government intervention.[22]

The myriad impacts of colonisation were further explored in Gilbert's later book, *Living Black: Blacks Talk to Kevin Gilbert*.[23] *Living Black* was based on a series of personal interviews undertaken by Gilbert in an attempt to describe the actual situation of Indigenous people in their own words. Through such testimonies the reader was able to glimpse the often insidious but pervasive racism endured by Indigenous people. Missions were likened to concentration camps,[24] and generations of Aboriginal people had grown up in tents on the fringes of country towns with few prospects of improving their circumstances.[25] Racism was often internalised by the victims and was manifest in a sense of hopelessness. Gilbert's antidote was a re-education of Aboriginal people, which would 'include a barrage of intensive positive propaganda about Aboriginal history, identity and culture to counteract the negative material that is constantly raining in on them from the major society at present'.[26]

When the Commonwealth failed to take advantage of the successful 1967 referendum and embark on a reform package for Indigenous people, the disillusionment within the Indigenous leadership became palpable.[27] Such bitter disappointment provided fuel for the emergence of Australian Black Power. This movement was fundamentally an attitudinal shift; one that encouraged pride in being Aboriginal and the view that Aboriginal people were best placed to solve their own problems.[28] The founders of Black Power were predominantly young activists in Melbourne, Sydney and Brisbane, who shared a belief in Indigenous self-determination and economic independence.[29]

Black Power would find expression in community controlled organisations, such as the Aboriginal Legal Service (ALS). After suffering years of police harassment, young activists such as Paul Coe established the first ALS in Redfern in 1970.[30] Black Power would also find expression in the Aboriginal Tent Embassy. The Embassy began as a response to Prime Minister McMahon's Australia Day speech, in which he ruled out Aboriginal land rights in the form of freehold title.[31] But it would quickly come to represent a nascent pan-Aboriginal movement.

---

[22]Gilbert (2013), p 198.
[23]Gilbert (1978).
[24]Gilbert (1978), p 57.
[25]Gilbert (1978), p 117–138.
[26]Gilbert (1978), p 3.
[27]Walker (1969) cited in Foley (2001).
[28]Lothian (2007), p 20.
[29]Foley (2001).
[30]Foley and Anderson (2006), p 89.
[31]Foley (2001).

The holistic approach to justice espoused by earlier generations found resonance in the Embassy's 'Five Point Plan':

1. Aboriginal ownership of all existing reserves and settlements (including rights to mineral deposits);
2. Ownership of areas of land in the capital cities (including mineral rights);
3. Preservation of all sacred sites in all parts of the continent;
4. Six million dollars in compensation; and
5. Full rights of statehood for the Northern Territory.[32]

Soon after, the fledgling Whitlam government adopted the policy of self-determination. This policy would be maintained by the Fraser, Hawke and Keating governments. While this era saw the conflagration of Indigenous community organisations, these bodies remained beholden to governments, which continued to exercise control over funding and policy direction.

Indigenous expressions of justice in the 1980s

The ability to become self-determining, the acquisition of land and the payment of compensation continued to emerge in Indigenous platforms created during the closing decades of the twentieth century. Among the most renowned of those documents was the Barunga Statement, presented to Prime Minister Hawke by leaders of the Central and Northern Land Councils at the 1988 Barunga Festival. The statement demanded recognition of rights to:

> Self determination and self management including the freedom to pursue our own economic, social, religious and cultural development;
> Permanent control and enjoyment of our ancestral lands;
> Compensation for the loss of use of our lands, there having been no extinction of original title;
> Protection of and control of access to our scared sites, sacred objects, artifacts, designs, knowledge and works of art;
> The return of the remains of our ancestors for burial in accordance with our traditions; and
> Respect for promotion of our Aboriginal identity, including the cultural, linguistic, religious and historical aspects, including the right to be educated in our own languages, and in our own culture and history ...[33]

The Barunga Statement also called on the Commonwealth to introduce a national system of land rights and negotiate a treaty or compact.[34] Although Prime Minister Hawke responded to the Barunga Statement with the promise of a treaty, that commitment was short-lived.[35]

---

[32]Robinson (1994), p 52.

[33]Attwood and Markus (1999), pp 316–317.

[34]Attwood and Markus (1999).

[35]Clayton-Dixon (2014).

The Aboriginal and Torres Strait Islander Commission

Tentative steps towards Indigenous self-determination were taken by the Commonwealth with the creation of the Aboriginal and Torres Strait Islander Commission (ATSIC). ATSIC replaced the Department of Aboriginal Affairs and the Aboriginal Development Commission, both of which had been criticised for not effectively responding to Indigenous disadvantage.[36] But ATSIC was not only a bureaucratic structure, it also included a new arm directly elected by Indigenous people. [37]

ATSIC's functions were three-fold: to provide advice to governments; to advocate on behalf of Indigenous people; and to fund and monitor Indigenous programs.[38] This amalgam of complex, and sometimes conflicting, roles 'beleaguered'[39] ATSIC until its demise in 2005. It is not the purpose of this article to discuss the relative strengths and weaknesses of ATSIC. Rather, this article will canvas ATSIC's contribution to the intellectual framework for Indigenous conceptions of justice, in particular, *Recognition, Rights and Reform: A Report to Government on the Native Title Social Justice Measures*.[40]

Recognition, Rights and Reform

The Native Title Social Justice Measures, also known as the Social Justice Package, represented the third tier of the Keating government's response to the *Mabo* decision. The first was the enactment of the *Native Title Act 1993* (Cth), the second was the creation of the Indigenous Land Fund.[41] *Recognition, Rights and Reform* was ATSIC's blueprint for the Social Justice Package. The Social Justice Package has never been delivered, as the Howard government refused to honour its predecessor's commitment. However, *Recognition, Rights and Reform* remains important because it was informed by what Indigenous people themselves considered to be necessary in order for them to receive justice.

In common with the platforms discussed above, *Recognition, Rights and Reform* advocated a holistic approach to justice. ATSIC described the fundamental aim of the report in the following terms:

> Our focus is on institutional, structural, collaborative, cooperative reform. It is about a fundamental shift from welfare to basic rights, from dependence to autonomy, from government assistance to power.[42]

Relationships between Indigenous people and governments were to be transformed by the legislative entrenchment of 'Principles for Indigenous Social Justice'. Those principles included the rights of Indigenous people to self-determination, recognition

---

[36]Ivanitz (1998), p 2.

[37]Ivanitz (2000), p 4.

[38]Cunningham and Baeza (2005), p 463.

[39]Chesterman and Galligan (1997), p 213.

[40]Aboriginal and Torres Strait Islander Commission (1995).

[41]Aboriginal and Torres Strait Islander Commission (1995).

[42]Aboriginal and Torres Strait Islander Commission (1995) Preface.

as the original owners of the land, and full equality.[43] ATSIC envisaged the payment of compensation which would take the form of a share in revenue generated from land, such as a percentage of land tax and mining royalties.[44] The ability for Indigenous people to exercise self-determination would be achieved through a variety of measures including regional governance.[45] That self-determination was to be achieved within existing democratic processes was evidenced by recommendations pertaining to the creation of Indigenous seats in parliament,[46] and incentives for greater Indigenous representation in local government.[47]

Holistic conceptions of justice also found expression in other forms of Indigenous literature in the 1980s and 1990s, such as novels. Indigenous writers often portray their relationships with their lands as dynamic and inextricable from the reclamation of stolen identity and the exercise of self-determination. One of the most successful forms of Indigenous literature at this time was the life story; exemplified by Sally Morgan's best-selling memoir, *My Place*.[48]

The book not only depicted Morgan's discovery of her Aboriginal heritage, but also the stories of two generations of her family who had suffered the impacts of child removal policies. In order to learn more about her identity, Morgan travelled to her grandmother's birthplace of Corunna Downs near Port Headland, Western Australia.[49] Morgan and her mother considered this journey to be a crucial step towards becoming self-actuated individuals.[50]

My Place sold over half a million copies,[51] and paved the way for other Aboriginal people to publish their stories. Reconciling with one's ancestral home, often after a long absence spanning decades, is a common theme of such literature.[52] Such texts reveal that relationships between Indigenous people and their lands cannot be extricated from issues such as the reclamation of identity and empowerment.

Part 2: Critical race theory

Critical race theory (CRT) is a revolutionary movement which seeks to challenge the racial hierarchy within American society. It began in the 1970s, when scholars such as Derrick Bell and Alan Freeman were concerned that the gains of the civil rights movement had stalled.[53] At the same time a stock story had emerged, in which racism had been relegated to the past. Although racism still existed, it had

[43]Aboriginal and Torres Strait Islander Commission (1995), [1.28].
[44]Aboriginal and Torres Strait Islander Commission (1995), [4.32] – [4.46].
[45]Aboriginal and Torres Strait Islander Commission (1995), [4.47] – [4.58].
[46]Aboriginal and Torres Strait Islander Commission (1995), recommendation 25.
[47]Aboriginal and Torres Strait Islander Commission (1995), recommendation 27.
[48]Morgan (1987).
[49]Morgan (1987), pp 276–296.
[50]Morgan (1987), p 296.
[51]Morgan (1987), Preface.
[52]See also Langford Ginibi (1994).
[53]Delgado and Stefancic (2013), p 2.

apparently become an aberration. In reality, however, African Americans remained steeped in poverty:

> While some blacks are doing very well – the true beneficiaries of the civil rights era – more than one third of all black people are mired in poverty that is degrading, dispiriting and destructive. Those in the middle-class have seen their progress halted and many are sliding back toward the low-income status they worked so hard to escape.[54]

Civil rights victories in the earlier part of the twentieth century had delivered only the illusion of meaningful change, because racism was so deeply ingrained in American society. Contemporary racism was no longer as overt as earlier Klan violence. Rather, it had become institutionalised and legitimised by 'neutral' laws and practices that treated histories of racial oppression as irrelevant.[55]

Although there is great diversity within the movement, most CRT scholars would subscribe to some foundational principles. First, hundreds of years of slavery and apartheid left behind a pervasive racial caste system. Second, CRT challenges the experience of white Americans as the norm.[56] Third, CRT questions the ability of the legal system to ever create a just society when racism is so widely tolerated.[57]

Related to the third principle is Derrick Bell's theory of interest convergence. Bell argued that legal advances for African Americans were only possible when such developments also served the interests of white Americans.[58] The decision of *Brown v Board of Education*,[59] which brought about the end of school segregation, was only possible because it represented a convergence of black and white interests. The latter was served because desegregation met the needs of American foreign policy in the 1950s. In the midst of the Cold War, America was anxious to win the hearts and minds of leaders in Asia and Africa; parts of the world that were in transition from colonisation and therefore deeply concerned by media coverage of racial oppression in America. Decisions such as *Brown* proved to the world that racism was not only taken seriously, but was being eradicated.[60]

Finally, CRT scholars seek to illuminate and challenge America's racial caste system by way of counter-storytelling. Much of what we consider to be reality is constructed through narratives, which are repeated so often that we come to believe that the status quo is inevitable, or the best situation in a less than perfect world.[61] The CRT response is storytelling that questions such complacency through its privileging of the lived experience of people of colour.[62] In a much quoted piece,

[54]Bell (1995), p 903.

[55]Bell (1971–1973).

[56]Cummings (2013), p 108.

[57]Cummings (2013).

[58]Bell (1980).

[59]*Brown v Board of Education* 347 US 483 (1954).

[60]Bell's argument was subsequently vindicated by historian Mary L Dudziak, see Dudziak (2013), p 136.

[61]Delgado (2013), p 72.

[62]Delgado (2013).

Mari Matsuda identified the benefits that outsider storytelling can bring to legal scholarship:[63]

> There is a standing concept in movements for social change. One needs to ask who has the real interest and the most information. Those who are oppressed in the present world can speak most eloquently of a better one. Their language will not be abstract, detached or inaccessible; their program will not be undefined. They will advance clear ideas about the next step to a better world. The experience of struggling against racism has taught much about struggle, about how real people can rise up, look power in the eye and turn it around.[64]

Critical race theory scholars engage with a rich body of sources, much of which is outside of conventional legal scholarship. By way of example, Paul Butler has argued that hip-hop offers insights that could improve the criminal justice system.[65] Hip-hop artists cast light on the impacts of high rates of incarceration of African Americans on poor communities.[66] In common with CRT scholars, hip-hop artists often argue that the law is structured in order to accommodate powerful interests at the top of America's racial hierarchy:

> Hip-hop often depicts incarceration as driven by profit rather than public safety. Its analysis is that it is socially expedient to warehouse people whose problems are difficult or expensive to treat, especially when economic benefits accrue to the (largely white and rural) communities where prisons frequently are situated.[67]

Critical race theory has also spawned fictitious narratives. By way of example, Bell's 'The Space Traders Solution',[68] is a science fiction that revolves around a proposal made by intergalactic visitors – panaceas for America's debt, energy and pollution crises – in exchange for the trade of every single black person in the country. The story is a powerful allegory for a history in which the rights of African Americans have been consistently sacrificed in order to accommodate the 'national interest'.

Part 3: Why should legal scholars engage with Indigenous literature?

The applicability of CRT to Australia

Race has its own complex history in Australia, beginning with the perverse notion that Indigenous people were so uncivilised as to lack any system of laws. This racist application of *terra nullius* would set the tone for Indigenous people's future relationships with governments and other Australians. As pointed out by Mick Dodson and Lisa Strelein, 'it is not sufficient to relegate the failure to respect

[63]Matsuda (1987).
[64]Matsuda (1987), pp 346–347.
[65]Butler (2013), p 533.
[66]Butler (2013), p 541.
[67]Butler (2013), p 543.
[68]Bell (1999).

Indigenous peoples as equals to the vagaries of history, because that history constantly informs Australia's identity, values and governance'.[69]

The law has invariably provided structure and legitimacy to the racism that imbues the foundations of Australian society. Although Indigenous people became British subjects when the Crown acquired sovereignty over what is now known as Australia, they were consistently denied the protection of the rule of law. Their lands were seized without compensation, and the dispossessed were vulnerable to frontier conflict. This brutality is still recent past. The last recorded atrocity was the Coniston Massacre; in which scores of Indigenous people in Central Australia were murdered by members of a police patrol in 1928. A federal inquiry into the killings exonerated those responsible.[70]

The law continued to normalise the oppression of Indigenous people throughout the twentieth century, under the guise of protectionist regimes. Protectionism was a form of wardship applicable only to Indigenous people. Although each state regime differed, the most enduring was the *Aboriginals Protection and Restriction of the Sale of Opium Act 1897* (Qld). This Act and its successors would enable the incarceration of Indigenous people on remote reserves, where their freedom of personal movement was curtailed and most aspects of life were subject to surveillance.[71]

When the High Court repudiated *terra nullius* in the *Mabo* decision, many believed that the legal system was embarking upon a new chapter of racial equality. However, Dominique Allen has argued that the *Mabo* decision was an example of Bell's interest convergence theory.[72] The decision served to neutralise international criticism of Australia's treatment of Indigenous people at a crucial point in the nation's history. Two years before the *Mabo* decision, Sydney had been selected for Australia's bid for the 2000 Olympics. Success was expected to generate AU$ 13 billion dollar windfall and create 100,000 jobs.[73] Unsurprisingly, the Australian government quickly publicised the *Mabo* decision as evidence of Australia's deference to international human rights standards.

Indigenous people, however, gained little from the *Mabo* decision. Two decades after the decision, Indigenous people are more likely than their fellow Australians to experience incarceration, have their child removed by social services, or suffer the loss of a loved one to suicide. This dilemma is not unlike that confronted by the founders of CRT in the 1970s. Bell and his colleagues had sought to create new approaches which would deal with racism that was so ingrained that it had become normalised. Just as CRT scholars have used outsider storytelling in order to expose systemic discrimination, Indigenous literature could provide a means of explaining why it is that landmark decisions such as *Mabo* failed to disrupt the status quo.

---

[69]Dodson and Strelein (2001).

[70]SBS News, 'Remembering the Coniston Massacre', http://www.sbs.com.au/news/article/2013/09/09/remembering-coniston-massacre-0, 9 September 2013.

[71]For a comprehensive historical analysis of the protectionist regime, see Kidd (2000).

[72]Allen (2007).

[73]Allen (2007), p 79.

How do Indigenous platforms compare with legal processes?

Why should legal scholars consider the work of Kevin Gilbert or the platform of the original Tent Embassy? Because Mari Matsuda's sentiments that those oppressed in the present world can speak most eloquently of a better one, lend themselves to Indigenous literature. Such platforms are neither abstract nor inaccessible. They speak of a program of wholesale reform to relationships between Indigenous people and the state, which would see Indigenous people gain mastery over their lives. Indigenous literature would allow us to move beyond the current approach of squeezing Indigenous aspirations into legal doctrine as a means of 'solving' Indigenous people's problems. Rather, it would spur scholars to build meaningful vehicles for change; vehicles that are rooted not in what lawyers think Indigenous people need, but what Indigenous people believe that they need.

Indigenous literature can also highlight the inadequacies of existing processes that are supposed to deliver a 'modicum of justice'[74] to Indigenous people; namely, those provided for under the *Native Title Act 1993* (Cth). Such processes bear little resemblance to the above platforms. Unlike holistic expressions of justice, a native title determination can define only rights and interests in lands and waters, and the holders of those rights.[75] It says nothing of the relationships between native title holders and governments. Self-determination, which for many such as the late Kevin Gilbert is indivisible from land, cannot be dealt with at all. No doubt native title has delivered some benefits to a minority of Indigenous people. However, any such gains have been a far cry from the 'fundamental shift' from dependence to autonomy foreshadowed in *Recognition, Rights and Reform*. Furthermore, such processes have made no real dint in the psychological harms experienced by Indigenous people in their daily lives, so vividly described by Kevin Gilbert.

Such processes are also counter to the aspirations of those Indigenous people who fought the monumental legal battles of the 1980s and 1990s. For such leaders, the litigation was not an end in itself, but only the latest means by which they and their communities sought to achieve mastery over their lives. The decision of *Koowarta v Bjelke-Petersen*[76] had its immediate beginnings in John Koowarta's campaign to buy the Archer River cattle station, which he was determined to run as a pastoral business.[77] But it was also one chapter of a long struggle by Koowarta's people, the Wik, to protect their land and way of life.[78] This struggle began in the seventeenth century, when the Wik fought Dutch explorers, and it would continue in the High Court, culminating in *Wik Peoples v Queensland*.[79]

We do not know what Eddie Mabo would have thought of the recognition processes under the *Native Title Act 1993* (Cth). But we should acknowledge that the litigation that carries his name was but one of his many contributions to the broader struggle for Indigenous rights. This included founding the Townsville Black

[74]Commonwealth of Australia (1993), *Parliamentary Debates*, House of Representatives, 16 November, 2877 (Paul Keating).

[75]*Native Title Act 1993* (Cth) s 225.

[76]*Koowarta v Bjelke-Petersen* (1982) 153 CLR 168.

[77]Woodley (1998).

[78]Collings (1997).

[79]*Wik Peoples v Queensland* (1996) 141 ALR 129.

Community School, and Mabo's involvement in the Aboriginal and Torres Strait Islander legal and medical services.[80] From such contributions it can be inferred that Mabo would have seen the recognition of native title as closely aligned with, and perhaps inextricable from, the pursuit of self-determination.

Finally, the native title recognition process does not allow for the resilience of the bonds between Indigenous people and their lands, which often finds reflection in Indigenous novels. In *Mabo*, Justice Brennan expressed the view that native title was extinguished when the 'tide of history had washed away any real acknowledgement of traditional law and any real observance of traditional customs'.[81] Justice Brennan's logic was at odds with the experiences of Sally Morgan, as described in *My Place*. Morgan had grown into adulthood unaware of her Aboriginal heritage, before finally travelling to her homelands as an adult. Her community not only embraced her, but incorporated Morgan into their matrix of family relationships.[82] If Indigenous people are, in fact, resurrecting their relationships with their lands after diasporas, then why can't the law accommodate this reality?

New questions for legal scholarship

One consequence of engagement with Indigenous literature is that legal scholars will be forced to consider new questions. For Indigenous litigants and their communities, the factual dispute that ignited the legal process does not end in the final paragraph of the judgment. Scholars need to consider what happened after the lawyers packed up their bags and went home. We should also ask ourselves the question – if legal processes are unwieldy to Indigenous conceptions of justice, and on occasion even harmful, then should Indigenous people resort to other measures?

This article takes the position that the decision whether or not to pursue litigation should always lie in the hands of Indigenous communities. However, Indigenous literature reveals that grassroots activism has often been an empowering and uniting experience. In her anthology, *Take Power Like This Old Man Here*,[83] Alexis Wright revealed the Herculean struggles by Aboriginal people in Central Australia to gain land rights in the 1980s. Charles Perkins considered that the turning point was the first land rights demonstration ever held in Alice Springs, in March 1976. It was a defining moment because the participants genuinely felt empowered:

> I think it was the beginning of the land rights movement in a very real sense. Everybody felt that they could play a role, even the poor buggers that came in with no money, no food, and walked barefoot and in rags down the streets of Alice Springs. We have had many dramatic events over the years, all worthwhile, but I think the march was the one that came right from out of the earth, from the grass roots … People brought everything with them, dogs, kids and bloody everything. They had swags on their backs and all sorts, it was a motley crew. No wonder everybody stared at us. But it was a revolution in the minds of lots of Aboriginals and white people, including the marchers. The marchers thought: 'Hey. What am I doing marching down the streets for land rights?

[80]Russell (2006), p 193.

[81]*Mabo v Queensland (No. 2)* (1992) 175 CLR 1 at 60 (Brennan J).

[82]Morgan (1987), pp 276–296.

[83]Wright (1998).

> Well! I should've been doing this before. I'm standing up for my land, I'm standing up for my culture and everybody around me seems to be doing the same so we must be doing the right thing'.[84]

This sense of empowerment that Perkins described was essential in order for Indigenous people and their land councils to breathe life into the *Aboriginal Land Rights (Northern Territory) Act 1976* (Cth). In the early days of the legislation, opponents openly hurled abuse at claimants, land council staff and even land commissioners. But in the face of such extraordinary prejudice and perhaps even hatred, Indigenous people and their land councils maintained an indomitable spirit. Perhaps one of the reasons why grassroots activism is so empowering is because it enables Indigenous people to exercise control over language. For many, secure title to land cannot be considered in isolation from the broader struggle for self-determination. That the law is yet to provide a framework for these aspirations is beside the point.

It seems trite to ask if the native title recognition process has been similarly empowering for Indigenous people. For most, native title simply isn't relevant because of the extinguishment and validation provisions of the *Native Title Act 1993* (Cth). For the minority of Indigenous peoples whose native title may still exist, the processes for recognition are rigorous and painfully slow.[85] Whereas grassroots movements tend to raise the self-esteem of Indigenous communities and promote solidarity, native title has proven to be highly divisive and linked to lateral violence.[86]

Arguably, grassroots activists have also been successful in projecting black voices to a broad audience because their platforms contain an element of humanity. The language is often raw and on occasion confronting, but always accessible. One of the most effective examples of such a movement was the Aboriginal Tent Embassy. The Embassy's proximity to the parliament forced some Labor MPs to engage with the question of land justice, on Indigenous terms.

It was not only politicians who were engaged, but also local residents. The writer's father participated in the Embassy and has often reflected on the trade union officials who would deliver cash donations that had been collected from work sites. In contrast, the native title recognition process is so complex and buried in layers of legalese that it remains inaccessible to all other than those who operate within the native title industry.

Conclusion

There are a number of compelling reasons why legal scholars should engage with Indigenous literature. Because such literature is so closely aligned with the sociopolitical milieu, it is a rich source of information in relation to what Indigenous people believe is necessary for them to receive redress for the injuries of colonisation. Over the past century, Indigenous platforms have consistently made at least three

---

[84]Perkins (1998), pp 19–20.

[85]*Western Australia v Ward* [2002] HCA 28 at 561.

[86]Aboriginal and Torres Strait Islander Social Justice Commissioner (2011), p 81.

indivisible demands – the realisation of self-determination, the creation of a land base, and the payment of compensation.

Processes such as those contained in the *Native Title Act* create only cracks in the status quo, and are a far cry from the long desired transformation of relationships between Indigenous people and the state. This desired transformation lies at the heart of Indigenous literature – from the AAPA's petition, to the writings of Kevin Gilbert, to ATSIC's ground-breaking report, *Recognition, Rights and Reform.*

CRT provides a theoretical foundation for the incorporation of such narratives into legal scholarship. By engaging with Indigenous literature, legal scholars will be challenged to confront the law's complicity in the continuing subjugation of Indigenous people, and devise new frameworks for the realisation of Indigenous self-determination. The prospect of such change is no doubt daunting for many. But unless we embark upon this difficult journey, the law will continue to be an instrument of colonisation.

References

Primary sources

Cases

Brown v Board of Education 347 US 483 (1954)
Koowarta v Bjelke-Petersen (1982) 39 ALR 417
Mabo v Queensland (No. 2) (1992) 175 CLR 1
Western Australia v Ward [2002] HCA 28
Wik Peoples v Queensland (1996) 141 ALR 129

Legislation

Aboriginal Land Rights (Northern Territory) Act 1976 (Cth)
Aboriginals Protection and Restriction of the Sale of Opium Act 1897 (Qld)
Native Title Act 1993 (Cth)
Racial Discrimination Act 1975 (Cth)

Parliamentary debates

Commonwealth of Australia (1993), *Parliamentary Debates*, House of Representatives, 16 November

Secondary sources

Aboriginal and Torres Strait Islander Commission (1995) *Recognition, Rights and Reform: A Report to Government on Native Title Social Justice Measures.* ATSIC Strategic Policy and Planning Branch.

Aboriginal and Torres Strait Islander Social Justice Commissioner (2011) *Native Title Report 2011*, Australian Human Rights Commission.

Dominique Allen (2007) 'Periodic Peaks of Progress: Applying Bell's Interest Convergence Theory to the *Mabo* Decision' 26 *University of Tasmania Law Review* 63.

Bain Attwood and Andrew Markus (1999) *The Struggle for Aboriginal Rights: A Documentary History*, Allen & Unwin.

Derrick Bell (1971–1973) 'Black Faith in a Racist Land: A Summary Review of Racism in American Law' 17 *Howard Law Journal* 300.

Derrick Bell (1995) 'Who's Afraid of Critical Race Theory?' 4 *University of Illinois Law Review* 893.

Derrick Bell (1999) 'The Power of Narrative' 23 *Legal Studies Forum* 315.

Derrick Bell (1980) '*Brown v Board of Education* and the Interest Convergence Dilemma' 93 *Harvard Law Review* 518.

Frank Brennan (1992) *Land Rights Queensland Style*, University of Queensland Press.

Richard Broome (2006) 'There Were Vegetables Every Year Mr Green Was Here: Right Behaviour and the Struggle for Autonomy at Coranderrk Aboriginal Reserve' 3(2) *History Australia*, http://journals.publishing.monash.edu.au/ojs/index.php/ha/article/view/382/394. doi:10.2104/ha060043

Paul Butler (2013) 'Toward a Hip-Hop Theory of Punishment' in Richard Delgado and Jean Stefancic (eds) *Critical Race Theory: The Cutting Edge*, Temple University Press.

Callum Clayton-Dixon (2014) 'Treaty Now: An Agreement Between Two Equals', http://tracker.org.au/2014/03/treaty-now-an-agreement-between-two-equals/ (link no longer active).

John Chesterman and Brian Galligan (1997) *Citizens Without Rights: Aborigines and Australian Citizenship*, Cambridge University Press.

Neva Collings (1997) 'The Wik: A History of Their 400 Year Struggle' 4 *Indigenous Law Bulletin* 4.

Andre Douglas Pond Cummings (2013) 'A Furious Kinship: Critical Race Theory and the Hip-Hop Nation' in Richard Delgado and Jean Stefancic (eds) *Critical Race Theory: The Cutting Edge*, Temple University Press.

Joan Cunningham and Juan I. Baeza (2005) 'An Experiment in Indigenous Social Policy: The Rise and Fall of Australia's Aboriginal and Torres Strait Islander Commission (ATSIC)' 33 (3) *Policy & Politics* 461.

Richard Delgado (2013) 'Storytelling for Oppositionists and Others: A Plea for Narrative' in Richard Delgado and Jean Stefancic (eds) *Critical Race Theory: The Cutting Edge*, Temple University Press.

Richard Delgado and Jean Stefancic (eds) (2013) *Critical Race Theory: The Cutting Edge*, Temple University Press.

Michael Dodson and Lisa Strelein (2001) 'Australia's Nation-building: Renegotiating the Relationship Between Indigenous Peoples and the State' 24(3) *UNSW Law Journal* 826.

Mary L Dudziak (2013) 'Desegregation as a Cold War Imperative' in Richard Delgado and Jean Stefancic (eds) *Critical Race Theory: The Cutting Edge*, Temple University Press.

Gary Foley (2001) 'Black Power in Redfern 1968–1972', *The Koori History Website*, http://www.kooriweb.org/foley/essays/essay_1.html, 5 October 2001.

Gary Foley and Tim Anderson (2006) 'Land Rights and Aboriginal Voices' 12 *Australian Journal of Human Rights* 83.

Kevin Gilbert (2013) *Because a White Man'll Never Do It*, 3rd edition, Angus & Robertson Australian Classics.

Kevin Gilbert (1978) *Living Black: Blacks Talk to Kevin Gilbert*, Penguin Books.

Michele Ivanitz (1998) *Straddling Two Worlds: ATSIC and the Management of Indigenous Policy*, Research Paper No. 6, Centre for Australian Public Sector Management, Griffith University.

Michele Ivanitz (2000) 'The Demise of ATSIC? Accountability and the Coalition Government' 59 *Australian Journal of Public Administration* 3.

Rosalind Kidd (2000) *The Way We Civilise: Aboriginal Affairs, The Untold Story*, University of Queensland Press.

Ruby Langford Ginibi (1994) *My Bundjalung People*, University of Queensland Press.

Kathy Lothian (2007) 'Moving Blackwards: Black Power and the Aboriginal Embassy' in Ingereth Macfarlane and Mark Hannah (eds) *Transgressions: Critical Australian Indigenous Histories*, ANU E-Press, http://press.anu.edu.au//aborig_history/transgressions/mobile_devices/ch02.html, accessed 11 November 2014.

Tony Martin (1983) 'Case Note: *Koowarta v Bjelke Petersen* (1982) 39 ALR 417' 13 *Federal Law Review* 360.

Mari J. Matsuda (1987) 'Looking to the Bottom: Critical Legal Studies and Reparations' 22 *Harvard Civil Rights – Civil Liberties Law Review* 323.

John Maynard (2003) 'Vision, Voice and Influence: The Rise of the Australian Aboriginal Progressive Association' 121 *Australian Historical Studies* 91. doi:10.1080/1031461030 8596238

Peter Michael (2012) 'Cape York Crusader Martha Koowarta Wins Land Rights Battle', *The Courier Mail*, http://www.couriermail.com.au/news/queensland/cape-crusader-wins-land-fight/story-e6freoof-1226364036460, 23 May 2012.

Sally Morgan (1987) *My Place*, Fremantle Arts Centre Press.

Oodgeroo Noonuccal (1962) 'Aboriginal Charter of Rights', *The Dawn is at Hand*, Australian Poetry Library, http://www.poetrylibrary.edu.au/poets/noonuccal-oodgeroo/aboriginal-charter-of-rights-0719030, accessed 11 November 2014.

Charles Perkins (1998) 'When We Started Marching' in Alexis Wright (ed) *Take Power like this Old Man Here: An Anthology of Writings Celebrating Twenty Years of Land Rights in Central Australia 1977–1997*, IAD Press.

Scott Robinson (1994) 'The Aboriginal Embassy: An Account of the Protests of 1972' 18 *Aboriginal History* 49.

Peter Russell (2006) *Recognising Aboriginal Title: The* Mabo *Case and Indigenous Resistance to English-Settler Colonialism*, University of New South Wales Press.

Geoffrey Sawer (1984) 'The External Affairs Power' 14 *Federal Law Review* 199.

Adam Shoemaker (1989) *Black Words White Page: Aboriginal Literature 1929–1988*, University of Queensland Press.

Penny Van Toorn (1999) 'Authors, Scribes and Owners: The Sociology of Nineteenth-century Aboriginal Writing on Coranderrk and Lake Condah Reserves' 13(3) *Continuum: Journal of Media and Cultural Studies* 333.

Penny Van Toorn (2006) *Writing Never Arrives Naked: Early Aboriginal Cultures of Writing in Australia*, Aboriginal Studies Press.

Kath Walker (1964) We Are Going, Jacaranda Press.

John Woodley (1998) 'John Koowarta – Mabo of the Mainland' 17(2) *Social Alternatives* 26.

Alexis Wright (1998) *Take Power Like This Old Man Here: An Anthology of Writings Celebrating Twenty Years of Land Rights in Central Australia, 1977–1997*, IAD Press.

Recovering the foundations of *Koowarta*: the struggle of the Aboriginal Land Fund Commission to purchase land in Queensland

Alexander Reilly

Law School, University of Adelaide, Australia

This article examines one of the stories underpinning *Koowarta v Bjelke-Petersen*; the story of the attempts of the Aboriginal Land Fund Commission (ALFC) to purchase land for Aboriginal communities in Queensland amid conflicting Commonwealth and state policies on Aboriginal rights. Through telling this story, the article reflects on legal historiography, on the role of legal judgments as official records of the events they document, and on how what is recorded in judgments becomes the official memory of events, marginalising and strategically forgetting other stories to achieve judgment and resolution. The story of the struggles of the ALFC to purchase land for Aboriginal people in Queensland disrupts a too easy memorialising of *Koowarta*, and presents an alternative source for remembering the events surrounding the *Koowarta* litigation, to deepen our appreciation of official and unofficial struggles for Aboriginal justice in the 1970s and 1980s.

Introduction

When we commemorate an event, we increase its significance in relation to other events. The act of commemoration itself alters our remembering of the past, and so it is with *Koowarta v Bjelke-Petersen*.[1] To establish *Koowarta* as a moment to be remembered, and even more significantly, as a 'turning point', opens a field of vision. Surrounding events are brought also into view, though they necessarily remain peripheral. Legal cases are a central reference point for remembering (and also forgetting) the issues to which they give rise.[2]

The historiographical presence and significance of legal cases is a cause for caution. There is a risk that the legal judgments replace the history of events to which they bear witness, that the events recorded in judgments take on a greater significance than they warrant, distorting our understanding of other related events. Unrepresented facts risk being forgotten, or worse, reinterpreted to reinforce the central narrative around unquestionable key moments. Whatever it is we remember in relation to *Koowarta* becomes the reference point for future remembering, and what we remember risks contributing to our forgetting of other conflicting stories. It was because of this risk that the French historian, Henry Rousso refused to

[1]*Koowarta v Bjelke-Petersen* (1982) 153 CLR 168.

[2]See, for example, Evans (2002); Rousso (2002); Reilly (2006).

participate as an expert historical witness in the Vichy trials in the 1990s.[3] He argued that historians' search for truth was compromised by participation in legal causes.[4]

The presence of *Koowarta* in the *Commonwealth Law Reports* itself signifies Aboriginal resistance to white colonisation. It facilitates particular memorialising of the man who gives the case its name. John Koowarta is elevated to a symbol of Aboriginal struggle for land rights. He becomes a symbolic 'Mabo for the mainland' regardless of the historiographic sense of this claim.[5]

The presence of *Koowarta* in the law reports hints at the complex layers of Indigenous resistance both in and outside the law. Positing *Koowarta* as a turning point offers the opportunity to cast our gaze around the central event of the case to understand more fully why it represents a significant turning point in law, and to engage in a deeper excavation of the other stories and moments associated with the name Koowarta. Without doing so, the case commemorates a name and an event in an 'excess of memory' which masks an 'excess of forgetting' elsewhere.[6]

While the confirmation of the validity and operation of the *Racial Discrimination Act* 1975 (Cth) (RDA) promised to protect existing Aboriginal rights from future denigration and discriminatory treatment, it did not provide a positive platform for protecting Aboriginal land rights. But for the declaration in *Mabo* of the role of the RDA in protecting native title rights from extinguishment after 1975, the RDA itself had little role in protecting Aboriginal land rights, illustrated dramatically by the Queensland government's ability to circumvent the result in *Koowarta* through declaring the Archer lease to be part of a national park. There was no memorialising of the case in 1992, on its tenth anniversary, as it was yet to embody its present significance; and, in 2002, on its twentieth anniversary, it was overshadowed by the deep uncertainty at the extent to which the *Native Title Act 1993* protected native title rights from extinguishment. *Koowarta* becomes a turning point on its thirtieth anniversary, as a retrospective act, when the time is ripe to manufacture new memories and new meaning.

This article examines one of the stories underpinning *Koowarta*, the story of the attempts of the Aboriginal Land Fund Commission (ALFC) to purchase land for Aboriginal communities in Queensland amid conflicting Commonwealth and state policies on Aboriginal rights. But for the determination of the Commission to pursue land purchases in Queensland in the face of a hostile Queensland government and a Commonwealth lacking resolve to support its efforts, the *Koowarta* litigation would not have occurred.

There is very little written about the ALFC. This is not surprising given its status as an administrative body. Creating an administrative body like the ALFC is a way of disciplining resistance – to keep it within civilised bounds. And so, the ALFC was to make purchases of land for Aboriginal communities that were agreed to by state governments and were aimed at aiding Aboriginal economic development. However, the ALFC revealed itself to be independently minded. As the story of the ALFC reveals, it believed that land purchases were important for cultural as well as

[3]Conan and Rousso (1998).

[4]Rousso (2002).

[5]Woodley (1998), p 26.

[6]Ricouer (2004), pp 449–450.

economic reasons and, in the case of Queensland, it was prepared to pursue purchases that were not agreed to by the state government. It was this preparedness that led to conflict between the Commonwealth and the states, which in turn led to the *Koowarta* litigation.

The story of the ALFC reveals a struggle for Aboriginal justice outside of the courts which made litigation possible, but also subverted its results. It is a trite observation that what is considered by courts in resolving claims is the distillation of a complex narrative into a linear historiography capable of assessment, judgment and resolution. The *Koowarta* litigation focused on a brief Cabinet memorandum of the Queensland government that revealed a policy of discouraging purchases of land by or for Aboriginal people. The memorandum expressed a breathtakingly racist policy, in clear contravention of the newly minted RDA. The brazenness of its discriminatory content meant there was no need to examine Queensland Aboriginal policy in detail in *Koowarta*, and the litigation could focus on the technical constitutional question of the extent of the Commonwealth's legislative power under s 51(xxix) of the Constitution.

There are several key themes in the story of the ALFC in Queensland that emerge around *Koowarta*. First, there is a conflict between Commonwealth and Queensland government policies over Aboriginal land rights. At this point in time, Queensland was alone among the states in opposing the sale of land to Aboriginal people, and in holding to a contradictory and unreconstructed policy towards the advancement of Aboriginal people. Second, there is a conflict between the ALFC and the Commonwealth as the ALFC pushed ahead with land purchases in Queensland while the Commonwealth government was more concerned to avoid conflict with the Queensland government on Aboriginal policy. Third, there is a story of how the RDA contributed to the revelation of the Queensland policy opposing purchases of land for Aboriginal peoples. These themes are explored in this article to disrupt a too linear reading of *Koowarta* and to encourage a broader remembering of the struggles for Aboriginal land rights in the 1970s and 1980s in Australia.

The Aboriginal Land Fund Commission

The ALFC was established by the Whitlam government in 1974. The idea for an Aboriginal land fund was first raised by Whitlam during the election campaign of 1972,[7] and was again raised as a recommendation in the second report of Justice Woodward's Aboriginal Land Rights Commission in July 1974.[8] The Whitlam government passed legislation creating the commission in that same year.[9] Unlike the later *Aboriginal Land Rights Act 1976* which provided for land rights claims only in the Northern Territory, the Commission was empowered to buy land for Aboriginal communities in all states and territories. Indigenous Australians from around the country whose lands were under state title could ask the ALFC to purchase land on their behalf and transfer the title to Indigenous corporations who

---

[7]Chartrand (1981), p 444.

[8]Chartrand (1981), p 443.

[9]*Aboriginal Land Fund Act 1974* (Cth).

were invested with the responsibility to manage the land. Therefore, although the states remained in control of Aboriginal land rights in the 1970s, the work of the ALFC had the potential to affect state policy through the purchase of land and, importantly, the commission's work brought to light the differences in state land policy in relation to Aboriginal land rights.

Whereas other recommendations emanating from the Woodward reports focused on returning traditional lands to Aboriginal people through the grant of freehold or leasehold title over land, the ALFC was able to take into account non-traditional economic and social needs of Aboriginal communities. Given its broad focus, it is not surprising that the commission was at the centre of a struggle between the precedence of Commonwealth and state policy on Aboriginal land rights. This struggle was particularly fierce in Queensland which was opposed to the purchase of land for Aboriginal communities both for traditional and non-traditional purposes.

The ALFC was established as a statutory body and operated within the Department of Aboriginal Affairs from 1974 to 1980. The original purpose of creating the commission as a separate statutory body was to distance the department from the politically contentious activity of purchasing land for Aboriginal peoples for which it had previously been responsible. The Liberal opposition supported the creation of the ALFC on the basis that it would be a more effective and responsible body for the purchase of land than the department.[10] The recommendation for an Aboriginal land fund was the first of Woodward's recommendations to be passed into law.[11]

The bipartisan support for the creation of the commission reflects that there was a commitment to land rights for Aboriginal and Torres Strait Islanders across the political spectrum at the Commonwealth level, consistent with the bipartisan support for constitutional change in 1967. However, as with constitutional change in 1967, the overt support for Aboriginal people contained qualifications. The independence of the ALFC enabled political parties to disavow any purchases that were controversial, while the ultimate control of the Minister for Aboriginal Affairs over decisions of the commission, and over its financial resources, enabled the government to constrain the commission's agenda of land purchases.

The ALFC was constituted of five commissioners who remained in office for the duration of the its 6 year existence. The commissioners were appointed part-time, and only received travel expenses and day-sitting fees. There were three Indigenous commissioners who were community leaders from different parts of Australia. Ernest (Ernie) Bridge was the Shire President of Halls Creek, Western Australia. Bridge later became a long standing Australian Labor Party (ALP) and independent Member of Parliament (MP) for the Kimberley in the WA Parliament (1993–2001). Bridge was the first Aboriginal person to be a Minister in a state or federal government in Australia.[12] Stumpy Martin Jampijinpa was a stockman on the Willowra pastoral lease in the Northern Territory. In 1960, with the support and encouragement of Jampijinpa, the leaseholder of Willowra, Edgar Parkinson, applied to the Northern Territory Administration to give the leased land back to

[10]Palmer (1988), pp 39–41.

[11]Chartrand (1981) p 446.

[12]'Ernie Bridge Dead at 76' *The West Australian*, https://au.news.yahoo.com/thewest/latest/a/16482280/ernie-bridge-dead-at-76/, 1 April 2013.

the Aboriginal residents, but the application was rejected. Jampijinpa continued to advocate for the purchase of Willowra and in 1972, while a member of the Interim Central Australian Aboriginal Rights Council, he secured a loan from the Commonwealth Department of Aboriginal Affairs for its purchase.[13] The experience with Willowra led Jampijinpa into official positions advocating for Aboriginal land rights, first on the ALFC (1974–80) and then on the Aboriginal Development Commission (1980–86).

Thomas Williams OBE was chosen as the chairman of the Aboriginal Advisory Council after its restructuring in the *Aborigines (Amendment) Act 1973* (NSW).[14] He was also the Director of Field Operations for the NSW Aboriginal Lands Trust and a member of the Aboriginal Relics Advisory Committee. In these roles he was involved in the transfer of reserve lands in NSW to Indigenous ownership.

Of the non-Indigenous commissioners, Neville Amy was the senior rural officer in the Commonwealth Development Bank of Australia. Amy brought to the commission expertise in purchasing pastoral properties.[15]

The commission was chaired by Charles Rowley, the renowned social scientist and advocate of Aboriginal rights. In 1964, Rowley had directed a research project on 'Aborigines in Australia' which highlighted the inequities facing Aboriginal Australians and was influential in the formulation of government policies promoting self-determination.[16] The Appendix to Justice Murphy's judgment in *Koowarta* lists among its sources on racial discrimination against Aboriginal Australians, two of Rowley's books; *The Destruction of Aboriginal Society* (1970) and *A Matter of Justice* (1979). At the time of his appointment to the commission, Rowley was the director of the Academy of Social Sciences at the Australian National University.

What is immediately obvious about the commissioners is the wealth of administrative experience they brought to the ALFC, including knowledge of rural land purchases, and their individual commitment to improving the rights and conditions of Aboriginal Australians prior to joining the commission. The Indigenous members of the ALFC all had experience in advocating for Aboriginal rights in official positions prior to joining the commission, and personal experience of fighting for land rights. These were not token appointments, but men capable of formulating an agenda for the ALFC independent of the Commonwealth government. Amy added important technical knowledge of land purchases in rural Australia and Rowley provided a general knowledge and vision of what might be achieved to improve Aboriginal rights and return Aboriginal communities to self-determination. Although the commission was intended to operate independently of government in its land purchasing decisions, reflected in its strong membership, under s 5(2) of the *Aboriginal Land Fund Act*, it was to perform its functions 'in accordance with any general directions given by the Minister'. Furthermore, the statutory authority granted to the ALFC was limited under s 4(2)(b) to 'acquir[ing], hold[ing] and dispos [ing] of real and personal property', and did not extend to dealing with any items on

---

[13]Vaarzon-Morel (2012).

[14]*New Dawn*, http://www.aiatsis.gov.au/collections/exhibitions/dawn/docs/v22/s04/September_1973.pdf, p 15, accessed 15 September 2014.

[15]Palmer (1998), p 43.

[16]Young (1986), p 3.

the land. This was a significant limitation on the ALFC in its purchase of pastoral properties, in which the moveable items such as machinery and stock were usually included in the purchase price.[17] In order to purchase a pastoral property, the ALFC had to approach the department to obtain additional funds to cover the cost of moveable items. Furthermore, the ALFC was only a purchasing agency, and had no authority or resources to cover costs associated with the management of a property after it had been purchased. This reliance on the department considerably affected the ALFC's independence and effectiveness.

The ALFC began with a budget of just under AU$2 million in its first year of operation in 1974, which was the unexpended balance of the Aboriginal Advancement Trust Account for land purchases in the Department of Aboriginal Affairs. In subsequent years, it had to fight for its allocation of funds from the department. The change of government in 1975 saw a dramatic tightening in the commission's budget. From 1976, the new coalition government required the ALFC to return unexpended funds to assist the department achieve its required budget savings. At first, the ALFC refused to release the funds. The struggle over finances resulted in the Minister for Aboriginal Affairs, Ian Viner, issuing a directive requiring the ALFC to consult with the Minister before 'entering into any new commitments to buy properties'.[18] This directive was reinforced in later communications from the Minister, and led to the ALFC questioning its independence.

The ALFC faced other constraints on its power to purchase land. Purchases were to be in rural areas, unless the ALFC consulted with the Minister for Aboriginal Affairs. The Department of Aboriginal Affairs required the ALFC to purchase on the open market, which meant it was limited to acquiring land that was available for sale and at a price within the ALFC's limited budget. The ALFC was limited to purchasing at a maximum price of 110 per cent of the valuation of a property, which meant that others interested in a property, such as mining companies, could easily outbid the ALFC if they were minded to prevent Aboriginal ownership.[19] Finally, the ALFC was to make purchases only at the request of Aboriginal communities. The ALFC was not, therefore, to purchase land in the expectation of a future interest in the land.[20] The ALFC did, however, bring to the attention of communities the availability of land for purchase.

Within these constraints, the ALFC developed its own purchasing priorities according to its broad policy goals. It was interested in purchasing land for the protection of Aboriginal culture and tradition, and also as a means of providing an economic base for Aboriginal communities in the national economy. As a result it was interested in purchasing land that had both economic and social value for communities. The most desirable land was land in which economic and cultural goals aligned – where economic activities supported or sustained cultural activities. However, the ALFC was interested in land which had no economic value. This accorded to Rowley's strongly held view that land purchases were primarily to provide the opportunity for Indigenous communities to make their own decisions

---

[17]Palmer (1988).

[18]Aboriginal Land Fund Commission (1977), pp 9–10.

[19]Palmer (1988), pp 46–47.

[20]Palmer (1988), p 46.

about their future needs.[21] It had to fight hard for the acceptance of land purchases for social reasons alone as the prevailing ideological position was a preference for economic viability.[22]

In furtherance of its policy of supporting the economic and social needs of communities, the ALFC took into account a number of factors in determining whether to purchase land. Many of these considerations were taken from the reports of the Aboriginal Land Rights Commission.[23] Key considerations included: the number of people claiming the land; the strength of tribal affiliation, and desire to live on the land; the cost of the purchase; the cost of providing services; and the viability of development schemes for the land.[24]

Fred Chaney took over from Viner as Minister for Aboriginal Affairs in early 1979. Chaney developed a better working relationship with the ALFC. He replaced the 1978 directive that required ministerial approval with one that was less onerous. The ALFC continued to pursue purchases throughout Australia until its abolition in 1980. Between June 1975 and June 1980 when it was abolished, the commission successfully completed 58 purchases of land, five of which were in Queensland. In terms of the total land area of purchases, there were large areas purchased in Western Australia, South Australia and the Northern Territory, and small areas in the other states.[25]

In 1980, Rowley said of the work of the commission:

> During the life of the Commission, the Commissioners' conviction that the purchase of property is vital for any substantial social and economic gain by the Aboriginal people was greatly strengthened. The importance of holding control of a safe home base may not be appreciated by those of us who have always had it – a place from which the person or the group cannot be removed at the whim of an individual or a government. Without this anchor in security neither economic success, nor gains in social cohesion are possible ... Aboriginal affairs are seen as welfare matters rather than matters of justice and politics, and governments approach welfare as a matter of the government cheque. So it proves easy to give out of pocket money, but difficult to transfer property in which to invest money and work. Yet a beginning was made through the Commission.[26]

In this reflection, Rowley articulates the rationale for the commission of supporting self-determination for Indigenous Australians. This was the promise of 1967, and the commission was the first substantive attempt by the Commonwealth government to achieve self-determination. Outside the Northern Territory, where the Aboriginal Land Rights Commission was responsible for the purchase and transfer of large areas of land to Indigenous traditional and freehold title, the work of the ALFC was the high point of Commonwealth efforts to realise land rights of Aboriginal communities.

---

[21]Young (1986), p 5.

[22]Palmer (1988), p 32.

[23]Aboriginal Land Rights Commission (1973, 1974). These two reports are often called *The Woodward Report*.

[24]Palmer (1988), pp 46–47.

[25]Palmer (1988), pp 150–151.

[26]Rowley (1981), pp 258–259.

Behind the result in *Koowarta* is a complex struggle for control of Aboriginal policy between Commonwealth and state governments, a struggle that was particularly intense in the 1970s following the successful referendum in 1967 which invested the Commonwealth with the power to make laws with respect to Indigenous issues under the races power. Although we now look on *Koowarta* as a significant point in the advancement of Aboriginal land rights, in an alternative historiography it signifies the lack of resolve of the Commonwealth government in advancing Aboriginal land rights, and the significant powers of resistance encountered by an ostensibly independent statutory authority to achieve its stated aims of purchasing land for Aboriginal economic and cultural purposes.

This last point is particularly significant in reflecting upon the ALFC. There is a fundamental contradiction faced by all government attempts to advance Aboriginal interests. As their starting point, governments confirm the validity of non-Indigenous law in using it to pursue Aboriginal rights, thus disavowing Aboriginal sovereignty and self-determination. So the ALFC, through pursuing land purchases for Aboriginal communities, implicitly accepted that the land was in need of purchase to become Aboriginal land. It also accepted that if a purchase was not successful for any reason then the land remained in non-Aboriginal ownership. Alternatively, if the purchase was successful, the underlying radical title remained in non-Indigenous possession, so that a government declaration of a national park could still undermine the purchase. A stronger position, more consonant with Indigenous sovereignty, is that land in which Aboriginal communities continue to work and reside is, and has always been, Aboriginal land, in no need of purchase according to the logic of an introduced legal system. The Indigenous and non-Indigenous commissioners on the ALFC could not entertain this possibility while on the commission.

The story of the ALFC reveals the ambivalence of the Commonwealth towards pursuing Aboriginal land rights in Queensland at the time. This is a story lost in the face of the litigation which pits the Commonwealth as a supporter of Aboriginal land rights against the State of Queensland. In fact, the Commonwealth government and several of its departments were themselves in conflict over the ALFC's attempt to purchase land in Queensland.

Unlike the Commonwealth's overt and strident effort to prevent the Tasmania government from damming the Franklin River a year later,[27] the Commonwealth was reluctant to pick a fight with Queensland over Indigenous policy that led to *Koowarta*. The contrast in the Commonwealth's resolve to confront the states in relation to environmental issues in *Commonwealth v Tasmania* ('*Tasmanian Dam*') and its resolve to confront Indigenous issues in *Koowarta* is reflected in how environmental policies were used in the resolution of the disputes in both cases. While in *Tasmanian Dam* the Commonwealth used the declaration of a heritage protection area to protect the Franklin and Gordon Rivers, the Queensland government successfully prevented the Aboriginal claimants in *Koowarta* from purchasing the Archer River lease by declaring the area a national park at the conclusion of the litigation.[28]

---

[27] *Commonwealth v Tasmania* (1983) 158 CLR 1.

[28] The use of environmental policy in Queensland to defeat Indigenous land rights following *Koowarta* provides an important reminder of why Aboriginal groups in Queensland are concerned about the effect of Wild Rivers legislation on their interests.

Queensland policy on Aboriginal land rights during the Bjelke-Petersen years

The head of the Queensland Department for Aboriginal and Islander Advancement, Pat Killoran determined Aboriginal policy in Queensland along with the Premier Bjelke-Petersen in the 1970s. Killoran had spent all his working life in the Department of Aboriginal and Islander Advancement, and carried forward the philosophy of assimilation developed in the department back in the nineteenth century. [29] The ultimate aim of Aboriginal policy was for Aboriginal people to leave their traditional lands and the reserves to which they had been relocated, and enter the general community.[30] This was to be achieved through a two-step process: initially segregation on reserves under a regime of strict regulation of the movement of Aboriginal peoples, and then a one-way move off reserves to live and work in the broader community. Although the ultimate goal was formal equality, Indigenous peoples in Queensland were subject to control over all aspects of their life not experienced by others.

Formal equality was used as a rhetorical device to undermine Indigenous claims to rights in Queensland. The government's Aboriginal policy was defined in the *Aborigines and Torres Strait Islanders' Affairs Act 1965*:

> All persons of Aboriginal descent will choose to attain a similar manner and standard of living to that of other Australians ... Any special measures taken are regarded as temporary measures ... intended to meet their need for special care and assistance to make the transition from one stage to another in such a way as will be favourable to their social, economic and political advancement.[31]

In relation to the purchase of land for Aboriginal people, Premier Bjelke-Petersen stated,

> Territorial acquisition en masse for Aborigines as a race ... stands in sharp contrast to the policy of Queensland where land rights are exactly the same for Aborigines and non Aborigines. Any Aborigine can hold the various tenures as many do, under the same legal rules and procedures which apply to everyone else.
>
> I want to make it clear to you that whilst in Queensland ethnic background is no disqualification from equal opportunity neither is it a qualification for privileged consideration over other citizens.[32]

Given its approach to equality, unsurprisingly the Queensland government was opposed to land purchases for Aboriginal groups. This was evident in a Queensland Cabinet decision of September 1972 which articulated the policy challenged in *Koowarta*:

---

[29]Ryan (1985).

[30]See, generally, Ryan (1985); Nettheim, (1976, 1978).

[31]Ryan (1985), pp 116–117.

[32]Brennan (1992), pp 11–12.

> The Queensland Government does not view favourably proposals to acquire large areas of additional freehold or leasehold land for development by Aborigines or Aboriginal groups in isolation.[33]

When Bjelke-Petersen became Premier of Queensland in 1968 there were approximately 31,000 Indigenous people living on 120 reserves, missions and settlements. The reserves were Crown land in remote areas set aside for Indigenous people to live until they died, or until they were ready to integrate into white society. The reserves could be cancelled through executive action and this happened whenever the government decided the land could be put to better use. For example, in 1959, the Weipa reserve was reduced from 354,828 hectares to 124 hectares to accommodate mining leases when bauxite was discovered on the reserve land.[34] People living at Mapoon on the Weipa reserve were forcibly moved to Bamaga, at the northern tip of Cape York.[35]

With no security of tenure over reserve land, the entitlement of Indigenous people to stay on the reserves was at the discretion of the Queensland government. Furthermore, Indigenous people on reserves were subject to a high level of control of their activities and movements. Aboriginal children were routinely removed from their parents at the age of four. Children attended European style schooling. If Indigenous people on the reserves did not comply with the strict regime of work and study, they were sent to Palm Island.[36] In the northern reserves, including Aurukun, Indigenous people were used as cheap seasonal labour in the pastoral industry. They were not paid award wages, and some wages were placed in a welfare fund.[37]

The central struggle over Indigenous land rights in Queensland related to extending Aboriginal control over their lives on reserves. The Commonwealth pursued a range of strategies to further Aboriginal rights on reserves. Under one strategy, the Commonwealth attempted to enter an agreement with the State of Queensland to transfer control of Aboriginal Affairs under the *Aboriginal Affairs (Arrangements With the States) Act 1973* (Cth).[38] Queensland strongly opposed this initiative, holding tightly to its control over reserve lands.

From the 1970s, the Commonwealth assisted Aboriginal communities in the Northern Territory to return to the bush to pursue their traditional life. This movement of communities to remote areas was known as the 'outstation movement'. The outstation movement began in Queensland on the Aurukun reserve, which was managed by the Presbyterian church. The Commonwealth supported the outstation movement by passing the *Aborigines and Torres Strait Islanders (Queensland Reserves and Communities Self-Management) Act 1978* (Cth) which allowed residents of a reserve to request self-management from the Commonwealth and for the Minister to make a declaration to this effect.[39] The Queensland government

---

[33]Palmer (1988), p 67.

[34]Brennan (1992), p 8.

[35]Brennan (1992), pp 8–9.

[36]Ryan (1985), p 117.

[37]Ryan (1985), p 117.

[38]Ryan (1985), p 121.

[39]Brennan (1992), p 12.

responded by simply changing the status of the land at Aurukun and Mornington Island from reserve land to local government land, to which Commonwealth legislation did not apply. The Commonwealth could have compulsorily acquired the reserve land under s 51(xxxi) of the Constitution, but was not prepared to do so in order to avoid an unknown compensation bill.[40]

The operation of reserves in Queensland was clearly out of step with movements towards the recognition of Aboriginal land rights in the rest of the country in the mid to late 1970s. The Queensland government was opposed both to attempts by Aboriginal peoples to return to traditional country and to them gaining control of land for the economic and social advancement of communities.[41]

In 1973, when the Whitlam Labor government entered agreements with the states to transfer state control over health, welfare, education and housing for Aboriginal peoples to a new Commonwealth Department of Aboriginal Affairs, Queensland did not participate. As Premier Bjelke-Petersen put it, 'Queensland is the only State that hasn't fallen for their soft soap about land rights'.[42]

Commonwealth attempts to address overt discrimination against Aboriginal people in the late 1970s through the enactment of the RDA were met with trenchant opposition from Queensland. Commonwealth Commissioner for Community Relations, Al Grassby described racial discrimination as 'widespread throughout the whole of Queensland' with the rights of Aboriginal and Islander persons being 'infringed extensively in a way which affects ... all aspects of their daily lives. Public facilities and public services are often denied Aboriginal and Islander people'.[43]

Grassby described the Queensland government as adopting 'a policy and practice of non-cooperation with the Commissioner for Community Relations. Correspondence is not acknowledged and not answered. Directions to attend compulsory conferences under the RDA 1975 are not complied with by those concerned'.[44] In its response to Commonwealth attempts to require attendance at compulsory mediation conferences under the RDA, Queensland routinely denied that it had acted in a discriminatory manner and denied the validity of the RDA.[45]

Only in early 1982, prior to the Brisbane Commonwealth Games, and well after the *Koowarta* litigation had commenced, did the Queensland state government outline a plan for the conversion of reserves into a different form of land tenure. The Queensland government proposed to vest title in lands in elected councils through 'Deeds of Grant in Trust' (DOGITs). DOGITs had a wide range of limitations on the ability of the trustees to control the land including that the deed could be revoked at any time by the governor-in-council. The one protection that existed was that any revocation had to be tabled in parliament and was thus subject to parliamentary disallowance.[46]

---

[40]Ryan, (1985), p 122; Brennan (1992), p 12.

[41]Smith (2003), p 30.

[42]Grassby (1981), p 11.

[43]Grassby (1981), p 3.

[44]Grassby, (1981), p 7.

[45]Grassby, (1981), p 7.

[46]Brennan (1992), pp 19–25.

Outside of reserve lands, the ALFC pursued a separate approach of purchasing land which Aboriginal people had identified as of traditional and economic value. The purchase of non-reserve land concerned the Queensland government for reasons different from the struggle over Aboriginal control of reserves. The reserves had always been a place for Aboriginal tradition to continue, but within a controlled and limited geographical area. The expectation was that the zone of separateness on reserves would diminish over time, and ultimately disappear altogether. The purchase of other land for Aboriginal people gave rise to the spectre of a growing area in which Aboriginal peoples could assert their autonomy and the continuation of their traditional way of life. This outcome was a direct challenge to the Queensland policy of assimilation.

In the legal historiography of *Koowarta*, the measures in Queensland Aboriginal policy are not discussed. It is not necessary for the court to raise them, even in a case concerning the application of the RDA, because the brief Cabinet note is sufficient to satisfy the criteria of discrimination under s 10 of the RDA. This is an example of the reductive quality of judicial historiography, whereby superfluous facts are erased, relieving the decision-maker from the need to account for a fuller story. In the case of *Koowarta*, it relieved the court of the uncomfortable responsibility of analysing and judging the full suite of Queensland Aboriginal policies against the criteria of the RDA.

ALFC and the purchase of the Archer River pastoral lease in Queensland

In 1974, John Koowarta, with other Aboriginal pastoral workers, approached the owner of the Archer River cattle station about selling the property to the Winychanam/Wik people to run it as a pastoral business.[47] The owner, who knew Koowarta as 'an experienced stockman who had worked at the station' agreed to the sale.[48] Koowarta then approached the ALFC and 'persuaded the Commission to buy it'.[49] In 1976, the ALFC completed negotiations for the purchase of the Archer River station. The purchase required the consent of the Queensland Minister for Lands to complete the transfer of the property. On 12 July, the Queensland Land Administration Commission (QLAC) formally refused the transfer of the Archer River holding without providing reasons.[50]

The ALFC sought a review of this decision and, in December 1976, the Queensland government confirmed its decision not to allow the transfer of the Archer River holding. The Minister for Lands stated the reason for the refusal to consent to the Archer River property in the following terms:

> The question of the proposed acquisition of Archer River Pastoral Holding comes within the ambit of declared Government policy expressed in Cabinet decision of September 1972, which stated: –
> 'The Queensland Government does not view favourably proposals to acquire large areas of additional freehold or leasehold land for development by Aborigines or Aboriginal groups in isolation.'

---

[47]Woodley (1998), p 26.

[48]Woodley (1998), p 26.

[49]Nettheim (2001), p 11.

[50]Palmer (1998), p 68.

> In light of this policy the recent development whereby the Aboriginal Land Fund Commission sought to acquire by transfer Archer River Pastoral Holding was reported in detail to State Cabinet, whereupon Cabinet said in June 1976 –
>
> (1) That Cabinet's policy regarding Aboriginal reserve lands ... remains unchanged.
> (2) That in accordance with such policy and as it is considered that sufficient land in Queensland is already reserved and available for use and benefit of Aborigines, no consent be given to the transfer of Archer River Pastoral Holding No. 4785 to the Aboriginal Land Fund Commission.[51]

These reasons for refusing the transfer brought to public light the policy of the Queensland Cabinet not to consent to purchases of land for Aboriginal communities. Although the ideological position of the Queensland government in relation to Aboriginal peoples was well known at the time, it was the persistence of the ALFC in pursuing the purchase of Archer River that led to the Queensland government revealing its untenable policy. The express failure to consent to the transfer moved the issue of Commonwealth property purchases for Aboriginal people into the realm of Commonwealth–state relations. The Queensland government was effectively rejecting the power of the ALFC, a Commonwealth government instrumentality, to purchase land contrary to state policy.

At this time, the ALFC was pursuing a range of options to overcome the Queensland government's objection to the purchase of the Archer River station. It requested and received support from the Minister for Aboriginal Affairs, who tried to negotiate a political solution. There were two avenues of legal challenge to the Queensland refusal to agree to the sale of the Archer River property. The first avenue was a direct challenge to the Queensland government's power to effectively veto the purchases by a Commonwealth government agency with express statutory authority to acquire land. Under s 21 of the *Aboriginal Land Fund Act 1974* (Cth), the ALFC was empowered to 'acquire by agreement any interest in land'. The requirement of purchase by agreement would likely be interpreted as extending to agreement of a state government as the holder of the radical title of land within the state. As a result the ALFC had no power to complete a purchase of land in the face of state government opposition. However, if 'agreement' was limited to agreement with the owner of land to purchase, s 21 might be read as a broad power of acquisition that would render the inconsistent exercise of a state ministerial power invalid under s 109 of the Commonwealth Constitution.[52] The second avenue was to attack the Queensland government's express policy to prevent purchases of land under the RDA. The ALFC lodged a complaint with the Commissioner for Community Relations, Al Grassby.[53] Under the RDA, the commissioner was required to conciliate complaints. Following the express statement of reasons for refusing to allow the acquisition of Archer River by the ALFC in December 1976,

---

[51] *Koowarta v Bjelke-Petersen* (1982) 153 CLR 168 at 176 (Gibbs CJ).

[52] Note that, under this broad interpretation of s 21, there might still be a question whether the Commonwealth law was invalid for violating the implied immunity doctrine in the Commonwealth Constitution.

[53] Nettheim (2001), p 11.

Grassby wrote to the Queensland Minister for Lands, Kenneth Tomkins, indicating that the refusal contravened the RDA.[54] Grassby received no response to this letter and, in 1979, issued directions for Tomkins, his predecessor, the Director of the Department of Aboriginal and Islanders Advancement and the chairman of the Land Administration Commission to attend a compulsory conference under the RDA to resolve the matter.

The Queensland Crown solicitor wrote a letter to Grassby explaining that the failure of Tomkins and others to attend was on the basis that the RDA was invalid and that the ALFC, being a body corporate, had no power to take and operate a grazing lease.[55] When Grassby's attempts at conciliation failed, he issued a certificate authorising court proceedings, the first ever such certificate to be issued.[56]

As is well known, the success of the *Koowarta* litigation did not lead to the Archer River property being transferred into Indigenous ownership. Instead, the Queensland government converted the property into a national park. This possibility had been mooted by the Queensland government in 1976 as a reason not to allow the sale of the property to proceed. The ALFC alleged at the time that Queensland was proposing the national park simply to deny the purchase of the property by Aboriginal peoples. In the face of this criticism the QLAC maintained that a proposal to convert Archer River into a national park had existed since 1975. However, the Queensland government was also actively encouraging the vendors of Archer River to approach the mining company Comalco as possible purchasers of the property, which seems to confirm that the proposed conversion of the property to a national park was no more than a cynical move to thwart the property moving into Aboriginal hands.[57]

Frank Brennan recounts introducing John Koowarta to Sir Ninian Stephen in February 1991, and how at that meeting Koowarta confirmed to Stephen that, 9 years after the judgment, he and his people still had not secured title to their land. This situation persisted until Koowarta died 6 months later, at which point, as Frank Brennan puts it, his legal file was closed.[58]

The ALFC continued to purchase properties in Queensland despite the federal tensions. In the middle of 1977, the Queensland and Commonwealth Ministers for Aboriginal Affairs struck an agreement that the ALFC should consult with the Queensland government about any possible future purchases. The reason given was that the ALFC could then learn of any information the department had of the state of the land, or of any future land use plans of the Queensland government. A plan to convert part of the Archer River property into a national park was used as evidence of the need for such consultation. The effect of requiring the ALFC to consult with state government departments was to undermine its independence in making decisions over purchases.[59] This was followed by an instruction from the

---

[54]Grassby (1981), p 11.

[55]Grassby (1981), p 11.

[56]Nettheim (2001), p 11.

[57]Palmer (1998), p 87.

[58]Brennan (1992), p 2.

[59]Palmer (1998), p 86.

Commonwealth Minister to the ALFC not to pursue the purchase of Glenore station in Queensland, which was interpreted as a directive not to pursue land purchases in Queensland at all.[60]

The Labor opposition in the Commonwealth parliament put pressure on the government over its apparent capitulation to Queensland in relation to ALFC purchases in the state. In response, the government focused on technical reasons why purchases could not go ahead and was not prepared to challenge the Queensland government position. On 25 July 1977, Viner wrote to Tomkins assuring him that the ALFC would not be pursuing the purchases of Glenore or Archer River.

Despite a clear instruction from the Minister not to pursue the purchase of Glenore, the ALFC continued to pursue the purchase. It rejected the Queensland government's position that the property needed considerable reparatory work and was not viable. When the property was put up for public auction again in November 1977, the ALFC authorised a solicitor to attend the auction and bid on its behalf. In this way it once again purchased the property, this time at nearly AU$200,000 below the asking price. It was only revealed that the ALFC was the purchaser when the contract of sale was signed. Once again, the Queensland Minister for Lands refused to consent to the transfer of the lease.

Following the failure of the Queensland Minister for Lands to consent to the second purchase of Glenore, the ALFC sought funds from Viner to pursue legal action under the RDA against Queensland to complete the sale. Viner responded negatively to this request:

> Your letter of 7 December 1977 was … the first advice to me that the Commission had taken relevant legal advice in respect of the Racial Discrimination Act. Not having been consulted on a matter of such evident policy significance, I am not prepared to give assurance that funds would be available.[61]

In pursuing the purchase of Glenore for a second time, the ALFC put itself in direct conflict with the express intentions of the Commonwealth Minister for Aboriginal Affairs, Ian Viner, and embarrassed the Minister both in his relations with the opposition in the Commonwealth parliament and in his dealings with the Queensland government. On 10 February 1978, Viner issued a directive requiring the ALFC to inform him of its activities and to only take a decision to purchase a property after it had received his views on key issues, including whether he was satisfied of the existence and identity of the relevant Indigenous community.[62] This restricted the effectiveness of the ALFC in achieving land purchases across Australia until relations with the department improved in early 1979 when Fred Chaney became the Minister for Aboriginal Affairs.[63] However, by this time, in its last two years of operation, the commission had significantly reduced funds to purchase land for Aboriginal communities.

---

[60]Palmer (1998), p 87.

[61]Palmer (1988), p 96.

[62]ALFC (1978), p 11.

[63]Palmer (1998), p 104.

From the perspective of the commission, the *Koowarta* case was, at best, a pyrrhic victory. It did not lead to successful land acquisition, and it resulted in a strident response from the Queensland government and a weakening of support from the commission's own Commonwealth Minister for Aboriginal Affairs. And yet we celebrate *Koowarta* today for its confirmation of the validity of the RDA and its subsequent power to prevent racially discriminatory practices of government and private individuals.

The place of *Koowarta* in the remembering of the legal struggle for Aboriginal land rights exemplifies another aspect of legal historiography – the requirement that, once judgment is delivered, the grievance must be forgotten. Rousso makes this point elegantly:

> Calling for moral, symbolic or judicial reparation after the heat of the moment implies that debts always have their price. Once paid, the debt should be settled, so that one can henceforth speak of forgetting, forgiving, or simply turning the page.[64]

There is no postscript to *Koowarta* drawing attention to the fact the response of the Queensland government to having its rejection of the purchase of the Archer pastoral lease was to prevent the purchase through a different administrative mechanism. There was no legal judgment of whether the declaration of a national park over the leasehold land was simply a means of blocking the purchase or was motivated by racially discriminatory attitudes. The fact that *Koowarta*, and subsequent legal cases, do not question these possibilities means they can be forgotten, and the case law stands as the official record and justification for this forgetting. Taking this a step further, as Heidegger does, this officially sanctioned forgetting is essential for the very possibility of documenting and remembering the central narrative in *Koowarta*.[65]

Conclusion

As the reconstruction of events past, our memory is dependent on the documentary record. That record is, itself, necessarily contested. Some documents are foregrounded, others buried and forgotten. As a result of their authority, accessibility, simple narrative line and perfect chronological ordering, legal judgments are powerful historiographies. Legal judgments are also the dominant, official, and, from an Indigenous perspective, colonial story of the events they memorialise. They focus on developments in the official law. So the significance of *Koowarta* is in the validity of the RDA, and not the success or otherwise of John Koowarta and the Winychanam/Wik people's struggle for land.

The legal record of the *Koowarta* case presents a particular version of the struggle for rights. It highlights a particular event, the moment when the RDA was declared to be a valid legal instrument to prevent the Queensland government from blocking a land purchase. In the legal story of Aboriginal land rights, this story is of undoubted significance. The legal historiography of Aboriginal rights reads as a slow but

[64] Rousso (2002), p 23.
[65] Ricouer (2004), p 442.

inexorable move towards greater justice and recognition, culminating in the great case of *Mabo*. *Koowarta* plays a crucial and particular part in this narrative. Without it, the declaration of common law native title in *Mabo* would have been of no practical consequence.

There is a danger, however, that this legal story turns our attention too readily from struggles on the margins. As with all prominent legal judgments, there is a rich back story to *Koowarta* with the potential to subvert the dominant narrative. Was the confirmation of the validity of the RDA significant for Aboriginal rights in Australia, or did it just lead to new administrative mechanisms through which government departments could continue to pursue a racist agenda? Did the judgment lead to a softening of Queensland policy or to renewed efforts to prevent Aboriginal purchases of land? Narratives of each possibility can be written with some force, with the ALFC featuring in each.

In attempting to purchase the Archer River property, the ALFC found itself in direct opposition to a conservative state government while in the employ of a government from the same political persuasion. It was pursuing the issue of Aboriginal land rights in Queensland much more vigorously than the Commonwealth Department of Aboriginal Affairs could or would. In fact, the federal government made efforts to keep the problem of land purchases out of public view. This perspective is not evident in the *Koowarta* case in which the Commonwealth and the state governments are pitted against each other in a struggle over the balance of legislative power in the federation.

The determination of the ALFC to pursue land purchases in Queensland against vociferous opposition from the state, and less than enthusiastic support from the Commonwealth Minister for Aboriginal Affairs was crucial to the *Koowarta* litigation occurring at all. It provided the administrative means for John Koowarta and the Winychanam/Wik people to pursue the Archer River lease. When John Koowarta approached the ALFC, he encountered a segment of government bureaucracy not only receptive to his claim, but prepared to champion the cause of land rights for his people. For this reason alone the story of the ALFC is worth telling. More significantly, however, as one of the stories underpinning *Koowarta*, the struggles of the ALFC to purchase land for Aboriginal people in Queensland leaves us with an alternative source for remembering the events surrounding the *Koowarta* litigation, deepening our appreciation of official and unofficial struggles for Aboriginal justice.

Acknowledgement

My sincere thanks to Ann Genovese for the opportunity to participate in the *Koowarta* symposium.

References

Primary sources

Cases

Commonwealth v Tasmania (1983) 158 CLR 1

Koowarta v Bjelke-Petersen (1982) 153 CLR 168

Legislation

Aboriginal Affairs (Arrangements With the States) Act 1973 (Cth)

Aborigines (Amendment) Act 1973 (NSW)

Aboriginal Land Fund Act 1974 (Cth)

Aboriginal Land Rights Act 1976 (Cth)
Aborigines and Torres Strait Islanders' Affairs Act 1965
Aborigines and Torres Strait Islanders (Queensland Reserves and Communities Self-Management) Act 1978 (Cth)
Native Title Act 1993 (Cth)
Racial Discrimination Act 1975 (Cth)

Secondary sources

Aboriginal Land Fund Commission (1978) *Annual Report 1977–1978*, Australian Government Publishing Service.
Aboriginal Land Rights Commission (1973) *First Report*, Australian Government Publishing Service, - Parliamentary Paper ; No.138/73.
Aboriginal Land Rights Commission (1974) *Second Report*, Australian Government Publishing Service, - Parliamentary Paper ; No.138/73.
Eric Conan and Henry Rousso (1998) *Vichy: An Ever-Present Past*, Dartmouth.
Al Grassby (1981) A Report by the Commissioner for Community Relations on Complaints of Racial Discrimination and Enquiries Under the Racial Discrimination Act 1975 for the Period October 31, 1975 to August 26, 1981 'Discrimination Against Aboriginals and Islanders in Queensland' Community Relations Paper No. 17.
Frank Brennan (1992) *Land Rights Queensland Style: The Struggle for Aboriginal Self-Management*, University of Queensland Press.
Philip Chartrand (1981) 'The Status of Aboriginal Land Rights in Australia' 19 *Alberta Law Review* 436.
Richard Evans (2002) 'History, Memory and the Law: The Historian as Expert Witness' 41 *History and Theory* 326. doi:10.1111/1468-2303.00209
Garth Nettheim (1976) 'Queensland's Laws for Aborigines' 1 *Legal Service Bulletin* 321.
Garth Nettheim (1978) 'A Matter of Management? The Prospect for Queensland's Aboriginals and Islanders' 2 *UNSW Law Journal* 314.
Garth Nettheim (2001) '2001 Sir Ninian Stephen Lecture' 5 *Newcastle Law Review* 3.
Ian Palmer (1988) *Buying Back the Land: Organisational Struggle and the Aboriginal Land Fund Commission*, Aboriginal Studies Press.
Alexander Reilly (2006) 'How Mabo Helps Us Forget' 6 *Macquarie Law Journal* 25.
Paul Ricouer (2004) *Memory, History, Forgetting*, University of Chicago Press.
Henry Rousso (2002) *The Haunting Past*, Ralph Schoolcraft tr, University of Pennsylvania Press.
Charles Rowley (1981) 'The Aboriginal Land Fund Commission, 1974–1980', in Nicolas Peterson (Ed), *Aboriginal Land Rights: A Handbook*, Australian Institute of Aboriginal Studies Press.
Lindall Ryan (1985) 'Aborigines and Torres Strait Islanders' in Allan Patience (Ed), *The Bjelke-Petersen Premiership 1968–1983: Issues in Public Policy*, Longman Cheshire, Melbourne.
Benjamin Smith (2003) 'Wither "Certainty" Coexistence, Change and Land Rights in Northern Queensland' 13 *Anthropological Forum* 27.
Petronella Vaarzon-Morel (2012) 'Tjampijinpa, 'Stumpy' Martin (1932–1986)', *Australian Dictionary of Biography*, National Centre of Biography, Australian National University, http://adb.anu.edu.au/biography/tjampijinpa-stumpy-martin-15660/text26856, accessed 8 October 2014.
John Woodley (1998) 'John Koowarta – Mabo of the Mainland' 17(2) *Social Alternatives* 26.
Elspeth Young (1986) 'Charles Rowley – A Fighter for Justice and Equality' 10 *Aboriginal History* 3.

Koowarta: constitutional landmark, transition point or missed opportunity?

Sean Brennan[a] and Megan Davis[b]

[a]*Gilbert + Tobin Centre of Public Law and Faculty of Law, University of New South Wales, Australia;* [b]*Indigenous Law Centre and Faculty of Law, University of New South Wales, Australia*

Beyond the immediate significance to Wik-Mungkan people and Aboriginal peoples more generally, *Koowarta v Bjelke-Petersen* was an important constitutional case for several reasons. First, it confirmed that the Australian parliament could enact national human rights laws binding on the states. Second, the decision showed how close the High Court of Australia in the early 1980s came to revisiting the propulsive centralism of the *Engineers* decision, a central tenet of Australian constitutional doctrine, but also exposed the elusiveness at the heart of the pro-federalist interpretation of the external affairs power, thereby setting the stage for the affirmation of central government power a year later in the *Tasmanian Dam* case. Third, the court failed to persuasively address credible arguments that the races power in s 51(xxvi) of the Constitution could support a national law prohibiting racial discrimination. The *Koowarta* decision was, in these three respects, simultaneously a landmark, a turning point and a missed opportunity. In a contemporary sense, when alterations to the Australian Constitution in respect of Aboriginal and Torres Strait Islander peoples are under active consideration, *Koowarta* underlines the importance of choosing amending words carefully – history suggests the court may not, of its own volition, bring a non-discriminatory mindset to the question of constitutional interpretation.

Introduction

Koowarta v Bjelke-Petersen ('*Koowarta*')[1] is a classical constitutional case because it involved three fundamental aspects of Australian constitutionalism: a fierce competition over the federal division of powers between Commonwealth and state; the tensions created by the division of authority between the executive, legislative and judicial arms of government, specifically in the making of treaties overseas and their implementation in domestic law; and the discretionary power of elected politicians to make public policy decisions pitted against the enjoyment by the Australian people of legally enforceable rights and freedoms.

In addition, *Koowarta* involved race and the then still unusual recourse to the courts by Aboriginal people in the hope of materially affecting their political and socio-economic position in Australian society. The federal Act involved in the case – the *Racial Discrimination Act 1975* (Cth) (RDA) – later proved decisive in the recognition and protection of Indigenous property rights, by prohibiting racial discrimination and

[1]*Koowarta v Bjelke-Petersen* (1982) 153 CLR 168.

binding the states in their treatment of native title.[2] In *Koowarta* this Act survived a constitutional challenge from the Queensland government by the slimmest margin.

This article focuses on aspects of the constitutional content and significance of the *Koowarta* decision and the judiciary's contribution to this country's still unresolved encounters with globalisation, race, Aboriginal issues and human rights protection. Part 1 of this paper will interrogate the majority's finding that a general law prohibiting racial discrimination cannot be sustained by s 51(xxvi) of the Constitution, the races power. Part 2 will analyse the high-stakes confrontation between federalism and internationalism regarding the external affairs power in s 51(xxix), emphasising the precarious nature of the states' rights argument that almost prevailed in the High Court. Finally, in assessing the constitutional significance of the judgment as a landmark, transition point or missed opportunity in Australian law and politics, this paper will consider *Koowarta* in the context of the current Indigenous constitutional reform process. As an important historical source on judicial behaviour – when matters of race attain constitutional significance in the courts – *Koowarta* suggests careful attention to text when attempting to steer the court towards non-discriminatory legal outcomes.

Part 1: The races power

In *Koowarta*, the Commonwealth argued that the RDA was supported by the parliament's power in s 51(xxvi) to make laws with respect to 'the people of any race for whom it is deemed necessary to make special laws'. By an emphatic majority of 5:1 (Mason J not deciding), the court held that the races power did not support a national law prohibiting discrimination on the basis of race. It is a conclusion that seems to us counterintuitive. In 1920, the High Court in *Amalgamated Society of Engineers v Adelaide Steamship Co Ltd* ('*Engineers*')[3] made clear that the words in s 51 of the Constitution granting the Commonwealth power to make laws in defined areas of jurisdiction should be given their ordinary natural meaning, not subjected to artificial limitations. Given the general width ascribed to the Commonwealth's constitutional powers by the High Court since the decision in *Engineers*, surely a races power in the Constitution supports a general law about discrimination on the basis of race? But, in the legal commentary that followed *Koowarta*, the court's conclusion on this issue attracted little attention or controversy.[4]

---

[2]The survival of the test case litigation to establish native title depended on the RDA overriding state legislation that would have otherwise nullified the court proceedings *(Mabo v Queensland (No 1)* (1988) 166 CLR 186). Subsequently, when the High Court affirmed the existence of native title, the harshness of common law rules of extinguishment without compensation was ameliorated after 30 October 1975 by the RDA *(Mabo v Queensland (No 2)* (1992) 175 CLR 1). Next, the existence of the RDA shaped political negotiations over national native title legislation, leading to a default standard of formal equality with freehold title for development proposals on native title land after 1 January 1994 (*Native Title Act 1993* (Cth) Part 2 Div 3). And then the attempt by the Western Australian government to legislatively diminish all native title rights in that state was foiled by the RDA, in tandem with the *Native Title Act* (*Western Australia v Commonwealth* (1995) 183 CLR 373).

[3]*Amalgamated Society of Engineers v Adelaide Steamship* Co Ltd (1920) 28 CLR 129.

[4]One senior constitutional authority, who had written about the races power decades earlier, prior to its amendment in the 1967 referendum, described the majority conclusion in *Koowarta* as 'sensible' (Sawer 1982, p 429). Another commentator described the Commonwealth's argument as 'circular' (Howard 1982, p 637). Generally, legal commentators focused on the external affairs power and gave little or no attention to the races power.

The finding by the court that the races power does not support a general law about discrimination on the basis of race can be interrogated from both an internal and external perspective. First, as a matter of legal doctrine, could the High Court credibly have arrived at the opposite conclusion? If it could have, then, second, what hindsight judgment can we fairly make about the fact that the court in 1982 did not so conclude; especially conscious that in the present day we have a constitutional reform process underway and the Prime Minister's Expert Panel on the Recognition of Aboriginal and Torres Strait Islander peoples in the Constitution (Expert Panel) recommended the inclusion in the Constitution of a racial non-discrimination clause?[5]

Internally, the doctrinal heart of this question is the presence of the word 'special' in the grant of power to the Commonwealth. Semantically, the 'people of any race' could mean people of all races, as Gibbs CJ conceded.[6] Remove the word 'special' from s 51(xxvi) for a moment and it is hard to refute that the RDA is a law with respect to the people of any race for whom it is deemed necessary to make laws, based on this concession that 'any' can mean 'all'. But the word 'special' is there. And it is not customary to overlook terms in the grant of a power. They are typically regarded as words of limitation.[7] In addition, there is a wider constitutional consideration hinted at by Stephen J in *Koowarta*.[8] If s 51(xxvi) is capable of supporting universal laws, provided they are deemed necessary for the people of all races, then the Commonwealth has a persons power at its disposal of quite formidable reach.[9] It is reasonable, therefore, to discipline the term 'any' by recognising that its co-location with the word 'special' puts operative limits on what otherwise might be the scope of s 51(xxvi). Gibbs CJ, however, went further than we would say was necessary in order to respect the text and guard against the floodgates potential of a persons power, by smuggling in the word 'one' at the end of the following passage:

> The opinion of Parliament that it is necessary to make a special law need not be evidenced by an express declaration to that effect; it may appear from the law itself. However, a law which applies equally to the people of all races is not a special law for the people of any one race.[10]

This interpolation eclipsed the very question before the court and obscured consideration of the special, perhaps unique, characteristics of the impugned legislation: a

---

[5]Expert Panel on Constitutional Recognition of Indigenous Australians (2012).

[6]*Koowarta v Bjelke-Petersen* (1982) 153 CLR 168 at 186–187.

[7]As Gaudron J later put it, when ascribing significance to the term 'necessary' in s 51(xxvi), 'the words "for whom it is deemed necessary to make special laws" must be given some operation. And they can only operate to impose some limit on what would otherwise be the scope of s 51(xxvi)' (*Kartinyeri v Commonwealth* (1998) 195 CLR 337 at 363–364).

[8]*Koowarta v Bjelke-Petersen* (1982) 153 CLR 168 at 209–210 (Stephen J): 'Most grants of power in s. 51 are defined in terms either of some class of activity, as with "trade and commerce with other countries" and "astronomical and meteorological observations", some common governmental power or function, as with "taxation", and "census and statistics", or some class of physical object, such as "lighthouses, lightships, beacons and buoys". In all such cases the subject-matter of the grant of power is more or less apparent and identifiable on its face. However, a grant of legislative power defined only by reference to a particular class of persons for whom laws may be made under it is inherently less precise as to its permitted subject-matter'.

[9]See *Strickland v Rocla Concrete Pipes Ltd* (1971) 124 CLR 468 at 507–508 (Menzies J).

[10]*Koowarta v Bjelke-Petersen* (1982) 153 CLR 168 at 187.

national law prohibiting discrimination on the basis of race. Stephen J, taking a slightly less restrictive line, interpreted 'any' to mean 'particular'.[11] He recognised that if 'two or more races ... share particular problems within the Australian community' this may necessitate a law 'applying equally to those several races' and such a law would 'not necessarily forfeit the character of a law under par. (xxvi) because it legislates for several races'.[12] He agreed with the majority judges, however, that a law 'for all peoples of the Commonwealth, regardless of race' could not derive constitutional support from s 51(xxvi).[13] That was so even if the law itself was about race (as with the RDA), because 'the coincidence that its subject-matter happens to match one of the words in par. (xxvi) will not of itself bring it within power'.[14]

The key question is whether, contrary to these interpretations, the RDA possesses a quality that could plausibly be described as 'special' in the context of s 51(xxvi). There are two arguments that can be made in the affirmative, both of which respect the textual constraint of the word 'special' and avoid the prospect of a person's power available on an unlimited basis to support universally applicable laws. The first such argument is an empirical one, based on the practical operation of the law. A law can be general on its face but, at the same time, special because of its significance to a particular group. To take an illustrative example, through much of the twentieth century Aboriginal people in Australia were subjected to legally-sanctioned discrimination in basic aspects of life such as residence, wages and voting rights when compared with other Australian citizens. The unwinding of discriminatory statutes in the second half of the twentieth century and the removal of s 127 from the Constitution in 1967 demonstrated the disproportionate importance of the principle of racial non-discrimination for Aboriginal people.[15]

There are some potential objections to this first line of argument. It depends on establishing the differential significance of a law across the Australian population. That may require fact-finding, a not unproblematic issue for the High Court in constitutional cases.[16] It may ultimately depend on judicial notice about the historical experience of Aboriginal people or non-Anglo-Saxon people in Australia and an interpretation of Australian history that some High Court judges may be normatively or methodologically disinclined to adopt.[17] But, significantly, without calling into question the technical ratio of *Koowarta* regarding the RDA, a 'general-

---

[11]*Koowarta v Bjelke-Petersen* (1982) 153 CLR 168 at 210: 'I regard the reference to special laws as confining what may be enacted under this paragraph to laws which are of their nature special to people of a particular race'.

[12]*Koowarta v Bjelke-Petersen* (1982) 153 CLR 168 at 210.

[13]*Koowarta v Bjelke-Petersen* (1982) 153 CLR 168 at 210: 'It must be because of their special needs or because of the special threat or problem which they present that the necessity for the law arises'. Indeed, as noted in French (2003), pp 193–194, Stephen J's language found its way into *Commonwealth v Tasmania* (1983) 158 CLR 1 and *Western Australia v Commonwealth* (1995) 183 CLR 373.

[14]*Koowarta v Bjelke-Petersen* (1982) 153 CLR 168 at 210.

[15]Expert Panel on Constitutional Recognition of Indigenous Australians (2012), ch 1.

[16]See Kenny (1990) and, more recently, Heydon (2012).

[17]In this respect, it is notable that Murphy J, who dissented on the races power issue, included in his judgment the observation that a 'considerable literature exists on the subject of racial discrimination against Aborigines' and listed a number of books, reports and articles in an Appendix to his judgment (*Koowarta v Bjelke-Petersen* (1982) 153 CLR 168 at 239, 242–243).

but-also-special' interpretation is essentially where the High Court ended up soon after *Koowarta* was decided in 1982. While it must be acknowledged that both *Commonwealth v Tasmania* ('*Tasmanian Dam*')[18] and *Western Australia v Commonwealth* ('*Native Title*')[19] concerned laws that expressly referred to Aboriginal people, nonetheless the court on both occasions chose to express itself in a generally worded proposition, not dependent on those specific provisions. The six-way joint judgment in the *Native Title* case, for example, said:[20]

> A special quality appears when the law confers a right or benefit or imposes an obligation or disadvantage especially on the people of a particular race. The law may be special even when it confers a benefit generally, provided the benefit is of special significance or importance to the people of a particular race.

As Robert French later put it, to be 'special' a law 'must have a differential operation upon the people of a particular race or a subgroup thereof' and the differential operation of the law may be established by 'its actual operation', not only by its terms. Further, a law 'can be special when it confers a general benefit which is of special significance or importance to the people of a particular race'.[21]

The ultimate objection to adopting a 'general-but-also-special' line of argument and characterising the RDA as a 'special' law might be a legalist one, that the court should avoid a 'political value judgment' about the needs of a particular race.[22] On the other hand, once the court has acknowledged that a 'special' character might arise from the operation of the law, it has made (and legitimised) that leap and inevitably involved itself in empirical and other interpretive endeavours regarding the experience or perspective of a given racial group in Australia. The first argument then is that the court in *Koowarta* could have characterised the RDA as 'special' because it is a law of particular significance to groups in Australia that have historically endured systemic discrimination on the basis of their race, such as Aboriginal people (of whom the plaintiff Mr Koowarta was one).

The second argument is more closely attuned to the generally legalistic ethos of the High Court: it finds another way of giving meaning to the text of s 51(xxvi), including the word 'special' that does not depend on the subjective historical experience or position of particular groups. A special law for the people of any race conceivably describes a law that takes race as its operative focus. The RDA is special because it makes the central attribute identified in the head of power relevant to each group to whom the law applies, considered as a race, and it relates legal rights, obligations, prohibitions and so on directly to that attribute. For each group united by race, this is a special law because it protects the group against discrimination on the basis of race. For the purposes of this analysis, although on its face the RDA is a universal law, each racial group is a distinct group the subject of a special law, because the non-discrimination principle protects them from conduct differentially

[18] *Commonwealth v Tasmania* (1983) 158 CLR 1.

[19] *Western Australia v Commonwealth* (1995) 183 CLR 373.

[20] *Western Australia v Commonwealth* (1995) 183 CLR 373 at 461.

[21] French (2003), p 204.

[22] To quote the court in *Western Australia v Commonwealth* (1995) 183 CLR 373 at 460 when it was clarifying the term 'necessary'.

applied to them as against other groups. That innate quality in the concept of race discrimination shows how limited the additional Commonwealth law-making space thereby created would be. Very few universal laws could claim this capacity of applying to each racial group specially as a racial group and thus the concerns about the uncontrolled scope of a person's power in s 51(xxvi) would be allayed.

Koowarta was the first time the High Court had to directly address the scope of the races power.[23] It was unburdened by precedent when it came to interpreting terms such as 'special'. And we have seen that the High Court did subsequently accept the idea that a general law might have a differential and particular significance for some groups. These factors suggest that a finding of validity in *Koowarta* would have been plausible. On the other hand, it was reasonable for the court to want to fence off the protean possibilities of a domestic power that applied to people rather than subject matters or activities. And it was plausible for the High Court to conclude that the term 'special' did not apply to a universal law because, as Stephen J put it, 'a law must be special in the sense that it is the particular race, or races, for whom it legislates that give rise to the occasion for its enactment'.[24] It is perhaps not surprising, then, that in 1982 the High Court, with its traditional legalism and restrictive constitutional fact-finding practices, rejected the first line of argument outlined above and declined an approach that would have involved socio-legal investigations into the differential effects of a law on particular groups within the community.

Nevertheless, the second argument rehearsed here received too little attention at the time. The races power was the invidious legacy of turn-of-the-century racist politics. The court in *Koowarta* was asked for the first time, 81 years later and after the 1967 referendum, to define the contemporary scope of the power. The word 'special' had undefined content and the court spent almost no time considering whether a law forbidding discrimination on the basis of race was not a constitutional 'coincidence' with the wording of the power, as Stephen J suggested[25] but, instead, to quote him again, a special law 'in the sense of having some special connexion with people of any race'.[26] In that respect *Koowarta* was a missed opportunity – to do what journalist David Marr has implored the court to do, when it can – that is, to help Australians face 'this country's intractable problems with race'.[27] Faced with the question whether the RDA could validly prevent a state government blocking land transfers to Aboriginal groups on the basis of their race, *Koowarta* presented the court with an opportunity. Using orthodox legal approaches it could, if not rehabilitate this disconcerting race-based presence in our Constitution, at least tilt it by confirming the power's capacity for positive laws relating to race. That was not to be. The Commonwealth legislation survived only because of the external affairs power and only by the barest margin.

---

[23]There was a passing reference to s 51(xxvi) in the pre-1967 decision of *Robtelmes v Brenan* (1906) 4 CLR 395 and in the post-1967 decision of *Strickland v Rocla Concrete Pipes Ltd* (1971) 124 CLR 468.

[24]*Koowarta v Bjelke-Petersen* (1982) 153 CLR 168 at 210.

[25]*Koowarta v Bjelke-Petersen* (1982) 153 CLR 168 at 210.

[26]*Koowarta v Bjelke-Petersen* (1982) 153 CLR 168 at 209.

[27]Marr (2013), p 59.

Part 2: The external affairs power

The other question before the High Court in *Koowarta* was whether the RDA, as a federal law implementing Australia's obligations under a multilateral treaty known as the *International Convention on the Elimination of All Forms of Racial Discrimination* (ICERD),[28] was a valid exercise of parliament's power in s 51(xxix) to legislate with respect to 'external affairs'. This confronted the court with a stark choice between federalism and the process we now refer to as 'globalisation'. Was it possible to accommodate simultaneously the internationalisation of domestic affairs at the United Nations and the belief that a federal system allocates some subject matters to state and not Commonwealth jurisdiction?

Stephen J attempted to bridge these two concerns with his requirement that the subject of a treaty itself be a matter of 'international concern'.[29] Racial discrimination easily satisfied that test, he said, because the idea of equality between the races 'has emerged as *the one which, more than any other, dominates the thoughts and actions of the post-World War II world*'.[30] Three other judges, in the majority on this issue (Mason, Murphy and Brennan JJ), would not permit federalist concerns (if they had any) to constrain their definition of 'external affairs'. They upheld the validity of the RDA under s 51(xxix) because, in their eyes, the international treaty self-evidently dealt with an external affair – the fact of multilateral negotiation and agreement being a conclusive demonstration. By contrast, the three minority judges (Gibbs CJ, with whom Aickin J agreed, and Wilson J) explicitly prioritised 'states rights' in finding that the term 'external affairs' did not extend to a law implementing obligations dealing with the domestic regulation of racially discriminatory conduct. As Gibbs CJ put it, 'a narrower interpretation of par. (xxix) would ... be more consistent with the federal principle upon which the Constitution is based'.[31]

It is not easy to pin down precisely why the minority found that the ICERD and the RDA lacked the requisite international character they said was present in earlier cases involving, for example, civil aviation.[32] This is especially so as the judges with federalist sympathies (including Stephen J) made some significant concessions in the course of their judgments. They acknowledged that 'many countries ... profess, a deep concern that human rights and fundamental freedoms should be observed, and that racial discrimination should be eliminated, throughout the world'.[33] They also affirmed that there is no closed category of permissible treaty topics – any subject matter can potentially be an external affair[34] – and that it is difficult 'to identify

[28] *International Convention on the Elimination on All Forms of Racial Discrimination*, opened for signature 7 March 1966, 660 UNTS 195 (entered into force 4 January 1969).

[29] *Koowarta v Bjelke-Petersen* (1982) 153 CLR 168 at 217.

[30] *Koowarta v Bjelke-Petersen* (1982) 153 CLR 168 at 220 [emphasis in the original].

[31] *Koowarta v Bjelke-Petersen* (1982) 153 CLR 168 at 200, Aickin J agreed with the reasons and conclusions of Gibbs CJ.

[32] *Koowarta v Bjelke-Petersen* (1982) 153 CLR 168 at 192 (Gibbs CJ).

[33] *Koowarta v Bjelke-Petersen* (1982) 153 CLR 168 at 201 (Gibbs CJ).

[34] Provided, Gibbs CJ said, 'that the manner in which it is treated in some way involves a relationship with other countries or with persons or things outside Australia' (*Koowarta v Bjelke-Petersen* (1982) 153 CLR 168 at 201).

subject-matters which are of their nature not of international but of only domestic concern'.[35] Such concessions forced the three minority judges in particular to construct arguments on shaky legal ground.

One of these vulnerabilities involved a challenge to the orthodoxy of the *Engineers* case[36] – that grants of Commonwealth power are not to be artificially constrained by a preconceived notion of 'federal balance'. The *Koowarta* minority posited that the careful division of powers between Commonwealth and state could influence the meaning given to a term in s 51; in this case 'external affairs'. It was the late twentieth century re-run of an occasionally recurring episode, more recently seen in the dissenting judgments of Kirby and Callinan JJ in *New South Wales v Commonwealth* ('*Work Choices*');[37] that is, where one or more members of the High Court risk the charge of heresy, revisit the propulsive centralism of *Engineers* and ask whether it admits of some nuanced qualification on federalist grounds.[38]

Here, *Koowarta*'s constitutional significance is that it was perhaps the most vulnerable moment for the *Engineers* doctrine because only three of seven judges rejected this state-friendly argument. Given the intervening change in the composition of the bench between 1982 and 1983, perhaps it is a little reductive to make the suggestion that follows. But, arguably, by revealing the elusiveness at the heart of this pro-federalist argument, *Koowarta* was also an important transition point to the reaffirmation of *Engineers* the following year in the *Tasmanian Dam* case. The greatest difficulty the proponents of the states rights view had in the *Koowarta* and the *Tasmanian Dam* cases was demonstrating a viable, persuasive and judicially manageable criterion for distinguishing between permissible and impermissible exercises of the power. In *Koowarta* they employed an artificial and unconvincing distinction: steadfastly insisting that an internal matter was not simultaneously an external affair, even when Australia's 'relations with other countries may be affected by the manner in which it conducts those domestic affairs'.[39]

The second vulnerability in the minority's argument was the proposition that something beyond mere entry into a *bona fide* international treaty was required to demonstrate an 'external affair'. Here, the unsteadiness in the argument began with deciding what that element was. For Wilson J it seemed to be about the law made by parliament.[40] The statute needed to show some external operation, and the RDA was purely domestic in its regulation of conduct. Wilson J's first difficulty, contrary to the implication in his judgment,[41] was precedent. Legislation that included very extensive regulation of domestic matters, such as civil aviation, had been twice upheld under s 51(xxix), albeit that foreign aircraft were also regulated by the same

[35]*Koowarta v Bjelke-Petersen* (1982) 153 CLR 168 at 217 (Stephen J). Indeed, Justice Wilson conceded that 'Australia is under an obligation to the world community "to prohibit and to eliminate racial discrimination"' and that racial equality was one of the dominant ideas of the post-World War II world (at 248).

[36]*Amalgamated Society of Engineers v Adelaide Steamship Co Ltd* (1920) 28 CLR 129.

[37]*New South Wales v Commonwealth* (2006) 229 CLR 1.

[38]For a recent discussion of whether the decision in *Williams v Commonwealth* (2012) 288 ALR 410 foreshadows a new challenge to this orthodoxy, see Hume et al (2013).

[39]*Koowarta v Bjelke-Petersen* (1982) 153 CLR 168 at 203 (Gibbs CJ).

[40]*Koowarta v Bjelke-Petersen* (1982) 153 CLR 168 at 251.

[41]*Koowarta v Bjelke-Petersen* (1982) 153 CLR 168 at 246–247.

law. His other problem was, as Gibbs CJ suggested, that the external affairs power seems logically to contemplate some domestic operation at least[42] – it is, after all, a power to make laws for the peace, order and good government of the Commonwealth.[43] On technical as well as practical grounds, the claim of mutual exclusivity between domestic laws and externally-facing laws was, in reality, difficult to plausibly maintain.

By comparison, the judicial trio of Gibbs CJ, Aickin and Stephen JJ said that the element of externality derived primarily from the subject matter of the international treaty.[44] The basic problem here was persuasively arguing that a *bona fide* treaty solemnly concluded between two or more nations does not involve an external affair in the sense of being a matter of international concern or significance.[45] An additional discomfort here for these more conservative members of the court was the need to engage in judicial interventionism of quite formidable proportions. Not only did they have to tangle with the authority of the *Engineers* case and its rejection of reserved state powers. They had also to abandon Diceyan deference to the judgments of elected politicians, as to what affects Australia's relations with other countries or constitutes an international concern. Once the constitutional judgment became the subtle judicial differentiation of matters affecting and not affecting Australia's international relations, separation of power issues (on grounds of both legitimacy and competence) reared its head.[46]

The minority judgments, and that of Stephen J in the centre of the *Koowarta* court, not only substituted a judicial assessment for the executive and parliamentary ones already made in Australia as to whether racial discrimination constituted an external affair, but, most radically, they sought to second guess and, in the case of the three minority judges, defy the assessment of the international community of nation states as to what constituted 'international', rather than internal, affairs.[47] This was despite the acceptance by Gibbs CJ that Australia 'is bound to make a report to an international body on domestic affairs' and 'its relations with other countries may be affected by the manner in which it conducts those domestic affairs'.[48] As both Gibbs CJ and Wilson J also noted in their dissents, the preamble to the ICERD emphasises that 'discrimination between human beings on the grounds of race, colour or ethnic origin is an obstacle to friendly and peaceful relations among nations':

> The existence of racial barriers is repugnant to the ideals of any human society. In substance the preamble [of the *International Convention on the Elimination of All Forms of Racial Discrimination*] testifies to the view that it is essential to the peace and

---

[42]See Dixon J in *R v Burgess, ex parte Henry* (1936) 55 CLR 608 at 669.

[43]*Koowarta v Bjelke-Petersen* (1982) 153 CLR 168 at 190.

[44]*Koowarta v Bjelke-Petersen* (1982) 153 CLR 168 at 201 (Gibbs CJ), at 216–217 (Stephen J).

[45]*Koowarta v Bjelke-Petersen* (1982) 153 CLR 168 at 229–230, 231 (Mason J): 'Agreement between nations to take common action in pursuit of a common objective evidences the existence of international concern and gives the subject-matter of a treaty the character which is international' (at 231).

[46]*Koowarta v Bjelke-Petersen* (1982) 153 CLR 168 at 229 (Mason J).

[47]*Koowarta v Bjelke-Petersen* (1982) 153 CLR 168 at 202 (Gibbs CJ).

[48]*Koowarta v Bjelke-Petersen* (1982) 153 CLR 168 at 203.

> well-being of the international community that the laws of a community apply to all the members of that community regardless of race.[49]

The activism of John Koowarta, the Commonwealth's legislative importation of international human rights principles and the Queensland government's resistance to those principles compelled several judges into re-assessing *Engineers*, one of the central doctrines of Australian constitutionalism. If the view shared by four judges here had taken hold, it could have changed the course of Australian constitutional law and its federal arrangements. Significant new limits on the legislative competence of the Commonwealth parliament to make national laws in various areas of public policy might have emerged, particularly if later High Court judges determined that the 'external affairs' power was not a special case all of its own. More immediately, a single vote the other way in *Koowarta* could have radically altered the legal and non-legal transformative power of constitutionalism for Aboriginal and Torres Strait Islander peoples.

Conclusion

Constitutional reform and the importance of wording

It is appropriate to conclude by considering the relevance of *Koowarta* to the current constitutional reform process in relation to Aboriginal and Torres Strait Islander peoples. Reform of the races power in s 51(xxvi) was a prominent feature of the Expert Panel's deliberations across 2011, and in the public consultations it carried out and the submissions it received from the public. Behind this was a widespread acceptance that the present power in s 51(xxvi) likely supports laws that discriminate against the people of any race and not just laws that are for their benefit.[50] The Expert Panel recommended the races power be repealed and a new 'section 51A' (with preambular words of 'recognition' followed by an operative head of power to make laws with respect to Aboriginal and Torres Strait Islander peoples) be inserted in the Constitution, along the following lines:

> Recognising that the continent and its islands now known as Australia were first occupied by Aboriginal and Torres Strait Islander peoples;
> Acknowledging the continuing relationship of Aboriginal and Torres Strait Islander peoples with their traditional lands and waters;
> Respecting the continuing cultures, languages and heritage of Aboriginal and Torres Strait Islander peoples;
> Acknowledging the need to secure the advancement of Aboriginal and Torres Strait Islander peoples;

---

[49] *Koowarta v Bjelke-Petersen* (1982) 153 CLR 168 at 244 (Wilson J), see also Mason J (at 235).

[50] *Kartinyeri v Commonwealth* (1998) 195 CLR 337. See also Robert French's post-1967 survey of High Court jurisprudence in relation to s 51(xxvi) (written prior to becoming Chief Justice of the High Court) where he says there is nothing in s 51(xxvi), 'other than the possibility of a limiting principle of uncertain scope, to prevent its adverse application to Australian citizens simply on the basis of their race' and there is 'little likelihood of any reversal of the now reasonably established proposition that the power may be used to discriminate against or for the benefit of the people of any race' (French 2003, p 206).

> the Parliament shall, subject to this Constitution, have power to make laws for the peace, order and good government of the Commonwealth with respect to Aboriginal and Torres Strait Islander peoples.

In addition, the Expert Panel recommended the insertion of a racial non-discrimination clause.[51]

The Expert Panel advocated for a new head of power with respect to Aboriginal and Torres Strait Islander peoples because it was persuaded that the existing provision must be deleted. A mere alteration would not displace its original intent and would continue to invite the court to make assessments based upon the racist historical foundation of the power.[52] The decision to express the power itself in language unqualified by concepts such as advancement or benefit, but coupled with preambular words of recognition, is both a nod to parliamentary sovereignty and an implicit invitation[53] to the court to respond constructively to 'this country's intractable problems with race'.

As a minority in a characteristically utilitarian democratic polity, Australia's 3 per cent Indigenous population confronts in the 97 per cent of the electorate that is non-Indigenous what Noel Pearson calls the elephant/mouse conundrum. The overwhelming view of the Indigenous community during the Expert Panel's consultation process was that, in such a context, the High Court plays a welcome and important role in scrutinising government action. The preference for constitutional reform, amongst those Indigenous people who share it, is frequently motivated by deterrence; that is, the expectation that, suitably constrained by law, a parliament will, at the very least, consult before legislating in a way that may be viewed as detrimental to Indigenous interests.[54] Of course, there are very real limitations to what constitutional reform alone can achieve, not least because fulfilling its promise may entail litigation. *Koowarta* itself exemplifies the hazards and complexity of litigation – the cost, the time delays, the stress experienced by John Koowarta and, notoriously in this particular case, the possibility of having a positive outcome reversed by political action.[55]

---

[51]Section 116A Prohibition of racial discrimination: '(1) The Commonwealth, a State or a Territory shall not discriminate on the grounds of race, colour or ethnic or national origin. (2) Subsection (1) does not preclude the making of laws or measures for the purpose of overcoming disadvantage, ameliorating the effects of past discrimination, or protecting the cultures, languages or heritage of any group'.

[52]French (2003), p 180.

[53]Twomey (2012) suggests the invitation is quite explicit.

[54]Note, however, the doubt recently cast by the High Court on a legal requirement to consult in a related but technically distinct situation, where the Commonwealth government defends a law held to be *prima facie* racially discriminatory, claiming that it falls into the exceptional category of a 'special measure' (*Maloney v The Queen* (2013) 298 ALR 308). The High Court was reluctant to attach determinative significance to whether consultation had occurred before the introduction of a measure to which criminal sanctions attached (e.g. French CJ at 317, Hayne J at 334, Crennan J at 345, Kiefel at 357, Bell J at 372–374 and Gageler J at 404–405).

[55]Queensland Premier Joh Bjelke-Petersen thwarted the anti-discrimination proceedings by declaring a national park over the pastoral land sought to be recovered by John Koowarta and the other Winychanam people, putting the land beyond reach until restorative action was finally taken by the Newman state government in May 2012.

The other salutary lesson from *Koowarta* (and, later, *Kartinyeri v Commonwealth*[56]) is the central importance of text and its interpretation. Reliance on the races power in *Koowarta* to give validity to the RDA failed because of the interpretation given to the solitary word 'special'. The words of a contemporary referendum proposal on the issues of race, Aboriginal and Torres Strait Islander peoples and/or non-discrimination will need to be highly directive to achieve their intended purpose because history discourages any assumption that the court will, of its own volition, bring a non-discriminatory mindset to the question of constitutional interpretation.[57] That said, and while a realistic appreciation of the constraints inherent in legal language and its interpretation is important, constitutional reform nonetheless can be a galvanising and channelling force for the community and can bring extra-legal benefits such as greater political mobilisation, media coverage, enhanced access to centres of political power and a heightened sense of identity.

The case brought by John Koowarta was a constitutional landmark because it confirmed that the Australian parliament could enact national human rights laws binding on the states. Pending any successful amendment of the Constitution in the near future, this is, despite its fragile legislative basis, a disproportionately significant proposition for Aboriginal and Torres Strait Islander peoples and the material effect of the RDA on the course of native title law is clear evidence for that.[58] *Koowarta* was also a near-landmark in that, for a moment, 60 years after the *Engineers* case, the court was poised to reconceptualise the most basic interpretive principle in Australian constitutional law. *Koowarta* was also an important turning point in the path to the opposite outcome, achieved only a year later in the *Tasmanian Dam* case when the centralists on the High Court reasserted by majority the rejection of federalism as a factor in the interpretation of Commonwealth powers – important, arguably, because the decision (and particularly the judgment of Stephen J) revealed the elusiveness of a judicial manageable criterion to adequately support the pro-federalist position.

Finally, we suggest that, in the first major case about races power, *Koowarta* was a missed opportunity to nudge the Constitution away from its nineteenth century racist origins, with a plausible reading of the word 'special' found in s 51(xxvi), and a conclusion that the RDA addresses a problem that is peculiar to the people of a particular race and does so severally through words of general application.

References

Primary sources

Cases

Amalgamated Society of Engineers v Adelaide Steamship Co Ltd (1920) 28 CLR 129

Kartinyeri v Commonwealth (1998) 195 CLR 337

Koowarta v Bjelke-Petersen (1982) 153 CLR 168

---

[56]*Kartinyeri v Commonwealth* (1998) 195 CLR 337.

[57]See Twomey (2012), pp 424–439. See also Parliamentary Joint Committee on Human Rights (2013), pp 21–31, which said, after *Maloney v The Queen* (2013) 298 ALR 308, that the High Court's interpretation of 'racial discrimination' (and the apparent absence of recognition of the concept of legitimate differential treatment) and of 'special measures' did not accord with recognised understandings under international law.

[58]See n 2 and Brennan (2002).

Mabo v Queensland (No 1) (1988) 166 CLR 186
Mabo v Queensland (No 2) (1992) 175 CLR 1
Maloney v The Queen (2013) 298 ALR 308
New South Wales v Commonwealth (2006) 229 CLR 1
R v Burgess, ex parte Henry (1936) 55 CLR 608
Robtelmes v Brenan (1906) 4 CLR 395
Strickland v Rocla Concrete Pipes Ltd (1971) 124 CLR 468
Commonwealth v Tasmania (1983) 158 CLR 1
Western Australia v Commonwealth (1995) 183 CLR 373
Williams v Commonwealth (2012) 288 ALR 410

Legislation
Native Title Act 1993 (Cth)
Racial Discrimination Act 1975 (Cth)

International instruments
International Convention on the Elimination of All Forms of Racial Discrimination 1965

Secondary sources
Sean Brennan (2002) 'Whitlam and the Value of Law in Indigenous Affairs: Lessons for the Contemporary Debate on Reconciliation and a Treaty?' in Jenny Hocking and Colleen Lewis (eds) *It's Time Again: Whitlam and Modern Labor*, Circa.
Expert Panel on Constitutional Recognition of Indigenous Australians (2012) *Recognising Aboriginal and Torres Strait Islander Peoples in the Constitution*, Commonwealth of Australia.
Robert French (2003) 'The Race Power: A Constitutional Chimera' in HP Lee and George Winterton (eds) *Australian Constitutional Landmarks*, Cambridge University Press.
Dyson Heydon (2012) 'Constitutional Facts' in *Upholding the Australian Constitution Volume 23*, Proceedings of the Twenty-second Conference of The Samuel Griffith Society.
Colin Howard (1982) '*Koowarta v Bjelke-Petersen and Others, Queensland v Commonwealth of Australia* – External Affairs Power' 13 *Melbourne University Law Review* 635.
David Hume et al (2013) 'Heresy in the High Court? Federalism as a Constraint on Commonwealth Power' 41 *Federal Law Review* 71
Susan Kenny (1990) 'Constitutional Fact Ascertainment' 1 *Public Law Review* 134.
David Marr (2013) *Panic*, Black Inc.
Parliamentary Joint Committee on Human Rights (2013) *Stronger Futures in the Northern Territory Act 2012 and Related Legislation, Eleventh Report of 2013*.
Geoffrey Sawer (1982) 'The External Affairs Powers of the Commonwealth and Koowarta's Case' 54 *Australian Quarterly* 428.
Anne Twomey (2012) 'The Race Power: Its Replacement and Interpretation' 40 *Federal Law Review* 413.

Practising law and politics in 1980s' Australia: the liberating effect of *Koowarta v Bjelke-Petersen*

Maureen Tehan

Melbourne Law School, University of Melbourne, Australia

As a lawyer working with Indigenous organisations in the central Australian region in the 1980s, the *Koowarta* case had an immediate impact which was both liberating and limiting. This article reviews the impact of the decision on the lawyer's practice from a personal, political and legal perspective, by considering *Koowarta*'s effect on three events or issues in the 1980s: the national land rights proposal; *Gerhardy v Brown*; and alcohol control and management. Based on that discussion, it considers *Koowarta*'s contemporary impact in land rights, native title, and alcohol management and control, drawing conclusions about the nature of lawyers' practice, the relationship of politics and law, and the conundrum of individual and communities' rights post *Koowarta*.

Introduction

Koowarta v Bjelke-Petersen[1] ('*Koowarta*') was a ground-breaking decision with both immediate and long-term consequences. Its immediate impact beyond its facts was to open up both legal and political possibilities for Indigenous people and those working with them. For example, the dynamics of dealing with state governments changed, but, more generally, so did the possibilities of using the legal system to reinforce entitlements to fair and equal treatment of individuals in the provision of entitlements and services. It opened up possibilities to use law to support Indigenous peoples' access to citizenship rights and to engage in civil society as equal participants in areas such as education, housing and land. However, its impact was varied and paradoxical. For example, *Koowarta* did not deal with the anomalies that the *Racial Discrimination Act 1975* (Cth) (RDA) threw up such as the protection to be afforded beneficial acts, for example land rights legislation, and the application of the 'special measures' provision of the Act more generally. This was left for later cases with variable and concerning results.

As a legal practitioner practising law in the central Australian region in the 1980s, my work was impacted by *Koowarta* in a variety of ways. *Koowarta* was something of a double-edged sword. On the one hand it was a liberating decision, changing forever the lawyer's 'tool box' and creating new possibilities for action. However, it also created impediments – to be managed and negotiated – particularly

[1] *Koowarta v Bjelke-Petersen* (1982) 153 CLR 168.

in relation to the formal equality approach and the attendant special measures provisions of the RDA. Working as a lawyer across the central Australian region around and across the borders of South Australia, Western Australia and the Northern Territory, much of the lawyer's work was associated with politico/legal issues around the *Pitjantjatjara Land Rights Act 1981* (SA) (PLRA)[2] and management of the land granted under that Act, the campaign for land rights in Western Australia and as a result the national land rights policy proposal, associated land access issues, particularly in relation to resource exploration and extraction, and broad issues of community concern such as the policy and legal response to alcohol abuse and its impact in communities.

In this article I take up the invitation to respond to *Koowarta* as memoir and encounter. Therefore, rather than conventionally focus on particular themes in *Koowarta* as the basis of a doctrinal analysis of the case, I reflect on the force and resonance of *Koowarta* in three disparate moments or events in the 1980s in which I was involved as a practising lawyer: the failed national land rights initiative of the Hawke government in the mid-1980s in which the federal government, for political reasons, declined to use the power that *Koowarta* reinforced, namely the power of the federal government to bind the states in relation to matters touched by the RDA, to introduce a national land rights scheme; the High Court's upholding both land rights legislation and the permit system in *Gerhardy v Brown* [3] ('*Gerhardy v Brown*') as special measures and the political consequences of that finding; and the paradoxes of liquor licensing restrictions for Indigenous communities in the central Australian region encompassing both discrimination and special measures under the RDA. Each of these seemingly disparate and unrelated legal and political encounters is bound together by the place of the lawyer and his or her office in the application of *Koowarta*, and this relationship is the dominant theme in this article. Each event is examined in turn, focusing both on the role of the lawyer and the power and paradoxes of *Koowarta*'s liberating impact at the time and subsequently. *Koowarta* has continued to impact the lives of Indigenous Australians, and each of the 1980s' events presaged key legal and political developments in the native title era: *Mabo v Queensland (No 1)* [4] ('*Mabo No 1*') and *Mabo v Queensland (No 2)* [5] ('*Mabo No 2*'); the *Native Title Act 1993* (Cth) and *Western Australia v Commonwealth*,[6] and the political and legal response to endemic issues around Indigenous disadvantage, particularly associated with alcohol and special measures recently considered in *Maloney v The Queen* ('*Maloney*').[7]

---

[2]Renamed and now known as the *Anangu Pitjantjatjara Yankunytjatjara Land Rights Act 1981* (SA). For convenience, the original name: *Pitjantjatjara Land Rights Act 1981* (SA) is used throughout this article.

[3]*Gerhardy v Brown* (1985) 159 CLR 70.

[4]*Mabo v Queensland (No 1)* (1988) 166 CLR 186.

[5]*Mabo v Queensland (No 2)* (1992) 175 CLR 1.

[6]*Western Australia v Commonwealth* (1995) 183 CLR 186.

[7]*Maloney v The Queen* (2013) 298 ALR 308.

National land rights?

Following the failure of the Yolgnu land claim in *Milirrpum v Nabalco*,[8] the Whitlam government initiated the Woodward Commission in 1973. The commission recommended a form of statutory land title for the Northern Territory.[9] The *Aboriginal Land Rights (Northern Territory) Act 1976* (Cth) (ALRA), based on Woodward's report, was ultimately passed by the Fraser government in 1976. Under the ALRA, land is held as inalienable freehold title by a land trust on behalf of the traditional owners of the land. Land has been either granted by the Minister upon the recommendation of the land commissioner following a claims process or existing Aboriginal reserves have been transferred via Schedule 1 of the ALRA. Despite many changes to the legislation over the years, traditional owners had and continue to have significant control over their land including a consent right (often referred to as a veto right) over mineral exploration and development on their land.[10]

Both South Australia and New South Wales had legislated for varying forms of land recognition in 1981 and 1983 respectively.[11] However, the overall landscape was one of little or no recognition, especially in Western Australia and Queensland. In response to this situation, the national land rights proposal of the Hawke government sought to extend the provisions of the ALRA beyond the obvious constitutional reach of the Commonwealth in the Northern Territory to the states.[12] While *Koowarta* made this possible, the national land rights proposal led to many years of controversy and fiery political debate, and ultimate failure.

The Hawke government had taken a national land rights scheme to the 1983 election, and in December 1983 the Minister for Aboriginal Affairs, Clyde Holding, moved a resolution setting out the principles that would 'guide the attitudes of the majority of Australians to Aboriginal Australians and of them to us'[13] and set out the principles to be embodied in land recognition legislation:

(i) Aboriginal land to be held under inalienable freehold title
(ii) protection of sacred sites
(iii) Aboriginal control in relation to mining on Aboriginal land (commonly referred to as a mining veto)
(iv) access to mining royalty equivalents
(v) compensation for lost land to be negotiated[14]

---

[8] *Milirrpum v Nabalco* (1971) 17 FLR 141.

[9] Woodward (1974).

[10] Controversies around the land management aspects of the ALRA and their operation extend beyond resource extraction and include issues such as leasing, individual titling and permits. While these are crucial to any assessment of the ALRA they are beyond the immediate scope of this article.

[11] *Pitjantjatjara Land Rights Act 1981* (SA) and *Aboriginal Land Rights Act 1983* (NSW).

[12] For a detailed consideration of the proposal, its prosecution, opposition and defeat, see Libby (1989).

[13] Commonwealth of Australia (1983) *Parliamentary Debates*, House of Representatives, 8 December, 3485 (Clyde Holding).

[14] Commonwealth of Australia (1983) *Parliamentary Debates*, House of Representatives, 8 December, 3485 (Clyde Holding).

This effectively replicated the ALRA, particularly in the contentious area of traditional owner control over resources development on their land.

Ultimately no Act was passed, but the 2 years following the statement were given to discussions and negotiations about the scheme in an environment of furious opposition by a variety of groups including the mining industry. This was particularly virulent in Western Australia. The following three examples of the campaign capture the intensity of opposition:

- advertisements on television 'showed a pair of black hands building a brick wall across the map of Western Australia and putting up a notice: 'Keep out – this land is part of Western Australia under Aboriginal claim';[15]
- home owners were told that 'your rights of ownership could be under threat';[16] and
- the Australian Mining Industry Council produced maps that provided visual impact of the model on prospective mining developments. Perhaps this was also code to reinforce fears of an 'Aboriginal takeover' of large parts of the Australian landmass.[17]

In late 1984 and early 1985 a series of opinion polls commissioned by various groups, including the government, recorded extraordinary opposition to land rights. For example, an Australian National Opinion Poll (ANOP) of Perth's northern suburbs showed that only 12 per cent agreed that the Western Australian government had done a good job on land rights.[18] Another poll in areas south of Perth showed that 90 per cent either strongly opposed (47 per cent) or opposed or were leaning to opposition (43 per cent).[19] A later national poll showed that 76 per cent opposed Aboriginal land rights.[20]

Along the way the Hawke government amended its model to remove the veto on mining and replaced it with an arbitrated scheme (similar to that in the PLRA) and indicated that it intended to bring the ALRA provisions into line with this proposal – not only weakening the national proposal but effectively winding back the strong provisions in the ALRA.[21] One effect of this was to produce divisions among Aboriginal parties with interests in the scheme and some groups, especially those in the Northern Territory, came to oppose the package.[22]

Western Australia was crucial in this episode. The Seaman land rights inquiry, established by the state Labor government in 1982, reported in late 1984,[23] and the Western Australian government, in its response, removed 'the mining veto and postponed the implementation of the model recommended by Seaman'.[24]

---

[15]McRae et al (1991), p 156.

[16]McRae et al (1991), p 156.

[17]Australian Mining Industry Council (1986); Libby (1989), p 136.

[18]Goot and Rowse (2007), p 70; see also Libby (1989).

[19]Goot and Rowse (2007), p 70

[20]Goot and Rowse (2007), p 73

[21]McRae et al (1991), p 156.

[22]Libby (1989), p 56.

[23]Seaman (1984).

[24]McRae et al (1991), p 156.

The federal government finally abandoned the model, with the Prime Minister suggesting that public opinion was the reason and stating that Australian society had become less compassionate than in previous years and that it would be counter-productive for his government to 'jump miles in front of "public opinion"'.[25] The recent release of Cabinet documents from 1986–87 suggests that the government's decision was at least in part due to the particular challenges in Western Australia and the influence of some Western Australian members because of the intense opposition to the proposal in that state. Commenting on the events of the time, Gareth Evans was quoted in the following terms: 'John Dawkins saying that … "he'd listened to Beazley's horror stories for the last three years and had we ignored them as we should have we'd at least have land rights legislation in place rather than the mess we'd got ourselves into"'.[26] It is suggested that 'Cabinet … endorsed its 1985 Preferred National Rights Model, but agreed to negotiate with Western Australia on non-legislative measures such as community funding and granting long leases to Aboriginal Reserves'.[27]

Following the Seaman report, the Western Australian government introduced its own watered down version of land rights legislation.[28] The Burke Labor government did not enjoy a majority in the Upper House, which failed to pass the Bill. Thus, Western Australia's opposition to land rights including the national land rights model prevailed.

In an interesting exercise of its powers under s 51(xxvi) of the Constitution, the Commonwealth legislated at the request of the Victorian government to pass the *Aboriginal Land (Lake Condah and Framlingham Forest) Act 1987* (Cth) which enabled the transfer of these areas of land to Aboriginal corporations. This overcame the opposition to such transfers by the opposition controlled Upper House in Victoria but was a poor substitute for the national land rights model.

Writing in 1991, Garth Nettheim noted that '*Koowarta* enabled the Federal government to implement a national land rights scheme'.[29] He pointed out that the power delivered by *Koowarta* meant that the Commonwealth could design a scheme that ensured delivery of land rights in some form. It could, for example, 'set minimum standards and rely on *Koowarta* to require State compliance'.[30] Each state would be expected to pass legislation that met the standards and, if it fell short, then the stronger Commonwealth legislation would override the state legislation. This is now a familiar mechanism for the exercise of Commonwealth power and was the mechanism used in the *Native Title Act 1993* (Cth), relying in part on the special measures provision of the RDA to achieve state compliance in relation to both recognition and protection of native title and regulation of future acts on native title land. This scheme was upheld in *Western Australia v Commonwealth* in which Western Australia challenged the validity of the *Native Title Act 1993* (Cth) and the

[25]*The Australian* (1986) 6 March cited in McRae et al (1991), p 157.

[26]Murphy (2014).

[27]Murphy (2014),

[28]*Aboriginal Lands Bill 1985* (WA).

[29]McCrae et al (1991), p 156.

[30]McCrae et al (1991), p 156.

Wororra peoples challenged the validity of the *Land (Title and Traditional Usage) Act 1993*(WA) – state legislation seeking to extinguish native title post *Mabo No 2*.

Interestingly, the native title experience confirmed that contested areas of land in the national land rights model debate has continued to be highly contested in the native title domain, and many native title determinations in fact cover those areas identified by the Australian Mining Industry Council (AMIC) in 1985 as the 'danger' areas under the national land rights model, particularly in Western Australia. However, any map of native title determinations does not show the variation in the native title rights included in a determination, the limitations on the control and management that native title holders enjoy under the *Native Title Act* and that not all land within the external boundaries of a determination is native title land. In most instances, the land and the rights attached are significantly less than those offered in the original national land rights scheme.

In spite of the promise presented by the High Court's confirmation of the Commonwealth's power deriving from the external affairs power and the RDA in *Koowarta*, the national land rights model was never introduced. There is no doubt that *Koowarta* provided the tools for those advocating for the national scheme and the constitutional power for the Commonwealth government to implement its plan, but the government failed to do so. This failure of the 1980's initiative was not a failure of law but a failure of politics, emphasising both the entanglement of law and politics in this field and that law alone is not enough. While *Koowarta* gave lawyers the tools that would enable land rights reform, in this instance it was the politician rather than the lawyer who failed.

Land rights, permits and race discrimination

The second event or moment in which *Koowarta* was significant for a practising lawyer was the case of *Gerhardy v Brown*, decided by the High Court in 1985.

This case concerned the validity of the South Australian PLRA and the permit provisions of that Act: were they inconsistent with ss 9 or 10 of the RDA or both ss 9 and 10 of the RDA and, if so, were they protected by the 'special measures' exemption in s 8 of the RDA.

Section 9 of the RDA makes it unlawful:

> [T]o do any act involving a distinction, exclusion, restriction or preference based on race, colour, descent or national or ethnic origin which has the purpose or effect of nullifying or impairing the recognition, enjoyment or exercise, on an equal footing, of any human right or fundamental freedom in the political, economic, social, cultural or any other field of public life.

Section 10 refers to the variable enjoyment of rights of people of a particular race:

> If, by reason of, or of a provision of, a law of the Commonwealth or of a State or Territory, persons of a particular race, colour or national or ethnic origin do not enjoy a right that is enjoyed by persons of another race, colour or national or ethnic origin, or enjoy a right to a more limited extent than persons of another race, colour or national or ethnic origin, then, notwithstanding anything in that law, persons of the first-mentioned race, colour or national or ethnic origin shall, by force of this section, enjoy that right to the same extent as persons of that other race, colour or national or ethnic origin.

Sections 9 and 10 do not apply if the act or lack of enjoyment is by reason of 'special measures taken for the sole purpose of securing adequate advancement of certain racial or ethnic groups or individuals requiring such protection as may be necessary in order to ensure such groups or individuals equal enjoyment or exercise of human rights and fundamental freedoms'.[31]

Collectively, these provisions protect a person from being treated less favourably than others because of their race in the enjoyment of 'any human right or fundamental freedom'. Any differential treatment may, however, be permitted if it is captured by s 8 of the RDA in that it is for the sole purpose of advancing a particular racial group so that they may ultimately enjoy equality at some point in the future. Thus, an otherwise discriminatory act or provision will not be unlawful if it is for this purpose.

The PLRA provided for the grant of an inalienable freehold title of the land to Anangu Pitjantjatjaraku (as it was then called), a body corporate constituted under the PLRA.[32] Anangu Pitjantjatjaraku comprised all 'Pitjantjatjaras', defined as: 'a) a member of the Pitjantjatjara, Yungkutatjara (sic) or Ngaanatjara (sic) people; and b) a traditional owner of the lands or a part of them'.[33] Subject to some limited exceptions, s 19 of the PLRA required that all people, other than Pitjantjatjaras (as defined in the PLRA) obtain permission from Anangu Pitjantjatjaraku, by 'instrument in writing' before entering the land.

The case arose when Reverend Bob Brown was charged with being on the Pitjantjatjara lands without a permit on 27 February 1982, less than a year after the Act had been assented to in 1981. The matter came before 'Mr Wayne Chivell SM sitting as the Oodnadatta Court of summary jurisdiction'.[34] Brown's argument was that the Act itself, but more particularly the permit provision, was invalid as it breached the RDA which, following the High Court's decision in *Koowarta*, bound the states.

Brown was an Aboriginal pastor. He was not a Pitjantjatjara as defined in the PLRA. There was a general understanding that Christian pastors could come onto the lands without a permit in order to preach and carry out their duties, but Brown's situation was more complex because of his involvement with a group called Mama Gurunpa. Loosely translated this means 'God's mining company'.[35] The company directors were mostly members of the Aboriginal Evangelical Fellowship (AEF).[36] Some, but by no means all, were Pitjantjatjaras under the PLRA.[37] This company had previously attended a meeting with Anangu Pitjantjatjaraku and suggested that, as an 'Aboriginal and a Christian enterprise, it should be involved in all exploration and mining on the lands'.[38] The meeting decided that Anangu Pitjantjatjaraku was the appropriate body to deal with government and mining companies and that if

---

[31] *Racial Discrimination Act 1975* (Cth) s 8.

[32] *Pitjantjatjara Land Rights Act 1981* (SA) ss 5, 15 and 17.

[33] *Pitjantjatjara Land Rights Act 1981* (SA) s 4.

[34] *Gerhardy v Brown* (1983) 34 SASR 452.

[35] Toyne and Vachon (1984), p 148.

[36] Toyne and Vachon (1984), p 148.

[37] Toyne and Vachon (1984), p 148.

[38] Toyne and Vachon (1984), p 148.

Mama Gurunpa wanted to be involved in exploration and mining it should proceed under the PLRA in the same way as other companies.[39]

Brown had been on the lands a number of times, combining both preaching and discussion of Mama Gurunpa.[40] He had been warned about discussing mining while on the land without a permit and so on this occasion when he was on the land without a permit and discussing mining, the executive of Anangu Pitjantjatjaraku asked the police to prosecute Brown.

As Toyne and Vachon wrote at the time,[41] Anangu seemed to have the view 'that he (Brown) shouldn't mix up Christian business with mining business'.[42] They also noted that 'the Crown's case was weak, and it was unlikely that Brown would have been convicted on the evidence'.[43] The defence, however, in what may have been a politically motivated action, wanted the matter 'determined beyond doubt'[44] and, at the request of the defendant, the matter was referred to the South Australian Supreme Court on a case stated by Chivell SM to determine certain questions of law. The weakness of the police case can be clearly seen in the case stated which is reproduced in full in the judgment of Millhouse J.[45] For example, there was no evidence that the lands had actually vested under the PLRA, that the constitution of Anangu Pitjantjatjaraku had been determined and approved as required by the PLRA, or that the executive (to whom a written application for a permit must be made) had been duly elected.[46] There was also evidence (set out in the case stated) indicating that there had been a range of discussions between Brown and Anangu including Donald Fraser, the chairman of Anangu Pitjantjatjaraku, who 'informed the defendant that there would be a meeting with Anungu [sic] Pitjantjatjaraku on 26th, 27th and 28th of February 1982 and that the defendant could attend that meeting'.[47] The case stated indicated that there was 'no reliable evidence that Fraser told the defendant that it was necessary to obtain permission in writing from Anungu [sic] Pitjantjatjaraku'.[48] On the weakness of the case, Millhouse J commented 'there were quite large gaps in the proof of the complainant's case'.[49] In spite of these weaknesses, the defendant proceeded on a case stated. The case stated asked questions of law, *inter alia*, in relation to the validity or restricted operation of the PLRA and, in particular, s 19 as a result of the operation of the RDA and whether the complaint fell within the valid operation of the PLRA.[50]

---

[39]Toyne and Vachon (1984), p 148.
[40]Toyne and Vachon (1984), p 148.
[41]Toyne and Vachon (1984), p 149.
[42]Toyne and Vachon (1984), p 149.
[43]Toyne and Vachon (1984), p 149.
[44]Toyne and Vachon (1984), p 149.
[45]*Gerhardy v Brown* (1983) 34 SASR 452.
[46]*Gerhardy v Brown* (1983) 34 SASR 452 at 452–453.
[47]*Gerhardy v Brown* (1983) 34 SASR 452 at 453.
[48]*Gerhardy v Brown* (1983) 34 SASR 452 at 454.
[49]*Gerhardy v Brown* (1983) 34 SASR 452 at 455.
[50]*Gerhardy v Brown* (1983) 34 SASR 452 at 455.

Millhouse J, at the urging of the defendant, approached the matter by considering the issue of validity first.[51] The defendant argued, and Millhouse J – making specific reference to *Koowarta*'s finding on the validity of the RDA[52] – accepted, that the permit provisions were invalid because they breached the RDA; that is, the permit provisions made a distinction based on race and were therefore invalid.[53] Millhouse J did not make any finding about the invalidity of the PLRA itself, although he did indicate in response to an argument put by counsel for the complainant that there was a distinction between a private title and the title granted under the PLRA, because under the PLRA a particular group based on their race had been granted land and that the right to enter the land was different from that in relation to 'private land' for which permission is not required to enter, but rather a person may 'order them off and they may then become a trespasser'.[54]

The South Australian government appealed Millhouse J's decision to the High Court. As we now know, the court answered 'No' to the question before it: 'Is the Pitjantjatjara Land Rights Act 1981 (SA) invalid or restricted in its operation by reason of the Racial Discrimination Act 1975 (Cth)?'[55] In summary, the permit provisions were valid because the PLRA, and therefore the permit provisions, were special measures, permitted under s 8(1) of the RDA.[56]

This is interesting for a number of reasons. Apart from confirmation that *Koowarta* confirmed the RDA as a valid law of the Commonwealth that bound the states,[57] and that s 10 of the RDA was not considered in *Koowarta*,[58] there is no reference to *Koowarta*. However, it is clear from the general tenor of the judgments that *Koowarta* is foundational for *Gerhardy v Brown*, even though the court was required to address the reach of s 10 of the RDA and the special measures provision in s 8 of the RDA, neither of which engaged the court in *Koowarta*. The issue of special measures was not considered by Millhouse J, but it was the crucial element in the High Court's view that the PLRA was valid. It was open to the court to take a broader view – that the protection of cultural and traditional land rights is not discriminatory in that they are property rights which are recognised and given effect through the mechanism of the grant of a fee simple title. This is the approach taken in the *Native Title Act 1993* (Cth)[59] and approved by the High Court in *Western Australia v Commonwealth*.[60] In *Gerhardy v Brown* all judges took the approach that the '"special measures" clause ... [legitimated] what would otherwise be

[51] *Gerhardy v Brown* (1983) 34 SASR 452 at 456.

[52] Reliance was also placed on the High Court's decision in *Viskauskas v Niland* (1983) 153 CLR 280 which had considered the application of the RDA to the states post *Koowarta*.

[53] *Gerhardy v Brown* (1983) 34 SASR 452 at 461.

[54] *Gerhardy v Brown* (1983) 34 SASR 452 at 461.

[55] *Gerhardy v Brown* (1985) 159 CLR 70 at 162.

[56] *Gerhardy v Brown* (1985) 159 CLR 70.

[57] *Gerhardy v Brown* (1985) 159 CLR 70 at 94 (Mason J), at 155 (Dawson J).

[58] *Gerhardy v Brown* (1985) 159 CLR 70 at 85 (Gibbs CJ).

[59] For example, Subdivision M *Native Title Act 1993* (Cth).

[60] *Western Australia v Commonwealth* (1995) 183 CLR 186 at 4456 (Mason CJ Brennan, Deane, Toohey, Gaudron and McHugh JJ).

discriminatory in law since they view the legislation without that clause as being discriminatory';[61] that is, it legitimated the PLRA itself as a special measure. While the broader approach would have delivered substantive equality without resort to special measures, the special measures provision was used as a means of addressing the impact of the formal equality approach: 'Formal equality before the law is an engine of oppression destructive of human dignity if the law entrenches inequalities "in the political, economic, social, cultural or any other field of public life"'.[62] Special measures provide 'a means by which the injustice or unreasonableness of formal equality can be diminished or avoided'.[63]

There was considerable discussion in most judgments about what might be required for a provision to be a special measure. In the context of the meaning of 'advancement' in Article 1(4) of the *International Convention on the Elimination of All Forms of Racial Discrimination* (and s 8 of the RDA), Brennan J was the only judge to refer specifically to the importance of the wishes of those for whom the special measures were introduced:

> The wishes of the beneficiaries for the measure are of great importance (perhaps essential) in determining whether a measure is taken for the purpose of securing their advancement. The dignity of the beneficiaries is impaired and they are not advanced by having an unwanted material benefit foisted on them.[64]

Of course, the wishes of the beneficiaries were not in issue in *Gerhardy v Brown* but, as will be seen below, were an important element in the argument in *Maloney*.

The decision of the court in *Gerhardy v Brown* was criticised at the time for 'accepting the "colour blind" theory of racial discrimination'.[65] Brownlie was particularly concerned with the court's 'inquiry in terms of the category of discrimination ... rather [than] in terms of reasonableness of the objectives, the proportionality of the means employed and the question whether a special measure involves unfairness between one group and another'.[66] There was also the disturbing view that the freehold land, granted in fee simple, was more public in nature than 'private title' and this had consequences for the broader response to the permit system that continued to be the subject of political discussion and activity in relation to both the PLRA and the *Aboriginal Land Rights (Northern Territory) Act 1976* (Cth) in 2006.[67] Emerging from both *Koowarta* and *Gerhardy v Brown* is the curious and paradoxical proposition that, without the RDA, *Koowarta* and the particular interpretation of the RDA and special measures in *Gerhardy v Brown*, there would have been no question of invalidity of the PLRA or the permit provisions.

My personal engagement with *Gerhardy v Brown* was focused on its aftermath – dealing with the response to it by Reverend Brown and his supporters. Much of the

---

[61]Brownlie (1985), p 112.

[62]*Gerhardy v Brown* (1985) 159 CLR 70 at 129 (Brennan J).

[63]*Gerhardy v Brown* (1985) 159 CLR 70 at 130 (Brennan J).

[64]*Gerhardy v Brown* (1985) 159 CLR 70 at 135 (Brennan J).

[65]McRae et al (1991), p 142; Sadurskzi (1986).

[66]Brownlie (1985), p 113.

[67]*Aboriginal Land Rights (Northern Territory) Amendment Act 2006* (Cth); *The Anangu Lands Paper Tracker* (2012a).

criticism revolved around a perceived conflict between Christianity and land rights.[68] As indicated above, a number of members of Mama Gurunpa were also members of the AEF. Some members of the AEF, although not necessarily members of Mama Gurunpa, held anti land rights views, expressed in such comments as 'saying yes to land rights is saying no to God' and 'a vote for the ALP is a vote for communism and the devil'.[69] Of course, there were many staunch Christian supporters of land rights and, post the decision, considerable time was spent responding to their requests for information or material in support of the decision. In particular, it was important to point out that the Reverend Brown had not been prosecuted because he was preaching the gospel. Rather, he had been prosecuted because, in spite of warnings, he had continued to promote Mama Gurunpa and its approach to mining on the Pitjantjatjara lands, an activity for which he required a permit.

Interestingly, and emphasising both the evidentiary problems with the case and the range of motivations of the defendant in seeking to have the permit provisions tested against the RDA, post the High Court decision, the prosecution of Reverend Brown did not proceed, notwithstanding the validity of s 19 of the PLRA. Following the case, there were some discussions about possible amendments to the PLRA in order to clarify who needed permits and in what circumstances, but these discussions did not lead to any amendments to the permit provisions at that time.[70]

The current position is that the PLRA is discriminatory legislation, but saved as a special measure. This is the result of *Koowarta* – subjecting state legislation to Commonwealth legislative authority – for better or worse. Reliance on special measures in this and other contexts raises issues of autonomy for the Aboriginal peoples affected by the measures and, in particular, whether their consent to the measures is required. It raises uncertainty about the effectiveness of the provisions as a means of addressing both positive and negative rights, and it may have the effect of criminalising behaviour of the intended beneficiaries of the measures. These issues and the court's approach to special measures has recently been reconsidered by the High Court in relation to alcohol management in *Maloney*.

Alcohol and race discrimination

The third moment or event also touches the paradoxical impact of the RDA and *Koowarta* and the possible unintended consequences for alcohol management in Aboriginal communities, and the operation of the special measures provisions of the RDA.

Alcohol management has long been the fulcrum of conflicting views about issues such as dry areas, supply limitations including take-away alcohol and limiting opening hours of licensed premises, banned drinkers' registers and the tension between community views about alcohol limits and individual desires in relation to alcohol consumption, among others. These directly engage issues of potential discrimination on the basis of race and the operation of the special measures provisions of the RDA.

[68]This opposition by certain groups has continued, see *The Anangu Lands Paper Tracker* (2012b).

[69]Toyne and Vachon (1984), p 148.

[70]Toyne (1977–1986).

The most recent example of these tensions occurred in *Maloney*, a case which challenged the validity of an alcohol management plan for Palm Island in Queensland and that raised the issue of whether consent, by those affected, to special measures is required, as well as the desirability of using special measures to criminalise otherwise racially discriminatory behaviour, albeit underpinned by the notion of 'advancement'.

The seeds of the issues in *Maloney* were present in the 1980s as communities and their advisers sought to grapple with the impacts of alcohol abuse and develop strategies for managing those impacts. Concern was expressed about alcohol sales across the central Australian region – northern South Australia, Western Australia and the southern Northern Territory – and action was taken in relation to alcohol sales in each of these jurisdictions. These actions were complex but, in each jurisdiction, the RDA, and therefore *Koowarta* and *Gerhardy v Brown*, were engaged. Many of these actions occurred in the Northern Territory where the reach of *Koowarta* in its impact on the states was less significant, but the prominence of the RDA, and the reach of the alcohol issue across state and territory borders, meant that *Koowarta* and the RDA continued to have an underlying impact on attempts to resolve alcohol management issues.

Reflecting on the history of alcohol regulation in the Northern Territory, Heather Douglas has recently noted that, following the passing of the assimilationist era, there was a 'collaboration approach, beginning in approximately 1963 when prohibition ended for Northern Territory Aboriginal people and they gained the right to vote (in 1964)'. This period, she suggests, 'lasted until around 1999 when the then Prime Minister passed a formal motion of something he described as "practical reconciliation"'.[71]

The alcohol issue should be seen in this context, and as part of an emerging discourse of autonomy and self-determination. Douglas has noted that 'one of the central tensions that has played out in alcohol regulation has been the issue of racial discrimination and its relevance to the creation of special laws for Aboriginal people … The tensions between individual rights and individual autonomy on the one hand and collective rights and collective autonomy on the other hand have also been key concerns in struggles to regulate Aboriginal drinking'.[72] Just as these tensions were at the heart of *Maloney*, they were also very evident in the 1980s as Pitjantjatjara communities sought to regulate the flow of alcohol into their communities. The case study of Curtin Springs Roadhouse exemplifies this.

The general Pitjantjatjara area is remote. It includes the lands granted under the PLRA, now known as the APY lands, several communities in the southwest of the Northern Territory and related communities in Western Australia, adjacent to the Northern Territory border. In these regions, although not on the Aboriginal lands in South Australia, the Northern Territory or Western Australia, there are, or were in the early 1980s, a number of liquor outlets with licences for on-premises drinking as well as take-away alcohol and from which alcohol found its way into Aboriginal communities.[73]

[71]Douglas (2007), p 4.

[72]Douglas (2007), p 4.

[73]These included Erldunda Roadhouse, Mount Ebenezer Roadhouse, Curtin Springs Roadhouse, Kulgera Hotel, Marla Bore Hotel/Motel, Yulara Tourist Resort as well as roadhouses between the community of Warburton and Laverton in Western Australia.

Concern among the Pitjantjatjara about alcohol was long standing. There is evidence that there was discussion at meetings of Pitjantjatjaras in 1979 about limiting the sale of alcohol from the various roadhouses adjacent or en route to their communities.[74] This flowed through to the 1980s and, as a result, there was much legal work implementing instructions from communities and regional organisations aimed at limiting the availability of alcohol from these various outlets in the Northern Territory, South Australia and Western Australia. Further, in 1987 the PLRA was amended to allow by-laws to be made 'restricting or prohibiting the consumption, possession, sale or supply of alcoholic liquor on the lands'[75] and by-laws in similar terms were gazetted in December 1987.[76]

While there were many challenges to licence conditions, and negotiations over the years with the various outlets, the Curtin Springs Roadhouse case provides an example of the difficulties in achieving limits and how the issues of the RDA and community versus individual concerns played out.

Historically, the licensee, Peter Severin did not sell alcohol to members of adjacent communities.[77] It was said that there was an agreement, perhaps informal, that he would limit take-away sales to local community members.[78] The existence of this agreement was relied upon by the Northern Territory Liquor Commission in its decision not to formalise limitations in licence conditions in 1984 following an application from the Pitjantjatjara Council to do so.[79]

Then, in 1987–88, alcohol gradually became available to local community members at the roadhouse – both as take-away and in the bar. Local communities, particularly but not exclusively women in those communities, were greatly concerned as they reported increased violence and community disturbances.[80]

There have been many reasons suggested for this change but the licensee himself said that there were three reasons: 'an arrangement to supply 13 communities with meat from his cattle station has been cancelled and he is unhappy about an application for an Aboriginal living area on the station'.[81] He also indicated that it would be unlawful because the refusal to sell would be discrimination. He recounted that he had refused sale of alcohol at some stage and this had caused him trouble with the Minister in Canberra and white do-gooders from down south: 'I was informed by the Minister for Aboriginal Affairs that if I didn't serve Aborigines alcohol, I'd be taken to court for discrimination'.[82]

Negotiations to reinstate the old scheme were unsuccessful. Agreements had been negotiated with other licensees in the area not to sell take-away to people from Pitjantjatjara and Ngaaanyatjarra communities in the Northern Territory, South Australia or Western Australia, but no such agreement could be negotiated with

[74]Toyne (1977–1986).

[75]*Pitjantjatjara Land Rights Act Amendment Act 1987* (SA) s 12(d).

[76]*South Australian Government Gazette* (1987), 3 December, p 1775.

[77]Peter Severin, licensee of Curtin Springs Roadhouse, quoted in Krien (2011).

[78]Cooke (1989), p 13.

[79]d'Abbs et al (1999), p 3.

[80]Cooke (1989), p 13.

[81]Cooke (1989), p 13.

[82]Peter Severin, licensee of Curtin Springs Roadhouse, quoted in Krien (2011).

Curtin Springs at that time. Therefore, in 1988, a challenge to licence conditions was instituted by the Pitjantjatjara Council on behalf of a number of its members. During a 2 month adjournment of the hearing of the challenge, an injunction to prevent sales based on a prospective nuisance action was sought in the Northern Territory Supreme Court. The injunction was sought on behalf of certain named residents of the Mutitjulu Community, which was the closest community to Curtin Springs. Therefore it was arguable that those community members' enjoyment of their land was affected by the adjacent Curtin Springs liquor outlet. While this was innovative and interesting, it was unsuccessful.[83]

The challenge to the licence conditions was ultimately also unsuccessful. The liquor commission (rather perversely given its approach in 1984 referred to above, namely that the existence of an agreement meant there was no need for the commission to impose conditions) found that there had never been an agreement between communities and the licensee in relation to the sale of alcohol.[84] The commission did not accept evidence about issues such as the link between availability of alcohol and consumption or the impact of resumed sales on the wellbeing of people in the communities. The licence was renewed without restrictions (as was that of the Erldunda Roadhouse).[85] What, then, could be done?

In 1990, the Ngaanyatjarra, Pitjantjatjara and Yankunytjatjara (NPY) Women's Council was very active with regard to this issue. The council held a meeting near the roadhouse and 300 women marched along Lassiter Highway to Curtin Springs.[86] At this point, the issue passed from a legal to a political one – the lawyers having failed to provide any solution. The problems continued, with a number of road deaths, which local communities linked to alcohol availability, and a complaint was lodged with the Northern Territory Liquor Commission seeking a 'cessation of take-away sales'.[87] In response, the liquor commission placed a limitation of six cans take-away on all customers.[88]

As the damage caused by the sales continued, the coroner held an inquest into a number of road deaths and found that they were related to alcohol sales from Curtin Springs.[89] A further complaint was lodged with the then liquor commissioner who sought to achieve voluntary restrictions at all liquor outlets in the region.[90] This was rejected by local communities as they took the view that it actually extended the availability of alcohol by opening up sales through outlets that previously did not sell at all.[91]

Apart from the contested issues around links between availability of alcohol and consumption, alcohol consumption and violence in communities and the reluctance

---

[83] *Malya Teamey and Ors v Peter Severin* Northern Territory Supreme Court No 887 of 1998 [1988] NTSC 78 22 December 1988.

[84] d'Abbs et al (1999), p 3.

[85] d'Abbs et al (1999), p 3.

[86] Ngaanyatjarra, Pitjantjatjara and Yankunytjatjara Women's Council (1990), p 23.

[87] d'Abbs et al (1999), p 3.

[88] d'Abbs et al (1999), p 3.

[89] Kavanagh (1999).

[90] Kavanagh (1999).

[91] d'Abbs et al (1999), p 4.

of licensees and the liquor commission to restrict sales, there was an underlying problem under the RDA: limiting the availability of alcohol on the basis of race. The Human Rights and Equal Opportunities Commission had first become involved in 1990 at the instigation of communities and their organisations, and they were again asked for advice in 1994 in relation to a proposed ban on all alcohol sales to community members.[92] The commission published the results of its inquiry in 1995[93] and gave some support to the idea that particular licence conditions might constitute 'special measures' under the RDA.[94]

At some point (after my involvement) there was a rapprochement between the licensee – not with the lawyers but with the NPY Women's Council. Negotiations were undertaken and a trial arrangement was agreed to. The Human Rights and Equal Opportunities Commission agreed to issue a 'special measures certificate' in respect of negotiated trial rules that prevented any take-away sales, but allowed drinking in the bar for specified hours for people from the various named communities or others travelling to them for a period of 6 months with the reverse – no drinking on the premises and a take-away limit of six cans for a further period of 6 months.[95] The special measures certificate provided comfort to the licensee in relation to his 'racial discrimination' concerns, although it is unclear what, if any, legal force it actually had.[96]

Following the trial, the parties again met and the licensee offered not to sell to community members at all. This was accepted, licence conditions agreed and a special measures certificate granted to cover the new conditions. The arrangement is still in place.[97]

The Curtin Springs case is full of the paradoxes and tensions referred to by Douglas,[98] and that emerge more broadly in the application of the RDA regime, with varying community and individual wishes, and the potential for protective acts, as expressions of community wishes, to be viewed as racially discriminatory. While these may be saved by the 'special measures' provision, one consequence of this is that individual acts may be criminalised. These tensions were played out most recently in the High Court decision in *Maloney*. Ms Maloney, a resident of Palm Island, was charged with being in possession of alcohol, contrary to s 168B of the *Liquor Act* 1992 (Qld) and Schedule 1R of the *Liquor Regulation 2002* (Qld) made thereunder. The regulation limited the amount and type of liquor that could be consumed in areas of Palm Island, the details of which were implemented under an alcohol management plan, instituted after some consultation with the community although with by no means unanimous support. Whether the regulation was a special measure was central to the decision, with Ms Maloney arguing that it was not a special measure in part because a special measure should be beneficial and agreed

92 d'Abbs et al (1999), p 4.

93 Race Discrimination Commissioner (1995).

94 Race Discrimination Commissioner (1995), pp 89–91.

95 Kavanagh (1999).

96 Race Discrimination Commissioner (1995), pp 89–91.

97 Krien (2011), p 9; Ngaanyatjarra, Pitjantjatjara and Yankunytjatjara Women's Council (2012).

98 Douglas (2007).

to by those affected, as suggested by Brennan J in *Gerhardy v Brown*.[99] Unlike *Gerhardy v Brown*, this special measure had the effect of criminalising the acts of the beneficiary of the special measure in circumstances where it was unclear that a majority of those affected agreed with the measure. There was evidence that some discussions had taken place between the community and government about the alcohol management plan, but there was no clear agreement on implementation of the plan.[100] Despite this, the court held that it was a special measure as the Queensland parliament and the executive considered it reasonably necessary for them to enjoy human rights to security of persons and protection against violence or bodily harm and to public health equally with other Queenslanders, indicating that agreement or consent was not a necessary element of a special measure.[101]

The Curtin Springs arrangement is an example of a community supported innovative response to the limitations imposed by the RDA in alcohol management, and *Maloney* is a living example of the paradoxes of the application of the RDA and reliance on special measures. While *Maloney* may preserve the measure, in that case the alcohol management plan, it may also have other consequences for Aboriginal autonomy and the enjoyment of citizenship rights in that behaviour is criminalised on the basis of 'advancement' without the consent of those for whom the potentially discriminatory measure was implemented.

Conclusion

There is no doubt that *Koowarta* was ground breaking. It provided the foundations for the application of the principle of freedom from discrimination on the basis of race, and extended that principle to all. It extended the reach of the Commonwealth to proscribe the power of the states to act in a racially discriminatory manner. *Mabo No 1* and *Mabo No 2* and their impacts on the states, requiring state compliance in land administration, thus limiting the extinguishing effects of state actions on native title, are major examples of the force of the *Koowarta* reasoning in this regard. It also created many paradoxes, most recently seen in *Maloney*.

As a practising lawyer at the time, the case opened a whole range of possibilities for dealings with what might be described as recalcitrant states, but it also created difficulties in finding solutions to enduring problems such as alcohol management. It created possibilities but also imposed additional limits to solutions for problems that Indigenous people might fashion for themselves. As a lawyer, these paradoxes of possibilities and limits were, and remain, central to proper practice of law in this intercultural context.

In spite of these issues, the full force of *Koowarta* has been apparent and effective when relied upon as the foundation of creative and ambitious political action to advance the rights and entitlements of Indigenous Australians. The entanglement of law and politics was, and remains, a central element of *Koowarta*, and its resonance

[99] *Gerhardy v Brown* (1985) 159 CLR 70 at 135 (Brennan J).

[100] *Maloney v The Queen* (2013) 298 ALR 308 for example at 319–320 (French CJ).

[101] *Maloney v The Queen* (2013) 298 ALR 308 at 324–325 (French CJ), at 337–338 (Hayne J), at 345–346 (Crennan J), at 358–359 (Keifel J), at 374 (Bell J), at 404–408.

has underpinned a changing dynamic at the intersection of law, politics and the rights of Indigenous Australians.

Acknowledgements

I would like to acknowledge the support of the Australian Research Council (LP0990125) and the work of researcher Ben Silverstein.

References

Primary sources

Cases

Gerhardy v Brown (1983) 34 SASR 452
Gerhardy v Brown (1985) 159 CLR 70
Koowarta v Bjelke-Petersen (1982) 153 CLR 168
Mabo v Queensland (No 1) (1988) 166 CLR 186
Mabo v Queensland (No 2) (1992) 175 CLR 1
Maloney v The Queen (2013) 298 ALR 308
Malya Teamey and Ors v Peter Severin Northern Territory Supreme Court No 887 of 1998 [1988] NTSC 78 22 December 1988
Milirrpum v Nabalco (1971) 17 FLR 141
Viskauskas v Niland (1983) 153 CLR 280
Western Australia v Commonwealth (1995) 183 CLR 186

Legislation

Aboriginal Lands Bill 1985 (WA)
Aboriginal Land (Lake Condah and Framlingham Forest) Act 1987 (Cth)
Aboriginal Land Rights Act 1983 (NSW)
Aboriginal Land Rights (Northern Territory) Act 1976 (Cth)
Aboriginal Land Rights (Northern Territory) Amendment Act 2006 (Cth)
Land (Title and Traditional Usage) Act 1993 (WA)
Liquor Act 1992 (Qld)
Liquor Regulation 2002 (Qld)
Native Title Act 1993 (Cth)
Pitjantjatjara Land Rights Act 1981 (SA) (renamed *Anangu Pitjantjatjara Yankunytjatjara Land Rights Act 1981* [SA])
Pitjantjatjara Land Rights Act Amendment Act 1987 (SA)
Racial Discrimination Act 1975 (Cth)

Parliamentary debates

Commonwealth of Australia (1983) *Parliamentary Debates*, House of Representatives, 8 December

International instruments

International Convention on the Elimination of All Forms of Racial Discrimination 1965

Secondary sources

The Anangu Lands Paper Tracker (2012a) 'APY Lands:The Permit System', http://www.papertracker.com.au/archived/apy-lands-the-permit-system/, accessed 15 May 2012.

The Anangu Lands Paper Tracker (2012b) 'APY Lands: The Permit System – Isolated Incidents From the Early 1980s', http://www.papertracker.com.au/archived/apy-lands-the-permit-system-isolated-incidents-from-the-early-1980s/, accessed 20 April 2012.

Australian Mining Industry Council (1986) *Mining and Access to Aboriginal Land: An Issue of National Importance*, AMIC.

Ian Brownlie (1985) 'The Rights of Peoples in Modern International Law' 9 *Bulletin of the Australian Society of Legal Philosophy* 104–119.

Karen Cooke (1989) 'A Culture Tries to Defend Itself From Alcohol Abuse' *The Age* 14 February.

Peter d'Abbs et al (1999) *Evaluation of Restrictions on the Sale of Alcohol from Curtin Springs Roadhouse Northern Territory*, Menzies School of Health Research.

Heather Douglas (2007) 'The Curse of "White Man's Water": Aboriginal People and the Control Of Alcohol' 4 *University of New England Law Journal* 3.

Murray Goot and Tim Rowse (2007) *Divided Nation? Indigenous Affairs and the Imagined Public*, Melbourne University Publishing.

Maggie Kavanagh (1999) 'Curtin Springs Roadhouse: Ten Years of Community Struggle' 4 (19) *Indigenous Law Bulletin* 15.

Anna Krien (2011) 'Booze Territory: The Crisis of Alcoholism' *The Monthly*, September, No 71 http://www.themonthly.com.au/issue/2011/september/1318218855/anna-krien/booze-territory, accessed 20 November 2012.

Ronald T Libby (1989) *Hawke's Law: The Politics of Mining and Aboriginal Land Rights in Australia*, University of Western Australia Press.

Heather McRae et al (1991) *Aboriginal Legal Issues*, The Law Book Company Limited.

Damien Murphy (2014) 'Cabinet Papers 1986–87: The Struggle for Indigenous Land Rights', *The Sydney Morning Herald*, http://www.smh.com.au/federal-politics/political-news/cabinet-papers-198687-the-struggle-for-indigenous-land-rights-20131228-3017r.html#ixzz2reXXbadU, 28 December 2013.

Ngaanyatjarra, Pitjantjatjara and Yankunytjatjara Women's Council (1990) *Minyma Tjuta Tjunguringkula Women Growing Strong Together*, Alice Springs.

Ngaanyatjarra, Pitjantjatjara and Yankunytjatjara Women's Council (2012) *NPY Women's Council Advocacy: Substance Abuse: Alcohol Fact Sheet 13*, http://www.npywc.org.au/wp-content/uploads/2012/01/13-Substance-Abuse-Alcohol.pdf, accessed 22 November 2012.

Race Discrimination Commissioner (1995) *Alcohol Report: Racial Discrimination Act 1975: Race Discrimination, Human Rights and Distribution of Alcohol.*

Paul Seaman (1984) *The Aboriginal Land Inquiry*, Government Printer.

Wojczech Sadurskzi (1986) '*Gerhardy v Brown* V. The Concept of Discrimination: Reflections on the Landmark Case That Wasn't' 11 *Sydney Law Review 5.*

Phillip Toyne (1977–1986) Papers National Library of Australia MS9024.

Phillip Toyne and Daniel Vachon (1984) *Growing Up The Country: The Pitjantjatjara Struggle for Their Land*, McPhee Gribble/Penguin Books, Australian Government Publishing Service.

Edward Woodward (1974) *Aboriginal Land Rights Commission Report 1974*, Australian Government Publishing Service.

Koowarta and the rival Indigenous international: our place as Indigenous peoples in the international

Mark McMillan

Melbourne Law School, Australia

Indigenous Australian nations have been interacting with each other since time immemorial. Ravi de Dosta posits that there was, and still is, an Indigenous transnationalism. This transnationalism is required between the Indigenous nations for our nations' sustainability and maintenance as distinct polities. The relationship between the Indigenous peoples of Australia and the Anglo-Australian legal system has been a difficult one to manage due to the denial of recognition of Indigenous jurisdiction by the Anglo-Australian legal system. Indigenous peoples have maintained our own recognition processes of each other *and* the Anglo-Australian legal system. The *Koowarta* decision of the High Court of Australia focused the Anglo-Australian legal system outwards towards the international order and the recognised Indigenous jurisdiction that exists outside of the borders of Australia and our Indigenous nations' borders. Indigenous people(s) have been participating in the international arena for decades. This paper explores the unique ways that the *Koowarta* decision brought together the Indigenous international, the international order and the domestic jurisdiction of the Anglo-Australian legal order, and how the decision has influenced the life of a Wiradjuri legal academic.

What are the possibilities of viewing *Koowarta* as part of an 'Indigenous international'?

The *Koowarta v Bjelke-Petersen*[1] decision was an historic moment where multiple jurisdictions were able to view each other. The jurisdictions that became aligned and viewed within the case were: the relationship between the international and domestic law; the relationship between Indigenous peoples (and our distinct jurisdictions) and the State of Queensland; the relationship between the Commonwealth and states; and the relationship between the international order and the Indigenous. The concept of the 'Indigenous international' is rooted in the existence and meaning of the Indigenous peoples in international law. Such a space provides for the historic and contemporary experiences of Indigenous peoples to found a focal and gathering point for each other and then simultaneously position those experiences against the nation states and capturing a place within the 'international' without falling into the 'domestic' spheres of individual nations.

In that moment it provided an opportunity to move away from the legal denial of existence of Indigenous peoples within Australia to a place of mutual recognition (by

[1]*Koowarta v Bjelke-Petersen* (1982) 153 CLR 168.

the states, the Commonwealth and Indigenous peoples). The existence of the Indigenous international shows that the international can provide an opportunity for rival jurisdictions to meet. Thirty years has passed since the High Court delivered its judgment. In many respects the Indigenous international has since this time become a focus of the international. There have been defined periods of international focus as well as more formal and permanent institutional features of the United Nations system: the working group on Indigenous populations;[2] the international decade of the world's Indigenous peoples;[3] the second international decade of the world's Indigenous peoples;[4] United Nations permanent forum on Indigenous issues;[5] special rapporteur on the rights of Indigenous peoples; the expert mechanism on the rights of Indigenous peoples[6]; and the *United Nations Declaration on the Rights of Indigenous Peoples 2007*.[7]

Within the storytelling of the Anglo-Australian legal system, in other words, in the practice of its jurisprudence, the High Court decision centres on a question of the limits of the external affairs powers and the constitutionality of domestic legislation intended to uphold international obligations, specifically, Australia's obligations under the *International Convention on the Elimination of All Forms of Racial Discrimination 1965* enacted in Australia as the *Racial Discrimination Act 1975* (Cth) (RDA). Overwhelmingly, scholarship and reflections of the case cast it as a moment of the 'increasing interdependence of the internal and the international life of a nation state'.[8] This relationship between the internal or 'domestic affairs' of a state and the international is a culmination of a 'globalising world' and the quickly evolving place of human rights as a consequence of the end of World War II and the practice of the United Nations. The case exposed the multiple jurisdictions that exist in Australia and internationally, and the plurality of those jurisdictions. To date, reflections on *Koowarta* only recognise the meeting point of two jurisdictions – the domestic and the international. Viewing *Koowarta* through the Indigenous international allows for this previously ignored jurisdiction to legitimately be placed back in its rightful constellation, alongside and interacting with the other jurisdictions that

[2]Established in 1982 pursuant to the United Nations Economic and Social Council resolution 1982/34: http://web.archive.org/web/20060211221540/; http://www.ohchr.org/english/issues/indigenous/groups/wgip.htm#mandate.

[3]Resolution adopted by the General Assembly 48/163, international decade of the world's Indigenous peoples: http://www.un-documents.net/a48r163.htm.

[4]Resolution adopted by the General Assembly 59/174.

[5]United Nations special rapporteur on the rights of Indigenous peoples: the Commission on Human Rights decided to appoint in 2001 a special rapporteur on the rights of Indigenous peoples, as part of the system of thematic special procedures. The special rapporteur's mandate was renewed by the Commission on Human Rights in 2004 and by the Human Rights Council in 2007: http://www.ohchr.org/en/issues/ipeoples/srindigenouspeoples/pages/sripeoplesindex.aspx.

[6]The expert mechanism provides the Human Rights Council with thematic advice, in the form of studies and research, on the rights of Indigenous peoples as directed by the council. The expert mechanism may also suggest proposals to the council for its consideration and approval: http://www.ohchr.org/en/issues/ipeoples/emrip/pages/emripindex.aspx.

[7]Resolution adopted by the General Assembly 61/295 on 13 September 2007: http://www.un.org/esa/socdev/unpfii/documents/DRIPS_en.pdf.

[8]Byrnes and Charlesworth (1985), p 622.

have long sought to deny the Indigenous international's existence. More importantly, viewing *Koowarta* through the Indigenous international may explain some of the complexities and conundrums existing within the other jurisdictions (and their particular relationships with one another) that actively sought the denial of the Indigenous peoples and, through that denial, the denial of the Indigenous international.

Viewing *Koowarta* as part of the Indigenous international is an ongoing, personal story. However, this personal story is not about recollections of a romanticised past whereby the Indigenous is historicised, fetishised and romanticised by others as a mechanism to review their own histories and their relationship with Indigenous peoples, nor is this article an autobiographical account of my personal perspectives as an Indigenous person. It is a borrowed technique that seeks to inform of the multiple jurisdictions that exist in the telling of accounts of the intersection of such jurisdictions. This is not a story merely of my personal journey, but an important exercise of personal practice of communal jurisdiction given to me through my birth into the Wiradjuri nation. This article is the practice of my jurisprudence as a Wiradjuri person. The activity of practising jurisprudence through storytelling is neither new nor novel. Christine Black and John Burrows[9] are Indigenous legal scholars and practitioners in both Indigenous and Western systems of law. They emphasise that this practice is not new or novel to them; rather, that practice through storytelling is as old as our societies themselves. The common law can also be seen as a vehicle of the practice of jurisprudence through storytelling. However, Black and Borrow's position is that telling stories, and thereby practising their jurisprudences, creates a meeting point. Both are skilled at creating those meeting places. By telling their stories, connecting to their Indigenous jurisprudences, they have distinctive starting and reference points to align with their own jurisprudences. The reference points that lead their stories are those of their Indigenous jurisdictions, and from these points they actively practice and thereby maintain their connection to it – by being part of it. They perpetuate their jurisdiction by doing so. In telling stories, Black and Borrows try to make sense of their own jurisprudences and how these connect with other jurisdictions. They achieve all of this by storytelling. Their personal accounts, narratives and experiences of multiple jurisdictions are guides to me on how to be active in the practice of my own Wiradjuri jurisprudence.

To practice Wiradjuri jurisprudence in this article I will be telling a series of stories – four vignettes. Christine Black's words about the Indigenous international resonate in my mind – I must be grounded in my law and jurisprudence in order for me to activate and be engaged in the meeting place of jurisdictions, I must know on which perspective I am basing my world views, I must know the law of my land. She said:

> But what is theory? I understand theory as nothing more than a story. Just as history is the story of the victor, not the defeated, so theory is a story that elucidates a people's

[9]Dr Christine Black is a Kombumerri and Munaljahlai woman: http://www.griffith.edu.au/environment-planning-architecture/griffith-centre-coastal-management/staff/christine-black; Professor John Borrows is Anishinabek (also called Ojibway or Chippewa). He is a member of the Chippewas of the Nawash First Nation from Georgian Bay, in the Lake Huron area of Ontario, Canada: http://www.law.umn.edu/facultyprofiles/borrowsj.html.

> sense of self. Like all stories, it is a matter of how much power it is given. So when reading a theory, one must ask, does this story tell me who I am? There are very few accounts of the 'thinking' of senior law people in Australia; rather, it becomes railroaded into the accepted 'oral history', that is, Australians want to read about the trials and tribulations and the hero's venture, not the law of the land and how it manifests and still governs these peoples' lives.[10]

As a boy, my first encounter with *Koowarta*, just days after the High Court determination, connected me to the Indigenous international. Learning about the case as a young man connected me as a Wiradjuri person living on country to a place outside of my existence. My initial connection to *Koowarta* as a boy has been through the storytelling between my grandmother and my mother. The coupling between me and the Indigenous international remains in my everyday experience. As a boy, the connection between *Koowarta* and the Indigenous international was far less significant than the connection is today for a Wiradjuri lawyer and lecturer. The significance of understanding rival jurisdictions in that moment of connection has become more profound. Viewing *Koowarta* through the lens of the Indigenous international opens up possibilities of a true meeting place for the rival jurisdictions of Indigenous peoples and nations in Australia and the Anglo-Australian legal order.

Vignette 1. 1982 and the car ride over Wiradjuri country

In 1982, when the *Koowarta* decision was handed down, the manner in which it was received by me as a 13 year old Wiradjuri boy is an important reminder of how, when different worlds/cosmologies/ontologies meet, there is a permanent bonding of the two. An inextricable link between them is forged and, with this, a requirement to maintain that link at the same time as retaining the separate and distinct jurisdictions. I maintain this link across three distinct, but interrelated spaces of my existence: country (Wiradjuri); international (Indigenous); and as a lawyer trained in Anglo-Australian law. They are distinct spaces that influence each other in my world.

On 11 May 1982 I was 13 years old. I was living in Trangie, New South Wales, with my Mum, Nan and siblings. The town of Trangie is 72 kilometres west of the regional city of Dubbo; both are on Wiradjuri country. The city and the town for me and my family was a meeting place of two worlds. We understood our existence as about 'walking in two worlds'. Walking in two worlds was something that my grandmother actually said to us, and she instilled its meaning in each of us from an early age. It was 'a gift' she would say. She always said this with such happiness. That being able to indeed walk in both worlds was such a special thing for us – her children and grandchildren. Being able to walk in these two worlds also carried responsibilities. Nan was very clear that such a gift was not just about what we could get from such a thing, but what we were required to do to inform each world of the other. Her happiness about our 'gift' was real. Upon reflection, I think that her happiness on our behalf was born from having herself been prevented for a large part of her life from walking in both worlds. Like many Aboriginal and Torres Strait

[10]Black (2011), p 358.

Islander peoples of my Nan's generation, the governments of the states and the Commonwealth denied them (Aboriginal and Torres Strait Islanders) the opportunity to be able to walk in both worlds – they were simply not allowed to participate in the life of the country. They were not allowed to vote, they were denied access to education and denied the possibility of attaining citizenship. It was made unlawful in the Anglo-Australian legal system for Aboriginal and Torres Strait Islanders to practice culture and speak their language that connected them to their country. Aboriginal and Torres Strait Islanders of my Nan's generation and ancestors were not allowed to become citizens and were, at the same time, not allowed to be who they were culturally. But to make sense of both worlds for us was very real and very practical. Nan always talked about the possibilities for us – and by possibilities I think she meant the opportunities that were being made available to our generation that was simply not thought of in her generation. Such opportunities were embedded, for me at least, in education and law. The responsibilities to participate in these opportunities were made fundamental responsibilities, so Nan schooled us. For me, accessing these opportunities became a fundamental responsibility to my Mum and Nan.

To explain geography is to explain connection to country. My great, great grandmother was born at, or near, what is now the town of Carcoar in central New South Wales. It is in the heart of Wiradjuri country. Gran, my great grandmother, was born on the banks of the Macquarie River at Dubbo, also on Wiradjuri country, 'the year the railroad came to Dubbo'. Nan, born in Trangie, was also connected to Wiradjuri through her own mother and grandmother and her own connection to country by being physically on it. Mum is also connected to Trangie. My siblings and I were also from Trangie. Gran, Nan and many of my relatives are buried at Trangie. My connection to country has been strong and remains so. We did not understand at the time that living on country is a precious thing. It may seem that we took for granted that we actually lived on country because my siblings and I learnt about our connections to place as a matter of course – or normality. Such was the subtlety of how we engaged with such connections and learning about responsibilities to country and others on it that it was not until I was a parent myself that I saw the significance of how we lived our lives.

We travelled to Dubbo from Trangie frequently. We did shopping in Dubbo and we played sport in Dubbo. On the weekend after the *Koowarta* decision had been handed down we were driving home from Dubbo where my brother and I had been playing football in the under 14s competition. We had a brown two-tone XB Ford Falcon, dark brown on the bottom and a lighter brown, almost beige, on the top. Inside the car the two seats were made of dark brown vinyl. Both were bench seats and we could fit three across the front seat and three (usually four) across the back seat. It was an automatic with the gear level on the 'column'. Importantly, there was an ashtray. It was the time when most adults I knew smoked. Nan smoked Viscount and Mum smoked Benson and Hedges. Mum had switched brands after spending some time with Kool.

It was a treat for my brother and I that, at the end of the game and on our way home, we could get take-away McDonald's. My sisters were not with us on this Saturday as they had netball games back at home in Trangie that weekend. The McDonald's was on the main road in Dubbo. After we had called in and got the order we headed back to Trangie. We headed west over the Thomas Ford bridge, a huge structure (for us) that spans the Macquarie River. Each time we would go over it we were reminded that just down on the banks was where Gran had been born. We were being reminded of our connection.

I was sitting in the back with my brother. Mum and Nan were in the front of the car talking while they had put the tape on. The windows were down while we headed out of Dubbo so that Mum and Nan were happily talking and smoking. My brother and I were greedily eating the McDonald's. The tape that Nan had put on and was playing in the background also had particular significance. I remember it well. I remember receiving the tape of various hits – '1982 with a bullet'. I had only just received it for my thirteenth birthday on 6 May, some five days before the decision was handed down in *Koowarta*. The album had on it a song that even at the time I thought was very moving. On side two there was the song 'What about me' by Moving Pictures. I asked Nan to start it there. The lyrics are poignant and were fitting for the period. As an angst-ridden teenager, Moving Pictures told the story of my life: 'What about me? It isn't fair, I've had enough, now I want my share, Can't you see, I wanna live, But you just take more than you give'. The lyrics also strike resonance with the case or, more importantly, with Aboriginal people's struggles that lie at the heart of the case.

We were just coming into Narromine. Narromine is a town half way between Dubbo and Trangie. It is a larger town than Trangie. As we approached Narromine from the Dubbo side Mum decided to take the 'by-pass way', which was just a route that skirted town without having to go down the main street. Taking the by-pass way we ended up near the river again. At Narromine there were lots of peppercorn trees lining one side of the road near the river. As we drove past the trees our windows were down, I recall the amazing smell of the peppercorn trees. The day was a typical Western Plains day. It was clear with the bluest of blue skies which still seem so 'big' to me. There were no clouds that day and set against the blue of the sky was the very distinct green of the peppercorn trees with the thick, dark trunk, and the red peppercorns. That smell of the peppercorn trees at that place is the one that can transport me 'home'. It was always at this place in Narromine that I get a strong feeling of connection. That day was no different.

The tape had long finished and by the time we were coming up to Narromine I was doing my usual 'I want to know everything' and was leaning forward with my arms folded on the top of the front bench seat listening to Mum and Nan. Mum and Nan were talking about a court case that involved Aboriginal people in Queensland. They knew about it because they were, at that stage, participating in land rights discussions in our town. The issue of land rights for Aboriginal people in New South Wales was gaining momentum and my family was participating in that push. One year later, New South Wales implemented the *Aboriginal Land Rights Act 1983* (NSW).

One thing that is so distinct was the tenor of the conversation. Mum and Nan were absolutely enlivened and animated about it. Words like 'rights', 'our land', 'discrimination', 'obligation', 'hero', 'Queensland', 'gerrymander' were being bandied about. At the time it was strange for me to witness a discussion about a court case. This conversation went on for a while. It survived the 'by-pass way' and Mum pointed the car towards Trangie from Narromine, and took the bend in the road at Narromine Airport – the last bend or curve in the road for 30 kilometres before we reached Trangie. What I learned later in law school – what my Mum and Nan were talking about in the car that day was the *Koowarta* case.

Vignette 2. Law school and the *Koowarta* case: the meeting of multiple jurisdictions

Ten years later, in 1992, I commenced my Anglo-Australian legal education at the University of New South Wales. The first assessment piece that I was required to do as part of my studies was a casenote. That casenote was on no other case than *Koowarta*. It was meant to be. Writing this casenote I was taken back to that time in the car. The casenote allowed me to reacquaint myself with the multiple connections made in the car between the local and the Indigenous international and the international more broadly; as well as between my Wiradjuri jurisdiction and the Indigenous international and international.

It was not until much later in life that I could identify that that moment at law school doing the casenote cemented my connection to the Indigenous international. It was a meeting point. I am lucky to be able to inhabit different jurisdictions. I also do not merely inhabit multiple jurisdictions. I am active in all of them. I freely move between and around them. This is part of the 'gift' that Nan often reminded us of.

The case became active in my life and remains so. I had to experience it to make sense of it. To make sense of the multiplicity going on within it there first had to be a story to tell about it. I had to connect Mr Koowarta's story as a way to attach my own jurisprudential lens to it. I had to read it as a lawyer, but also as a Wiradjuri jurist, in order to locate his story and understand how he exercised his own jurisprudence.

Legal cases where Indigenous peoples are discussed as a subsidiary question to the main issue are not a new phenomenon. The legal principle in issue rarely concerns any specific Indigenous person or Indigenous peoples more generally. Nevertheless, the experiences that Indigenous peoples have of the principles being discussed in those cases might be brought into the Anglo-Australian legal system. Such instances may indeed provide a meeting place where the impact of the laws on Indigenous peoples, and the way they experience them, may be better understood. However, the law and legal cases that invoke Indigenous experiences to get to the 'legal issue' in the particular matter seldom seem to actually create a meeting place for the Indigenous person or Indigenous peoples. The prescriptive nature of the processes of law, including the rules of evidence, mostly inhibit or prohibit the Indigenous experience, and are conveyed in a way that can impede a meeting point. This prescription may also impede the capacity to convey the story at all – or the opportunity of the Indigenous person to actually tell *their* story.

As a lawyer reading *Koowarta*[11] I find it difficult to find Mr Koowarta's story. That is, it is difficult to find Mr Koowarta's own story about his experiences of the law and the refusal of Queensland to transfer land to the Commonwealth, in his words and his world view. Analyses of the case in legal text books or commentaries often refer to it as a 'victory' for Mr Koowarta. This is consistent with the binary way in which legal education sees cases in terms of winning or losing. My first question, even in 1992, was: how is such a statement measured? Ultimately, Mr

[11] *Koowarta v Bjelke-Petersen* (1982) 153 CLR 168.

Koowarta was still denied access to his land – a place in which he was connected, a place that founded and maintained his identity. It is not through the case that we are able to find out about his circumstance before, during or after the High Court's decision.

To become a 'victor', Mr Koowarta had to be discriminated against and that discrimination harmed him and his people. In fact, the spirit of the law in question was harmful to Aboriginal and Torres Strait Islander peoples. The discrimination of Mr Koowarta by the State of Queensland spoke of the relationship between Aboriginal and Torres Strait Islander people and the settler state which is mired by the history and experiences of colonisation. In order to be in a position to have such a 'victory' Mr Koowarta was required to relive the harm so that 'legal issues' of the colonial legal system could be adjudicated. What was to be adjudicated exactly? For me, the larger issue to be analysed was about the legal system itself and what it was restrained from doing to Aboriginal and Torres Strait Islander peoples. Such adjudication was complicated further by the fact that, previous to this case, the law was actually allowed to (and indeed did) treat Aboriginal and Torres Strait Islander peoples in a discriminatory way with the consequence of harming them, cruelly. Mr Koowarta relived that harm. It was a moment in time when his decision to publicly state his harm – exerting his own jurisprudence – reverberated within Aboriginal and Torres Strait Islander communities and the broader Australian community.

The judgment, and its silence about/concerning the relationship of Mr Koowarta and his land, impacted me as a Wiradjuri person and as a would-be lawyer who wanted to focus on human rights and Indigenous peoples. Mr Koowarta might not have been able to tell his story in his own way; but the case, and Mr Koowarta's bravery in participating, created a meeting place. I think that meeting place is one of hope.

What this case did for me, as lawyer, was to understand the importance of international law – the relationship between the international and the 'Indigenous'; the relationship between the domestic and international law; and the evolving voice of Indigenous peoples in the international arena. It also opened up the possibility for Indigenous voices and experiences at the international level to inform the Anglo-Australian legal system about the relationship that is required to exist as a matter of law between Indigenous peoples and the state.

Understanding that there are connections between Indigenous peoples and international law has, for me, become a meeting point of itself. An example of this connection has been the rights of Indigenous peoples and the specific and general obligations on nation states to give effect to those rights. Indigenous peoples from around the world participated as equals with nation states to negotiate the text of the *United Nations Declaration on the Rights of Indigenous Peoples 2007* over a 25 year period. That meeting point allows me to create a meeting place of laws, legal systems, and thus of legal plurality itself. Such a point also places my Wiradjuri experiences, existences, ontologies and epistemologies (Wiradjuri jurisdiction) outside of the gaze of the Anglo-Australian legal system. As well as Wiradjuri jurisdiction, in Australia all Indigenous peoples' individual (nation) jurisdictions are separated from the connection to the Anglo-Australian legal system for our mere existence.

Shaunnagh Dorsett and Shaun McVeigh describe how the structure of different existences can be explained by an understanding of 'jurisdiction'. That is, that people –

as individuals and as collectives – exist in a relational way to each. Therefore, to be able to understand them, there is a need to understand the 'structure' of the way those people/collectives relate outwards. Jurisdiction is an outward expression of the internal structure of a particular existence. In order to understand a jurisdictional boundary or meeting point there must be a recognition of the structured existences of the other to observe (and respect) its jurisdiction. More importantly, Dorsett and McVeigh assert that jurisdiction or 'speaking the law' is an activity that must be practised to be maintained.[12] Jurisdictional thinking may allow for a better explanation for how our lives, our existences (through our laws) are structured.[13] An extension of jurisdictional thinking is to place Indigenous peoples distinctly apart from the jurisdiction of the nation state. That is not to deny the existence of the nation state. Jurisdictional thinking in this way does not bind Indigenous peoples to the nation state for their own existences. Jurisdictions, according to Dorsett and McVeigh, can come into existence in many ways at different times and, accordingly, some 'jurisdictions' are in existence before others.[14] It is what happens to the relationship between the jurisdictions that excites me about the possibilities of jurisdictional thinking.

This jurisdictional thinking, in the context of the multiple relationships that were being viewed in *Koowarta* (the international/domestic/racial) allows Indigenous people to assert what we know and live every day – that our jurisdictions exist outside of and have been practised long before being exposed to the Anglo-Australian jurisdiction. We practise our jurisprudence to maintain our distinctive jurisdictions. Further, our jurisdictions are not reliant on the Anglo-Australian jurisdiction to be maintained as distinct jurisdictions. And, as a result of the evolving relationships (including the movement in technologies of jurisdiction[15] of the Anglo-Australian and international jurisdictions), a more nuanced understanding of the codependence of jurisdictions can be promulgated. The technologies of jurisdiction that Dorsett and McVeigh allude to are the practices that are employed within a jurisdiction that is required to maintain it. The practices may change or adapt over time to respond to changing circumstances of the jurisdiction. One example of one such technology is the use of precedent in the common law of Australia to perpetuate the common law doctrine of *terra nullius*. However, the doctrine was removed from the common law system and a particular practice had to be adapted to achieve it.

The international arena provides a place where the Indigenous jurisdictions are not dependent on the jurisdiction of the nation state to exist. The international confirmed this with the *United Nations Declaration on the Rights of Indigenous Peoples* where it was affirmed that Indigenous peoples have rights to exist as societies just because they are Indigenous peoples. The recognition of Indigenous peoples is not required by individual nation states for their existence. The nation states are obligated to give proper effect and enjoyment to Indigenous peoples of those rights – and not to interfere with them. The mere existence of the international order is also evidence and acknowledgment of multiple jurisdictions. The International system can also be the meeting place and creation of the Indigenous/nation state

[12]Dorsett and McVeigh (2012).

[13]Dorsett and McVeigh (2012).

[14]Dorsett and McVeigh (2012).

[15]Dorsett and McVeigh (2012), p 56.

relationship as envisioned with the *United Nations Declaration of the Rights of Indigenous Peoples* that, in effect, sought to create very distinctive relationships with Indigenous peoples and the nation states that have Indigenous populations.

The willingness to hear the voices of Indigenous peoples – that have authority to speak about their jurisdictions – was an unexpected by-product of the *Koowarta* legacy. As stated earlier, Mr Koowarta's story had difficulty being heard throughout the case. It was in the immediate time after the case that Mr Koowarta and his dire story became fully known. The case itself did not provide an opportunity for Mr Koowarta to actually tell his story, nor the enormity of the harm inflicted on him and the Wik peoples over the denial of access (and ownership) of his/their lands. The denial of the opportunity to tell his story was because the case could only deal with the jurisdictional relationships between the national/state (Queensland)/international that reinforced the technologies of jurisdiction. Moreover, the case represented a seismic shift in the jurisdictional relationship between the international and the state and, as a necessary extension, the relationship between the Commonwealth and Queensland. None of these relationships were inclusive, let alone cognizant of an Indigenous perspective or jurisdiction. The case started out as being a reshaping of the *status quo* – that Indigenous peoples are only subjects to the Anglo-Australian jurisdiction. Indigenous were not what was being adjudicated (or valued) in the case. The case, for me, was about whether the laws or actions of Queensland would have an effect on the relationship between Australia and the rest of world. Therein lies the reason why Mr Koowarta was seen as a hero by my mother and grandmother – because he was able to bring his Indigenous jurisdiction into focus. This, for Mum and Nan, held out the hope that our jurisdiction may be capable of being heard and exercised in the future.

For Aboriginal people, it may be seen as an instance of using the Anglo-Australian legal apparatus to state what cannot and should not be done to us. For me, the Indigenous experience was not about the relationship between the international and national. It was about using the legal system to place Indigenous experiences of the legal system itself to allow non-Indigenous people to make sense of their own system. By bringing matters before the court, of what cannot and should not be done to Aboriginal people by the law itself, two things are achieved. First, it allows non-Indigenous people to see the effects of law and the effects of Indigenous peoples by reference to its failings to treat Indigenous people respectfully and equally. In other words, it allows non-Indigenous people the opportunity to make sense (or observe the non-sense) of their legal system by referencing the Indigenous experience to 'their' law. Second, it allows Indigenous peoples to state that the jurisdiction being asserted (that is, that laws are actions that can be done to us) is only one of the dimensions that Indigenous peoples experience – one type of jurisdiction. The existence of the 'Indigenous' by its very nature allows for multiple jurisdictions to operate within and over Indigenous peoples.

This conception of multiple jurisdictions – whether it be the international and national, or the impact of federation on the relationship between the Commonwealth and states – is used extensively by lawyers, academics and legislators to read, interpret and analyse *Koowarta*. However, such reading, interpretation and analysis leave out the Indigenous jurisdiction. There is no requirement for Indigenous jurisdiction to exist when it comes to the way in which the Anglo-Australian system operates with respect to Indigenous peoples. It allows the system to make sense of itself by how it actually treats Indigenous peoples. That is why Mr Koowarta was brave. He allowed a mirror to be held up to the legal system. The only question that Mr Koowarta posed for the Anglo-Australia legal jurisdiction was 'do you want to treat us [Aboriginal people] this way?' The response was entirely internal to that jurisdiction. However, the internal operations of the Anglo-Australian legal jurisdiction (between the Commonwealth and Queensland) was dramatically impacted by the relationships of jurisdiction external to it. That external jurisdictional relationship was between the Indigenous and the international jurisdictions. Mr Koowarta wanted this to occur. By drawing on the international, Mr Koowarta provided a meeting place – a meeting place of jurisdictions of which Indigenous jurisdictions became an essential understanding of the jurisdictional relationships.

How was the case and the jurisdictional relationships reflected back to the Anglo-Australian legal system? How was the jurisdictional relationships reflected back through particular technologies of jurisprudence of this case?[16] What was a 'traditional' response to the case? It would appear that the traditional approach to the case in the reporting of it was part of the technology of the jurisprudence of the Anglo-Australian legal system. It also appears that the case was not about Mr Koowarta; rather, it was about an issue between the Commonwealth and the states through the development of a human rights framework that, in this instance, was reflected in the *International Convention for the Elimination of All Forms of Racial Discrimination 1965* (ICERD).[17] The legal question was whether Queensland could be prevented from discriminating against Indigenous peoples. The law was a reflection of three things: (1) Queensland sought to treat Aboriginal and Torres Strait Islander people terribly and the Commonwealth did not like the RDA operating in this way; (2) the operation of the law of Queensland violated Australia's obligations and therefore affected the relationship of the Commonwealth and other nations; and (3) the jurisdictional relationship between the Commonwealth and states when there are issues that are deemed 'international' – in particular the question of which laws will take precedence. Stated differently, what is one of the technologies of jurisdictions (what are the rules) that give clear direction to the distribution of authority between the jurisdictions? I have yet to find a case or 'legal' analysis that has the Indigenous experience as its starting point.

In an article written in 1985, Professor Hilary Charlesworth (co-authored with Professor Andrew Byrnes) wrote of the critical moment – jurisprudentially – that human rights norms that existed in the international legal order were necessarily being re-evaluated and re-positioned with respect to their application and relationship to Australia's domestic legal order. In emphasising what can be described as a new and different, even radical, approach to how scholars were viewing and analysing the case, they positioned and chastised the *status quo*, that nation states in the operation of their 'domestic' sovereignty had the right to implement laws and policies that were racially discriminatory. By grounding their analysis in international human rights norms they shifted the emphasis from the right of nation states

---

[16]Dorsett and McVeigh (2012).

[17]Australia is a signatory to the convention. Australia provided internal effect to the convention by implementing the RDA. The convention can be accessed at https://www.humanrights.gov.au/international-convention-elimination-all-forms-racial-discrimination-icerd.

to act as a matter of right in their own domestic jurisdictions towards the question of what the obligations of such states are to their people and the international community. They rightly and boldly stated: 'non-discrimination on racial grounds is accepted as a rule of *jus cogens*, a norm from which no derogation is permitted at international law'.[18]

The analysis by Charlesworth and Byrnes of, not only the relationship between the international and Australia, but the relationship of a federated Australia with the external and internal order, was innovative and superb. With particular reference to the complex relationships for a 'federated' Australian state Charlesworth and Brynes provided to Indigenous peoples another way to understand where our relationship to the three other jurisdictions (international, national and state) may be placed with respect to each of them singularly and collectively. Nicely, Charlesworth and Byrnes locate the majorities' decision as resisting any incompatibility between federalism and Australia's 'effective participation in the international community … They bring Australian jurisprudence in this respect firmly into the modern age'.[19] In concluding, the authors assert that: 'A state in a federation simply cannot isolate itself from international law'.[20]

It is this demand to bring Australian jurisprudence into the modern age that is of most utility to Indigenous peoples and our experiences. It is in the 'modern age', jurisprudentially and practically, that Indigenous peoples have come to have our own voice – stating our own jurisdictions. It was a very strong movement that predates the heavy influence that international human rights law had in the *Mabo No 2*[21] case some 10 years after *Koowarta*. It makes me wonder, as a lawyer, what influence the *Koowarta* decision had on the legal team representing Mr Mabo and the other plaintiffs.

Mr Koowarta's story being told through the lens of a Wiradjuri international human rights lawyer reminds me of what Nin Tomas, a Māori activist and academic, suggests about the importance of the possibilities of the Indigenous voice. She suggested that by articulating how we might organise as Indigenous peoples – she references Māori peoples – will make us real. We are not relegated into the wallpaper of cases, or the psyche of the legal consciousness. This, she said, 'invites and perhaps challenges the reader to engage with a Māori/Indigenous perspective they may not have previously considered, and to accept that there are other ways of thinking, measuring, and analysing existence other than from within a Western sovereignty paradigm'.[22]

I found a home in 'law' in that casenote. That sense of belonging is not rooted in which law I am most qualified to participate in. I am qualified to participate in both and have a legitimacy and responsibility to both. I find that this sense of belonging now comes with 'the gift' that Nan talked about. To be able to 'walk in both worlds' she called it. I am also excited by the possibilities of law. The excitement comes from the possibility to explain one system of law to another; to explain concepts that allow

[18]Byrnes and Charlesworth (1985), p 632.

[19]Byrnes and Charlesworth (1985), p 640.

[20]Byrnes and Charlesworth (1985), p 640.

[21]*Mabo v Queensland (No 2)* (1992) 175 CLR 1.

[22]Tomas (2013), p 220.

for a better understanding of experiences of law. The possibilities of law are best explained when existing with and experiencing things other than law. For me, existing in both worlds has allowed for the Anglo-Australian law to be seen as a site of possibility – and hope. Julie Evans and Ann Genovese have best summed up the possibility of law or the understanding of the possibilities: '[L]aw is not the only terrain on which to think through, imagine and enact other ways of living justly together. Working both within and beyond law at once recognizes and challenges its thrall, opening up pathways to alternative determinations, to possibilities "other than the ones we have today"'.[23]

Vignette 3. The personal: Professor Hilary Charlesworth, *Koowarta* and me

To be able to experience the law differently is not confined to the experience of Indigenous peoples. Professor Hilary Charlesworth's personal experiences with the *Koowarta* case have led to many intersections that can be described as alternative possibilities. Professor Charlesworth's personal experience with the case was as an Associate to Sir Ninian Stephen. Sir Ninian was a High Court justice at the time and his decision was the 'swing vote' in the *Koowarta* case. She has since had an influence as a world leading scholar in international human rights and its relationship to Australian jurisprudence. She also taught me, as a law student, international human rights law at the Australian National University where I completed my Bachelor of Laws degree. Professor Charlesworth's personal involvement in this case and my life has, of itself, become a meeting point.

The meeting of the international and domestic is such an important nexus for me to be able to formulate and articulate 'possibilities'. Professor Charlesworth's view of the new nature of the relationship between the international and the domestic was not orthodox at the time. Since that time, Professor Charlesworth's insistence of placing a greater emphasis on the international in our domestic jurisdictions has been realised, in particular in the High Court's use of international human rights norms as justification for unsettling the doctrine of *terra nullius* in *Mabo No 2*.[24] Professor Charlesworth has maintained a very strong view about the connection between the local and global: between Australia and the international order. She has described the urgency and necessity of the relationship:

> My central argument is that the Australian legal system will be impoverished unless it becomes more receptive to international law in the twenty-first century … In this lecture in Sir Ninian's honour, I want to argue that, as judges make decisions in an increasingly complex world, they need to consider the important source of principles and norms provided by international law. I do not wish to suggest an unthinking embrace of all international legal rules, but rather that they be seriously considered as a resource in the task that faces us all of thinking globally and acting locally.[25]

---

[23]Evans et al (2013), p 1.

[24]*Mabo v Queensland (No 2)* (1992) 175 CLR 1.

[25]Charlesworth (2002), p 15.

Vignette 4. Indigenous international and Indigenous transnationalism: the politics of Indigenous experiences in the international

Associate Professor Ravi de Costa and my life also have personal connections and intersections. He now resides in Canada. However, from the outside he reflects back to Australia our jurisprudence and simultaneously situates the Indigenous international and the politics of Indigenous transnationalism. Ravi de Costa studied with Professor Mick Dodson, and it was he who encouraged me to utilise the work and direction of Ravi de Costa and to undertake postgraduate studies at the University of Arizona with Professors Robert A. Williams Jr and James Anaya. The exceptional work of de Costa promotes the possibility of the international to deal with issues that the domestic cannot, or will not confront.[26]

Indigenous participation in the 'international' has been as old as us. What must be made clear is what 'international' we refer to and what created it. There are, and have been, Indigenous nations (otherwise called societies) on the landmass that is now named Australia for millennia. Native title law in Australia expressly recognises Aboriginal and Torres Strait Islander societies prior to European contact. The existence of our nations is not new. Such recognition of pre-existing jurisdictions can be found in our Indigenous nations' laws (such as the practice of Yindjamara in Wiradjuri) and the Anglo-Australian legal system (land rights legislation in New South Wales and the Northern Territory, the constitutions of the states of Victoria, New South Wales, Queensland and South Australia). In order to sustain the individual nations over millennia there was, and still remains, a very strong sense of the international. That is one international that is often overlooked when Indigenous transnationalism is referred to. However, its potency is now more evident. The continuing recognition by Indigenous nations within Australia creates a collective jurisdiction – this international collective jurisdiction is as old as the individual nations. The collective jurisdiction is the practice of the exercising of jurisdictions to, and for, other Indigenous nations, which provides the momentum for continuing practice and exercise of jurisdiction and the development of jurisprudence. It allows the assertion of such jurisdiction away from the Anglo-Australian legal system or the nation-state international order. This kind of Indigenous transnationalism perpetuates our jurisdictions. Christine Black refers to the positioning of law to the landscape as the essence of our jurisdictions: '[L]aw is posited in the landscape at the time of creation and to understand the law there must be a meaningful engagement with the landscape – or, as it is termed in Aboriginal Australia, "The Land is the Source of the Law"'.[27]

The Indigenous transnationalism that sustains us as distinct Indigenous nations within the confines of Australia is different to Indigenous transnationalism which sees Indigenous participation outside the borders of the Australian nation state. Ravi de Costa says of this: 'Indigenous transnationalism describes the political activities of indigenous peoples that exceed the bounded culture and politics of the Australian nation-state'.[28]

---

[26]de Costa (2006), p 5.

[27]Black et al (2007), p 308.

[28]de Costa (2006), pp 2–3.

De Costa explains that Indigenous peoples view the international in a particular way and that Indigenous transnationalism is an old phenomenon – the 'newness' is in the enquiry into Indigenous transnationalism. He posits that, despite the importance and prominence of nation states in peoples' lives, 'transnational analysis demonstrates that nation-states do not completely account for the reality of human experience'.[29] Where the international and the Indigenous international intersect, de Costa's 'transnational' is a mechanism that 'indigenous peoples have appealed to external powers in order to restrain colonial and national authorities and to have their claims heard'.[30]

Higher authority, according to de Costa, can be conceptualised as deriving from two sources; first, a set of broad norms or universal values and, second, from a body that can enforce these norms.[31] De Costa suggests that these concepts are interwoven, there is 'a productive relationship between the two, where appeals to particular norms and values help create and legitimise an enforcing body and where using international organisations and institutions helps spread awareness of and support for the values on which they are founded … indigenous transnationalism … indicates many indigenous peoples' commitment to a universal order of experience and justice; one in which indigenous and other peoples can coexist'.[32]

The relationship between the international and domestic has seen Indigenous participation. That participation has seen the influence of the international on Indigenous experiences in Australia. By connecting Indigenous Australians' experiences to other Indigenous experiences outside of Australia has had multiple effects. It has allowed for different political discussions and activities in Australia; a more connected Indigenous movement around the world; the possibility to look at and solve problems differently when experienced and positioned outside of Australia.

The influence of the international on the expression and experiences of Indigenous Australians was taking root in international agreement making. De Costa highlights that the International Labour Organization's (ILO's) *Convention 107 – Indigenous and Tribal Populations Convention 1957* (ILO 107) had profound impacts on the political discourse in Australia between Indigenous and non-Indigenous governments. De Costa suggests that ILO 107 'had a galvanising and coordinating effect on the Aboriginal movement in Australia'.[33] He also located the centrality of the principles of ILO 107 into the national discussion and activism of Indigenous Australians in the 1960s. According to de Costa, even though there was resistance – legally and politically – to international law in the domestic Anglo-Australian legal order, human rights norms had been internalised into Indigenous activism in Australia.[34]

ILO 107 was a first attempt to codify international obligations of states in respect of Indigenous and tribal populations, and was the first international convention on the subject, adopted by the ILO at the request of the United Nations.

---

[29]de Costa (2006), p 4.

[30]de Costa (2006).

[31]de Costa (2006).

[32]de Costa (2006), p 5.

[33]de Costa (2006), pp 83–85.

[34]de Costa (2006).

International conventions are between nation states. However, the international provides a place where different experiences and jurisdictions can be articulated. It is also a place where a particular issue that is seen to exist only in the 'domestic' sphere has the possibility of being seen differently. Again, de Costa brilliantly articulates this connection that working outside of the political nation – where there may be limited capacity to deal with particular problems – there exists a place that holds out hope of different rationalities being able to deal with such issues. One particular possibility of the international, according to de Costa, is a movement away from seeing nation states as the only valid source of value or place of action. In other words, the international may be a place where old binaries of authority may be challengeable and provide new ways of solving old problems. De Costa deliberately places Indigenous transnationalism at the core of the Indigenous international and internationals' meeting place. The hope of Indigenous transnationalism is 'an effort to broaden our sense of what forms of human association and interaction are possible'.[35]

This was certainly true for Indigenous experiences in Australia. Indigenous peoples in Australia were having particular political experiences. One of the political strategies of Indigenous peoples was to connect our struggles with a polity outside of the nation state. De Costa demonstrates a deliberate connection between the two: 'The Tent Embassy as a transnational indigenous movement demonstrates its domestic and international duality, "explicitly connecting Aboriginality to the main currents of world politics"'.[36]

There was a political connection between the domestic and the international that was commenced before *Koowarta*. Indeed, the *Koowarta* case was predicated on the legal connection between the domestic and international by the operation of the RDA. Indigenous peoples combined the political and the legal by connecting to the international. This turning to the international order was also being done simultaneously to challenging experiences of Indigenous peoples in the Anglo-Australian legal system.

Back to 1982: the completion of the journey home, to country, to law and its jurisprudence

The long stretch of straight road between Narromine and Trangie was coming to an end. The curve to the left that took us over the Goan waterhole – the place where my great grandmother camped – took us into Trangie. We were home. Even then I knew that hearing that story in the car was a significant point in my life. I am still passing on those stories of Mr Koowarta's bravery as told through my Mum and Nan.

Now, as an academic lawyer, I have different opportunities to inform the legal system of Indigenous experiences. Like Christine Black and John Borrows I had to tell the story of my jurisprudence.

---

[35]de Costa (2006), p 170.

[36]de Costa (2006), p 5.

Acknowledgements

Special thanks to Dr Ann Genovese, Cosima McCrae and the Melbourne Law School Law Library Research Service.

References

Primary Sources

Aboriginal Land Rights Act 1983 (NSW)
ILO Convention 107 – Indigenous and Tribal Populations Convention 1957
International Convention on the Elimination of All Forms of Racial Discrimination 1965
Koowarta v Bjelke-Petersen (1982) 153 CLR 168
Mabo v Queensland (No 2) (1992) 175 CLR 1
Racial Discrimination Act 1975 (Cth)
United Nations Declaration on the Rights of Indigenous Peoples 2007

Secondary Sources

Christine Black (2011) 'Maturing Australia Through Australian Aboriginal Narrative Law' 110(2) *South Atlantic Quarterly* 347. doi:10.1215/00382876-1162489

Christine Black et al (2007) 'Of The South' 16(2) *Griffith Law Review* 299. doi:10.1080/10383441.2007.10854592

Andrew Byrnes and Hilary Charlesworth (1985) 'Federalism and the International Legal Order: Recent Developments in Australia' 79 *American Journal of International Law* 622. doi:10.2307/2201890

Hilary Charlesworth (2002) 'International Law and Australian Law in the 21st Century' 6 *Newcastle Law Review* 1.

Ravi de Costa (2006) *Higher Authority*, UNSW Press.

Shaunnagh Dorsett and Shaun McVeigh (2012) *Jurisdiction*, Routledge.

Julie Evans et al (2013) 'Sovereignty: Frontiers of Possibility' in Julie Evans et al (eds) *Sovereignty: Frontiers of Possibility*, University of Hawai'i Press.

Nin Tomas (2013) 'Māori Concepts and Practices of *Rangatiratanga*' in Julie Evans et al (eds) *Sovereignty: Frontiers of Possibility*, University of Hawai'i Press.

Koowarta: a vital turning point for Aboriginal rights and Australia
Summing up the symposium

The Hon Michael Kirby AC CMG

Look up, my people
The Dawn is breaking
The World is waking
To a bright new day
Where none defame us
No restriction tame us
Nor colour shame us
Nor sneer dismay.
Kath Walker (Oodgeroo of the Nunuccal)

Song of Hope

A time for reflection

At the time of this symposium in May 2012, Australia faced another occasion for reflection about its Indigenous peoples and their relationship with the law. The country had before it (as it still does) the report of a panel on the desirability of change to the Australian Constitution, so as to re-express provisions relating to Aboriginal Australians and to insert a preamble, acknowledging their special place in our nation.[1] In ongoing fragile political circumstances would any referendum fail and thereby add discouragement to the hopes of Indigenous advancement?[2] Hope and fear of failure are the twin companions of this journey.

Looking backwards, it is now 45 years since, on 27 May 1967, a referendum was held that approved amendments to the Constitution to remove some of the provisions in the original document that were thought to discriminate against Aboriginals. The referendum was carried by the affirmative votes of the Australian electors.

[1]Expert Panel on Constitutional Recognition of Indigenous Australians (2012). The proposal is still under consideration at the time of publication.

[2]Note that, since 2012, the moves towards a constitutional amendment for Indigenous recognition have continued. In March 2014 the Australian government established a panel to conduct a review into public support for Indigenous constitutional recognition: Minister for Indigenous Affairs Media Release, 'Next Step Towards Indigenous Constitutional Recognition' http://minister.indigenous.gov.au/media/2014-03-28/next-step-towards-indigenous-constitutional-recognition, 28 March 2014.

Overwhelmingly they favoured the changes.[3] Optimistically, Australians hoped that the goodwill, signalled by such a positive vote, was a sign that a page had been turned forever in the history of this country. We hoped that, with one resolve, we could move beyond the past: beyond the 'the pain and sorrow'[4] of violence, dispossession, prejudice and disadvantage. We hoped that we would adopt new laws to protect the basic rights, dignity and economic wellbeing of the Indigenous people of Australia.

Since the referendum, and the resulting amendments to the Constitution,[5] there have been enactments and court decisions of great importance for the journey that Australians recognised they had to take. The national apology in the Federal Parliament in 2008 was an important high point, rich in symbolism and grace.[6] Similarly, amendments to state constitutions have been important high points – although the amendments have generally been premised on the express requirement that they do not give rise to justiciable rights.[7]

Court proceedings have provided a key opportunity for heroes from Indigenous communities to challenge legal injustice and thereby facilitate a modernisation of Australia's laws. Certain cases, and the heroes behind them, have left a permanent mark on the Australian Constitution and how the nation views itself. John Koowarta, Eddie Mabo, the Wik and their communities are examples of such heroes. In having the leadership, courage and determination to challenge indifference to inequality, these heroes have initiated a process of change beyond narrow power circles. They have played a vital role in instigating processes leading to reconciliation and greater equality for the Indigenous people of Australia.

Some of the court decisions since 1967 have not, in their result, proved favourable to the interests of Aboriginals. Of these, I would mention most particularly *Kartinyeri v Commonwealth* ('*Kartinyeri*'),[8] *Yorta Yorta v Victoria* ('*Yorta Yorta*')[9] and *Wurridjal v Commonwealth* ('*Wurridjal*'),[10] all decisions of the High Court of Australia. The first rejected Justice Lionel Murphy's historical view that the amendment to the Constitution, consequent on the 1967 referendum, when it empowered the Federal Parliament to make laws 'with respect to the people of any race ... *for* whom it is deemed necessary to make special laws' was to be read so that

[3]The referendum was carried in every state of Australia. The proposal received 89.3 per cent of all votes (and 90.8 per cent of valid votes nationally). This was over 10 per cent more than any other referendum before or since, see Blackshield and Williams (1998) p 1186.

[4]A reference to Oodgeroo of the Noonuccal and the report of National Aboriginal Day Observance Committee (1974).

[5]Effected by *Constitutional Alteration (Aboriginals) 1967* (Cth).

[6]Commonwealth of Australia (2008) *Parliamentary Debates*, House of Representatives, 13 February, 166–177 (The Hon. Kevin Rudd MP, Prime Minister). See also Rudd (2008).

[7]The following state constitutions have included the express requirement that amendments recognising Indigenous Australians do not give rise to justiciable rights: *Constitution Act 1975* (Vic) s 1A(3); *Constitution of Queensland 2001* (Qld) s 3A; *Constitution Act 1902* (NSW) s 2(3); *Constitution Act 1934* (SA) s 2(3). Note that the *Constitution Act 1889* (WA) and the *Constitution Act 1934* (Tas) have not been amended to recognise Indigenous Australians.

[8]*Kartinyeri v Commonwealth* (1998) 195 CLR 337.

[9]*Members of the Yorta Yorta Aboriginal Community v State of Victoria and Others* (2002) 214 CLR 422.

[10]*Wurridjal v Commonwealth* (2009) 237 CLR 309.

the words '*for* whom' were confined to mean 'for the benefit of whom' such laws were deemed necessary.[11] Only Gaudron J[12] and I[13] were attracted to such an interpretation. In *Yorta Yorta*, in joint reasons, Gaudron J and I dissented (as Black CJ had done in the federal court)[14] in relation to the way in which Aboriginals, claiming native title rights, could prove continuity of interest in the land of their forebears. And in *Wurridjal*, over my sole dissent, the High Court upheld the constitutional validity of the federal legislation authorising what has become known as the 'Northern Territory intervention'. This imposes special restrictions and controls on Aboriginals in that territory reminiscent of the special protectorates of the nineteenth century colonial patriarchy. By the time that case was decided, in 2009, Gaudron J had departed the High Court of Australia. As, indeed, I also soon myself did. *Wurridjal* was the last decision I made, and the last judgment delivered, as a Justice of the High Court.[15]

Despite these decisions, and doubtless many others, three judgments of the High Court since the referendum have generally been hailed, in Aboriginal and other circles, as advancing the legal and economic interests of Australia's Indigenous peoples. These were, first, *Koowarta v Bjelke-Petersen* ('*Koowarta*'),[16] which upheld the challenge to the validity of the actions of the Queensland government inconsistent with the *Aboriginal Land Fund Act 1974* (Cth) and the *Racial Discrimination Act 1975* (Cth) (RDA). Second, *Mabo v Queensland (No 2)* ('*Mabo No 2*'),[17] which upheld 'native title' as a legal possibility in the Australian system of land law. And, third, *Wik Peoples v Queensland* ('*Wik*'),[18] which endorsed the compatibility of 'native title', as upheld in *Mabo No 2* and given effect by federal legislation,[19] alongside pastoral leases over vast areas of the Australian continent, granted under state and territory laws, mostly prior to the decision in *Mabo No 2*.

The *Koowarta* decision was delivered 30 years ago, on 11 May 1982. The *Mabo No 2* decision was delivered on 3 June 1992, 20 years ago. The *Mabo No 2* decision is much better known than either *Koowarta* or *Wik*. On 7 May 2012, the Australian Broadcasting Corporation broadcast a special edition of its *Four Corners* program dedicated to reflections on *Mabo No 2*. Several university conferences on that decision have also been convened on the topic.[20] Yet, without the earlier decision of

[11]This opinion was first expressed by Murphy J. in *Koowarta v Bjelke-Petersen* (1982) 153 CLR 168. It was revisited in the *Hindmarsh Bridge* case but rejected by a majority.

[12]*Kartinyeri v Commonwealth* (1998) 195 CLR 337 at 367 [44].

[13]*Kartinyeri v Commonwealth* (1998) 195 CLR 337 at 411–414 [155]–[158].

[14]*Members of the Yorta Yorta Aboriginal Community v Victoria and Others* (2001) 110 FCR 244.

[15]*Wurridjal v Commonwealth* (2009) 237 CLR 309.

[16]*Koowarta v Bjelke-Petersen* (1982) 153 CLR 168.

[17]*Mabo v Queensland (No 2)* (1992) 175 CLR 1.

[18]*Wik Peoples v Queensland* (1996) 187 CLR 1.

[19]*Native Title Act 1993* (Cth).

[20]Including a conference on *Mabo* at the University of Queensland on 31 May 2012. A feature length film, 'Mabo', premiered in Sydney on 7 June 2012 as part of the Sydney Film Festival 2012.

the High Court in *Koowarta*, it is doubtful that the *Mabo No 2* decision, and particularly that in *Wik*, would have had much impact at all.

If, in *Koowarta*, the RDA had been held invalid, the protection of federal law against the threatened 'bucket loads' of extinguishment of native title would have been missing. The general principle in *Mabo No 2*, and the specific extension of the ruling in *Wik* to pastoral leases, would probably have been rendered nugatory. State and territory laws, and state executive action, would quickly have swept the dreams of native title into the dust can of lost hopes. Unless prevented by federal laws,[21] state laws and actions might have attempted to restore the *status quo ante*, before the suggested 'heresy' of Eddie Mabo's native title had arrived on the scene and spread like a wildflower in the Australian legal desert.

At this time of anniversaries, we should therefore remember Eddie Koiki Mabo and his struggles in the courts of Australia.[22] However, we should also remember the earlier struggles of John Koowarta to uphold the validity of the RDA. And to use that Act to strike down, as invalid, the inconsistent move of the government of Queensland Premier, Joh Bjelke-Petersen, to frustrate John Koowarta's search for legal rights in his traditional lands: rights potentially of great cultural importance to the spirits of the Winchyanam people from whom John Koowarta sprang. But also rights potentially important to the economic and social survival of Indigenous communities in the often hostile environment of contemporary Australia.

The *Koowarta* case

The people behind the great test cases that come to the highest courts in the land are rarely, if ever, known to the judges or, indeed, to the general community. When they have died, respect must be paid to sensibilities and religious customs and to the inhibitions that exist, in some Aboriginal circles, upon reproducing their photographs and images.

Eddie Koiki Mabo is such an important figure in the history of Australia that it is inevitable that books, filmed documentaries and even feature films will portray him and his family for us to look at his real or simulated features. As is well known, although Eddie Mabo lived to see the first decision of the High Court in his long litigious saga,[23] he died just a few months before the announcement of the second decision that will forever carry his name into the history books. We listen to Eddie Mabo's story and that of his people. We stare at his image and at the actors as they attempt to reproduce his determination, strength and resilience. Although justice in his case came after his death, he had already won a number of moral victories against discrimination on the grounds of his race. And the same is true of John Koowarta.

There is much less public knowledge of this earlier hero in the struggle of Australia's Indigenous peoples to establish legal entitlements over their traditional

[21]Or unless the federal law was suspended as provided by the *Northern Territory National Emergency Response Act 2007* (Cth). See *Wurridjal v Commonwealth* (2009) 237 CLR 309 at 372–375 [133]–[143] and 432–434 [332]–[340].

[22]Told in Keon-Cohen (2011).

[23]*Mabo v Queensland* (1988) 166 CLR 186 ('*Mabo No 1*').

lands. However, Marcia Langton has begun the process of correcting this gap in our knowledge.[24] She has explained the derivation of his name and the links that his name gives to the leech and the dingo; symbols that John Koowarta embraced and affirmed.

John Koowarta wanted support from the Aboriginal Land Fund Commission (ALFC). That body had been established under federal law, enacted by the Federal Parliament, with bipartisan support, during the Whitlam government. John Koowarta asked the ALFC to purchase a pastoral lease in North Queensland, on the Archer River in the Wik country. Neither John Koowarta nor his community had the capital to acquire the holding. However, the ALFC had been established to support this process. He and other members of the clan requested the commission to acquire the lease so as to enable the land to be used by and for the members of his clan for their traditional purposes and for their immediate contemporary livelihood. The commission acceded to this request and set about allocating funds to permit the request to be fulfilled.

The ALFC was comprised of resolute members, five in number; three were of Aboriginal descent and two were not. However, there was no recorded disagreement within the commission about affording the funds necessary to fulfil John Koowarta's dream. The excellent and detailed examination in this special issue of *Griffith Law Review* by Associate Professor Alexander Reilly[25] of the University of Adelaide Law School, has explains the struggle that then unfolded between the commission and officials of the government of Queensland, led by Premier Bjelke-Petersen. This is a story of the bricks and mortar necessary for the advancement of the dignity and legal and economic entitlements of Indigenous peoples in Australia.

Under s 4(2) of the *Land Act 1962* (Qld) any sale or transfer of the Archer River pastoral holding was subject to the veto of the Minister for Lands of the State of Queensland. The solicitors for the ALFC secured approval to the transfer of the then leases. They then sought the Minister's permission for the transfer. In the optimistic times that had followed the referendum on Aboriginal rights in 1967, the creation of the commission, the appropriation of federal funds, the agreement of the current land holder and the desires of John Koowarta, there was an air of optimism and expectation that the Minister's approval would be forthcoming.

However, in June 1976, the government officials of Queensland indicated that the Minister had rejected the transfer. He withheld his permission. He was pressed for reasons, which he took a long time to deliver. This showed once again the unreasonableness of permitting officials, acting under statutory power, a legal exemption from the obligation to provide reasons for their official acts.[26] The politics of the situation, rather than the state of the common or statute law, ultimately forced the Minister to provide reasons. Those reasons were blunt:

> The question of the proposed acquisition of Archer River Pastoral Holdings comes within the ambit of declared Government policy expressed in cabinet decisions of September 1972, which stated – 'The Queensland Government does not view favourably

---

[24]Langton (2014).

[25]Reilly (2014).

[26]*Public Service Board of NSW v Osmond* (1986) 159 CLR 656, reversing *Osmond v Public Service Board of NSW* [1984] 3 NSWLR 477(CA).

proposals to acquire large areas of additional freehold or leasehold land for development by Aborigines or Aboriginal groups in isolation'.[27]

Because this stated policy had been affirmed and reaffirmed by the Queensland Cabinet, John Koowarta concluded that he and his community were being denied an entitlement by reason of their Aboriginal race, colour or ethnic origin. Guided by excellent lawyers, led by the late Ron Castan QC of the Melbourne Bar (who was later also to act for Eddie Mabo), John Koowarta decided to initiate proceedings in the High Court of Australia, invoking the RDA. This federal enactment makes any discriminatory acts based on racial grounds illegal.

John Koowarta's action immediately led the State of Queensland, for its part, to challenge the constitutional validity of the RDA. That challenge, in turn, led Mr Koowarta to argue that the Act was valid as a special law based on the races power (s 51[xxvi]), as it had been amended in the 1967 referendum. He also based his argument on the external affairs power (s 51[xxix]) in the Australian Constitution.

A majority of the High Court (Gibbs CJ with Stephen, Aicken and Wilson JJ) rejected John Koowarta's reliance on the races power. However, another majority (Stephen, Mason, Murphy and Brennan JJ) upheld the validity of the RDA based on the external affairs power. They did so for reasons which they severally expressed.

The narrowest expression was that of Stephen J whose vote was to prove determinative. It was to the effect that 'external affairs' in the Constitution included reference to the public engagement of the national government with other nations, things or circumstances outside Australia. Justice Stephen held that it was not enough that a challenged law should give effect to a treaty obligation. Nor was it necessarily excluded because the subject was not one provided for expressly in a treaty to which Australia was a party.[28] By referring to developments occurring in international law since the 1945 United Nations Charter, Stephen J recognised the growing significance for international law of the global prohibition upon racial discrimination. Following World War II, such prohibition was a central purpose of international law. As he put it: '[It is a purpose] which, more than any other, dominates the thoughts and actions of the post-World War II world'.[29] A similar point was later to be made by Brennan J in *Mabo No 2* when explaining and justifying his decision and giving reasons in that case.[30]

Normally, judges, lawyers and the public generally are afforded few insights into the modes of thinking of decision-makers in courts such as the High Court of Australia, other than those provided by the written reasons delivered by the justices in support of the orders that they propose on judgment day. In *Mabo No 2*, however, a few tiny glimmers of extra light were provided as to his reasoning and approach by former Chief Justice, Sir Anthony Mason, in an interview that he recently granted to

[27]*Koowarta v Bjelke-Petersen* (1982) 153 CLR 168 at 20 (Gibbs CJ).

[28]*Koowarta v Bjelke-Petersen* (1982) 153 CLR 168 at 217–218.

[29]*Koowarta v Bjelke-Petersen* (1982) 153 CLR 168 at 220.

[30]*Mabo v Queensland (No 2)* (1992) 175 CLR 1 at 42: 'It is contrary both to international standards and to the fundamental values of our common law to entrench a discriminatory rule which, because of the supposed position on the scale of social organisation of the indigenous inhabitants of a settled colony, denies them a right to occupy their traditional land. See also *Advisory Opinion on Western Sahara* [1975] ICJR at 39, 85–86.

the *Four Corners* team. In the case of John Koowarta's proceedings, a small number of additional clues have been provided by Professor Hilary Charlesworth, Director of the Centre for International Governance and Justice and Professor & ARC Laureate Fellow at ANU College of Asia and the Pacific and ANU College of Law.[31]

When *Koowarta* was decided, Professor Charlesworth was serving as one of the Associates (clerks) to Stephen J. Justice Stephen's appointment as Governor-General of Australia, to succeed Sir Zelman Cowen, had already been announced by Prime Minister Malcolm Fraser at the time of argument in *Koowarta.* With customary propriety, Stephen J offered to stand aside if any party objected to his participation in the *Koowarta* case. None did. As we now know, had the Queensland government objected, legal history would have been different. The *Koowarta* ruling, upholding the validity of the RDA on the basis of the external affairs power, would not have been made, at least at that time. Absent an established foundation for the validity of that Act, the Queensland government's veto would arguably have stood. Absent a later, equivalent ruling, the barrier revealed in *Koowarta* against unfavourable state government or territorial laws or executive actions, unfavourable to Australia's Aboriginals by reference to their race, might well have been legally valid.

In the High Court chambers, the young Hilary Charlesworth endeavoured unsuccessfully to persuade Stephen J to change his view that the validity of the federal RDA could not be founded in the basis of the races power under the Constitution. However, her early interest in international law was stimulated by the broad view that Stephen J took of the developing head of constitutional power relevant to that topic. And of the sheer necessity, in the modern world, of arming the federal government and parliament in Australia with full and appropriate powers to deal effectively with the international community, by treaty and otherwise, and with the growing body of global laws.

The fascination with international law, nurtured in the Stephen chambers in Canberra, was to lead Hilary Charlesworth into a distinguished career as a professor of international law. This was recognised most recently by her appointment as a judge *ad hoc* of the International Court of Justice.[32] She contests that there was any disparity between the essential reasoning for the ambit of the external affairs power given by Stephen J and that offered by Mason, Murphy and Brennan JJ. Basically, all of them were sympathetic to the necessities of Australia's playing a full role as a member of the emerging system of law. All of them were attentive to the impact of international law on domestic (including constitutional) law. All of them appreciated the obligations of the new world legal order to safeguard peace and security, by defending universal human rights at home and abroad. After the Holocaust and the repeated instances of racial genocide, the majority of the justices of the High Court of Australia were aware that this was at the very core of international law; that

---

[31]Charlesworth (2014).

[32]Hilary Charlesworth was chosen to sit as judge *ad hoc* in *Whaling in the Antarctic (Australia v Japan) (Judgment)* [2014] ICJ Rep 1. See also joint media release: Attorney General and Minister for Foreign Affairs, 'Australian appointed to International Court of Justice for Australia's whaling case against Japan' http://foreignminister.gov.au/releases/Pages/2011/kr_mr_110325a.aspx?ministerid=2, 25 March 2011.

Australia could not be a full participant in the new world order, combating racism, if it were missing from the table because of any constitutional incapacity.

As Professor Charlesworth has observed, the events since the *Koowarta* decision of the High Court have not borne out the optimistic predictions about the relationship between Australia's constitutional law and international law back in 1982, particularly the international law of human rights.[33] Still, the decisions of the High Court of Australia since *Koowarta* have generally supported the broad ambit of that head of power. They have done so notwithstanding its potential to undermine some of the federal attributes of our Constitution.[34]

The lines drawn by the High Court to mark off the *permissible* ambit of external affairs from the *impermissible* are often disputed and sometimes disputable.[35] There is, of course, a point beyond which the external affairs power cannot be pushed, appearing as it does in a constitution whose federal character is an essential and over-arching theme. But the importance of the *Koowarta* case was that it upheld the deployment of the external affairs power in our constitution in a matter that directly impacted upon the laws and executive activities of state governments. And it did so in the context of basic human rights that had previously been seen as essentially ones of purely national and domestic concerns. Because there will be no going back on this wider vision of the Australian Constitution and its engagement in the world, John Koowarta left an indelible mark on the Constitution. The same was true in Eddie Mabo's case. These insights, necessary to their cases in the High Court, were to prove yet another gift of the Indigenous people to the modernisation of Australia's laws and of the nation's view of itself.

The risks of test cases

John Koowarta's test case, like the later proceedings of the *Wik* case that it foreshadowed, was decided by the narrowest of margins in the High Court: four Justices to three.

---

[33]See Charlesworth (2014); cf *Al Kateb v Godwin* (2004) 219 CLR 562 at 589–594 [62]–[72] (McHugh J), at 617–630 [152]–[191] (Kirby J); see also *Roach v Electoral Commission* (2007) 233 CLR 162 at 177–179[13]–[19] (Gleeson CJ), at 224–226[181]–[182] (Heydon J).

[34]See, for example, *XYZ v Commonwealth* (2006) 227 CLR 532; *Vasiljkovic v Commonwealth* (2006) 227 CLR 614; *Thomas v Mowbray* (2007) 233 CLR 307; *R. v Wei Tang* (2008) 237 CLR 1 at 40 [84].

[35]See, for example, *XYZ v Commonwealth* (2006) 227 CLR 532 at 612 [226] (Callinan and Heydon JJ); *Thomas v Mowbray* (2007) 233 CLR 307 at 402–411 [269]–[294] (Kirby J); see also *New South Wales v Commonwealth* [2006] 229 CLR 1 ('*Work Choices*' case). The industrial relations power in the Australian Constitution s 51(xxxv), like the acquisitions power in s 51(xxxi), is conferred subject to a condition. In the first category it is that disputes must be settled by the independent process of conciliation and arbitration. In the second, it is that property may only be acquired 'on just terms'. At least since 1921, the High Court of Australia has insisted upon an ample and plenary interpretation of the grants of federal power, without inhibitions adopted by reference to implied or reserved powers of the states said to arise from federalism, see *Amalgamated Society of Engineers v Adelaide Steamship Co Ltd* (1920) 28 CLR 129; (1921) 29 CLR 406 (PC). However, previously it had been settled law that the *Engineers* doctrine was modified where the constitutional power was granted subject to a condition. This, and much else, proved unpersuasive to the majority in the *Work Choices* case, see at 208 [494] ff.

Over the years there have been many similar outcomes where the composition of the court at a particular time has been vital to the outcome of a case. The *Wik* case came up for decision in 1996, the first year of my appointment to the High Court. Had another nominated lawyer been appointed in my stead, the outcome might have been different. Legal formalists often like to believe, and even teach, that the law is wholly objective; that its discipline is a pure science; that outcomes are always predetermined. However, experience in Australia, as elsewhere, often shows the contrary. Appointments, especially to a final national and constitutional court, are therefore always important. As Professor Julius Stone, my great law teacher demonstrated in my youth, judges, especially appellate judges, and particularly justices of the High Court, necessarily give effect to legal values in their decisions. Their approaches, opinions and life experiences inevitably influence the outcome of their cases. This happens when the judges are faced (through ambiguity or imprecision) with 'leeways for choice' that they must resolve in deciding a case.[36]

This is why the Australian Constitution, like that of other common law countries, rightly reserves the appointment of judges to the elected executive government. It is in this way that governments, reflecting the changing values and aspirations of the Australian people over time, influence judicial outcomes long after the appointing ministers have departed the Treasury benches. Far from being illicit or objectionable, this is exactly how the Constitution is meant to work. Party political allegiance is, and should be, irrelevant to judicial appointment. But values and philosophy are the very essence of the judicial role.

In Australia, conservative federal governments generally know this well. They give effect to it without embarrassment. It was Deputy Prime Minister Tim Fischer who, after attacking the majority of the High Court for its decision in the *Wik* case, called bluntly for the appointment of 'capital C conservative[s]'.[37] This was a call that was fulfilled. On the other hand, governments of the Australian Labor Party have frequently been neglectful, apologetic or casual about the power of judicial appointment. Of course, it is usually easier to find 'capital C conservatives' amongst appointable lawyers than it is to find candidates who are, or have become, liberals and legal realists. And, in any case, Labor governments can sometimes be more conservative over values than Coalition ones, as we all know.

With the departure of Justices Gummow, Heydon and Crennan from the High Court of Australia, three vacancies arise which will have to be filled. By our traditions, once the vacancies are filled, the appointed judges have nothing to do with politics or politicians. Yet *Koowarta*, *Mabo No 2*, *Wik* and countless other cases, before and since, reveal the importance of every appointment to the High Court and to other superior courts in Australia. The importance is magnified in Australia because the final court comprises but seven human actors. This is smaller than every equivalent national final court, save for New Zealand. Of course, some Labor appointees, after their appointment, turn out to be legal conservatives and formalists. Some Coalition appointments emerge as strong liberals and legal realists. But the point I make is that there is no escaping the importance of the constitutional

[36]Stone (1946); see also Stone (1966), p 649.

[37]Tim Fischer quoted in *The Age*, 6 March 1997, p A6; *Courier Mail* 5 March 1997, p 1; *Canberra Times*, 8 March 1997, p 17; cf Kirby (1998), p 605.

power of judicial appointment. If a single one of the majority participating judges in *Koowarta* or *Wik* had held a contrary view, the history of the legal rights of Aboriginal Australians would have been significantly different.

It is this fact that demonstrates how risky test cases can sometimes be for advancing the interests of Aboriginal Australians, including in the High Court. Not only is much dependent on the judges. Much also depends on the other actors in the drama. John Koowarta and Eddie Mabo were fortunate to have had the services of Ron Castan and his team of lawyers. The Wik peoples were fortunate in the advocacy of Walter Sofronoff, Sir Maurice Byers, J.W. Greenwood and their team. This is not to say that the opponents were poorly represented; quite the contrary. But governments and wealthy interests can usually secure top lawyers. Vulnerable litigants, with few resources, are often dependent on *pro bono* lawyers who are willing to discount, or waive, their fees and to act in the interest of their vision of justice.

Another risk in the equation is sometimes presented by the approaches of governments and other actors in the administration of public institutions.[38] We now know how important, in the *Koowarta* case, was the decision of the ALFC to exercise its powers in support of John Koowarta and his community. According to recent research, the commission faced not only the vehement opposition of the Queensland government against what it saw as the Trojan horse of international ideas invading their constitutional space. It also felt pressure from the Minister for Aboriginal Affairs in the Fraser government seeking to reduce the tensions over Aboriginal rights that were emerging in Queensland. This was especially significant because of the provisions of their statute, which obliged the ALFC to carry out the performance of its functions 'under the general direction of the Minister'.[39] Presumably because the political pressure was never formalised as a legal direction, the commission stuck to its guns. It pressed on with its challenge. And then the federal government's lawyers felt obliged, as the Commonwealth usually does, to intervene to support the constitutional validity of what the commission was seeking to do. Which is what then happened.

Counter factual speculation is possible. What if the federal Minister had given a direction to the ALFC to back off, so as to avoid political confrontation with Queensland? What if the commission, by its statute, had not included a majority of Aboriginal members? What if those members had lacked the courage and determination to press on with, and to fund, the constitutional challenge to the Queensland government's stance? Once again, the risks of a test case are revealed. Courage, determination, means and luck are vital ingredients for success.

The timing of litigation, as of legislation, can also be vital. The setting for the significant decisions in *Koowarta, Mabo No 2* and *Wik* was undoubtedly fixed by the overwhelming vote of the electors in the 1967 constitutional referendum. This created a new national Zeitgeist – a spirit of the times in the law – to which at least a majority of the justices were not impervious.

---

[38] Reilly (2014).

[39] *Aboriginal Land Fund Act1974* (Cth) s 5(2): 'The Commission shall perform its functions in accordance with any general directions given by the Minister'.

Some Aboriginal leaders have been critical about other ill-timed and poorly mounted challenges presented by private individuals, such as in *Coe v Commonwealth*.[40] The litigation that challenged the Northern Territory intervention has also been questioned, on the basis that it was doomed to fail, as legally it did. On the other hand, there may sometimes be merit in a challenge to orthodoxy by individuals approaching the independent courts. The political process in Australia is now substantially controlled by the ever dwindling numbers of Australians who join the major political parties. Because of the power that they exert over elective government, a disjuncture exists between democratic theory and political power realities.[41] The right of individuals to subject public power to questioning, and to public and legal scrutiny, is an important feature of freedom. I am far from convinced that the *Wurridjal* case, which contested the constitutional validity of the Northern Territory intervention, was ill conceived or untimely. The decision and the dissent stand, at least, as a sharp reminder of the vulnerability of Australia's Indigenous people to the invocation of the Constitution, as it is presently interpreted, in ways that specially disadvantage the rights of Aboriginals when compared to those of every other race or ethnicity in the nation. When important principles are involved, the symbolism of subjecting power to judicial accountability can be potent, at least in the long term. So it will prove in due time with the Northern Territory intervention.

Judicial or political?

Just the same, Eddie Mabo died before his challenge to the rejection of land rights was finally decided. Although John Koowarta succeeded before the High Court, his family's claims to their land were effectively stymied for a time by designation of the land as a national park and by manoeuvres that occurred both before and after his death in 1991. In fact, it was not until 2011 that Premier Anna Bligh in Queensland confirmed the decision to revoke a section of the Mungka Kadju National Park, in preparation for its return to John Koowarta's community. And her successor, Premier Campbell Newman, has recently concluded this legal process by presenting the title documents to John Koowarta's community. It took 30 years to vindicate the success that John Koowarta won in the High Court. But finally it happened.

Nicole Watson, a law lecturer and a member of the Birri Gubba people, has asked a pertinent question: why should Australia's Aboriginal people place their trust in a legal and judicial process that rarely delivers justice that is either practical or timely?[42] She points out that, in the aftermath of *Mabo No 2*, *Yorta Yorta* and other decisions, actual access by Aboriginal Australian's to economic benefits from 'native title' has been very difficult to attain. It has been problematic to prove,

---

[40] *Coe v Commonwealth* (1993) 118 ALR 193 (Wiradjuri claim); *Coe v Commonwealth of Australia and Government of the United Kingdom* (1978) 18 ALR 592; *Coe v Commonwealth* (1979) 24 ALR 118.

[41] Mason (2005) p 69; cf Kirby (2006) pp 312–313.

[42] Watson (2014).

expensive to litigate and contested by powerful interests in the mining and extractive industries; as well as divisive within Indigenous communities themselves.[43]

Given the dimension of the disadvantages still so clearly faced by urban, regional, rural and remote communities of Aboriginal Australians, why should economic *benefits* accrue to a comparative few just because of the chance consideration of provable ancestry, where the *burdens* in terms of health, housing, education and imprisonment rates are so widespread? Was a different solution to Australia's poor record of Indigenous disadvantage not possible? Has the attainment of that different approach been set back, rather than advanced, by the well meaning interventions of the courts in *Koowarta, Mabo No 2* and *Wik*? These are serious questions. They demand an answer.

If, in the heady aftermath of the 1967 referendum, we were starting again, what would hindsight suggest that we should have done in Australia? Probably, our parliament should have struck with bold legislation while the iron was hot. We should have moved quickly to include a preambular acknowledgement of the Aboriginal and Indigenous peoples in the Australian Constitution. Embarked on a process to create a properly representative, national body of all Australia's Indigenes. Plunged into a negotiation of a treaty which, after all, was common British practice with dispossessed peoples or their princes even in Canada and the American settlements. This would probably have happened but for the mistaken belief of the early governors and settlers that Australia was *terra nullius*. Any such treaty would have addressed the material disadvantages of the Indigenous peoples, viewed as a whole and from a perspective of a comparison with the majority population.

In a proper exercise to respect the self determination, promised to every 'people' by international law,[44] Australians should probably have created a much larger body with greater resources than the ALFC. One with proper powers to establish a national equality fund, designed to improve rapidly the conditions of all of this country's Aboriginals and Torres Strait Islanders. By this I mean all, not just those who could trace their ancestry's claims to identified undemised Crown land. With goodwill and great effort, had we done these things immediately after the 1967 referendum, we would probably now be much further advanced. A return to paternalistic, unconsulted, impositions such as the Northern Territory intervention would then probably have been unnecessary. With a little luck, we might have been able to consign the races power in our Constitution to the historic relic that it represents.

But we did none of these things.

This was *despite* (or perhaps even *because of*) the fact that Australia was one of the oldest electoral democracies in the world, with forms of responsible government dating back at least to 1856, and with legislatures created even earlier. We were paralysed by substantial inertia and hostility that remained just below the surface.

Courts do not initiate litigation. Except in plainly hopeless cases, they have very limited power to rebuff it. This is the background against which we must understand the initiatives taken by the courts in *Koowarta*, *Mabo No 2* and *Wik*. The courts

[43]Langton (2014).

[44]See, for example, *International Covenant on Civil and Political Rights* 1966, Art 1; *International Covenanton Economic Social and Cultural Rights* 1966, Art 1; see also now *United Nations Convention on the Rights of Indigenous People 2007*.

simply respond to cases brought to them for decision by others. Under our conventions, courts could not respond to such claims by conceiving and substituting a better one. And so we entered into the era of land rights cases and highly complex legislation. That is where we now find ourselves. Our solution may not address generically the burden of Aboriginal disadvantage. Yet to John Koowarta, Eddie Mabo, the Wik, and their communities, recognition of their land rights has been both precious and long overdue.

The benefits of native title may have proved divisive – and certainly they were less than a panacea for the variety of Indigenous peoples often in desperate need. Still there is no doubt that the discovery and affirmation of native title found in *Mabo No 2*, protected from extinguishment by the ruling in *Koowarta*, and extended and clarified in *Wik*, did advance the civil, community and economic interests of Australia's Indigenous peoples. Associate Professor Maureen Tehan[45] illustrates this truth by reference to lines on the map of the continent, drawn from her long experience with the Pitjantjatjara and Ngaanyatjatjarra peoples. Very large segments of the Australian land mass are now subject to recognised native title claims. These may not yet – or ever – embrace the majority of our Indigenous peoples. But they do extend to many. Judicial consideration of the outstanding claims is continuing. Responsibility, power and economic benefits are flowing to native title owners and the communities they serve. Whilst it is true that some Indigenous people have had it lucky, that is a common feature of life for the rest of Australia's citizens. In Professor Tehan's word, for a legal practitioner like her in the 1980s, working in remote communities, the decision in *Koowarta* was the first step. It changed the lawyers' 'toolbox', though its impact was to prove varied and, sometimes, paradoxical.

But sadly, the Federal Parliaments and governments failed to follow up *Koowarta* and to introduce a grand national response. The hope of the early days was replaced by a resuscitation of the permit system, upheld in *Gehardy v Brown*.[46] This was followed by special liquor and other controls of a distinctly paternalistic kind – culminating in the Northern Territory intervention. Viewed in this context, the continued journey taken by the courts in recognising and upholding native title rights is scarcely surprising. Courts in Australia are law-makers, but only in the minor key. They are limited to resolving the legal cases brought through their doors. They cannot invent or change the cases brought to them. But they can bring their independent powers to bear in deciding them.

Nicole Watson says that she yearns for the activism of the Tent Embassy in Canberra, for street protests and political action by Aboriginal leaders. No one would doubt the importance of such initiatives. They will certainly continue in Australia. But the inescapable fact for the tiny fraction of Australians who are, and identify as, Indigenous, in a population often indifferent and sometimes hostile, is that there must be space for both political and legal initiatives. The question is not either/or. Each process has its advantages and disadvantages. Whilst the disadvantages of costs, delays and follow up of court orders are illustrated in *Koowarta*, *Mabo No 2*, and *Wik* the advantages, as shown by a number of leading cases, are many:

---

[45]Tehan (2014).

[46]*Gerhardy v Brown* (1985) 159 CLR 70.

- they initiate a process of change which lies outside the compromises and deals effected by those who wield the levers of power in the narrow circle of purely political activism;
- at their core lie the judicial institutions of a free society. They can draw upon earlier judicial principles to uphold notions of liberty and equality that do not necessarily bend to the pressures of party power-play and political influence;
- courts introduce a random element into the power dynamic. They do this precisely because their process can be initiated by private individuals beyond the 'usual suspects' of partisan political activists and because they cannot be controlled by politicians;
- courts are more likely to be influenced by notions of justice, equality and principle than the forces of compromise that influence and control purely political decisions;
- courts can enforce their orders and generally their decisions will eventually be obeyed and upheld in Australia, both for legal and political reasons; and
- courts inject into political discourse decisions which themselves then interact with politics. Judgments can necessitate prompt legislative action, just as the *Mabo No 2* and *Wik* decisions of the High Court of Australia led to immediate legislative action on the part of the Federal Parliament.

It is natural for judges and lawyers like me to want to think optimistically about their discipline and its institutions. Some of this euphoria must give way to realism and to the changing moods of different decades. Nevertheless, we should not write off the courts of Australia as continuing, significant players in the process leading to reconciliation, justice and greater equality for Australia's Indigenous peoples. The record of the courts is patchy, it is true. But the stories of empowerment told by Aboriginal Australians who were acquainted with the decisions in *Koowarta*, *Mabo No 2* and *Wik*[47] reveal how greatly court decisions can act as a personal catalyst. They can help to mobilise self confidence and pride in the leadership and courage of heroes who have gone before. And they can re-enforce a determination to continue and extend their efforts. Large struggles usually come on multiple fronts. Although the courts will sometimes fail, in Australia they cannot be ignored nor are they destined always to disappoint. The record of the past 30 years since *Koowarta*, and that decision itself with *Mabo No 2* and *Wik*, establish the contrary.

Rallying points and new initiatives

A reflection on the 45 years since the referendum, the 30 years since *Koowarta* and the 20 years since *Mabo No 2* shows, I suggest, this much. Progress in Aboriginal advancement in Australia remains painfully slow. A symbol of this fact can be found in the hugely disproportionate rates of imprisonment of Aboriginal citizens, especially the young. Although Aboriginals are just over 2.2 per cent of the population they are 50 per cent of those in the juvenile justice system.[48] So shocking are these statistics that, exceptionally, the Governor of New South Wales (Professor

[47]Such as was mentioned by McMillan (2014).
[48]Susskind (2012).

Marie Bashir), used her office to convene and encourage fellow citizens who demanded action, fresh and radical thinking, and real change.[49]

We recognise now that the issues affecting Aboriginal citizens are interrelated, not neatly divided like different departmental and ministerial responsibilities. Homelessness and poor housing is connected with problems of nutrition and access to clean water. These deprivations, in turn, are related to the Aboriginal health crisis. The health impediments are interrelated with poor educational opportunities, truancy and despair. Australians of goodwill on all sides of politics want to see action. But the landscape is messy. Initiatives are often disappointing in their outcomes and counterproductive in their execution. In these circumstances, there is both room and a need for multiple initiatives from all branches of government – legislative, executive and judicial – and from the private sector, the educational institutions, the churches and civil society. Above all from Indigenous peoples themselves, from whom must come the solutions to endemic disadvantage, that the rest of the population can support and sustain.

Despite the doctrinal quandaries[50] and the occasional deficiency of the judicial decisions in Australia concerning Aboriginals, the fact remains that court proceedings and their aftermath have constituted an important opportunity for heroes who have emerged from the Indigenous communities and been recognised, in full dignity, by their fellow citizens because they have refused to accept indifference and hostility as an answer to legal injustice.

John Koowarta was such a hero. So was Eddie Mabo. So were the Wik. And there are other heroes; many of their faces were seen in the recent documentary about the negotiations that followed the *Mabo No 2* decision of the High Court. Lowitja O'Donoghue was there at that time. There have been others. Marcia Langton, Roberta Sykes, Mick and Patrick Dodson, Larissa Behrendt, Tom Calma, Noel Pearson and many others.

Increasing numbers of younger heroes are now entering the legal and academic professions. Political action is essential. Legal action and court judgments can also occasionally quicken the pace. Theoretical and conceptual analysis of where we are, where we have come from, and where we might be in another 30 years is critical. This is the role for everyone to play in this long drawn-out journey. For example, ideas for future political and judicial action in Australia will surely come from the reports and recommendations of Megan Davis – a young hero. She was recently elected by the General Assembly of the United Nations as special rapporteur for the world on Indigenous peoples. We should listen to her and learn from her reports. But you will search the newsprint and electronic media for any report of this appointment, notable for Australia, and a compliment to its Indigenous community.

Above all, it is necessary for Aboriginals themselves to speak out; and to be listened to respectfully, attentively. I hope that, in my lifetime, I do not see another initiative like the Northern Territory intervention. This was pressed forward with suspect motives, within eight weeks of a federal election and with no consultation in its design with the Aboriginal peoples and the Indigenous communities most

[49]The Governor of New South Wales, H.E. Professor Marie Bashir, convened the launch of an initiative at Government House Sydney on 2 May 2012.

[50]This is pointed out by Brennan and Davis (2014).

affected, despite the recommendation that consultation was an absolute prerequisite for an effective and just initiative.[51]

To the heroes of Indigenous Australians of the past – John Koowarta and Eddie Koiki Mabo, and other brothers and sisters – honour and praise. To the heroes who struggled but did not succeed – respect and thanks for standing your ground. To the heroes still amongst us – encourage and recommitment. To the heroes yet to come – a song of hope.

See plain the promise
Dark freedom-lover!
Night's nearly over
And though long the climb
New rights will greet us
New mateship meet us
And joy complete us
In our new Dream Time.

To our father's fathers
The pain, the sorrow.
To our children's children
The bright tomorrow

Song of Hope

Acknowledgements

The author acknowledges the use of comments of two anonymous reviewers.

References

Primary sources

Australian cases

Al Kateb v Godwin (2004) 219 CLR 562
Amalgamated Society of Engineers v Adelaide Steamship Co Ltd (1920) 28 CLR 129
Coe v Commonwealth (1979) 24 ALR 118
Coe v Commonwealth (1993) 118 ALR 193
Coe v Commonwealth of Australia and Government of the United Kingdom (1978) 18 ALR 592
Gerhardy v Brown (1985) 159 CLR 70
Kartinyeri v Commonwealth (1998) 195 CLR 337
Koowarta v Bjelke-Petersen (1982) 153 CLR 168
Mabo v Queensland (No 1) (1988) 166 CLR 186
Mabo v Queensland (No 2) (1992) 175 CLR 1
Members of the Yorta Yorta Aboriginal Community v State of Victoria and Others (2001) 110 FCR 244
Members of the Yorta Yorta Aboriginal Community v State of Victoria and Others (2002) 214 CLR 422

[51]For a discussion of the Northern Territory Board of Inquiry's Report on the Protection of Aboriginal Children from Sexual Abuse, *Ampe Akelyernemane Meke Mekarle – Little Children Are Sacred*, see *Wurridjal v Commonwealth* (2009) 237 CLR 309 at 398–399 [226]–[232]. Full consultation with the Aboriginal communities affected was a central part of the recommendation of the Northern Territory Committee of Enquiry, whose report was purportedly the trigger for the Northern Territory intervention.

New South Wales v Commonwealth [2006] 229 CLR 1
Osmond v Public Service Board of NSW [1984] 3 NSWLR 477(CA)
Public Service Board of NSW v Osmond (1986) 159 CLR 656
R v Wei Tang (2008) 237 CLR 1
Roach v Electoral Commission (2007) 233 CLR 162
Thomas v Mowbray (2007) 233 CLR 307
Vasiljkovic v Commonwealth (2006) 227 CLR 614.
Wik Peoples v Queensland (1996) 187 CLR 1
Wurridjal v Commonwealth (2009) 237 CLR 309
XYZ v Commonwealth (2006) 227 CLR 532

International cases
Advisory Opinion on Western Sahara [1975] ICJR
Whaling in the Antarctic (Australia v Japan) (Judgment) [2014] ICJ Rep 1

Legislation
Aboriginal Land Fund Act 1974 (Cth)
Constitution Act 1902 (NSW)
Constitution of Queensland 2001 (Qld)
Constitution Act 1934 (SA)
Constitution Act 1934 (Tas)
Constitution Act 1975 (Vic)
Constitution Act 1889 (WA)
Constitutional Alteration (Aboriginals)1967 (Cth)
Land Act 1962 (Qld)
Native Title Act 1993 (Cth)
Northern Territory National Emergency Response Act 2007 (Cth)

Parliamentary debates
Commonwealth of Australia (2008) *Parliamentary Debates*, House of Representatives, 13 February

International instruments
International Covenant on Civil and Political Rights 1966
International Covenant on Economic Social and Cultural Rights 1966
United Nations Charter 1945
United Nations Convention on the Rights of Indigenous People 2007

Secondary sources

Tony Blackshield and George Williams (1998) *Australian Constitutional Law and Theory: Commentary and Materials*, 2nd edition, Federation Press.
Hilary Charlesworth (2014) 'Internal and External Affairs: The *Koowarta* Case in Context' 23(1) *Griffith Law Review* 35.
Expert Panel on Constitutional Recognition of Indigenous Australians (2012) *Recognising Aboriginal and Torres Strait Islander Peoples in the Constitution*
Sean Brennan and Megan Davis (2014) '*Koowarta*: Constitutional Landmark, Transition Point or Missed Opportunity? 23(1) *Griffith Law Review* 79.
Bryan Keon-Cohen (2011) *Mabo in the Courts – Islander Tradition to Native Title – A Memoir*, Chancery Bold.
Michael Kirby (1998) 'Attacks on Judges – A Universal Phenomenon' 72 *Australian Law Journal* 599.
Michael Kirby (2006) 'Law Reform, Human Rights and Modern Governance: Australia's Debt to Lord Scarman' 80 *Australian Law Journal* 299.
Marcia Langton (2012) 'Koowarta: A Warrior for Justice' 23(1) *Griffith Law Review* 16.
Anthony Mason (2005) 'Democracy and the Law: The State of the Australian Political System' 43 *Law Society Journal (NSW)* 68.

Mark McMillan (2012) 'Koowarta and the Rival Indigienous International: Our Place as Indigenous Peoples in the International' 23(1) *Griffith Law Review* 110.
Oodgeroo Noonuccal & National Aboriginal Day Observance Committee (1974) *A Song of Hope*, National Aboriginal Day Observance Committee.
Alexander Reilly (2012) 'Recovering the Foundations of *Koowarta*: The Struggle of the Aboriginal Land Fund Commission to Purchase Land in Queensland' 23(1) *Griffith Law Review* 61.
Kevin Rudd (2008) 'Federal Government Apologies' 7 *Indigenous Law Bulletin* 2.
Julius Stone (1946) *The Province and Function of Law*, Maitland.
Julius Stone (1966) *Social Dimensions of Law and Justice*, Maitland.
Anne Susskind (2012) 'Focus on Prevention, Not Punishment, for Young Aboriginal People' 50 *Law Society Journal (NSW)* 29.
Maureen Tehan (2012) 'Practising Law and Politics in 1980s' Australia: the Liberating Effect of *Koowarta v Bjelke-Petersen*' 23(1) *Griffith Law Review* 92.
Nicole Watson (2014) 'Justice in Whose Eyes: Why Lawyers Sould Read Black Australian Literature' 23(1) *Griffith Law Review* 44.

Reflections on legal issues in the Tasmanian Dams Case

The Hon Sir Anthony Mason AC KBE GBM

The Hon Sir Anthony Mason AC KBE GBM is a Non-Permanent Judge of the Hong Kong Court of Final Appeal and a Distinguished Visiting Fellow of the Australian National University College of Law

Synopsis

The purpose of this paper is to identify the principal issues which arose for decision in the *Tasmanian Dams Case* and review the way in which they were resolved. The principal issue concerned the scope of the external affairs power (s.51(xxix). Did the power extend to the implementation of the World Heritage Convention by prohibiting the construction of the dams in the World Heritage Area when the Convention obligations related to matters*within*Australia? By a majority of four to three the Court answered the question in the affirmative, applying the broad interpretation of Commonwealth legislative powers earlier mandated by the*Engineers Case*. Other issues related to the corporations power (s.51(xx)) and the race power (s.51(xxvi). By majority the Court held that the Tasmanian Hydro-Electric Commission was a 'trading corporation' within s.51 (xx) so that the Commonwealth could legislate with respect to it. By majority the Court also held that ss. 8 and 11 of the *World Heritage Properties Conservation Act*, because they protected indigenous sites and artefacts, were a valid exercise of the power to legislate with respect to 'people of any race for whom it is deemed necessary to make special laws'.

I begin my remarks by refuting as strongly as I can any commentary that challenges the correctness of the public statement by Gibbs CJ on behalf of the Court that the Justices in *Tasmanian Dams*[1] were not concerned with the question whether it was desirable that the dam should or should not be constructed. For my part, I have no hesitation in rejecting the suggestion that my decision reflected or was motivated by any view of the undesirability or otherwise of constructing the dam. And I have no doubt that this was the position of all my colleagues. We were concerned solely with the legal issues.

If you were to ask a different question – 'were the Justices influenced by their general views about the scope of Commonwealth powers vis-à -vis the States?' you *might* – and I stress the word '*might*' – get a different answer. But that is a different and very difficult question which it would not be relevant or appropriate to explore to-day.

My comments on the *Tasmanian Dams* Case present a legal and constitutional perspective on the case. The object of my remarks is to show

[1]*Commonwealth v Tasmania* (1983) 158 CLR 1 ('*Tasmanian Dams*').

(1) that the division of judicial opinion in the case on the external affairs power (s.51 (xxix) – it was a majority of four to three – reflected in a revised version, the historic conflict of opinion that surrounded the interpretation of the Australian Constitution in its early days;
(2) that the case was resolved in conformity with the principle of constitutional interpretation that has prevailed ever since the *Engineers Case*[2];
(3) that, in principle, the decision was dictated by the Court's earlier decisions in *R v Burgess; ex parte Henry*[3] and *Koowarta*[4];
(4) that proposition (3) above turned largely on the question of what Stephen J. meant in *Koowarta* when he said that a treaty, in order to attract the legislative power to implement its provisions, must deal with a matter 'of international concern'[5].

I shall refer very briefly to the corporations power (s.51(xx)) and the race power (s.51 (xxvi)) and the application by my colleague and panel member, Michael Black, for leave to intervene on behalf of the Tasmanian Wilderness Society.

Interpretation of the Australian Constitution before the *Engineers Case*

The interpretation of the Constitution by the original High Court featured two doctrines the effect of which was to elevate the status of the States to that of 'sovereign' and to preserve State powers.

The second of these doctrines, the reserved powers doctrine stressed the limited nature of the powers conferred upon the Commonwealth by the Constitution and the preservation of the powers of the States by s.107. The doctrine led to the conclusion that there was reserved to the States an exclusive capacity to regulate all matters within their 'domestic affairs'. One illustration of the doctrine was that the limited nature of the trade and commerce power (s.51(i)) mandated the conclusion that the Commonwealth had no capacity to interfere with trade and commerce solely within the limits of a State[6]. The reserved powers doctrine probably served Australia well in the early years of Federation before the State-based communities were transformed into a nation (with a sense of national identity) and a national economy. This recognition of this change lies at the heart of Windeyer J's controversial explanation in the *Payroll Tax Case*[7] of the decision in the *Engineers Case*[8].

The Engineers interpretation

The *Engineers Case* rejected the two doctrines favoured by the original High Court and adopted the interpretation favoured by Isaacs and Higgins JJ who had been

[2] *Amalgamated Society of Engineers v Adelaide Steamship Co* Ltd (1920) 28 CLR 129.
[3] (1936) 55 CLR 608.
[4] *Koowarta v Bjelke-Petersen* (1982) 153 CLR 168 (*'Koowarta'*).
[5] *Koowarta v Bjelke-Petersen* (1982) 153 CLR 168. at 216–217.
[6] *Attorney-General (NSW) v Brewery Employees Union of NSW* (1908) 6 CLR 469.
[7] *Victoria v Commonwealth* (1971) 122 CLR 353 at 396.
[8] *Amalgamated Society of Engineers v Adelaide Steamship Co Ltd* (1920) 28 CLR 129.

dissenters in the *inter se* cases decided after their appointment. It is said, correctly, that the decision adopted a literal interpretation of the legislative powers conferred on the Commonwealth and pointed to the supremacy of a Commonwealth law over a State law recognised by s.109. The joint judgment in that case, while adopting a literal interpretation, did not qualify the fundamental principle that Commonwealth powers are to be given a broad and liberal construction.[9]

The arguments for invalidity directed to s.51(xxix) and the objections to them

The unsuccessful arguments presented on behalf of the State of Tasmania and its supporters in the *Tasmanian Dams Case,* in particular the argument invoking federalism and the federal balance, rested substantially on a revised version of the view of the Constitution that had prevailed in the early years of Federation. The federalism argument was that the expansion of the external affairs power so that it enabled the Commonwealth to legislate on a matter that was the subject of a treaty entered into by the Commonwealth, if it required action only in relation to domestic affairs in Australia, would cut across the division of powers made by the Constitution and the consequence would be to substantially alter the 'federal balance' created by the Constitution.

The arguments are closely related. Indeed, they are different sides of the same coin. The flaw in the arguments is that neither the doctrine of reserved powers nor the concept of federalism nor the concept of federal balance points to any particular powers which are preserved by the Constitution for the States.

The minority judgments sought to overcome this problem by asserting that it was inherent in the Constitution that some (undefined) areas of legislative powers must exclusively be preserved for the States at any given time and that an unlimited federal legislative power with respect to external affairs would have the potential to deny the States any area of exclusive power by reason of the Commonwealth's power to enter into a treaty on any topic. There are a number of answers to this elusive proposition which seeks to treat the treaty-making power along with s.51 (xxix) as an unlimited source of legislative power. First, there must be an international treaty; secondly, entry into it must be entered into *bona fide*; and, thirdly, exercise of federal power must be confined to the strict implementation of treaty obligations or treaty provisions. In other words, the ratification of a treaty does not confer an unlimited legislative power on the Commonwealth with respect to the general subject matter of the treaty e.g. the elimination of racial discrimination or preservation of the national heritage, being the subject matter of the Conventions considered in *Koowarta* and *Tasmanian Dams.*

The minority's argument based on federalism led them to an interpretation of s.51 (xxix) which confined the legislative power to implementation of a treaty which deals with a matter 'of international concern'. According to the minority, neither the making nor the implementation of the *World Heritage Act*[10] was a matter of international concern.

[9] *Jumbunna Coal Mine NL v Victorian Coal Miners' Association* (1908) 6 CLR 309 at 367–368.
[10] *World Heritage Properties Conservation Act 1983* (Cth) ('*World Heritage Act*').

This was the limitation insisted upon by Stephen J. in *Koowarta*. As he was one of the four majority judges in *Koowarta,* this limitation formed an element of the *ratio* in that case. The problem with this requirement is that it involves the Court 'second-guessing' the executive and making a sensitive judgment on an issue which it is ill-equipped to decide.

Gibbs C J acknowledged that the requirement that the subject matter of the treaty be of 'international concern' was an imprecise test and that he would have preferred one which was more precise[11]. His view was that the test depended on the extent to which the matter is regarded by the nations of the world as a proper subject for international action and on the extent to which it will affect Australia's relations with other countries. Nevertheless, having accepted the test, he then applied it and found that the World Heritage Convention[12] did not answer the test. He advanced a *melange* of reasons to support this conclusion i.e. no imposition of *specific* obligations to safeguard the heritage, the requirements were purely internal to Australia and Australia's relations with other countries would not be affected by whatever Australia did or did not do.[13] The last consideration mentioned was a bold prediction for a judge to make.

Notwithstanding *Koowarta*, the minority preferred to say that the external affairs power did not extend to the implementation of a treaty which was directed *purely* to matters within Australia and seemed to lack the degree of international concern which was evident in *Koowarta*. The minority required that treaty obligations or the law implementing those obligations involve a relationship with other countries or persons or things outside Australia[14]. The problem with this approach is that the legislative power under s.51(xxix) would extend to such matters without the need for a treaty.

The minority also held that the external affairs power extended only to the implementation of obligations imposed by a treaty and that the power was not attracted because the Convention did not impose obligations. Brennan J, a member of the majority, held that the power did not extend to implementation of every provision in a treaty and that, in such a situation, it would be necessary to consider whether the subject was of international concern. He considered, however, that the 'international concern' requirement was satisfied in the *Tasmanian Dams Case*, as did other members of the majority.

The *Industrial Relations Act Case*[15] is contrary to the views recorded in the previous paragraph. The Court in that case held that the power extended to the implementation of ILO recommendations (including draft conventions) relating to minimum wages, equal remuneration, discrimination, termination of employment, parental leave and the right to strike, even though the Constitution imposed no obligation to comply with recommendations. The existence of 'international concern' was not a condition of the power to implement an ILO recommendation.

---

[11] *Commonwealth v Tasmania* (1983) 158 CLR at 101.

[12] *Convention for the Protection of the World Cultural and Natural Heritage*, opened for signature 16 November 1972, 1037 UNTS 151, (entered into force 17 December 1975).

[13] *Commonwealth v Tasmania* (1983) 158 CLR at 101–102.

[14] *Commonwealth v Tasmania* (1983) 158 CLR at 312.

[15] *Victoria v Commonwealth* (1996) 187 CLR 416.

In reaching this conclusion the joint judgment rejected a submission that the power was limited to a treaty dealing with a matter of international concern. This submission was based on the argument that *Tasmanian Dams* was explicable on the footing that the majority held that it involved a matter of international concern. The joint judgment in the *Industrial Relations Case* held that to read *Tasmanian Dams* in the manner suggested would be to ignore the way in which the case was decided. As notification of a treaty does not convert its provisions into domestic law, an exercise of the legislative power would have been contemplated by the framers of the Constitution to bring this about. There is nothing to suggest that the framers contemplated that implementation of a treaty was a matter for the exercise of State legislative power.

Of course, in 1900 matters which were the subject of international agreement were far more limited than they were in 1983, though in the *Industrial Relations Case*[16] it was pointed out that the range of international conventions before 1900 was more extensive than one might have expected. Nevertheless in 1900 it would not have been foreseen that treaties would deal with such matters as were dealt with by the Conventions which arose for consideration in *Koowarta* and *Tasmanian Dams*. The expansion in the range of matters dealt with by international treaties is simply the consequence of increased and expanded international activity and could not constitute a reason for denying to the Commonwealth the exercise of a legislative power which has always been exercised for the purpose of implementing a treaty.

It is said by some that *Tasmanian Dams* is still a controversial decision notwithstanding its subsequent endorsement. This is evidently because it is thought, as Dawson J has suggested, that to attract s.51(xxix) the law must operate on something *external to* Australia.

It must be said that events since 1983 provide no support at all to the suggestion that the decision would open the way to Australia's entering into treaties on such a scale that the Commonwealth legislative powers would extend substantially beyond those powers conferred upon it by the Constitution. Nor has there been any sign of entry into such treaties simply for the purpose of expanding Commonwealth legislative powers.

Corporations power (s.51(xx)

A majority of four to two Justices held that the Tasmanian Hydro-Electric Commission was a trading corporation within the meaning of s.51(xx) and s. 10(i) of the *World Heritage Properties Conservation Act 1983* (Cth) because it engaged in substantial trading activities in selling electricity. Further, it was held that the purpose of constructing the dam and associated works was to further its trading activities in selling electricity.

The race power s.51 (xxvi)

A majority of the Court in *Tasmanian Dams* held that ss.8 and 11 of the *World Heritage Properties Conservation Act 1983* (Cth) were a valid exercise of the power

[16] *Victoria v Commonwealth* (1996) 187 CLR 416 at 479.

to legislate with respect to the 'people of any race for whom it is deemed necessary to make special laws'. The provisions in question protected sites and artefacts which were of significance to the whole of mankind as well as to people of the aboriginal race. It was not material that the provisions required that the items protected were of significance to the whole of mankind so long as they protected the cultural heritage of people of the aboriginal race.

Intervention by the Tasmanian Wilderness Society

My fellow panellist Michael Black sought leave to intervene in the hearing on behalf of the Society, an entity whose object was to protect the environment. The Court did not grant the application but ruled that what Mr Black said in support of the application would be treated as having been said by an *amicus curiae*. Michael Black's short address in support of intervention was a brilliant cameo performance as I remarked to others at the time. But I do not agree with the comment which I read somewhere recently that Michael's address won the case for the Commonwealth. That comment was in my view an exercise in myth-making. Of course, I can only speak for myself but I would be surprised if my judicial colleagues were to disagree with me on this point. In saying that I do not wish to detract from what I considered at the time to be an exceptional feat of advocacy. Counsel very often overlook the dramatic impact that a short condensed address will have. That said, Michael Black's address took advantage of the lengthy submissions made by Sir Maurice Byers QC. and Gaudron QC in support of the Commonwealth legislation.

Cases
Amalgamated Society of Engineers v Adelaide Steamship Co Ltd (1920) 28 CLR 129
Attorney-General (NSW) v Brewery Employees Union of NSW (1908) 6 CLR 469
Commonwealth v Tasmania (1983) 158 CLR 1
Jumbunna Coal Mine NL v Victorian Coal Miners' Association (1908) 6 CLR 309
Koowarta v Bjelke-Petersen (1982) 153 CLR 168
R v Burgess; ex parte Henry (1936) 55 CLR 608
Victoria v Commonwealth (1971) 122 CLR 353
Victoria v Commonwealth (1996) 187 CLR 416

Legislation
Commonwealth of Australia Constitution Act (Cth)
Convention for the Protection of the World Cultural and Natural Heritage, opened for signature 16 November 1972, 1037 UNTS 151, (entered into force 17 December 1975)
World Heritage Properties Conservation Act 1983 (Cth)

The *Tasmanian Dam Case*: an advocate's memoir

The Hon Michael Black AC QC[1]

Melbourne Law School, Australia

An advocate's memoir[2] of The *Tasmanian Dam Case* outlines important elements of the context in which the case was argued and explains the importance of context to understanding the case and its place in the development of the law. The memoir gives an account of events that preceded the hearing and an account, as seen from the bar table, of the course of argument and particularly the application of the Tasmanian Wilderness Society for leave to intervene and the oral submissions made on its behalf on the final day of hearing, heard by the Court as the submissions of an amicus curia. The author makes some observations about practise before the High Court in Canberra in the 1980s and the importance of its establishment there in 1981 to the development of an Australian Bar and an Australian legal profession.

The controversies that the courts resolve, and by which our law develops, are inevitably the distinctive products of their time and place. From an advocate's viewpoint context is a key to understanding why the conduct of a case took a particular course, why some points were pressed and not others and why issues that seem obvious or even unimportant now assumed central importance then. Yet even the critical elements of the context fade quickly from public and private memory, a circumstance highlighted in the writer's mind by reflections about a case argued some 30 years earlier.

The sharpness of the controversy that gave rise to the constitutional issues the High Court had to consider in the *Commonwealth v Tasmania (The Tasmanian Dam Case)*[3] is reflected in the opening lines of the reasons for judgment of the Chief Justice, Sir Harry Gibbs. The Chief Justice outlined the direct conflict between, on the one hand, Tasmanian legislation authorising the construction of a dam on the Gordon river below its junction with the Franklin, considered necessary by Tasmania to generate electricity at low cost to achieve economic growth and employment and, on the other hand, the Commonwealth Act and regulations which

---

[1]Barrister 1964–1990, Chief Justice of the Federal Court of Australia 1991–2010; Inaugural Judge in Residence, Melbourne Law School, 2012; Inaugural Chair, Legal Services Council.

[2]There are restraints in writing about a case in which the writer appeared as counsel. It has seemed to me however that the events recalled here are mostly sufficiently public and the lapse of time sufficiently great to loosen the restraints. I have referred to some incidents of little or no apparent importance in themselves because they speak of their times and the work of advocates in those times. On the other hand there is of course much of importance that has been omitted; as will be evident, this is not intended as a comprehensive account.

[3](1983) 158 CLR 1.

would stop its construction so as to preserve aboriginal archaeological sites and prevent damage to a wilderness area of great natural significance such as to satisfy criteria for inclusion on the World Heritage List.

So stated, it is hard to imagine, in the context of the Australian federal system, a more striking conflict in both constitutional and political terms. Its intensity is reflected again in the emphatic statements by the Chief Justice, in the second paragraph of his judgment:

> No lawyer will need to be told that in these proceedings, the Court is not called upon to decide whether the Gordon below the Franklin Scheme ought to proceed. It is not for the Court to weigh the economic needs of Tasmania against the possible damage that will be caused to the archaeological sites and the wilderness area if the construction of the dam proceeds. The wisdom and expediency of the two competing courses are matters of policy for the governments to consider, and not for the Court. We are concerned with a strictly legal question – whether the Commonwealth regulations and the Commonwealth statute are within constitutional power.[4]

The intensity of the controversy is also reflected in the short explanatory statement that, for the first time in its history,[5] the Court published to make it clear to the public what the questions before the Court for decision were and what the effect of its decision was. In its statement the Court emphasised that they were strictly legal questions: that '[t]he Court is in no way concerned with the question whether it is desirable or undesirable, either on the whole or from any particular point of view, that the construction of the dam should proceed' and that '[t]he assessment of the possible advantages and disadvantages of constructing the dam, and the balancing of the one against the other, are not matters for the Court, and the Court's judgment does not reflect any view of the merits of the dispute'.[6]

Social and historical context

Any matter before the High Court as the final interpreter of the Constitution is, of its nature, important. But in Australia, unlike in the United States, it has been very unusual for constitutional issues to excite passionate and widespread public controversy. Rarely, if ever, has the controversy been so passionate or of concern to so many people and to so many diverse interests as it was here.

Moreover the controversy about economic development and its impact upon indigenous and environmental values was overlain by a more fundamental controversy about the respective rights and functions of the component parts of the Australian federation. Already a divisive political issue in Tasmania, the controversy became a national issue in the 1983 federal election held on 5 March, following a double dissolution. The incoming Prime Minister, Mr Bob Hawke, had promised that under his

---

[4](1983) 158 CLR at 60.

[5]Some years later the publication of explanatory statements by the High Court and by some other superior courts became routine. They have an important function in explaining the work of the courts to the public especially now that there is ready access to them via court websites.

[6](1983) 158 CLR at 58–59.

government the Commonwealth would bring a stop to work on the dam. The new government now took steps to do so.

An event a few weeks later heightened the tensions. On 7 April a Mirage 111 interceptor aircraft of the RAAF was seen – and no doubt heard – flying low over the Franklin River. It was on a reconnaissance mission authorised by the Commonwealth Attorney-General (without the knowledge of the Minister for Defence) to find out whether Tasmania was continuing with the project despite the Commonwealth direction that it stop. The Mirage flight provoked outrage but on following day there was another flight – this time by a F-111C supersonic swing-wing bomber, flying unseen and unheard at 30,000 feet. Soon afterwards, however, a Sydney newspaper broke the story on its front page. There was uproar in the Commonwealth Parliament and more outrage by those opposed to the Commonwealth's actions – military aircraft deployed against a State![7]

As well as institutional conflict there was of course personal conflict between the protesters, who sought to blockade the remote worksites, and the Tasmanian authorities who sought to remove them. There was also conflict between the protesters and the workers, who saw the actions of the protesters as threatening their jobs. Many people were arrested[8] and many spent time in jail, including the leader of the Tasmanian Wilderness Society Incorporated, Dr Bob Brown. The depth of feeling was conveyed eloquently by a Tasmanian graduate student at the symposium at which this paper was presented when she recalled that in Tasmania at that time 'many a Sunday lunch ended in tears, with a family divided'.

The intensity of these divisions is no longer widely remembered in mainland Australia, although the memories run deeper in Tasmania, perhaps kept alive by the long-running controversies about the timber industry in that State. The substantial portion of the Australian population aged under about 35 will of course have no memory at all of these events.

An understanding of the political, economic and social issues that underlay the constitutional issues before the High Court is, however, essential for a full appreciation of many aspects of the case, including the context of the Court's ground-breaking explanatory statement and some of the passages in the judgments. The broader historical context of a changing Australian society and a changing local and international world view, including increasing concerns about the natural environment, must also be considered. Because this is an advocate's memoir, the examples I have

---

[7]The flights were the origin of the nickname 'Biggles' given to the Attorney-General (Senator Gareth Evans) by the media. The incident led to Senator Evans coining the expression 'The streaker's defence' for his observation that 'It seemed like a good idea at the time'. Some years later, when as counsel for the Commonwealth in the Lemonthyme and Southern Forests litigation before the High Court, I accompanied the Solicitor-General and Chris Maxwell on a flight over the wilderness area, our aircraft was a brightly colored helicopter of the Tasmania Police.

[8]Some 1500 were arrested and 600 jailed: Bob Brown (2012) 'Why I Am a Green' http://www.bobbrown.org.au/why_i_am_a_green. Pierre Slicer later wryly observed that he was (ie, later became) the 'only judge in Australia ... who's been refused bail by his own Chief Justice': ABC News Online, 'Marking 25 Years of the Franklin River Decision' http://www.abc.net.au/news/2008-07-01/marking-25-years-of-the-franklin-river-decision/2490228, 13 April 2010.

chosen to convey something of the context of those changing times concern cases in which I was involved as counsel.

Instances of discrimination for which remedies did not then exist come particularly to mind as illustrations of those times. Although the 1970s saw changes in the position of women in the workforce and in society more generally, direct and overt discrimination on the ground of marital status remained common, even to the extent that some women still lost their jobs upon marriage. As counsel for a Commonwealth Minister intervening in an industrial case in 1978 I was unable to secure a remedy for a young librarian who, in accordance with the policy of her employer, was dismissed when she married.[9] Some of the States enacted sex discrimination legislation during the 1970s but not all did. In the same period I acted for a leasee in a property matter in which there had been overt discrimination on the ground of race but for which the law then provided no remedy (although, in this instance, justice was done by a rather technical reliance on common law principles). More broadly, the laws relating to marriage and divorce in the early 1970s still allowed for serious injustices to women and sometimes, as in a case I recall well, founded upon a hypocritical double standard.

Another marker of social change was the abolition of the death penalty; it had only been 20 years since the dramatic, and constitutionally historic, order of the High Court of Australia restraining the execution of a prisoner in Victoria, fixed for the following day despite a pending application for special leave to appeal.[10] Counsel of my generation had clients who had been sentenced to death. Those of us who practised in other fields knew barristers who had been deeply affected by the sentence of death imposed upon a client in whose defence they had been unsuccessful. Although the hanging of Ronald Ryan in Victoria in 1967 marked a decisive change in community attitudes throughout Australia, as late as 1983 the penalty was still on the statute book in one State, Western Australia, from which it was not removed until the following year.

Changes more directly relevant to the controversy before the Court in the *Tasmanian Dam Case* included increasing concerns about the conservation of the natural environment. These had already been evident in Tasmania during the 1960s when there were protests aimed at preventing the flooding (the so-called 'enlargement') of Lake Pedder for hydro-electric power generation. The protests were unsuccessful but the wider environmental movement in Australia has been traced to them.

There was also growing concern about the conservation of the marine environment, and particularly about commercial whaling which had been carried on in Australian waters since colonial times and still continued out of Cheynes Beach near Albany in Western Australia. The change came in 1978 when, after a sustained campaign against whaling, the Commonwealth established an *Inquiry into Whales and Whaling* headed by Sir Sydney Frost whose report recommended the prohibition of commercial whaling in Australian waters. The recommendation was accepted and legislation soon followed.[11]

---

[9]See, eg, Kirkby (2011); *In re Municipal Officers Association of Australia* (1978) 203 CAR 584.

[10]*Tait v The Queen* (1962) 108 CLR 620. (I was present in the Court in Melbourne, my future master, E D Lloyd, being junior counsel to John Starke QC for the petitioner, David Scott).

[11]Frost (1978); *Whale Protection Act 1980* (Cth). I had a brief for the whales (that is, Project Jonah Inc.). The Project Jonah submission included an argument based on the common law and the onus of proof in criminal cases applicable, we argued, because the extinction of a

Despite, however, emerging issues about international aspects of the environment, such as whales and whaling and – reflecting the times – atmospheric nuclear tests, there was not a strong sense of the environment as a self-evident matter of international concern such as we might understand it to be today in a time of widespread concern about climate change and its global causes.

The concept of a 'world heritage' – with an emphasis on 'world' – was then new to the general public even though the World Heritage Convention had been adopted by UNESCO in 1972 and had been ratified by Australia (one of the first countries to do so). There were some earlier examples of international heritage protection such as treaties for the protection of historic sites against artillery bombardment but they were little known[12] and as late as 1983 the concept was still developing.

A quite different contextual element, directly relevant to the constitutional setting of the *Tasmanian Dam Case* and of great importance to an understanding of the case, was the continued enlargement of the areas of Commonwealth activity, particularly during the 1970s.[13] There was a strong feeling in the States that the Commonwealth was becoming dominant in the daily lives of citizens at the expense of the powers, functions and status of the States.[14]

Brief to seek leave to intervene and to apply for an injunction

It was, therefore, in a changing but still rather different world that, early in May 1983, I was briefed with another member of the Victorian Bar, Bryan Keon-Cohen[15] to appear on behalf of the Tasmanian Wilderness Society Incorporated at the hearing of the *Tasmanian Dam Case*. The case was listed for hearing before the High Court in Canberra some three weeks later, on 31 May.

We were briefed by Mr Pierre Slicer, a Hobart solicitor who had been active in opposition to the dam. He appointed Mr Lincoln Siliakis, a solicitor in his practice, to be our instructing solicitor in court. We all worked very much as a team. The leader of our client was, of course, Dr Bob Brown.

The brief presented considerable challenges since the Tasmanian Wilderness Society was not a party to the matters before the High Court and had no right to be heard. If we

---

species was fundamental and irreversible. We would now recognise the argument as embodying the precautionary principle.

[12] *Convention (II) with respect to the Laws and Customs of War on Land* opened for signature 29 July 1899, 187 CTS 429 (entered into force 4 September 1900) annex art 27 ('In sieges and bombardments all necessary steps should be taken to spare as far as possible edifices devoted to religion, art, science, and charity, ... provided they are not used at the same time for military purposes.'); *Convention (IV) with respect to the Laws and Customs of War on Land* opened for signature 18 October 1907, 205 CTS 277 (entered into force 26 January 1910) annex art 27 (substituting 'must' in place of 'should'); *Convention for the Protection of Cultural Property in the Event of Armed Conflict* opened for signature 14 May 1954, 249 UNTS 240 (entered into force 7 August 1956).

[13] By the late 1970s extensive new areas of federal practice had developed, particularly in the fields of commercial and administrative law.

[14] The introduction of a national *Family Law Act 1975* (Cth) with 'no fault' divorce was a big step by the Commonwealth. There were other notable examples in the fields of trade practices and consumer protection.

[15] Now Dr Bryan Keon-Cohen AM QC.

were to be heard it would have to be in the exercise of the Court's discretion. Our approach therefore would be to make an application to intervene; if successful, this might give us some status in the proceeding and some opportunity to be heard.

Courts did not favour the grant of leave to intervene at that time. Generally, applications for such leave are still not encouraged for reasons that include the risk of duplication of arguments, the wasting of time and a lack of focus resulting from the intervener not having a direct interest in the subject matter of the litigation. Moreover, in a case arising from an intense public controversy the High Court would naturally not want an intervention to become a platform for irrelevant, time-wasting or 'political' submissions. A perception that a party wanted to intervene for the purpose of making, in effect, a political broadcast to the wider world would be fatal.

Our application to intervene therefore had to be prepared on the footing that it would be principled, short and to the point.[16] Our intervention, if leave were granted, would likewise have to be short and absolutely to the point and, preferably, not a duplication of anything others had said. We determined that any oral submission we made, if leave were granted, would be limited to 10 minutes.

There was another challenge: we had instructions to apply for an injunction to stop further work on the project. A challenge indeed, although not lacking a respectable foundation since the challenged Act specifically conferred standing to apply for such an injunction upon 'an interested person' and the Tasmanian Wilderness Society fell within that definition.[17] Of course, if the Commonwealth were to succeed in its foreshadowed injunction application ours would have become unnecessary.

The evening of the hearing

As our team assembled in Canberra on Monday 30 May, the day before the case was listed for hearing, we did not know at what point in the proceedings our application for leave to intervene might be heard, although there was a distinct likelihood that it would be on the first day. Nor did we have any idea when, if at all, we might be called upon to make our submissions in support of the validity of the Act and the regulations. The injunction application was another concern. So our strategy had to be thought through and our arguments fully prepared and ready to be presented at any time.

University House was the preferred lodging for many of us who appeared before the High Court in those days and so it was with the *Tasmanian Dam Case*. In the rather austere but studious rooms there were late nights of writing and revising for the rest of that week and in the week that followed.[18]

---

[16]See Kenny (1998); Mason (1998); Willheim (2010). See also *Australian Conservation Foundation Inc. v Commonwealth* (1980) 146 CLR 493 and *Onus v Alcoa of Australia Ltd* (1981) 149 CLR 27.

[17]*World Heritage Properties Conservation Act 1983* (Cth) s 14(1). On 'interested persons' see, eg, *Australian Conservation Foundation Inc. v Commonwealth* (1980) 146 CLR 493 at 528, 530–531 (Gibbs J); *Onus v Alcoa of Australia Ltd* (1981) 149 CLR 27 at 35–39 (Gibbs CJ).

[18]On the then recently developed practice of the three-page outline, already at that point something of an art form, see Bennett (2001) and Brennan (2001). In the early 1980s it was common for these outlines to be revised and revised again well into the night on the eve of a hearing, The technology of the day would allow for the final version to be printed in the hotel room on a portable electric typewriter, ready for photocopying the following morning.

On the evening before the hearing, however, there was little time for any further preparation since there was a meeting to be attended with the client's numerous members and supporters. The meeting, which was essentially a public meeting, was at a venue in Civic (central Canberra) that I can no longer place. Whatever the venue was, it was packed.

We were invited to address the gathering. We explained in broad terms the challenges we faced and the essence of the submissions we would seek leave to make to the Court. We answered quite a few questions about the case and what we hoped would be our role in it.

Court etiquette and Sir Garfield Barwick's ties

There was also the potentially delicate matter of court etiquette to be addressed. All courts prefer – and if the deviation from the desired norm is too great will insist upon – dress that is appropriate to the occasion. Under the heading 'Court etiquette' the High Court's website today gently advises that 'you should be adequately neatly dressed, including footwear' and that 'inappropriate clothing may not be worn'.

Obviously enough what is 'appropriate clothing' varies with the times. In 1983 it included, for men, a jacket and tie. Attending court without a tie was definitely 'inappropriate'. In fact, in Melbourne at that time informal assistance was provided to those who attended without a tie, as law students of the 1980s were likely to do. Just inside the public entrance to Court One in Melbourne there was kept, on a wire coat hanger, a collection of ties of the width and patterns fashionable in the 1950s. They were said to be discards from the wardrobe of the previous Chief Justice, Sir Garfield Barwick. The collection was administered with charm and dignity by Mr Cole, the fondly remembered court crier of the High Court, who would offer them to students and others who came tieless to watch the proceedings.

Ties were not the dress item of choice for the mostly young gathering of concerned people at the meeting. But the possible problem went deeper than ties; given the highly discretionary nature of the application we were to make, the passions involved, and the certainty that the High Court would wish to appear to be utterly remote from the political side of the controversy, it was highly undesirable that any of our client's members or supporters should turn up in court the next day in anything resembling protest clothing. We were especially concerned that there should be no prominent displays of the ubiquitous bright yellow 'No Dam' triangles which many of the audience were keen to wear. And, of course, 'No Dam' placards had to be left behind.

The large audience listened with good humour, in the always-calm presence of Dr Bob Brown. It was very good for us to meet them and to answer their questions and for them to meet us. This, we felt, was the law at work as it should be; but would our application, perhaps to be made the following morning, nevertheless be fruitless?

The hearing begins

And so the day arrived: Tuesday 31 May 1983. The matters had been prepared and set down for hearing with remarkable speed, considering that the proceedings had been commenced only eight weeks earlier, on 4 April.[19]

The case was to be heard in the principal courtroom, Court One, of the new High Court building which had been opened by the Queen two years earlier, almost to the day.

To my mind, Court One was and is an architectural triumph; an almost perfect setting for counsel to engage intellectually and closely with a court of seven justices whilst at the same time providing fine facilities for the public to witness the administration of justice at the highest level. It was and is a place of space, of dignity and of light, enhanced by fine craftsmanship and artistry; a place for the rule of law and a place of which Australians can feel proud. (My suggestion to those who do not like the exterior of the building – my own view is that it is superb – is to experience the building from the inside first, absorbing the remarkable unity of light and space.)

There is always a sense of occasion when the seven justices constitute a full High Court and the Court assembles for the hearing of an important case. On 31 May 1983, the sense of occasion was especially notable. This was, on any view, a very important case and there was not a spare seat in the court. The diverse audience included many members and supporters of our client.

At 10.15 precisely the court was opened. The opening was in the usual manner of that time, the procedure itself creating a sense of drama and anticipation even, I suspect, for those who had experienced it many times. The court crier commanded all present to stand and remain standing. The seven justices filed onto the Bench, took their places, exchanged bows with counsel at the bar table and took their seats. Everyone else remained standing whilst the crier opened the Court:

> All persons having any manner of business before the High Court of Australia are commanded to draw nigh, give their attendance and they shall be heard! God Save the Queen!

Then, much less dramatically: 'Be seated please'.

Counsel announce their appearances

The Associate to the Chief Justice then 'called' the case by reading the names of the parties to each of the matters before the court. Counsel announced their appearances

---

[19]Three proceedings were before the Court: Action No C6 of 1983 (the Commonwealth seeking to restrain Tasmania from proceeding with the works on the basis that they were prohibited by the World Heritage (Western Tasmania Wilderness) Regulations made under *National Parks and Wildlife Conservation Act 1975* (Cth) s 69); Action No C8 of 1983 (Attorney-General of Tasmania seeking a declaration that those regulations were invalid); Action No C12 of 1983 (the Commonwealth seeking to restrain Tasmania from proceeding with the works on the basis that they were prohibited under the *World Heritage Properties Conservation Act 1983* (Cth)). On sources of jurisdiction, see *Australian Constitution* ss 75 and 76.

to the Court, that is to say the leading counsel for each party informed the Court of the party for which he or she appeared and with whom as their junior counsel.

The case was remarkable for the large number of counsel and for the eminence of the many Queen's Counsel involved. Appearing for the Commonwealth, the Solicitor-General, Sir Maurice Byers QC, led another Queen's Counsel Mr Ron Castan QC, and two juniors. For the State of Tasmania Mr R J Ellicott QC led two Queen's Counsel and three juniors (one of them being Professor Leslie Zines). As leading counsel for the Hydro Electricity Commission of Tasmania, Mr Ellicott led another Queen's Counsel, Mr James Merralls QC and a junior. Ms Mary Gaudron QC, Solicitor-General for NSW, appearing for the Attorney-General for New South Wales intervening in support of the Commonwealth, led two other counsel. Mr David Jackson QC appeared with a junior counsel for the Attorney-General for Queensland intervening in support of Tasmania. Mr Gerard Nash appeared for the Attorney-General for the State Victoria, intervening in support of the Commonwealth.

Many of those at the Bar table later become judges

Of the 20 counsel, at least 10 subsequently held high judicial office.[20] Two became members of the High Court of Australia, Mr Murray Gleeson QC as Chief Justice, having first served as Chief Justice of New South Wales between 1988 and 1997. Three others also became State or federal Chief Justices and one of them also subsequently became the Governor of Tasmania. Of the three women appearing as counsel, Ms Mary Gaudron QC, Solicitor-General, subsequently became a Justice of the High Court, junior counsel for the Commonwealth, Ms Susan Kenny (later Dr Susan Kenny QC), became a member of the Victorian Court of Appeal (the first woman to be so appointed) and subsequently a judge of the Federal Court of Australia, and junior counsel for Queensland, Mrs Margaret White, became a judge of the Supreme Court of Queensland and subsequently a member of the Queensland Court of Appeal. The circumstance that three women appeared as counsel is itself noteworthy having regard to the rarity of female counsel being retained in leading cases at that time. At least one other lawyer involved in the case was later appointed to judicial office: Mr Pierre Slicer, our instructing solicitor, later became a judge of the Supreme Court of Tasmania and, subsequently, a judge of the Court of Appeal of Samoa.[21]

---

[20]An eleventh, Mr F M Douglas QC, was appointed to the Court of Appeal for Fiji in April 2009 but served in that office for less than a week. The Court of which he was a member, having declared that the 2006 military coup in Fiji was illegal, effectively ceased to exist since shortly after its decision was given the *Fijian Constitution (Constitution of the Republic of Fiji)* was suspended and the judges dismissed.

[21]But for his untimely passing, the second member of the Commonwealth team, Mr Ron Castan QC, would most likely have been appointed to high judicial office. He later led my junior in the *Tasmanian Dam Case*, Bryan Keon-Cohen, as counsel for Eddie Mabo in *Mabo v Queensland [No 1]* (1988) 166 CLR 186 and *Mabo v Queensland [No 2]* (1992) 175 CLR 1. (Mrs Margaret White, junior counsel for Queensland, also appeared as junior counsel for Queensland in *Mabo*.)

The Tasmanian Wilderness Society Inc. seeks leave to intervene

Counsel for the principal parties and for the intervening Attorneys-General having announced their appearances, it was then for me, as senior counsel for the Tasmanian Wilderness Society, to announce our appearance on its behalf seeking the leave of the Court to intervene to support the validity of the Act and the regulations.[22] The response of the Chief Justice was immediate: 'On what grounds?'

And so it was that the first submission in the *Tasmanian Dam Case* was made on behalf of the Tasmanian Wilderness Society. Our application, which occupies only three pages of the first day's transcript, was made on four grounds. The first, which provoked no comment from the Court, was that the Society had a direct interest in the validity of the Act because, as an 'interested person', the Act gave it standing to seek an injunction. It therefore, so it was argued, had a direct interest for the reason that if the Act were held to be invalid the Society would lose a legal right to approach the Court. The second argument was that the Society had an interest, admittedly less direct, in the validity of the regulations by reason of a commercial interest it claimed it had in the land in dispute.[23] The third and fourth grounds, which did provoke comments from the Chief Justice, relied upon the Society's special interest and knowledge of the subject matter and its consequent capacity to offer a new perspective to the argument that the legislation was a valid exercise of the external affairs power. To this the Chief Justice somewhat tartly commented: 'The only perspective we want is the perspective which the Constitution requires'. The final point – made as succinctly as the others – was that any submission we made would be short and very much to the point. Our intervention would not prolong the proceedings. (It was of course important, as a demonstration of the reality of that contention, perceived to be fundamental to our chances of success, that the application for leave to intervene itself should be very succinct.)

As soon as I had completed our submission, and without discussion with the other members of the Court, the Chief Justice announced that the Court would reserve its decision on our application and that, 'if [we] were so minded, at the close of the subsequent arguments [we] might renew the application' which could be considered then in the light of the Court's 'fuller knowledge'.

'May we remain?' I asked. 'Of course' replied the Chief Justice, and so we did, at a small table placed behind the main bar table, for the remainder of that day and for the six further days of the hearing.

---

[22]Our argument essentially supported the Commonwealth's submissions about the external affairs power but included a more refined articulation of s 51(29) argument, specifically about the meaning and significance of world heritage – as pointing to universal value shared by all of humanity which only endures if the protected site exists as a living and enduring resource – and that Australia's standing in the international community is connected to protecting world heritage sites within Australia. See *Tasmanian Dam Case* (1983) 153 CLR 1 at 50. The argument formally supported the other grounds argued by the Commonwealth.

[23]This commercial interest was mentioned by Mason J in *Tasmanian Wilderness Society v Fraser* (1982) 153 CLR 270 at 273, though Mason J did not rule on the Society's standing in that challenge.

Tasmania puts its case

Although we had not been given leave to intervene, our application had not been rejected and substantial points had – we thought – been made about the legitimacy of the 'interest' (in a legal sense) claimed by our client. Moreover, our team remained in court, robed and ready to argue on behalf of the Society.

Almost all of the first day, the whole of the second and third days, and a substantial part of the morning of the fourth day were occupied by the address of Mr Ellicott on behalf of Tasmania. The duration of the leading argument for Tasmania was unusual, as was the infrequency of questions from the bench. At that time, as now, submissions before the High Court generally proceeded quickly with much interaction between the Bench and counsel. Indeed, the interaction during argument between counsel and individual justices is one of the highlights of High Court advocacy, presenting an opportunity to counsel to resolve doubts and to change opinions. Although there were some such interchanges in this case, they were substantially fewer than, and generally different in nature from, those that normally seen in the High Court.

A few paragraphs could not do justice to Mr Ellicott's arguments or indeed to any of the other arguments in the case. But in the context of a symposium with 'turning points' in its title, it is fair to say that it was of the essence of the Ellicott argument that the Constitution – indeed the Federation – was at a turning point. Were the impugned legislation and regulations valid, no part of Australia would be safe from the control of the Commonwealth, it was contended.[24] For example, 'the Sydney Harbour Bridge, the Opera House and Circular Quay' could be considered part of the world's natural and cultural heritage and could, through the impugned law, be placed under the control of the federal Minister. Areas in the Blue Mountains could be covered: 'Already, Lord Howe Island and Willandra Lakes in western New South Wales, the Great Barrier Reef and the Kakadu National Park have been listed in the World Heritage List'.

Mr Ellicott gave many examples of treaties entered into by the Commonwealth which, he said, if allowed to form the basis for the exercise of Commonwealth power, would intrude far into the everyday life of the States in fields utterly foreign to the division of legislative powers envisaged by the Constitution.[25]

Towards the end of the second day Mr Ellicott again stressed the federal nature of the Constitution and that it was the people of the States who formed 'this one indissoluble federal Commonwealth, the peoples of the States'. He concluded the day's argument with observations that I quote in full because they capture something of the moment[26]:

---

[24]*Commonwealth v Tasmania* [1983] HCATrans 24 (3 June 1983), p 330.

[25]Even the regulation of professional fees? At a Bar dinner in Melbourne the previous Saturday, the after-dinner speaker entertained the audience by claiming that Attorney-General Gareth Evans (who was present as a guest) had in mind a Barristers' Fees Tribunal, the joke being his supposed choice of its members. The sober observation that there was no Commonwealth head of power for such a tribunal was answered by a further proposal – a Barristers' Fees Treaty between Australia and Vanuatu. This jest achieved considerable currency, which we did not welcome. An unhelpful extreme; but what indeed were the limits?

[26]As happens when great issues are before a court, there were other moments during the hearing when the importance of the issues was felt in the courtroom – perhaps a shared sense of history in the making. When I attempted to describe this to a participant in a very important recent case, she replied that she knew exactly what I meant. During the hearing of her case, she said, she had 'felt the Constitution shift on its axis'.

> Your Honours, I know that what I have said has been tinged with emotion, but I have said it simply because I believe there is a moment in the work of the Court which is of such tremendous importance to this nation, when the question of power, which is so vital to its development and to its people, becomes a slightly emotional matter and all of us are human.

And then, perhaps incongruously, but only to those unfamiliar with the ways of barristers and which did not lessen the impact of what he had just said: 'Your Honours, I notice it is 4.15'.[27]

When asked by the Chief Justice how much of the following day he thought he 'would need to occupy' Mr Ellicott said that he would try to finish by lunchtime.

Mr Ellicott was a very experienced and powerful advocate, a former Attorney-General and a former Solicitor-General and completely at home in the High Court. The force of his submissions did not, however, attract the supporters of the Tasmanian Wilderness Society and by the end of the second day very few remained.

As Mr Ellicott's argument progressed it seemed to some of us that Sir Maurice Byers, another very powerful advocate but with a very different style, was unwell. As someone put it, the great Sir Maurice seemed to wilt, and it was known amongst our team that Mr Ron Castan QC was ready to present the argument for the Commonwealth should that become necessary. Whatever the cause of Sir Maurice's apparent indisposition, his recovery seemed to be concurrent with the appearance in court, soon afterwards, of Lady Byers. She sat in the public area a row or two behind where Sir Maurice was seated at the bar table and he rapidly improved. When, eventually,[28] it came to the Commonwealth's turn to put its case the Solicitor-General was in his usual fine form once again.

Mr Ellicott concluded his submission mid-morning on the fourth day and it was now the turn of Mr Murray Gleeson QC to argue that the so-called race power[29] did not support the Act or the regulations. It was in the opening minutes of his submission that he argued that the race power could not support the legislation for the reason that the Tasmanian aborigines were a distinct race of people and that, as he put it, 'the facts also seem to indicate that the former race is now extinct'.

Certainly what Murray Gleeson said had an immediate impact. Some of those present were noticeably shocked. The atmosphere in the court has been described as 'freezing'. The transcript, however, shows that this was not his primary argument.[30] It was acknowledged that the facts on that issue were contested and the quite lengthy and his closely reasoned principal argument proceeded on the footing that the contested facts about the aboriginal people of Tasmania might ultimately be decided in favour of the Commonwealth.

When the Court resumed on the following Tuesday Mr S Walmsley of the New South Wales Bar, briefed by our instructing solicitor, sought leave to intervene on behalf of Ms Heather Sculthorpe and the Tasmanian Aboriginal Centre

---

[27] *Commonwealth v Tasmania* [1983] HCATrans 22 (1 June 1983), p 213 (day two of the hearing).

[28] On day six of the hearing: *Commonwealth v Tasmania* [1983] HCATrans 26 (8 June 1983).

[29] *Australian Constitution* s 51(26).

[30] See *Commonwealth v Tasmania* [1983] HCATrans 24 (3 June 1983), p 361ff.

Incorporated.[31] He informed the Court that one purpose of his application was to correct Mr Gleeson's suggestion on Friday afternoon that the Tasmanian Aborigines had ceased to exist as a race. Accepting that Mr Gleeson's statement was now disputed and noting the intervention, Gibbs CJ reiterated that the Court was yet to decide whether any facts needed to be canvassed.[32]

'Humour' 'interventions' and 'interruptions'

As noted, there was much less interchange between counsel and the Bench than might normally be expected in a case before the High Court. The submissions were longer and it seemed that there were far fewer interventions – some counsel unwisely see them as 'interruptions' – than usual. Judicial interventions can take many forms and the art of the advocate is of course to use the responses to advance his or her case – or at least to keep it afloat and on a more or less even keel.

Despite the seriousness of the issues, there were a few exchanges of the type that seem – I emphasise 'seem' – to do no more than lighten the work of the day. For example, when Sir Maurice Byers told the Court that he did not want to go much further with a particular line of argument but was nevertheless proceeding 'without being unduly obdurate' the response from Gibbs CJ was: 'You are never *unduly* obdurate, Sir Maurice', to which Sir Maurice replied 'Your Honour means *very* obdurate'. He then continued to develop his point anyway.

On an earlier occasion a reference by Mr Merralls to a tendency to treat *Huddart Parker & Co Pty Ltd v Moorehead*,[33] (an important early case about the corporations power) as a 'museum piece' provoked the response from Mason J: 'Is it not?'[34] Mr Merralls did not treat this as a light-hearted exchange, replying that *Huddart Parker*, properly understood, was alive and that what had happened in a later case was that it had been 'stripped of a coat of varnish that had been imposed by the reserved State powers doctrine'. He continued: 'but that when that coat of varnish is removed it will be found, as I hope I shall demonstrate from reference …' at which point Mason J interrupted, saying that he 'would have thought "torpedoed and sunk with all hands" might have been a more accurate description'.[35] (Huddart Parker was an Australian coastal shipping line of an earlier era.) Mr Merralls was of course quite undeterred. There were later references to the case, some of them apparently whimsical, including Sir Maurice's observation: 'Your Honours must have read it [*Huddart Parker*] so often and with such devotion that the prospect of reading it again is a very wearisome task', continuing nevertheless: 'But might I just say this …'[36] And on the final day of the hearing, Mr Ellicott, a leader of the New South Wales Bar, could not resist referring to the River Yarra when responding to one of my submissions about places of beauty. 'Beauty', he said, can be anywhere;

---

[31] *Commonwealth v Tasmania* [1983] HCATrans 26 (8 June 1983), p 517ff.

[32] See further the exchange between Mr Ellicott and Gibbs CJ: *Commonwealth v Tasmania* [1983] HCATrans 26 (8 June 1983), pp 519–520.

[33] (1909) 8 CLR 330 (hereafter '*Huddart Parker*').

[34] *Commonwealth v Tasmania* [1983] HCATrans 24 (3 June 1983), p 394.

[35] *Commonwealth v Tasmania* [1983] HCATrans 24 (3 June 1983), p 394.

[36] *Commonwealth v Tasmania* [1983] HCATrans 27 (9 June 1983), p 628.

you could get these feelings of beauty on Sydney Harbour – 'you can get them *even* on the banks of the Yarra'.[37]

At the bar table; 'Breakfast at Boffins'

There is often a sense of community at the bar table during the hearing of a case, especially during a long case as, by High Court precedent, this certainly was.[38] Sometimes the competing causes intrude upon the relationships but more often not. As I recall it, relations between the 20 counsel at the bar table remained cordial throughout the case, with a lunchtime football game to take its place amongst the Bar's stories of events on circuit.

In this respect it is worth noting that the hearing of cases by the High Court in Canberra after its establishment there in May 1981 was influential in the development of the sense of an Australian Bar and an Australian legal profession. Members of both sides of the profession throughout Australia who were involved in cases before the High Court there would now meet each other in Canberra, much as they might have done on a country circuit. Breakfast or dinner at 'Boffins', the name then as now of the restaurant at University House, and at other popular places of lodging was often the occasion for social contact with barristers and solicitors from other States. The *Tasmanian Dam Case*, during which practitioners from four States worked in the same building and stayed in the same city for two weeks, is a good example of that development. There were many others in that era, and of course since. (In the previous year the High Court had begun the practice of inviting all newly appointed Queen's Counsel and Senior Counsel to come to Canberra on the same day at the beginning of the new legal year to announce their appointments to the Court, the development of an earlier tradition in which the announcements were made when the Court visited counsel's home State.)

'Tell the Court that the trees are hurting'

The passions of those involved in the protests to save the Gordon below the Franklin came through to the Wilderness Society team in our room on the practitioners' floor of the High Court. My junior, Bryan Keon-Cohen, had rafted down the Franklin some weeks earlier. When he did so, we had already been briefed on behalf of the Society to appear in the High Court, a fact apparently known to the protesters he met on the Franklin. They had expressed their relief that 'they' would be represented in the High Court and, moreover, by someone they had met and who knew the river.

A consequence of this contact was that Bryan received several communications, including some by a radio link from the Franklin wilderness. These included a specific instruction 'from the clients' to inform the Court that 'the trees are hurting

[37] *Commonwealth v Tasmania* [1983] HCATrans 28 (10 June 1983), p 786 (emphasis added).

[38] Landmark long cases include the *Bank of New South Wales v Commonwealth* (1948) 76 CLR 1 (39 hearing days before the High Court and 36 hearing days before the Privy Council); *Australian Communist Party v Commonwealth* (1951) 83 CLR 1 (24 hearing days). Reflecting the modern practice, the *Workchoices* case – *New South Wales v Commonwealth* (2006) 229 CLR 1 – whilst famous for producing one of the longest judgments to date and the most number of counsel appearing (39 in total), had only four days of hearings. See Bennett (2001).

and fearful'. Bryan told me that he had assured the caller that 'Mr Black would make sure that the Court understood'. There were other such communications with the third member of the team, our invaluable instructing solicitor Lincoln Siliakis. He was with us for the whole of the hearing.

As far as I know, Bryan was the only person directly involved in arguing the case who had ever been on (or even near) the Franklin River.[39] The possible exception might have been Mr Peter Underwood, the sole Tasmanian counsel on the Commonwealth side, a brief that apparently made him very unpopular in some circles in his home State.[40] It was of course this lack of any general familiarity with the physical subject matter of the case that we sought to address in our submissions.

The injunction application

At the conclusion of his argument on Thursday 9 June (the second last day of the hearing) Sir Maurice Byers raised with the Court the Commonwealth's two applications for an interim injunction.[41] He said that the Commonwealth, subject to the Court's views as to the appropriate course, would wish those matters to be dealt with. The Chief Justice's response was that the Court had decided to give expedited attention to the case and that it hoped – although it could not guarantee – to give its judgment before the end of the Brisbane sittings: within about three weeks. In those circumstances 'having regard to the obvious disadvantages entailed in sitting to hear the contested application for an interlocutory injunction' did the Commonwealth press the application?[42] Wisely and appropriately, the Commonwealth did not.

The final day, Friday 10 June: the Tasmanian Wilderness Society makes its submission

The final day began with a resumption of the address by Gerard Nash on behalf of Victoria. In something of a departure from the way the hearing had proceeded, Mr Nash was questioned closely by two members of the Court about aspects of his submission that there were limits to matters of international concern when it came to the natural, as opposed to the cultural, heritage of mankind.

Immediately upon the conclusion of Mr Nash's address we were called upon – in the ordinary way: 'Yes, Mr Black?' said the Chief Justice.

In essence, we explained that we wished to renew the application to intervene and to make a short submission as to why, on the *narrowest* view of the external affairs power, the Act and the Convention had characteristics that brought it within that power.[43] We also wanted to say something in answer to aspects of the submissions made on behalf of Victoria. The response of the Chief Justice was: 'Perhaps you

---

[39]Pierre Slicer, our instructing solicitor, had of course been in the area and had been arrested there, as had Dr Brown. Lincoln Siliakis was also familiar with the area

[40]It also made us unpopular in some circles in Victoria, including with some at the Bar. Our families received abusive phone calls whilst we were away in Canberra.

[41]*Commonwealth v Tasmania* [1983] HCATrans 27 (9 June 2013), p 712f.

[42]*Commonwealth v Tasmania* [1983] HCATrans 27 (9 June 2013), p 713.

[43]*Commonwealth v Tasmania* [1983] HCATrans 28 (10 June 1983), p 739ff.

should proceed and we can reserve the question whether we should allow you to intervene'.[44]

Before proceeding to the submission I informed the Court that if intervention were allowed we intended to ask the Court to look at some published photographs of the area. It was emphasised that they simply depicted what was there, even though they were taken from books that were 'very controversial'.[45] The response from the Chief Justice was that the photographs could do no more than 'inflame our minds with irrelevancies'.[46]

My reply to the Chief Justice has been reported in a way that suggests it was rather cheeky, as if said: 'They are not *that* sort of photograph!' In fact, the transcript reveals a more measured and courteous response notwithstanding that the quoted words were used – or at least that is how I recall it. The point of course was that if the elements of the world's heritage in issue had been the cave paintings at Lascaux or Leonardo da Vinci's 'The Last Supper' they would be well-known and their great significance as part of the heritage of mankind – a matter of international concern we would argue – deeply and instinctively appreciated. Moreover, if needed, authoritative illustrations could be found in any serious library. (The transformative access provided by the internet was still well in the future.) Although this was not put before the Court specifically, the fact of the matter was that – in all probability – the only people present in the Court who had any first-hand knowledge of the unique qualities of the area, other than the few remaining Tasmanian Wilderness Society members and supporters,[47] were my junior and our instructing solicitor. The view of the Chief Justice, however, very firmly expressed, was that it could not be relevant for the court to know how beautiful the area was. 'We can assume its beauty'.[48]

The submission that followed[49] was, as promised, short. It occupies some six pages of the 797 pages of the transcript of the seven days of the hearing. There was only one intervention, an observation – supportive of a point we were making – by Murphy J.

Because it was essential to keep the submission very short, the sharpness of the legal point that we sought to make emerges most clearly when the submissions are read in conjunction with the outline we handed up to the Court. The outline was itself very short: one and a half pages of carefully constructed propositions, well within the strict limit of three A4 pages.[50] Essentially, our submission was that even on the narrowest view of the external affairs power, as it was now understood, the relevant subject matter of the Act and the regulations, namely the protection of the

---

[44]*Commonwealth v Tasmania* [1983] HCATrans 28 (10 June 1983), p 737.

[45]The expression 'very controversial' seems very odd 30 years later. The expression, like much else, is of course a reflection of the times and of circumstances forgotten.

[46]*Commonwealth v Tasmania* [1983] HCATrans 28 (10 June 1983), p 737.

[47]See fn 41 and also the reference to Mr Peter Underwood.

[48]*Commonwealth v Tasmania* [1983] HCATrans 28 (10 June 1983), p 737.

[49]Ernst Willheim has recently characterised the submission as one of introducing 'legislative facts' about the 'value of the Tasmanian wilderness' for the Court's consideration: Willheim (2010) 10 n 30.

[50]The use of the larger foolscap sheets, still in the State courts, was seen as cheating and not allowed. Single line spacing was seen as cheating too.

world's cultural and natural heritage, was of its very nature international in character, that the subject matter necessarily affected Australia's relations with other countries and, further, that the manner in which the subject matter was treated involved a relationship with other countries or with persons or things outside Australia. These three propositions, all expressed within the first paragraph of the outline, were developed in the next three. The outline contained just five paragraphs. In essence, we argued that when the truly international character of the subject matter was recognised, it was apparent that the central point of principle had been decided by the Court the previous year in *Koowarta v Bjelke-Petersen*.[51] In support of that proposition we gave particular attention to the 'international character' of the subject matter considered by Stephen J in *Koowarta*. It followed of course that on our argument the Court was not presented with a turning point at all.[52]

And so having been in the court for the whole of the hearing, on the last day a submission had been made by counsel retained on behalf of the Tasmanian Wilderness Society. But in what capacity had we addressed the Court? Gibbs CJ said:

> Mr Black, we did not formally rule as to whether you could intervene or not. There is no need to do so, we could treat what you have said as having been said by an amicus curia [sic] and that would suffice, would it not?[53]

The question did not invite an answer but perhaps the rather informal response: 'Your Honour, so long as we could say it …' reveals the sense of relief that I had been able to address the court as counsel briefed by a client whose members passionately wanted to be heard.

Submissions in reply and a brief note about the delivery of judgment

There then followed a short and powerful submission in reply by Mr Merralls, then another by Mr Gleeson and finally the reply of Mr Ellicott.

At the conclusion of his submission in reply Mr Ellicott expressed what I am sure were the sentiments of all present when he said: '… I thank the Court for the time that it has given to the case and the way it has.' The Chief Justice thanked Mr Ellicott and announced, in the ordinary way: 'The Court will consider the matter'. The Court then adjourned.

It had been a remarkable hearing and the remarkable sequel, perhaps not appreciated fully even by lawyers, was that only four weeks later, at its Brisbane sittings and having heard the other cases set down for hearing in the meantime, the Court delivered judgment. There were seven separate judgments totalling 272 pages. They occupy an entire volume of the *Commonwealth Law Reports*.

As it happened, and to my great regret, I was unable to be present for the delivery of judgment, a momentous occasion on all accounts described by Dr Bob Brown on the day of the symposium.

---

[51](1982) 153 CLR 168.

[52]At least in relation to the external affairs power; we did not address the corporations power.

[53]*Commonwealth v Tasmania* [1983] HCATrans 28 (10 June 1983), p 745.

From an advocate's viewpoint the case was a remarkable experience. Writing about it some 30 years later emphasises the importance of understanding the circumstances in which cases are argued and also brings to mind the fragility of parts of the historical record particularly the illuminating matters of fine detail. It brings to mind too the challenges and the great satisfactions that are part of an advocate's professional life.

Reference List

Statutes and Treaties

Australian Constitution

Convention for the Protection of Cultural Property in the Event of Armed Conflict opened for signature 14 May 1954, 249 UNTS 240 (entered into force 7 August 1956)

Convention (II) with respect to the Laws and Customs of War on Land opened for signature 29 July 1899, 187 CTS 429 (entered into force 4 September 1900)

Convention (IV) with respect to the Laws and Customs of War on Land opened for signature 18 October 1907, 205 CTS 277 (entered into force 26 January 1910)

Family Law Act 1975 (Cth)

National Parks and Wildlife Conservation Act 1975 (Cth)

Whale Protection Act 1980 (Cth)

World Heritage Properties Conservation Act 1983 (Cth)

World Heritage (Western Tasmania Wilderness) Regulations 1983 (Cth)

Case Law

Australian Communist Party v Commonwealth (1951) 83 CLR 1

Australian Conservation Foundation Inc. v Commonwealth (1980) 146 CLR 493

Bank of New South Wales v Commonwealth (1948) 76 CLR 1

Commonwealth v Tasmania (1983) 158 CLR 1

Huddart Parker & Co Pty Ltd v Moorehead (1909) 8 CLR 330

In re Municipal Officers Association of Australia (1978) 203 CAR 584

Koowarta v Bjelke-Petersen (1982) 153 CLR 168

Mabo v Queensland [No 1] (1988) 166 CLR 186

Mabo v Queensland [No 2] (1992) 175 CLR 1

New South Wales v Commonwealth (2006) 229 CLR 1

Onus v Alcoa of Australia Ltd (1981) 149 CLR 27

Tait v The Queen (1962) 108 CLR 620

Tasmanian Wilderness Society v Fraser (1982) 153 CLR 270

Hearing Transcripts

Commonwealth v Tasmania [1983] HCATrans 22 (1 June 1983)

Commonwealth v Tasmania [1983] HCATrans 24 (3 June 1983)

Commonwealth v Tasmania [1983] HCATrans 26 (8 June 1983)

Commonwealth v Tasmania [1983] HCATrans 27 (9 June 1983)

Commonwealth v Tasmania [1983] HCATrans 28 (10 June 1983)

Secondary Sources

ABC News Online, 'Marking 25 Years of the Franklin River Decision', http://www.abc.net.au/news/2008-07-01/marking-25-years-of-the-franklin-river-decision/2490228, 13 April 2010.

David Bennett (2001) 'Argument before the Court' in Michael Coper, Tony Blackshield and George Williams (eds) *The Oxford Companion to the High Court of Australia*, Oxford University Press.

Sir Gerard Brennan (2001) 'Decision-Making Process' in Michael Coper, Tony Blackshield and George Williams (eds) *The Oxford Companion to the High Court of Australia*, Oxford University Press.

Bob Brown (2012) 'Why I Am a Green' http://www.bobbrown.org.au/why_i_am_a_green

Sir Sydney Frost (1978) *Inquiry into Whales and Whaling (Australia)*, Australian Government Publishing Service.

Justice Susan Kenny (1998) 'Interveners and *Amici Curiae* in the High Court' 20 *Adelaide Law Review* 159.

Diane Kirkby (2011) 'Sex Discrimination, Workplace Opportunities and Law's Transformative Promise' 34 *Australian Feminist Law Journal* 127.

Sir Anthony Mason (1998) 'Interveners and *Amici Curiae* in the High Court: A Comment' 20 *Adelaide Law Review* 173.

Ernst Willheim (2010) '*Amici Curiae* and Access to Constitutional Justice in the High Court of Australia' 22 *Bond Law Review* 126.

Limitlessness in Australian Constitutional Legal Narrative: The memory of Black's Address in the *Tasmanian Dam Case*

Rebecca LaForgia

Law School, University of Adelaide

Given that clashes of federalism and the interpretation of powers are often the predominant themes in Australian constitutional culture, an especially intriguing element in the address of Michael Black QC, representing the Tasmanian Wilderness Society, in the High Court *Tasmanian Dam case* is the idea that there was something evocative and poetic that was said in a constitutional setting. This article does not replicate Black's legal argument directly or in its entirety, but instead gives a close examination of the text, with a view to engaging with the performance, or the spirit and the emotion, that pervades the address and evokes a concept of limitlessness in connections between self and nature. In reading Black's address, the purpose of this article is to re-create and expand on three deliberate steps contained within the oratory, which lead to this experience of limitlessness.

> And limitless are leaves stiff or drooping in the fields,
> And brown ants in the little wells beneath them.
> — Walt Whitman, *Song of Myself*

On the retirement of the Hon Michael Black AC QC from his long-held position as Chief Justice of the Federal Court of Australia, there were many references to the lasting legacy of his address to the High Court in the *Tasmanian Dam case*.[1] I was intrigued, given the length and significance of the former Chief Justice's legal career, that his address as a relatively young barrister had retained a presence in the memories of those who had heard it or heard about it.[2] An especially intriguing element in Black's *amicus curiae* address to the Court was the idea that there was something lasting and evocative that was said in a constitutional setting. Australian constitutional law, although it has had many seminal cases,[3] is often expressed as clashes of federalism, as interpretation of powers, but evocative and moving oratory has not been a dominant part of the constitutional culture.[4] From reading second-hand accounts of Black's address, it seemed it was an example of what White would

[1] *Commonwealth v Tasmania* (1983) 158 CLR 1 ('*Tasmanian Dam Case*'). For accounts of Black's legacy, see especially Black et al. (2010); Douglas (2010).

[2] This article hereafter refers to Chief Justice Black as Black.

[3] Lee and Winterton (2003), p 267.

[4] Lee and Winterton (2003), p xxix.

call the legal imagination at work – a narrative or perhaps a work of art, or even a performance 'at its best'.[5]

The contribution of this article is not to replicate Black's legal argument directly or in its entirety. Instead, the contribution is to give a close examination of the text, with a view to engaging with the performance, or the spirit and the emotion, that pervaded the address. I address this particular approach in part one, which deals with memory, narrative and performance. Here, I am inspired by the words of Margalit in his *The Ethics of Memory*, where he suggests that it is '*knowledge from the past*' and 'not necessarily knowledge *about* the past' which can define memory.[6] My guiding question, therefore, is what knowledge can be gained from this celebrated address?

Outline of arguments in the paper

The argument of this article is that there are three particular insights which build upon each other which are structurally part of Black's address. They are particular to the context of *Tasmanian Dams case*,[7] that is, being an environmental case which had attracted great political and social activism, participation and emotion, both for and against the protection of the Franklin-Lower Gordon Wild Rivers National Park.[8] The first insight is that Black accepts the inadequacy around the power of words to describe the truth and beauty of the River. This is an intriguing idea in a legal context, which of course often only relies on words. However, it is an important observation that is made by Black, because it inherently sets the tone of what follows as one of limitation. In an address to the Court which is based on representing the position of the Tasmanian Wilderness Society,[9] there is always the possibility that any form of address could risk becoming sentimental or too emotional and thereby distorting the reality of the political and legal struggle at hand. By calling into question or even renouncing the ability of words to ever convey either the representation of nature or legal arguments about the protection of nature, Black creates a humility in his address. It is this humility which gives the address's tone a sense of groundedness. This becomes important in listening to the text. Even though we are reading it many years later, we can hear the tone in which his subsequent arguments are delivered because of this preliminary acknowledgement that anything that he says will simply not be enough. The second insight that Black then provides is constructivist in orientation. Quoting from the *Unesco Constitution*,[10] he argues that 'wars begin in the minds of men'.[11]

---

[5]White (1973), p xxxv.

[6]Margalit (2004), p 14 (original emphasis).

[7](1983) 158 CLR 1.

[8]Coper (1983); Gibbs (2001); Zines (2001, 2003). See also Carrick (2013), where he interviews, inter alia, Bob Brown.

[9]Keyzer (2010), p 10; Zines (2003), p 267.

[10]*Constitution of the United Nations Educational, Scientific and Cultural Organisation*, opened for signature 16 November 1945, 4 UNTS 275 (entered into force 4 November 1946) ('*Unesco Constitution*').

[11]Transcript of Proceedings, *Commonwealth v Tasmania* (High Court of Australia, Gibbs CJ, Mason, Murphy, Wilson, Brennan, Deane and Dawson JJ, 10 June 1983) at 739 (M Black QC).

This idea of reality being constructed and highly contested in the 'minds of men' creates a keyhole in the very fabric of the legal argument itself. Black has through this assertion lifted the veil of legal authority itself, for if everything is made in the minds of men, then, inter alia, the High Court's authority, indeed the very fact that the audience keeps sitting there listening,[12] to the legal argument, the legal texts and the structure of society itself are constructed phenomena.[13] For the audience listening to this quote by Black, and if they accepted it, then their agency is increased, because any line that separates them from the High Court is in their own 'minds'. Black, through this method – and it will be further explored in this article – gives for that moment, at least, the audience an intimacy with the High Court. As Ball puts it,

> An audience is no less important to courtroom action. In court, there are potentially three audiences: spectators, jury and judge. While these participants are more specifically the subject of constitutional protection than is courtroom design, it need scarcely be said that this protection has not been tied to their character as audience whose presence is necessary to consummate a theatrical event.[14]

Here the audience is differently composed than Ball, who was discussing the 'theatre' of courts in the American context, suggests; however, the point is still relevant. This article argues, then, that Black breaks what is known in performance as the 'fourth wall', namely, inviting the audience in.[15]

The last observation which is made from Black's address is the way in which he deals with the concept of what is phrased 'limitlessness'. The concept of limitlessness had been entwined in the legal arguments that had been presented to the court over the interpretation of the external affairs power.[16] There was the question of whether

---

[12]To listen to the 'narrative of law' is to 'perhaps finally pay attention to the fact that issues of telling and listening ... find their ultimate commentary in the judicial opinion . . .': Brooks (2006), p 26.

[13]White (1985), p 121.

[14]Ball (1975), p 86.

[15]On the idea of performance, see Butler (1988), p 527: 'the links between a theatrical and a social role are complex and the distinctions not easily drawn (Bruce Wilshire points out the limits of the comparison in *Role-Playing and Identity: The Limits of Theatre as Metaphor*) . . .' We could make the same observation here, in terms of the link of performance and examining the court room address by Black. However, given its status as a memory, the observations are evocative of what occurred rather than a linear legal argument. The analogy with theatre metaphor breaking the fourth wall therefore works to introduce the special way in which Black introduced the presence of the audience. On co-construction, see also White (1985), p 121: 'One great merit of reading texts as compositions, made by composers, is that we affirm that we are composers too . . .'

[16]Limitlessness is a concept that is used within the *Tasmanian Dams case* (see, eg, Appleby (2007), pp 16, 32. For instance, the term 'limitless' was invoked in relation to the question of the characterisation of the external affairs power (Appleby (2007), p 32, citing, inter alia, *Tasmanian Dams case* (1983) 158 CLR 1, 99-100 (Gibbs CJ), 197 (Wilson J)). Limitlessness, however, also relates to the concept of boundless connections between people in a legal or a political context (Koskenniemi (2001), p 506; Young (2013)). Black was evoking this particular concept of limitlessness. Although this article does not argue that Black solved the problem of the form or content of limitless connections, it does argue that what he did do was contribute in a constitutional setting to grappling with the concept and thus for a moment

any treaty could enliven the power, and if so, the resultant limitlessness of the Commonwealth's power and its capacity perhaps to destroy federalism was a concern within the legal arguments presented to the High Court. But Black came at the concept of limitlessness from a different direction. He accepted that the external affairs power may be constrained to those treaties of 'international concern', and therefore he centred on what international concern means.

However unlike arguments in the past as to international concern, Black's argument was not limited by ideas of sovereignty.[17] For Black, what made something an international concern was not whether one state was interested in a matter occurring in another state, which in the context of this case was Tasmania, and was concerned about the treatment of the Gordon below Franklin dam. Rather Black argued that international concern happens because individuals are connected with nature, and if nature is destroyed, then individuals, wherever they may be across the world, are affected. This concept of limitless connection, as argued by Black, between individuals and between individuals and nature is a truly courageous and evocative concept. For that moment, his argument was that anyone, wherever they were geographically situated, would care about the destruction of nature, and therefore it was inherently international. The contribution of this aspect of his narrative is to emphasise that if we go back in time and imagine listening at this point, we can imagine, as does the audience, understanding exactly what he meant.[18] This is the last – and most important – aspect of the memory of Black's address, because, at least for that moment, as the last section of this article will suggest, we can imagine the audience understanding the conception of limitlessness he was speaking about, and therefore, through their eyes we ourselves over 30 years later can share in that memory as well. The ability to comprehend limitlessness is done in communion with others. This is the core memory of Black's address.

Why then would we take these three entwining arguments from Black and draw this knowledge from them? Because the ideas that he spoke of are still pressing today. While this article will not examine theories of limitlessness, it is instructive to underscore how limitlessness is present, although not necessarily acted on, in social, political and cultural responses to issues regarding the environment, trade, labour, consumerism, violence, gender, migration and asylum seekers – limitlessness is the simple but often difficult idea that something that happens elsewhere matters

---

he successfully evoked what such a connection would be. Such a grappling with an elusive concept such as limitlessness in a constitutional context is worth recording and exploring.

[17]See generally Coper (1983), pp 6–7; Zines (2003), pp 268–271. See also the excellent overview of 'international concern' in Edson (2008). Against arguments that the 'international concern doctrine' represents 'a radical expansion of s 51(xxix) as presently understood' (Edson (2007), p 270), Edson concludes (at 314): 'However, the ultimate touchstone of validity has remained constant; namely, the capacity of a matter to affect Australia's international relations. Once it is accepted that this is precisely what is conveyed by the notion of "international concern", it becomes clear that there is nothing new for the Court to be concerned about'. The overview provides a summary of the idea that international concern was seen as sovereignty rather than individuals generating international concern as Black was arguing.

[18]On the idea of imagination, see McNay (1994), pp 187–188: 'The creativity is a recurrent if somewhat submerged theme in the work of continental social theorists and philosophers such as Paul Ricoeur, Cornelius Castoriadis, Michel de Certeau and Alain Touraine. By emphasizing the creative dimensions of action, these authors highlight, in different ways, how even the most normative forms of behaviour presuppose imaginative elements'.

because we are connected. It is still one of the most difficult conceptual realizations for humans. Koskenniemi (in the context of international law) calls this movement towards enlargement of meaning and horizons of connection under the law a democratic question, because ultimately, democracy is in 'constant expansion'.[19] Iris Marion Young offers the same views again in an international setting, arguing for political idea of 'responsibility for justice',[20] which we all share. White speaks of 'limitless connections', almost as a memory of child-like innocence: 'Consider in this context a child's unbelieving horror at being told about war, and how suddenly empty seem our accounts of the justifications that engage our grown-up world so completely . . . .' Having evoked the pain of emptiness, White offers this timely observation: 'This capacity for complete, if momentary, identification with others will to some degree be left behind as the child grows up. But in all of us the memory at least should remain of a simple voice stating, a simple self hearing, a central truth'.[21]

Black's address, I want to suggest, is a core memory in Australian constitutional life, because it introduced a conception of 'international society', and at least just for that moment, and perhaps the moment in which we read the address, we can see limitlessness, an evocative and difficult concept to understand or comprehend. In reading Black's address, the purpose of this article is to re-create the three steps in oratory which lead to this experience of limitlessness.

Memory, narrative and performance

Before examining Black's steps to limitlessness, it is instructive to elucidate the method through which this article examines his address. The transcript of the case has only recently become available due to the generosity of the High Court when I approached them about this project.[22] The fact that his transcript has only publicly become available as a shared resource means that it is somewhat of a new memory. The *Tasmanian Dam case*[23] itself has been interpreted and reinterpreted, and it is a pre-eminent constitutional case in Australia's constitutional history. The purpose is not to suggest that Black's argument sheds new light on the case. Rather, the purpose is to consider his address as a memory from the case, and provide something quite distinct from a legal or a historical analysis.

In his seminal work, *The Ethics of Memory*, Avishai Margalit makes several observations about memory. Beginning with an analysis of what it means for a society to have a memory, Margalit draws a parallel with the individual and the role

---

[19]Koskenniemi (2001), p 506.

[20]Young (2013).

[21]White (1985), p 120.

[22]Bucholtz (2000), p 1439 underscores the reflexive quality of 'naturalized transcription'. However, I should note that in terms of access to the transcripts that they were not publically available prior to starting this project. I approached the High Court and they sent them to me and then placed them on Austlii. I am grateful for their democratisation of this resource. I would add here that a reference to the transcript can be found in Zines (2003), p 267. See http://www.austlii.edu.au/au/other/HCATrans/1983/ where the transcripts can be located. The subject of this article is the (10 June transcript).

[23](1983) 158 CLR 1.

that memory plays in that context. He also draws from the Gnostics, Plato and Freud to voice the idea that through remembering one can enter into freedom and full consciousness.[24] Taking these metaphors, he explores the healing idea of memory for a communal or a societal memory.[25] His exploration of these concepts sits very much outside of our historical inspired memory. 'Memory then is knowledge from the past. It is not necessarily knowledge about the past'.[26] Margalit notes that 'a constitution is a constitutive part of the community's shared memory', and as such, '[d]emocracy can and should include backward-looking emotions and attitudes as well, such as forgiveness and gratitude'.[27]

In this context the backward-looking memory from the *Tasmanian Dam case*[28] is indeed the poetry or the art, the beauty in Black's final address. To recall that the constitutional court can contain something of the poetic,[29] that despite its often (but not always) dry nature of legal reasoning, it does represent moments of art as evidenced in Black's address. Therefore, the way in which this article deals with language is also free and evocative and thereby consistent with Black's address.[30] For as Margalit notes, 'So far, I have talked of metaphors and images rather than arguments and premises. This is as it should be. Our thinking about memory is in the *grip of powerful images . . .*'[31]

The idea of remembering Black's narrative is to be free to bring in imagery, evocative language, indeed imaginative leaps, and try and gain something from imagining being back listening to his address. In order to achieve this, the text is approached in a chronological manner. Each ordering idea is quoted and then that ordering idea is explored.[32]

What follows in this article is an exploration of the memory and narrative of Black as represented in the *Tasmanian Dam* transcript. It is a memory that was not represented in the judgment, yet it will be argued that the memory deserves to be remembered. This therefore orientates the exploration of the text. The guiding question in this article is what can we learn from Black's address? As such, the memory is more in the nature of the visual, impressionistic, trying to listen to his performance while working from his words. It is a fluid exploration of the transcription, for, as Feldman et al have noted, 'the terms *narrative* and *story* are often used interchangeably'.[33] This is the approach in this article, namely, to combine elements of narrative and story, but with particular attention to how the elements reveal memories and moments of art. In the words of Brooks,

[24]Gnostics: Margalit (2004), p 1; Plato: Margalit (2004), p 2; Freud: Margalit (2004), pp 2–4.

[25]Margalit (2004), p 5.

[26]Margalit (2004), p 14.

[27]Margalit (2004), p 12.

[28](1983) 158 CLR 1.

[29]On poetry and the law, see generally White (1985), pp 107–138.

[30]Margalit (2004), p 6.

[31]Margalit (2004), p 6 (emphasis added).

[32]Franzosi (1998), p 526 (quoting Vladimir Propp's *Morphology of the Folktale*): 'The sequence of events has its own laws'.

[33]Feldman et al (2004) p 149 (original emphasis). For an interesting overview of narrative research, see Smeyers and Verhesschen (2001).

'Narratology . . . distinguishes between events in the world and the ways in which they are presented in narratives. It pays attention to the parts of the narrative and how they combine in a plot'.[34] This article creates a written memory of both the narrative and from this narrative the story of Black's address in *Tasmanian Dam*.

The transcript is also approached as a performance imbued with symbolic sociopolitical meanings.[35] As Butler observes, drawing on the work of George Herbert Mead and others, an effort 'to explain the mundane way in which social agents *constitute* social reality through language, gesture, and all manner of symbolic social sign'.[36] Black is a performer, he has presence and is introduced to the audience, both us as the historical figure and the one who is reading the transcript at the beginning of the hearing. Chief Justice Gibbs' acknowledgment of Black's physical presence in the following exchange:

> GIBBS CJ: Yes. Thank you, Mr Black. Mr Black, the Court will reserve its decision on your application. If you are so-minded at the close of the subsequent arguments you may renew your application and we can consider it then in the light of our fuller knowledge.
> MR BLACK: May it please the Court. *May we remain*?
> GIBBS CJ: *Of course*.[37]

Black remained and we do not come back to him until ten days later when Chief Justice Gibbs recalls his 'existence':

> GIBBS CJ: No, well, it [ie the Court] will not sit beyond tomorrow, so counsel could shape — *we have not forgotten your existence*, Mr Black. We will deal with your application tomorrow.[38]

We have the sense of Black waiting patiently for his time. When his time comes he has only a brief moment to make his case, but his formal status as an intervener on behalf of the Tasmanian Wilderness Society is never ruled on.

> GIBBS CJ: Mr Black, *we did not formally rule as to whether you could intervene or not*. There is no need to do so, we could treat what you have said as having been said by an amicus curia [sic] and that would suffice, would it not?

---

[34]Brooks (2006), p 2.

[35]White (1985), p 117: 'The world often presents cases no mind could anticipate, in circumstances no one could wholly foresee, and in such instances the meaning the law gives to its governing words must be new (however the case is decided) ... And the meaning given by the law to its central terms has a deeply performative aspect as well.'

[36]Butler (1988), p 519 (original emphasis).

[37]Transcript of Proceedings, *Commonwealth v Tasmania* (High Court of Australia, Gibbs CJ, Mason, Murphy, Wilson, Brennan, Deane and Dawson JJ, 31 May 1983) at 7 (emphasis added).

[38]Transcript of Proceedings, *Commonwealth v Tasmania* (High Court of Australia, Gibbs CJ, Mason, Murphy, Wilson, Brennan, Deane and Dawson JJ, 9 June 1983) at 725 (emphasis added).

MR BLACK: May it please the Court. Your Honour, *so long as we could say it*, may it please the Court.
GIBBS CJ: Yes, thank you, Mr Black. . . .[39]

The analysis regarding Black's three core arguments that follows in the following sections of this article has assumed and, indeed, imagined some contextual background:[40] it has imagined that Black has patiently listened to the hearing, that he feels the intensity of the *one* brief opportunity he is given rather than the luxury of an advocate with the time to work into an argument. It also imagines the importance of his presence as he 'remains'[41] and his attitude of gratitude 'as long as we could say it'.[42] In this re-imagining of the day, there is an 'audience',[43] that is, Members of the Tasmanian Wilderness Society and others are watching him, the judiciary and audience are listening.[44] If there was no audience then, there is now as we the readers embark on watching his performance through the transcripts. The analysis that follows considers his narrative embedded in the transcript as a memory of his performance that day. Indeed, performance can exert an expansive pressure on interactions with an audience.[45] The objective of examining a transcript, as Franzosi states, is not so much to ask 'What is the story?', i.e. the arguments that were run, but rather '*Why* is the story told?'[46] The following three sections seek to evoke and relive the moment and lessons from the address drawing from his words and ideas to understand why it was told, and therefore why it is important to retell.

---

[39]Transcript of Proceedings, *Commonwealth v Tasmania* (High Court of Australia, Gibbs CJ, Mason, Murphy, Wilson, Brennan, Deane and Dawson JJ, 10 June 1983) at 745 (emphasis added).

[40]The above discussion is 'foregrounding' for the narrative analysis that follows. On the concept of foregrounding, see Franzosi (1998), p 532. The description of the case's background by Black in an ABC Radio National Law Report interview in 2013 is more legalistic than the transcript of his argument itself suggests. As Black said in the interview (Carrick (2013)), when describing the 'crux' of his argument: 'The argument was very short and it was based almost entirely on the earlier High Court decision in Koowarta and Bjelke-Petersen, and basically said if you apply what came out of that case to the circumstances of the Tasmanian dam case, then the law should be held to be a valid exercise of the power to make laws with respect to external affairs.'

[41]Transcript of Proceedings, *Commonwealth v Tasmania* (High Court of Australia, Gibbs CJ, Mason, Murphy, Wilson, Brennan, Deane and Dawson JJ, 31 May 1983) at 7 (M Black QC).

[42]Transcript of Proceedings, *Commonwealth v Tasmania* (High Court of Australia, Gibbs CJ, Mason, Murphy, Wilson, Brennan, Deane and Dawson JJ, 10 June 1983) at 745 (M Black QC).

[43]See Ball (1975).

[44]I could find no record of the member of Tasmanian Wilderness Society being there but I have taken the liberty of imagining there was an audience – friends of the court, or *amici curiae* – watching him. Pelias and VanOoosting (1987), p 220 (original emphasis): '"aesthetic communication" may be defined in terms of *effects* or *response*. Ever since Plato banished the poet from his ideal Republic, theorists have been interested in the social, ethical, political, and aesthetic effects of artistic discourse upon listeners and readers'.

[45]In the 'field' of 'performance', as Schechner notes, '[t]he whole constellation of events, most of them passing unnoticed, that takes place in both performers and audience from the time the first spectator enters the field of the performance — the precinct where the theatre takes place — to the time the last spectator leaves.' Schechner (1973), p 8.

[46]Franzosi (1998), p 532 (emphasis added).

Memory one: The limited nature of words for 'nature' – creating a tone of reflection and humility

Black begins his address to the Court by seeking to introduce photographs of the Franklin River; however, Chief Justice Gibbs rejects this for fear the photographs would 'inflame' the justices' minds'.[47] This rejection was followed by a robust yet humble response from Black:

> Your Honour, not 'inflame' Your Honours' minds; and they are certainly not that sort of photograph, and they are not desired to be put forward for that purpose, Your Honour. But, Your Honours, this is part of Australia. If we were talking about the pyramids, or Leonardo's Last Supper, or Lascaux, all of which are on the list, if the Court did not know them, it could look them up. Now, Your Honour, this is a very special part of Australia and, in the crudest way only, *a photograph can perhaps tell more than words. And, Your Honours only have words.*[48]

At this point, Black must have felt very keenly about the idea that he had the burden of translating the beauty of the Franklin River to the Court. Yet he was conceding that his arguments were and would be limited, and that he needed 'more than words'. This, although at the time was part of a plea to the Court to introduce the visual, in fact worked an important point in establishing tone. Tone in a performance is difficult to glean when you are reading the text some 30 years after the event.[49] Nonetheless, through the above extract we have, perhaps, a tone of desperation and inherent humility in that Black was quite sure that he could not describe, without the visual, the beauty of the area in the proposed Gordon Below Franklin dam scheme. Perhaps he was hoping to introduce silence, observation and a shared sense of what he was speaking about to the Court. He had lost this capacity, and in so doing, all that he had was his own words to follow.

This concept of a humble tone is important when considering idealism or utopian conceptions. Often, the thing that has to be mitigated against with idealism is a sense of disconnection or preaching to the audience or judges. The arguments that were to be made by Black were not based on utilitarianism or proportionality, nor were they grounded in any authoritative legal text. He was firmly entering into a terrain of the more evocative, spiritual, poetic, into the terrain that he had hoped that the visual would naturally usher him into. The recognition that he needed an aid and the

---

[47]Gibbs CJ: 'Yes. The photographs could do no more than inflame our minds with irrelevancies, could they?' Transcript of Proceedings, *Commonwealth v Tasmania* (High Court of Australia, Gibbs CJ, Mason, Murphy, Wilson, Brennan, Deane and Dawson JJ, 10 June 1983) at 737. See also Zines (2003), p 267. See also Gibbs CJ : '...it cannot be relevant, can it, for us to know how beautiful the area is. We can assume its beauty'. p 737. There is an interesting parallel, the words of Black, like the visual he sought to introduce, have been 'lost' until their public release. See footnote 22 for further details.

[48]Transcript of Proceedings, *Commonwealth v Tasmania* (High Court of Australia, Gibbs CJ, Mason, Murphy, Wilson, Brennan, Deane and Dawson JJ, 10 June 1983) at 737 (emphasis added).

[49]Anderson and Pildes (2000), p 1507: 'To interpret what an action means, we try to identify what the agent is doing. Deeds are identified, not by mere physical descriptions of bodily movement, but by the intentions that they express and that give them meaning. Interpretation is a matter of making sense of the speech or action in its context.'

hesitation that he expressed about the limits of words make this a very human journey, and naturally grounded the idealism which followed. We have the sense that he is about to do his best, knowing inherently it will never quite capture what he wants. This makes us, his readers, already on his side. He is precisely the opposite of someone who is looking down from the pulpit or taking on an air of arrogant advocacy. He is already expressing his humanness and limitations, which is communication through 'nonverbal information'.[50] In his own way he is setting a tone. This enables, right from the beginning, the sharing of this memory with Black, and we can imagine listening to his concession and perhaps feeling empathy in terms of the task that is before him. What it also does is to enable us to read the following arguments, which are quite radical with its egalitarian and humble rendition.

Memory two: Everyone is part of the Courtroom (For a moment) — Black's introduction of social constructivism

Black's core submission was that the protection of the Franklin River and surrounding rain forests was an 'international concern'. This use of the concept of international concern is familiar in the *Tasmanian Dam* context. As was well known, the Court had yet to finally establish whether any treaty could enliven the external affairs power, or whether it was limited to a treaty of international concern. Black, through addressing the Court on international concern, was presumably hedging his legal argument, so that if the Court did not endorse the expansive position of the external affairs power encompassing any treaty, his arguments would still be considered. Yet what is interesting about Black's address is that his conception of international concern is radical. Indeed, although he operates within the scope of the restrictive interpretation of the external affairs power, his approach to international concern as a concept is anything but restrictive. He uses the language of international concern, in fact it will be argued, to create limitless connections, and an idea of international society, rather than one based purely on the interests of sovereign states.

Black, when identifying Australia's obligations under the *Convention for the Protection of the World Cultural and Natural Heritage*,[51] and, inter alia, quoting the *Unesco Constitution*, introduces constructivism as a lens to address the Court. Elucidating the subject-matter of the Commonwealth's legislative and related efforts to implement Australia's obligations,[52] Black identifies the critical core of the need to protect world heritage:

> [T]he subject-matter is international because the recognition by the international community of a world heritage and the co-operation of that community for its protection advances the first object of international relations, namely, peace, and that was recognized by the nations of the world when they emerged from one of their darkest

[50] Ball (1975), p 102.

[51] *Convention for the Protection of the World Cultural and Natural Heritage*, opened for signature 16 November 1972, 1037 UNTS 151 (entered into force 17 December 1975).

[52] *National Parks and Wildlife Conservation Act 1975* (Cth); *World Heritage Properties Conservation Act 1983* (Cth); *World Heritage (Western Tasmania Wilderness) Regulations 1983* (Cth).

> hours in 1945 when they said, in the constitution of UNESCO, 'Since wars begin in the minds of men, it is in the minds of men that the defences of peace must be constructed'. And they said one other thing that has not been cited to the Court, I think — I think Your Honour Mr Justice Murphy referred to it — but, later down in the preamble, they said this — that, 'A peace based exclusively upon the political and economic arrangements of governments would not be a peace which would secure the unanimous, lasting and sincere support of the peoples of the world and that the peace must, therefore, be founded, if it is not to fail, upon the intellectual and moral solidarity of mankind', and we say, in our respectful submission, that mankind's own heritage — its overall heritage — is an aspect of — and a fundamental aspect of — its intellectual and moral solidarity.[53]

This is an allusion to a deep sense of constructivism, a world in which our identity, our fears, our futures are made in our minds. It is both a collective and an individual constructivism. Constructivists regard 'knowledge and truth as created not discovered by the mind',[54] and maintain that there is no necessary conflict between realism and relativism.[55] 'One can believe that concepts are constructed rather than discovered yet maintain that they correspond to something real in the world'.[56] In expressing the idea the creation of war but also peace is in the minds of people, Black is addressing the Court from this lens of constructivism.

If the audience believes Black on this point, they are pulled into, and indeed they could be seen to, have co-created the very jurisdiction of the High Court.[57] The audience in sitting and observing is giving over to the authority of the Court, but it is the very belief of the audience in the authority of the Court which is creating the Court's authority itself. That is the logical line of thought from the lens of constructivism. In a sense, then, Black's performance can be seen to break the 'fourth wall'.[58] In essence, the fourth wall is a performative idea in which there is a normally a wall between the performer and the 'audience'.[59] That wall enables the performance to occur as though in 'real life' with the observer looking on. As Jacobson et al put it:

---

[53]Transcript of Proceedings, *Commonwealth v Tasmania* (High Court of Australia, Gibbs CJ, Mason, Murphy, Wilson, Brennan, Deane and Dawson JJ, 10 June 1983) at 739.

[54]Andrews (2012), p 40. Regarding the epistemological dimensions of social constructivism, see Roy (2005), p 101: 'Recent work by philosophers such as Evelyn Fox Keller (1992), Sandra Harding (1998) and others have shown quite persuasively that the 'reality' that testifies to such correspondence is itself a result of choice and suppression and not the dissemination of 'pure light of knowledge' as some might suppose. Earlier, Michel Foucault's (1972) work on the human sciences had revealed the intimate relations between power and knowledge, showing how discourse operates to produce accepted truths. Given the depth and extent of this critical literature, only the die-hard realist can maintain that communication is merely a matter of the acquisition and deployment of codes.'

[55]Andrews (2012), pp 41–45.

[56]Andrews (2012) p 40.

[57]Note also that constructivist analysis of language in a constitutional setting. See Anderson and Pildes (2000), p 1575, citing Charles Taylor's essays 'Language and Human Nature' and 'Theories of Meaning' in volume 1 of his *Human Agency and Language: Philosophical Papers.*

[58]On the expansive use of the term 'fourth wall' in a non-theatre context, see generally Quinlan and Duggleby (2009).

[59]On courtroom and theatre, and specifically the audience, see Ball (1975), pp 86–88.

> The naturalistic theatre's fourth wall made it possible for the actors to behave on stage as they would in a real room, in real life, and the audience could observe the fiction 'as if they were observing real life. The imaginary fourth wall between the audience and the acting characters enabled a more direct interacting between the characters . . .[60]

To break this fourth wall it is, in other words,

> necessary to drop the assumption that there is a fourth wall cutting the audience off from the stage, and the consequent illusion that the stage acting is taking place in reality, and without an audience. That being so, it is possible for the actor in principle to address the audience direct.[61]

This is indeed what Black's constructivism achieved. If those listening believed or internalised the point Black was making, then naturally they were included in the courtroom – the fourth wall was broken[62] – for Black's address assumed that their very minds created and were responsible for the Court's authority.[63]

It is interesting to note that Black's jurisdictional pedigree was never formally established, and that he was never actually awarded formal intervener status. However, he was present within the courtroom. Chief Justice Gibbs said the Court has 'not forgotten' Mr Black, thus bringing him within the presence of the Court. His uncertain status, his capacity to address the Court as *amicus curiae* on behalf of the Tasmanian Wilderness Society,[64] operates as a keyhole to let in, through his constructivist lens, others that also have simply been present and waiting, but to whom the words I have 'not forgotten' you would not have been uttered by the Chief Justice. It was Black as a type of bridge between audience and legal actors who then invited the audience, whether members of the Tasmanian Wilderness Society or others, as watchers and listeners to see themselves as co-creators of the judicial world, and therefore also of the authority of the Court.[65] It is precisely this audience involvement which proves pivotal to enlivening the final point made by Black. He has articulated a conception of law that echoes what White sought to achieve in his seminal work *Heracles' Bow*, namely, a 'sense of the law as a social and cultural activity, as something we do with our minds, with language and with each other'. Law is seen not a mechanical institutional exercise 'but as a kind of rhetorical and literary activity'.[66]

---

[60]Jacobsen et al (2006).

[61]Jacobsen et al (2006).

[62]This is the operative conclusion to the use of the theatre metaphor as espoused by Ball (1975), p 109. It is more consistent with arguments regarding 'enlarging the mind' and 'inducing creativity' (see Ball (1975) pp 103, 104).

[63]Jacobsen et al (2006).

[64]Keyzer (2010), p 104.

[65]Dorsett and McVeigh (2012), p 5: 'Jurisdictional thought and practice provides the visible (and occasionally invisible) forms that law takes'.

[66]White (1985), p x.

Memory 3: Limitlessness

The core of Black's final argument concerns the concept of limitlessness in connections between self and nature. Black suggests, and it is worth taking his narrative in full, that we are connected to nature, and that every individual feels this connection and the loss of it wherever they may be.

> Now, what we say is that there is a special relationship, a very special relationship between man and his cultural and natural heritage. It is more than a mere intellectual or emotional concern. One's heritage is part of one. If it is lost, one loses. What one loses may be much more valuable a loss to man than the loss of a chattel, in the loss of the interests that the law, traditionally, has protected. And we do not wish to go through the whole World Heritage List and would not be permitted to. But, may we take three examples? The cave paintings at Lascaux, Leonardo da Vinci's Last Supper and part of the natural heritage, the Galapagos Islands. Can it be said that if any of those things were lost or destroyed that nothing would be *lost as part of one*? And, we submit, it cannot be said.
>
> What it is that would be lost I find impossible to define. All that we do assert, with respect, is that something very important — a very important part of people would be lost. And it would not be lost only within Australia, *it would be lost throughout the world.* And the Australian law, we say, by protecting this thing, protects interests outside Australia and therein, we submit, lies a relationship between Australia and things and persons outside Australia. It is a relationship in the mind, at one level, and it is a physical relationship in the other, because things that could be enjoyed for their physical attributes would, actually, be lost if the heritage were lost.[67]

A certain quality resonates in Black's address; he uses poetic language to cement the idea of feeling and connection with nature. Following immediately on from the above narrative, Black remarks:

> May we paraphrase something that John Dunne [sic] said nearly 400 years ago? 'Any loss of man's heritage diminishes me because I am involved in mankind'. We say, that protection against that sort of diminution is the essence of an international relationship because the matter is international. And we say, too, that this is a different sort of protection to the sort of protection of human rights that the minority — some of Your Honours dealt with — in Koowarta.[68]

Black's contribution to the idea of a human identity is reminiscent of Taylor's conception of authenticity. As Taylor said in *The Malaise of Modernity*, 'Authenticity is not the enemy of demands that emanate from beyond the self; it supposes such demands'.[69] The weightiness of authenticity as a concept aside, it is important to note that Black's brief account to the Court of limitless connection is not a philosophy but instead is an *assertion* of connection between self and nature. What is

---

[67]Transcript of Proceedings, *Commonwealth v Tasmania* (High Court of Australia, Gibbs CJ, Mason, Murphy, Wilson, Brennan, Deane and Dawson JJ, 10 June 1983) at 743 (emphasis added).

[68]Transcript of Proceedings, *Commonwealth v Tasmania* (High Court of Australia, Gibbs CJ, Mason, Murphy, Wilson, Brennan, Deane and Dawson JJ, 10 June 1983) at 743.

[69]Quoted in Frank (2002), p 112.

important to recall is that Black has brought the audience in.[70] We do not need to be limited to conceiving the validity of his assertion of limitless connection through our own eyes or in a philosophical or detached sense. We can imagine the audience listening to this assertion about the Franklin River, and if we imagine them listening, we can also imagine that they *would not* have stood up in shock saying, 'I do not understand what you are saying. This is incomprehensible'.[71] The audience is given the role, through their presence and comprehension of Black's address to the Court, to 'hail' into existence the idea of limitless connections between self and nature.[72]

Most people in that courtroom would not have misunderstood what Black was saying about the Franklin River. For that moment, he himself had constructed that reality which happened to include the whole world, the Franklin River and everyone in the Court. Therefore, the idea and the validity of limitlessness is mediated through imagining those listening to his address.[73] The memory that we take from his address is the knowledge that limitlessness can and did exist at that moment in that courtroom.[74] The limitlessness was understood and comprehended, and therefore *is not* an impossibility of the mind.[75] This comprehension or belief may only have been held onto briefly, perhaps it shattered when Black sat down, but in re-reading the address and imagining the audience listening, we can have a sense of holding on to it again.

Conclusion

Australian constitutional law often does not have these poetic memories within it, and yet Black's address did not last simply because it was beautiful but because it

---

[70]On the role of communication in forming relationships with the audience and bringing them in, see Anderson and Pildes (2000), pp 1571-2.

[71]See not this observation but the concept of imagining the responses of an audience in Butler (1988), p 528. See also Taylor (1980), p 298 (original emphasis): 'Language is shaped by speech and so can only grow up in a speech community. The language I speak, the web which I can never fully dominate and oversee, can never be just *my* language, it is always largely *our* language'. He continues in the next paragraph: 'This opens up another field of the constitutive functions of language'.

[72]Through imagining the lack of outrage, and the existence of understanding of those in the audience, Black's address works to 'hail' the idea into existence. Black has enabled the audience, through actively including them, to interpellate, or to become an authority for the point he is making. On interpellation and the use of the term 'hail', see generally Webb, Schirato and Danaher (2002), p 9: 'In other words, this involves not so much predicting history as helping to make it through a process that is very close to what Louis Althusser describes as 'interpellation'. For Althusser, identity comes into being when it is interpellated, or 'hailed' by someone in authority – for instance, when a member of the police force calls out, 'Hey you!' to someone in the street, and that person acknowledges the hailing (even if it is by running away).'

[73]On the mediation of limitlessness, see Anderson and Pildes (2000), p 1572.

[74]See generally Werman (1986), p 134.

[75]On the 'oceanic' sensations evoked by the sense of limitlessness, see Vermorel (2009), p 1244. See also Saarinen (2012). The above impossibility is often critiqued not simply from pragmatism or the practical difficulty of the realisation of limitlessness, but from a rejection of the 'oceanic' feeling as naïve. See Simmonds (2006) p 130: 'Rolland made to Freud's neglect of what Rolland considered to be "the true source of religious feeling," namely the oceanic feeling.'

was imbued with commitment to make the audience part of the poetic memories. The address lasted, as this article has argued, because of the three oratory steps that Black took. The first was to create a tone of humility, the second was to invite the audience within the Court and the third was to invite the audience in as a witness and co-creator to the radical idea of limitless connection. Their very witness proved the possibility of that idea. It is a narrative, a memory, in part filled in with my own imaginative steps, but going back to the original text – Black's address – supports this reading. Such a reading is important because 'hearing the moral impulse in other's stories enable us to be become part of their struggle to re-enchant a disenchanted world'.[76] Robert Cover states that, 'No set of legal institutions or prescriptions exist apart from the narratives that locate it and give it meaning. For every constitution there is an epic . . .'[77] Black's address was not a constitutional epic. Instead, it is a story contained and indeed until recently entombed within the epic of what became the decision in the *Tasmanian Dam case*.[78] This article has presented a constitutional story worth telling – a story about the memory of re-imagining the moment of comprehension and belief (if only for the briefest time) over limitless connections between ourselves and nature.

Acknowledgements

My sincere gratitude to the excellent editing provided by Dr Kim Sorensen and thanks also to the constructive comments provided in the referee reports.

References

Primary Legal Sources

Commonwealth v Tasmania (1983) 158 CLR 1.
Constitution of the United Nations Educational, Scientific and Cultural Organisation, opened for signature 16 November 1945, 4 UNTS 275 (entered into force 4 November 1946).
Convention for the Protection of the World Cultural and Natural Heritage, opened for signature 16 November 1972, 1037 UNTS 151 (entered into force 17 December 1975).
National Parks and Wildlife Conservation Act 1975 (Cth).
Transcript of Proceedings, *Commonwealth v Tasmania* (High Court of Australia, Gibbs CJ, Mason, Murphy, Wilson, Brennan, Deane and Dawson JJ, 31 May 1983).
Transcript of Proceedings, *Commonwealth v Tasmania* (High Court of Australia, Gibbs CJ, Mason, Murphy, Wilson, Brennan, Deane and Dawson JJ, 9 June 1983).
Transcript of Proceedings, *Commonwealth v Tasmania* (High Court of Australia, Gibbs CJ, Mason, Murphy, Wilson, Brennan, Deane and Dawson JJ, 10 June 1983).
World Heritage Properties Conservation Act 1983 (Cth).
World Heritage (Western Tasmania Wilderness) Regulations 1983 (Cth).

Secondary Sources

Elizabeth S Anderson and Richard H Pildes (2000) 148 *University of Pennsylvania Law Review* 1503.
Tom Andrews (2012) 'What is Social Constructionism?' 11 *Grounded Theory Review* 39.

---

[76]Frank (2002), p 116. This 'struggle' is inextricably linked with themes of 'disenchantment' with modernity and the attenuation of authenticity. Frank (2002), p 109 (citing Weber's *From Max Weber*): 'At the core of Weber's understanding of modernity is the idea of disenchantment.' See also Frank's discussion of Taylor, in Frank (2002), p 112.

[77]Cover (1983), p 4.

[78](1983) 158 CLR 1.

Gabrielle Appleby (2007) 'Proportionality and Federalism: Can Australia Learn From the European Community, the US and Canada?' 26 *University of Tasmania Law Review* 1.
Milner S Ball (1975) 'The Play's the Thing: An Unscientific Reflection on Courts Under the Rubric of Theater' 28 *Stanford Law Review* 81.
Michael Black et al (2010) 'Transcript of Ceremonial Sitting of the Full Court on the Occasion of the Opening of the New Ceremonial Court and Farewell to the Honourable Michael Black AC Chief Justice, Federal Court of Australia' 7 *Federal Judicial Scholarship*, http://www.austlii.edu.au/au/journals/FedJSchol/2010/7.html.
Peter Brooks (2006) 'Narrative Transactions — Does the Law Need a Narratology?' 18 *Yale Journal of Law & the Humanities* 1.
Mary Bucholtz (2000) 'The Politics of Transcription' 32 *Journal of Pragmatics* 1439.
Judith Butler (1988) 'Performative Acts and Gender Constitution: An Essay in Phenomenology and Feminist Theory' 40 *Theatre Journal* 519.
Damien Carrick (2013) 'Wilderness Case that Changed Course of Federal Power' (interview with Bob Brown, Michael Black and Lee Godden) *ABC Radio National Law Report*, 2 July 2013, http://www.abc.net.au/radionational/programs/lawreport/tasmanian-dams-30-years/4793690#transcript.
Michael Coper (1983) *The Franklin Dam Case*, Butterworths.
Robert M Cover (1983) 'The Supreme Court 1982 Term — Foreword: *Nomos and Narrative*' 97 *Harvard Law Review* 4.
Shaunnagh Dorsett and Shaun McVeigh (2012) *Jurisdiction*, Routledge.
Richard Douglas (2010) 'Ceremonial Farewell for the Hon Justice Michael Black AC' (speech delivered on 26 February 2010, at a ceremonial sitting of the Federal Court in Brisbane) *Hearsay: The Journal of the Bar Association of Queensland*, March 2010, http://www.hearsay.org.au/index.php?option=com_content&task=view&id=720&Itemid=48.
Elise Edson (2008) 'Section 51(xxix) of the *Australian Constitution* and "Matters of International Concern": Is There Anything to be Concerned About?' 29 *Adelaide Law Review* 269.
Martha S Feldman et al (2004) 'Making Sense of Stories: A Rhetorical Approach to Narrative Analysis' 14 *Journal of Public Administration Research and Theory* 147.
Arthur W Frank (2002) 'Why Study People's Stories? The Dialogical Ethics of Narrative Analysis' 1 *International Journal of Qualitative Methods* 109.
Roberto Franzosi (1998) 'Narrative Analysis — Or Why (and How) Sociologists Should Be Interested in Narrative' 24 *Annual Review of Sociology* 517.
Harry Gibbs (2001) 'External Affairs Power: A Critical Analysis' in Tony Blackshield, Michael Coper and George Williams (eds) *The Oxford Companion to the High Court of Australia*, Oxford University Press.
Torild Jacobsen et al (2006) 'Analysis of Role-Play in Medical Communication Training Using a Theatrical Device the Fourth Wall' 6 *BMC Medical Education*, http://www.biomedcentral.com/1472-6920/6/51.
Patrick Keyzer (2010) *Open Constitutional Courts*, Federation Press.
Martii Koskenniemi (2001) *The Gentler Civilizer of Nations: The Rise and Fall of International Law 1870–1960*, Cambridge University Press.
HP Lee and George Winterton (eds) *Australian Constitutional Landmarks*, Cambridge University Press.
Avishai Margalit (2004) *The Ethics of Memory,* paperback edn, Harvard University Press.
Lois McNay (1999) 'Subject, Psyche and Agency: The Work of Judith Butler' 16 *Theory, Culture & Society*, 175.
Ronald J Pelias and James VanOosting (1987) 'A Paradigm for Performance Studies' 73 *Quarterly Journal of Speech* 219.
Elizabeth Quinlan and Wendy Duggleby (2009) '"Breaking the Fourth Wall": Activating Hope Through Participatory Theatre with Family Caregivers' 4 *International Journal of Qualitative Studies on Health and Well-Being* 207.
Kaustuv Roy (2005) 'On Sense and Nonsense: Looking Beyond the Literacy Wars' 39 *Journal of Philosophy of Education* 99.
Jussi Antti Saarinen (2012) 'The Oceanic State: A Conceptual Elucidation in Terms of Modal Contact' 93 *International Journal of Psychoanalysis* 939.

Richard Schechner (1973) 'Drama, Script, Theatre, and Performance' 17(3) *The Drama Review: TDR* 5.
Janette Graetz Simmonds (2006) 'The Oceanic Feeling and a Sea Change: Historical Challenges to Reductionist Attitudes to Religion and Spirit From Within Psychoanalysis' 23 *Psychoanalytic Psychology* 128.
Paul Smeyers and Piet Verhesschen (2001) 'Narrative Analysis as Philosophical Research: Bridging the Gap Between the Empirical and the Conceptual' 14 *International Journal of Qualitative Studies in Education* 71.
Charles Taylor (1980) 'Theories of Meaning' 13 *Man and World* 281.
Henri Vermorel (2009) 'The Presence of Spinoza in the Exchanges between Sigmund Freud and Romain Rolland' 90 *International Journal of Psychoanalysis* 1235.
David S Werman (1986) 'On the Nature of the Oceanic Experience' 34 *Journal of the American Psychoanalytic Association* 123.
James B White (1973) *The Legal Imagination: Studies in the Nature of Legal Thought and Expression*, Little, Brown and Company.
James Boyd White (1985) *Heracles' Bow: Essays on the Rhetoric and Poetics of the Law*, University of Wisconsin Press.
Iris Marion Young (2011) *Responsibility for Justice*, Oxford University Press.
Leslie Zines (2001) 'External Affairs Power' in Tony Blackshield, Michael Coper and George Williams (eds) *The Oxford Companion to the High Court of Australia*, Oxford University Press.
Leslie Zines (2003) 'The *Tasmanian Dam Case*' in HP Lee and George Winterton (eds) *Australian Constitutional Landmarks*, Cambridge University Press.

Experiences of coming to law: An Interview with Bob Brown on the Tasmanian wilderness society as client in the *Tasmanian Dam Case*

Martin Clark

Melbourne Law School, Melbourne, Australia

While histories of law tend to examine the lawyers and judges involved through readings of the texts of transcripts and judgments, this contribution contextualises and presents a different and rarer artefact: the recollections of a client seeking to become part of a divisive, nationally significant case. The text here is a transcript that combines two interviews I conducted with Dr Bob Brown about his experience as head of the Tasmanian Wilderness Society when it sought to appear as *amicus curiae* before the High Court in the *Tasmanian Dam Case.* As an historical artefact, this interview tells a story of coming to law: Brown's recollections and explanation of the Wilderness Society's aims, expectations and experience before, during and after the matter. This contribution contextualises and presents the interview. To conclude, it suggests that among many readings of this text, it can be usefully read as a story about legalism; here, the encounter and disjuncture between environmental values and legal form.

Introduction

Histories of law tend to examine the lawyers and judges involved through readings of the texts of transcripts and judgments. This contribution presents a different kind of transcript to tell a different kind of story about the *Tasmanian Dam Case*.[1] This rarer artefact holds the recollections of a client seeking to become part of a divisive case of national significance, in at least a political and legal sense. The text combines two interviews I conducted with Dr Bob Brown about his experience as head of the Tasmanian Wilderness Society during its involvement as *amicus curiae* before the High Court in the case.[2] The first interview was conducted immediately after the first panel of the 'Turning Points' Symposium that comprised Dr Brown, Michael Black and Sir Anthony Mason. This interview draws out Brown's general account of the Wilderness Society's story, and much of its content reiterated the story that had just

---

BA(Hons)/LLB(Hons) (Melb), MPhil Candidate and Research Fellow, Melbourne Law School. My thanks to Ann Genovese and the anonymous reviewers for comments, to Dr Bob Brown, Michael Black AC QC and Sir Anthony Mason AC KBE GBM QC for their generous involvement in interviews for this project, and to Miranda Stewart for instigating this project for the Melbourne Law School High Court Blog, *Opinions on High*. See Martin Clark, 'Remembering the *Tasmanian Dam Case*' on *Opinions on High* (24 July 2013) http://blogs.unimelb.edu.au/opinionsonhigh/2013/07/24/clark-tasmanian-dam/. All errors remain my own.

[1] *Commonwealth v Tasmania* (1983) 158 CLR 1.

[2] Bob Brown, Interview recorded in Melbourne (28 June 2013) and Bob Brown, Interview recorded in Melbourne (12 September 2014).

been delivered to the audience at the Symposium.[3] The second interview took place over a year later by telephone, with a contribution to this issue of the *Griffith Law Review* in mind, and involved questions focused on Brown's experience as a client working with Michael Black as counsel for the Wilderness Society.The combined interviews tell a story about the experience of coming to law: deciding to seek to become part of an important matter; instructing counsel and discussing the preparing of submissions; attending the hearings; and witnessing the aftermath of judgment.

Interview

MC: Tell us a bit about your role in the Franklin Dam protests, and in the case later.

BB: Well in 1975, I was asked if I would go floating down the Franklin River, which had not been rafted in these new inflatable rafts, by Paul Smith, who was a forester in Tasmania, and he'd asked lots of other people and no one had been silly enough to say yes, but I did. And in early '76 we floated down the river and I was stunned by the wild beauty of the place.

Paul had all the contour levels of where the dams were going to flood – four dams – and the series would flood the river end-to-end. It was the last great river in southern Australia which was untouched. So, the campaign began. We went back the next year with a Bolex wind-up movie camera and got that footage onto Tasmanian television.

By the end of the 70s, most Tasmanians were opposed to the dam. That was unprecedented because they had always been strongly pro-dam. But, the Hydro [Electric Commission] then moved in. We effectively released their plans in '79, but after that along came the campaign. We knew that would be tough. They'd absolutely overrun the campaigns to save Lake Pedder 10 years earlier.[4]

Two things had changed, however. Colour television had come in, and we knew that getting colour pictures of this wilderness to people's lounge rooms in Tasmania and around Australia was going to be pivotal, because nothing could speak stronger for the river than itself. And the second thing was that the Whitlam Government had signed the *World Heritage Convention* which had then come into, you know, had been devised with Australia strongly behind it, so there was an external treaty power which didn't exist at the time of Lake Pedder. And we had that in mind, although the area wasn't world heritage.

The first world heritage areas were declared in Australia in 1982: the Barrier Reef, the Willandra Lakes in New South Wales, and Lord Howe Island, if I remember correctly. And the Franklin was hotly disputed and they wanted to build a dam there. In May 1982, Robin Gray, the whispering bulldozer Liberal premier of Tasmania came in, and within two months he had bulldozers, well in July of that year, he had bulldozers moving into the Franklin Valley.

[3]It was conducted with the intention of publishing it in a piece on the symposium for the Melbourne Law School's High Court Blog, *Opinions on High*: see Martin Clark, 'Remembering the *Tasmanian Dam Case*' (24 July 2013) http://blogs.unimelb.edu.au/opinionsonhigh/2013/07/24/clark-tasmanian-dam/

[4]On the Lake Pedder litigation, see Lindgren (1996) p 270.

It seemed hopeless. We had the three newspapers in Tasmania, the unions, except for the ETU [Electrical Trade Union], the business sector, both houses of Parliament, both political parties, all in the favour of the dam. We came to Canberra and the then Prime Minister, Mr Malcolm Fraser, said it was a state matter. We had one effort in the High Court, we tried to argue that the Commonwealth should not be lending money to Tasmania to damage a potential world heritage area, and that was thrown out on a Friday afternoon; got short shrift.[5]

So it seemed that there was nowhere to go. But we kept planning for a peaceful protest. That was the difference from Lake Pedder. They had decided not to. After all, environmentalism is an across-the-spectrum thing; it's good, law-abiding citizens who don't want to be crossing the line. But we did, and on the day the world heritage listing was accorded to the Franklin and Gordon river system as well as the rest of southwest Tasmania in Paris, the blockade began, 14 December 1982.

MC: When and why did the Wilderness Society turn to lawyers to support their campaign in the Franklin?

BB: Because the issue after the election of the Hawke Government in March 1983 was going to the High Court. The Gray government refused to back down, despite offers from Hawke of $500 million compensation. By the way, Tasmania ended up getting less than $300 million, as a result of the intransigence of the Premier Robin Gray, and lost over $200 million in potential compensation. But it was then a case of the Federal Government ordering that the Dam be stopped, and the State Government joined by several other state governments taking the matter to the High Court. Well, we campaigned for seven years on the issue, and we were going to leave no stone unturned, including no legal stone. So we engaged Michael Black et al., to join the court case on our behalf.

MC: Prior to the Tasmanian Dam case, what kind of relationship had the movement had with lawyers and legal advisers? Was this a new avenue or simply because the opportunity had come up?

BB: There had been a very intricate relationship over the years, in particular during the blockade where hundreds of people were arrested. We had a suite of voluntary lawyers helping process hundreds of arrests, and to work out a legal defence, which in the long run was successful: on a technicality of the law being drafted the way it was, nobody was convicted in the blockade cases, although 600 or so were arrested.

MC: These were generally Tasmanian lawyers?

BB: Yes they were, they were primarily Tasmanian lawyers at that stage.

MC: Were they part of the conservation movement at that stage, or did they become so after the arrests?

BB: They got involved as a result of the blockade case. For example Pierre Slicer, who was one of those who helped out later [in *Tasmanian Dams*] and went on to become a Supreme Court judge, and was arrested himself at the same time as I was. So they became involved as the campaign grew. And that included the Aboriginal interests being defended in the courts, and the Aboriginal people who were arrested

[5] *Tasmanian Wilderness Society Inc v Fraser* (1982) 153 CLR 270.

on the Franklin being defended by their own. They had lawyers who were sympathetic who were defending them in the courts, which I'm sure had a flow on effect for their efforts to be involved the High Court case as well.[6]

MC: So would you say there was something like a Wilderness society legal team that coalesced around the initial arrests but then went on to work on the High Court case?

BB: No I think they were separate. When it came to the High Court case our legal team, headed by Michael Black, was centred in Melbourne. And this would have come out of a mutual interest being shown by lawyers in various aspects. I might add here that we had looked at the legislation, for example, the Democrats sponsored legislation for World Heritage Protection, the *World Heritage Properties Protection Act*, which had been formulated in Canberra to give effect to the *World Heritage Convention*. So we had people giving us legal advice about what the Government was doing, and where the Government was, during the Fraser years. In Canberra, we had voluntary people offering legal advice, Henry Burmester was one of those, right back in those days, but we had people offering legal advice because they were concerned about the flooding of the Franklin. But when it came to the High Court case … and I don't remember exactly how this evolved: we had a very vigorous Tasmanian Wilderness Society group in Melbourne headed up by Karen Alexander – but Michael Black became our representative or our advocate in the High Court with a team of others of course. It was a fresh thing; it was separate to the blockade and the earlier legal advice we had got about what was happening in Canberra as to whether what the Federal Government was doing was legal – by ignoring the Convention during the Fraser years.

There had been a debate well before the High Court case about whether the Federal Government had the power to intervene in Tasmania. The Fraser Government decided not to take that action, but the Hawke Government decided to take that action, that was the difference between the two governments. But the matter as to whether the Commonwealth had an overriding power through the Convention to stop the Dam had been debated before that election in March 1983, and was a matter of considerable media interest.

MC: On Michael Black, how did you come to engage him? Can you remember meeting him for the first time? Do you know why it was he who was retained particularly?

BB: Of course at that time it was long before he became a judge, and he was in Melbourne but no I don't remember exactly how his services became engaged. But I do remember meeting him in Melbourne – we came to Melbourne to meet up with him to discuss the issue and to see what could be done. And it was a very difficult task for Michael Black: he had myself and others from the Wilderness Society insisting the river should be saved for its environmental amenity, and he had the task of explaining to us that this wasn't about environmental amenity, but about

---

[6]See 'SM Dismisses Dams Trespass Case' *The Canberra Times* (3 February 1983). Police later dropped the remaining charges on the basis that the costs of proving each case would far outweigh the fines reaped: 'Charges against Dam Protesters Dropped' *The Canberra Times* (14 May 1983).

Commonwealth powers based on the convention, as against State powers of land management.

MC: How did those conversations play out? Did it take a while for him to convince others that you had to take the constitutional route, and not the environmental amenity approach?

BB: Oh no, he was the legal expert and he was always an absolute gentleman and a very good advocate. We respected him enormously. But he had to contend with this huge frustration and that culminated in us putting together the seven photo albums of the Franklin and insisting that the poor guy put these up to the Bench. And the Chief Justice saying those famous words 'I think not Mr Black, we won't be looking at those albums lest the Court have its mind inflamed by irrelevancies'.

MC: And when he agreed to do that, I suppose it would have taken some convincing on your part?

BB: Yes it did, but it was always a pleasant exchange. And in retrospect it was a mightily courageous example of representing his clients, who were not going to be satisfied until they saw for themselves that his advice was good: the Court was not going to see these photographs. This was of course in the days when you had to fly everything around. There was no email or anything like that. So the job of getting those albums together was huge. And it had to be done very, very quickly, so for us it was a major task. In fact, it was a very good diversion for the energy of the organisation and the environmentalists while the slow, ponderous, almost inscrutable legal argument was played out in the High Court.

MC: On the issue of preparing the submissions, how long did that process take? Was it over a period of weeks, or was it a relatively quick set of meetings with Michael Black?

BB: No, the government changed in March and the case was in May, so we had some weeks. And at the same time, the Federal Government through the Australian Federal Police had engaged our services to help gather evidence, hence the famous F-111 flyover under the authority of Gareth Evans, which was a masterstroke of absurdity. He never consulted us about it and at any given day we could fly a light plane at very low level over the Dam and we had stacks of pictures, and the Federal Police were liaising with us, getting whatever evidence it was that their attorneys needed. Of course they had to establish that the Dam works were proceeding. It was blatantly obvious: it was on television every night. But nevertheless for the purposes of the Court it had to be established, and not that the Tasmanian Government was going to deny it; it was insisting on its right to proceed.

MC: How did the Tasmanian Wilderness Society think about becoming an intervener in a High Court case? This is a relatively new move from an environmental group. Was it politically or legally important? Or was it simply a question of Michael Black saying 'this is how we need to get in'?

BB: Yes, we were taking his advice: this was all foreign territory. We were non-plussed by the legal requirements, and effectively we were sidelined, and it was very hard to take. We wanted to be in there, showing what a disaster this scheme was. And except insofar as the new Commonwealth Government was committed to stopping the disaster, the black letter law wasn't about what this meant for the

Franklin River wilderness itself, or the values of wilderness for example. It was just whether the Commonwealth had the right to protect the property by ordering the State Government to get out of there. So it was Commonwealth versus State and we were on the sideline, and Michael Black showed not just great legal competence, but extraordinary interpersonal wherewithal to keep his more than enthusiastic clients satisfied in very difficult circumstances.

We took turns in going and sitting in and listening to the dry argument going on in the Court. We came to the realisation that this was on a matter of law that was not going to take into account environmental values *per se*, and we just had to put up with it. There was nothing we could do about that.[7]

MC: Despite the people who were intimately involved in the case feeling sidelined, do you think that the general public impression was that this was in fact a victory and achievement by the Wilderness Society, rather that it being a case between the State and the Commonwealth?

BB: The outcome for the public when it was announced in Brisbane was simply about saving the Franklin and the wilderness. The thing that had changed so many votes and got so many people involved. It wasn't about the law at all. It was about the nation having made a decision to protect a national heirloom. That's what was being celebrated. The anthem 'Let the Franklin Flow' was played all over the country and people jigged and danced about that. There wasn't too much analysis about the balance of powers or too many intricate looks at what the seven judges had said on various points, for example on the powers relating to Aboriginal people, as against the powers relating to the environment, as against the powers relating to the international covenant; and not just the international covenant but international *covenants*, that gave the Commonwealth the 4:3 decision ultimately.

MC: Tell us a bit about your experience when the judgment was handed down by the High Court in Brisbane.

BB: We were very anxious. I had been told by a senior legal entity who had visited Canberra, that 'it was okay Bob, you'll be okay'. But, I wasn't of a mind to accept it. So it was high anxiety. The dam was being built. You have to remember that the Gray Government in those days had—in dollars of those days—had spent $70 million on this dam: a huge investment. There were hundreds, if not thousands, of people working on these dams: bulldozing roads into the wilderness, pursuing the actual, moving towards the actual dam site. They had run into trouble with the geology, which slowed them up, and then the cold winter of 1982 slowed them up further.

But in those circumstances we flew to Brisbane where the High Court ruling was to be handed down on 1 July 1983. Our plane was struck with lightning as we took off from Melbourne, and rather than the deep freeze which Tasmania was experiencing, it was 26 degrees on that fateful day.

The High Court was packed, the High Court room in Brisbane. The judges read out their orders, and it took quite a long time, and we sort of had a running sheet on our laps and slowly it emerged that we were going to get a 4:3 judgment in favour of

[7]The entire transcript of proceedings was recently made available on Austlii: see http://www.austlii.edu.au/au/other/HCATrans/1983/. Michael Black's submissions are contained in *Commonwealth v Tasmania* [1983] HCATrans 28 (10 June 1983).

the Commonwealth power under the external affairs/treaties and corporation's power to stop the dam. So there was a rising tide of excitement in the courtroom, and suddenly a man in yellow saffron robes got up and ran across the Court yelling 'No Dams!' and he was promptly evicted.

But outside, great excitement. A journalist handed me a bottle of champagne and said 'shake this up, Bob', and I said no, I'd refuse, because I knew there'd be great anger among the pro-dam contingent back in Tasmania. But as we flew from Brisbane to Sydney to Melbourne to Hobart on the trip back that night, in Sydney Airport in the transit area there was more than a hundred people with 'No Dam' banners and singing Shane Howard's anthem 'Let the Franklin Flow', which was in the hit parade at the time, and, you know, it's just a pivotal expression of the excitement there was, right across Australia, because, remember, 6,000 people had gone to Strahan [in Tasmania], including, for example, 50 or 60 people from Western Australia, and a lot of people from the Northern Territory. Right across this country there had been training classes for people in non-violence, in every capital city and in provincial cities there were branches of the Wilderness Society. And 6000 people in Strahan, and 1300 were arrested, 600 went to Risdon Prison. But millions had an opinion on this, and untold numbers had changed their vote at the election on 5 March [1983] to bring in the Hawke Government, there were other issues, as there ever are, but the Dams issue was one of those pivotal issues.

So, great excitement across the country. And here in Sydney Airport a woman came up and said 'I've got a flat in Blacktown in the western suburbs in Sydney. I was doing my ironing at 11 o'clock this morning, and I heard screaming in the flat next door' and instead of ringing the police, she started screaming too, because she knew the news had come through that the Franklin had been saved. People were just jubilant about it.

It had been such a long, anxiety-ridden road through the campaigning days, through the election, a pivotal election, with a huge campaign with the combined environment groups of Australia: the Conservation Foundation, the Wilderness Society, the other conservation councils and groups right across the country campaigning in marginal seats. And then, this long way to the High Court hearings in May in 1983, and then the judgment on the first of July, so there it was 'No Dams', the headlines on the second of July, and right across the morning news with the exception of the Hobart *Mercury*. And the river flows free to the sea, and to the great employment, economic and environmental benefit of modern Tasmania.

MC: It was such an astonishing victory, but thinking about the conservation movement globally, do you think there have been other similar court cases?

BB: Well yes, I had justified anxiety about the High Court in Australia, because the year before in a 7:0 judgment of the High Court of Norway, in the matter of the Alta Dam, and a thousand people had been arrested in the far north of Norway trying to stop a dam on the Alta River, their court had ruled seven to zero that the dam should proceed. And so we knew about that. There had been several court cases in the USA. And of course Lake Pedder, and the wanton destruction of one of the most beautiful places on earth, in Lake Pedder was looming over us, so we could take nothing for granted. And nor did we.

MC: In the wake of the decision, do you think the environmental movement generally thought that legal avenues were worth pursuing in the future? Or was the attempt to be an intervener in a big case just particular to the Franklin Dam case, and was not going to be helpful in the future?

BB: No it was absolutely the former – it awakened the environmental movement. It wasn't the first time this had happened. There had been a huge legal stoush over Lake Pedder for example, where the Attorney-General for Tasmania had resigned because the legislation to flood Lake Pedder had come after the legislation to create a national park there, and when this was pointed out by legal entities, the Attorney-General had to give a fiat to the environmental movement to intervene to challenge in that case, and the Premier didn't like it, so the Attorney-General resigned, the Premier put in retrospective legislation and then the Attorney-General came back on again. There was a huge furore over that, with the Bishop of Hobart, among others, condemning the politicians for what they were doing. But the outcome of *Tasmanian Dams* was that it was thought that in future the nation would protect its top heritage: human and environmental. And we're now just seeing with the passage of time, 35 years later, that politics will trump the law, and all those powers are being handed back to the States. If we had what the Abbott Government is doing now in place then, the Franklin long ago would have been flooded.

Comment

As with all historical sources, there are multiple stories to be read in a single text. As a scholar of public law and legal theory, one of the stories I take to be prominent is a story about the encounter with legalism. In a famous articulation by the political theorist Judith Shklar, legalism is an ethical attitude that sees moral conduct as a question of rule following, and moral relationships as primarily ones of duties and corresponding rights outlined through rules. These rules are not necessarily clearly articulated as such, even when they are consistently followed both inside and outside courts.[8] Though writing on legal theory, Shklar is not a lawyer. She gives an outsider's view, aiming to suggest 'alternative ways of thinking about law'.[9] These interviews tell a story of another outsider seeking to suggest an alternative way of thinking about law.

In the *Tasmanian Dam Case* and *Tasmanian Wilderness Society v Fraser* before it, the Wilderness Society grasped at an alternative to legalism in the values of environmentalism. The Wilderness Society's expectation was that those values might carry the day, even as its members realised slowly that questions of law would inevitably displace them. It sought to appear before the Court to draw the Court's attention to the natural significance of the area and to bring environmentalism into contact with legal reasoning. The decision to attempt to intervene in the proceedings was part strategy and part opportunism; to be part of the legal event that was capable of finally resolving the issue originally spurred by mass popular protests started by the Wilderness Society in Tasmania that spread across Australia. The experience was one of gradually appreciating the strictures of law. As the process of preparing the submissions commenced the Wilderness Society quickly deferred to the legal expertise of Michael Black. They began to appreciate that the case would not turn on the things they cared about, but instead black letter law. Throughout the

[8]Shklar (1964) p 1.
[9]Shklar (1964) pp vii–viii.

experience of the hearings, the Wilderness Society remained somewhat indignant but also optimistic. They listened to the 'dry argument' that preceded Michael Black's final submissions with fading eagerness in the hope that somewhere arguments based the natural environment, wilderness, beauty and significance for humankind would be mentioned by at least one of the many barristers speaking throughout the days of hearings. Initially both hopeful and wary of the mysterious workings of law, once that mystery turned to mind-numbing drudgery it became clear that their values are not and cannot be the ones that inspire the barristers and judges speaking in the courtroom: 'we just had to put up with it'. Nonetheless they had convinced Michael Black to begin their oral submissions in the way their environmental values demanded – by seeking to present the Court with images of the area to demonstrate its natural beauty, famously rejected by Gibbs CJ: 'The photographs could do no more than inflame our minds with irrelevancies'.[10] Black's attempt to put images before the Court transgressed a code that had not been articulated – that is, until Gibbs CJ does so, almost in shock[11]– precisely because it is so pervasively understood: constitutional matters are about words alone. The Wilderness Society was only satisfied of the reality of law's strictness when the Court itself declined to see the photographs it had spent weeks preparing. In the end, bringing the Court's mind to those questions in a less 'inflammatory' way had to occur through words.[12] What followed then was Michael Black's poetic rumination on natural significance and what humanity values about the world it inhabits, still presented in visual terms, but in the orthodox mode of reasoned oral argument. While in the end the case did not turn on any of the Wilderness Society's arguments, it could still emerge from the Court sharing in the victory and claiming the outcome as a vindication of their views and campaign and that justice had been done, even if not through the route it thought was most important.

In reading the interview as a story about legalism I do not suggest that the Wilderness Society's experience impugns the procedures of receiving *amicus curiae*, deciding constitutional matters, or the outcome of the *Tasmanian Dam Case*, or that the Wilderness Society's visions of justice and morality ought to have trumped careful consideration of constitutional principles, the powers and competencies of parliaments of Australia and the texts of statutes and conventions. Its value is both different from and greater than providing another instance for further legal arguments on those topics. As a text recollecting the experience of coming to law – between expectation and reality – it reveals much about the role of courts in Australian public life, and another view of the meaning of the *Tasmanian Dam Case* besides a purely legal meaning.

Reference List

Primary Legal Sources

Tasmanian Wilderness Society Inc v Fraser (1982) 153 CLR 270.
Commonwealth v Tasmania (1983) 158 CLR 1.

[10] *Commonwealth v Tasmania* [1983] HCATrans 28 (10 June 1983) at 737. See also Black (2015), in this issue.

[11] See Black (2015), in this issue.

[12] *Commonwealth v Tasmania* [1983] HCATrans 28 (10 June 1983) at 737–738.

Secondary Sources

Michael Black (2015) 'The Tasmanian Dam Case: An Advocate's Memoire' 24 *Griffith Law Review* (in press).
Justice K E Lindgren (1996) 'Standing and the State' in PD Finn, *Essays on Law and Government, Volume 2: The Citizen and the State in the Courts*, LBC Information Services.
Judith Shklar (1964) *Legalism*, Harvard University Press.

Nineteen eighty three: A jurisographic report on *Commonwealth v Tasmania*

Ann Genovese and Shaun McVeigh

Melbourne Law School, University of Melbourne

The question we ask in this essay is quite direct: did the Tasmanian Dams case change the conduct of jurisprudence in Australia? To reflect on that question, we stand to the side of the review of the events of 1983 as constitutional decision, and present the jurisprudence of Dams and 1983 in terms of the incidents of legal thinking in the conduct of the office of the jurisprudent. Writing as jurisographers, we reflect historically on the conduct of office of the jurist and jurisprudent, and the writing of jurisprudence. Our account here provides a brief chronicle and record of the patchwork of law projects and engagements that pattern the events of Dams into the scholarly work of jurists in Australian universities.

On the 30th Anniversary of the High Court's decision in *Commonwealth v Tasmania* ('*Dams*'),[1] we were part of a meeting of jurists and jurisprudents at Melbourne Law School who gathered together to consider the significance of the case to Australian legal life. Our contribution to that gathering, and the question we ask now in this essay, is quite direct: did the *Dams* case change the conduct of jurisprudence in Australia? To reflect on that question, we stand to the side of the review of the events of 1983 as constitutional decision. It is clear that *Dams* has not been received only, or simply, as a doctrinal story about law's techniques. Our approach is to report how jurisprudents, those who care for the conduct of law within Australian universities, did (and did not) address *Dams* in their writing. Our response is that the jurisprudence of 1983, like the judgment itself, does not tell a dramatic story of a nation coming of age, nor does it offer a coherent teleology of the development of an Australian jurisprudence. Instead, we present the jurisprudence of *Dams* and 1983 in terms of the incidents of legal thinking in the conduct of the office of the jurisprudent. These accounts, we suggest, are taken up in a variety of different ways, but not yet cast as a jurisprudence that takes itself to be distinctly Australian in its concerns and forms of address to peoples and land, in time and place.

Our report, with its attention to forms of writing, shares concerns with legal sociologists (who might examine the everyday practices of legal academics and lawyers through textual production), or with legal historians (who might examine the texts of legal scholars in the past to offer description of the origins and changing

---

[1] *Commonwealth v Tasmania* (1983) 158 CLR 1(hereafter '*Dams*').

character of institutions, doctrine, or professional membership and allegiance). But in choosing to think with and write about the conduct of office in our address to jurisprudential writing we are aligning ourselves with a particular, different tradition. This tradition, as the historian and philosopher Pierre Hadot notes, has been uninterrupted from the Greeks to our own time, and is concerned with the question: 'How should I conduct a life?'[2] Within this tradition, conduct of office means something quite straightforward: that there is a relation between the status and official *persona* of a subject (their office as philosopher, soldier, judge, administrator, priest or jurisprudent) – and the conduct of their everyday human existence. This relation shapes the attitudes, obligations and responsibilities that are required to adequately conduct their official life. Within the conduct of life tradition, these attitudes, obligations and responsibilities are best learned, and taught, through conscious and productive activity, or exercise: often, and significantly, the art of writing.[3] It is through such practices and arts that the holder of an office offers training, to self and others, in how to consciously form an official life, as well as to remind that choosing the forms and expressions of that life's conduct comes both with costs, and possibilities. For jurisprudents working within this tradition, the central question in their own writing, and in their examination of the writing of others, can be cast as 'how can I conduct a lawful life?' By addressing the writing of jurisprudents from this tradition, we diverge from those interested in interpreting the writing of legal academics to examine its pedagogical intent, or benefit. Our concern is to examine how university jurisprudents take up their office through the practice of writing, and to show how that writing recommends to others, and deciphers for themselves, what it means to be responsible for their law. In this way, our orientation, and interest in the arts of writing, belong more to the traditions offered by Weber's *Politics as a Vocation* (1919), rather than expositions of the professionalisation of lawyers.[4]

Our own account of 1983, both our question, and idiom in which we write, is also a contribution to the project of the writing of histories of legal thought. We are interested, for example, in drawing the tradition of conduct into conversation with the tradition of legal critique. By reflecting historically on the conduct of office of the jurist and jurisprudent, and the writing of jurisprudence, we write as jurisographers. The duties that attach to the office of jurisographer involve examining how jurisprudence was written, thought and practiced in time and place, and paying attention to how those traditions have been inherited.[5]

While there are varied, and more elaborated, ways of writing about the conduct of lawful life as a practice of jurisography, our account here takes the form of report. As a report, it is limited in scope and ambition by its form: part record or chronicle and part commentary on style and genre. In order to establish a chronicle of the jurisprudence of the case, we hold the jurisprudence of 1983 apart from the present to gain some historical sense of what was happening in the domain of jurisprudence

---

[2]Hadot (1995) pp 264–274; Hadot (2002) pp 253–270.

[3]Hadot (2001) pp 22–34.

[4]Weber (2004).

[5]Genovese (2013), pp 41–44; Genovese (2014a); Genovese (2014b); McVeigh (2014); Dorsett and McVeigh (2014).

and journal publishing at that time. This is hardly the limit, or only forum, of jurisprudential thinking.[6] Similarly, the sources we examine are not the limit, or only forums for examples of legal writing in 1983. We focus in particular on the academic legal journals, particularly those that began their life in the early 1980s. This is not to disregard the political importance of other publications, in particular bulletins of community legal centres, or the more traditional Law Society newsletters. Our selection of sources is necessarily partial, chosen because they emanate from law schools, rather than the profession, and as such provide a means to examine the institutional position, and the fashioning of the office and *personae* of the university jurist and jurisprudent and their genres of scholarship. Our account, then, does not take up a formal narrative, or exhaustive review of available materials of 1983. Rather, it reports on the patchwork of law projects and engagements that pattern the events of *Dams* into Australian law, or at least the scholarly work of jurists in Australian universities.

Our report has three parts. First, we return to the specific commentary written in 1983 on the *Dams* case. This enables us to report on the shape and nature of the case as a concern of conduct of the office of jurist and jurisprudent. Second, we address a 'slice' of the publishing life of the legal academy in 1983. Third, by way of conclusion, we address three essays that stand out from, although are not entirely at odds with, other juristic writings of 1983. In retrospect, it is the gestures, animation and ripostes of the *Aboriginal Legal Bulletin,* Tony Blackshield, and Lionel Murphy that enable us to view genres of jurisprudence written after 1983 as something distinct, or at least distinctively Australian. These three contributions to the jurisprudence of 1983 provide a point of engagement between the conducts of life that animated the political disputes crystallised in the proposed building of the Franklin River dam, and the conduct of office of jurists who wrote specifically about *Dams* as an event of law.

1983: Canberra and Hobart

The office of the jurist and jurisprudent is long established, and has recognised, if disputed, duties. At their broadest these duties are to care for the law: its conduct, order, purpose and justice. In more material ways it is to explain the law, to transmit that explanation in a written form; and in doing so to consider the implications of law as authorised. As analyst, historian and critic these duties of the jurisprudent have always been carried out in their writing toward different audiences: court, university, and the general public. To the court, the jurisprudent has duties as a counsellor: to be a careful expositor of what the court has decided; and a cautious advisor as to the implications of that law. To the university, the jurisprudent has duties as a scholar: to produce expositions of law which carry the traditions of knowledge, and the rhetorical forms of scholarly engagement. And to the public (however we institute the public), the jurisprudent has duties of publicity, to transmit their writing about law.

On 1 July 1983, the High Court, for the first time, gave their own public summary of the outcome of a case. Chief Justice Gibbs pointedly reminds that the

---

[6]See n 86.

summary of *Dams* does not extend to 'providing a complete or authoritative exposition of the decision, which must be gathered from the judgment published'.[7] The 'gathering', and the exposition, is exactly the task undertaken in 1983 by those jurisprudents who chose to directly reflect on the judgment. Michael Coper's extended preface to the published full text decision by Butterworths in 1983 is one example.[8] Our report considers two others. The first are the papers produced at a seminar held at the Faculty of Law, the Australian National University (ANU), Canberra, in December 1983. The other is an edited book produced from a series of lectures held at the Law School, University of Tasmania, in Hobart, throughout 1983.

Clearly in 1983 the story of advocacy and politics, inside and outside of the court room in the *Dams* case, was predicated on contests about states' rights, and also state identities. The place of the enunciation and commentary on law also matters to the performance of the duties of jurisprudent, and we note that the only juristic writings of 1983 directly about *Dams* are Canberra and Hobart stories. In 1983, it is worth remembering, there were only 10 law schools in Australia, and each carried a particular duty, and particular institutional concerns, because of their location and history. The ANU, for example, was established in 1946 as Australia's first national university. It fostered engagement with government, science, and industry, and was open to research collaborations between disciplines to meet the challenges of a post war Australia. The establishment of the Academy of Social Sciences and the Research School of Social Sciences (RSSS) were central to that project. The Law School, which began in 1960, was committed in terms of personnel and scholarship, to the establishment and furtherance of those aims.[9] The one-day seminar at the ANU on the Dams case in 1983 was positioned as a Socratic debate and staged a provocation and response. The speakers and discussants were largely connected with the ANU and schooled, as might be expected, in the links between law and government. They included Geoffrey Sawer (foundation professor at ANU Law School), Dennis Rose (then principal advisor of the office of Attorney-General), Michael Crommelin (then reader in law at the University of Melbourne), and Geoffrey Lindell (then senior lecturer in law at the ANU).[10] Collectively, their jurisprudence, unsurprisingly, was directed toward the community of constitutional and public lawyers, and was concerned with explaining the implications of the Court's constitutional reasoning for the legal life of Federated Australia. The papers were published in the *Federal Law Review* in December 1983, a leading journal of Australian public law, that joins the work and writings of advocates, bureaucrats, and scholars, and the publication was officially launched (in 1985) at a celebratory dinner in Canberra, by the Secretary of the Attorney-General's Department, Pat Brazil.[11]

---

[7]*Dams* (1983) 158 CLR 1 at 30 (Gibbs CJ).

[8]Coper (1983), pp 1–26.

[9]Macintyre (2010); Foster and Varghese (1996).

[10]Note the edition is dated as (1983–84) as it was published at the end of year: (1983–84), 14 *Federal Law Review* 198–257 [hereafter '*FLR* (1983')]

[11]'A-G's Department Head Speaks on "the Dam Case and all that",' *Australian Law News*, July 1985, pp 22–23.

The University of Tasmania, in contrast to the ANU, was founded in 1890. The Law School, established in 1893, is the fourth oldest in the country, and like most colonial institutions, was designed to serve, train and educate the local community.[12] Throughout 1983, the Law School hosted a series of lectures about the legal and political events in the South-West of Tasmania. The lectures took place during the dispute, were given predominantly by members of the Law School,[13] and visitors to the Law School in 1983 (Brian Galligan, then lecturer in political science at ANU, Tony Blackshield, then Professor of Legal Studies at La Trobe University). The essays addressed prominently (although not solely) local concerns, including the legal ramifications of the arrests of protestors, and the implications of a state problem being redressed by domestic and international laws. After the July 1983 decision in the High Court, the papers were revised, and produced by the University of Tasmania as a book, – then a more open and accessible format than a journal. The book, edited by the head of the law School, Dr Muthucumaraswamy Sornarajah, was not called Tasmanian Dams but *The South West Dam Dispute: The Legal and Political Issues*.[14]

We note that the writers represented in these publications (with one exception, Kate Warner at the University of Tasmania), are male. We also note that many have travelled outside of Australia for further legal education.[15] The jurisprudence offered quietly joins the transnational, as a set of concerns, styles and duties in part inherited as a British colonial and common law tradition and in part inherited as a Realist and Federalist tradition from North America.[16]

Canberra

The contributors to the *Federal Law Review* generally, we think, present themselves as 'legalists' (or better legists).[17] In an Australian context 'legalism' is

[12]Davis (1993).

[13]Ernest Braybrooke had recently retired from La Trobe Law School, and had a temporary appointment at the Law School, University of Tasmania as a Visiting Professor (see Douglas (1989)).

[14]Sornarajah (1983a).

[15]For example: Geoffrey Sawer (1910–96), was educated at Melbourne University, and Tony Blackshield at the University of Sydney, and Kate Warner at the University of Tasmania. Dennis Rose (1936–2008) was educated at Tasmania and at Oxford; Michael Crommelin at the University of Queensland and the University of British Columbia; Muthucumaraswamy Sornarajagh at the Universities of Ceylon, Yale, and London; Ernest Braybrooke at the Universities of Western Australia, New Zealand, and at Columbia; and Brian Galligan (the only non-lawyer represented in the collection, but a specialist in the politics of the High Court) studied economics and commerce at the University of Queensland, then took a PhD in political science at the University of Toronto. Note that qualifications extracted from published articles in Sornarajah (1983a) and *FLR* (1983).

[16]For an overview of the influences on the generation of legal scholars working in the 1940s–60s in Australia, see Bartie (2010).

[17]We use the term in a general sense. The term 'legist' more properly relates to mediaeval lawyers who act as advisors to Feudal princes and monarchs. The term also referred to university researchers in law; see Kelley (1970), p 195 ff. For a modern usage see, for example, Goodrich (2004).

understood as related to distinct practices of adjudication, interpretation and exegesis ('strict legalism').[18] For critics, legalism is often considered a false ideology and practice – a way of masking reality. In political scientist Judith Shklar's famous book *Legalism* (1964), however, she relates legalism both to the way in which following rules is a morally appropriate way of being in the world, and a distinct ethos of the legal profession that addresses issues through the analysis of rules and rule following.[19] We note that legalism understood in this way is also a practice, and presentation, of a conduct of office; and is observable as such in the writings of the jurists represented in the *FLR* in 1983. These jurists' training is one of propriety in observing the law and of separating the law from what it is not. Their cumulative task after the *Dams* decision in *FLR* is to ensure that what law is remains properly so. Together, although discussing different aspects of the decision, the jurisprudents who gathered in Canberra are conscientious in expositing that despite 'political' or 'policy' or 'factual' aspects raised in and by this case, that the technical and doctrinal activities undertaken by the court were a fulfilment of judicial duties, and executed responsibly within the conventions of Australian constitutional practice.[20] At the same time, they are careful to question, rhetorically, but cautiously ('with due respect')[21] the implications of this judicial practice. In particular, they think with and through Australia's legal history – a narrative of how law conducts the transition from Imperial Colony to Federated nation- to consider the relations between states and the Commonwealth, and the State and the world, that the case does not answer. They ask: Does the decision clarify what federalism does in, and for, 'Australia'? If Australia is the signatory to an international convention, what does that suggest for how the Commonwealth might respond to recalcitrant or unruly states that refuse to act lawfully with that Convention? Could the High Court have achieved the same result in this case by returning the law to the nationhood power? To what extent does the decision broaden the scope and application of both the corporations power and the races power?[22] Geoffrey Sawer's contribution exemplifies the conduct of the legists in the *FLR*. As a foundation professor at ANU Law School, and an early member of the Australian Social Science Research Council, Sawer had long been instrumental in formalising the institutional relationships of law with the social sciences, translating the practices of law and government to each other at the ANU, and publicising the meaning of law as government to a general audience in his writing.[23] In his 1983 paper on the External Affairs power, Sawer did not direct discussion to a doctrinal exegesis of the past, present, and future of s 51 (xxix). His precise question was

[18]See Goldsworthy (2006).

[19]Shkalr (1964).

[20]'Preface' to the articles by Sawer, Lindell, Saunders, and Zines, *FLR* (1983) prefacing p 199.

[21]For example, Rose (1983b), p 218; Rose (1983a), p 256.

[22]These are considerations in: Sawer (1983); Crommelin (1983); Lindell (1983) 219. Lindell and Rose (1983a) both consider s 51 (xx) and s51 (xxvi) as doctrinal questions to be read in tandem as persons powers, and in terms of implied limitations. Rose concludes his discussion for example by arguing that if limitations were to be read on the corporations power after *Dams* 'consistency would require the same conclusion on s 51 xxvi) so far as it concerns laws controlling…the conduct of people of any race': Rose (1983a), 257.

[23]For overview and examples of Sawer's work and influence: Sawer (1968); Cranston (1980).

how, and to what extent, the *Dams* (and its obiter) might make any difference, if at all, to the legislative and executive practices of the Commonwealth.[24]

Understood as part of the performance of a conduct of office, we note that the concern with the formation of Australian law across institutional forums shows not only the range of duties of the legist, but what responsibilities they have to Australia-as place of law in the performance, writing and enunciation of their concerns.

Hobart

Where the contributors to the *FLR* were writing as advisors to government officials and lawyers, the articles collected in the *South West Dam Dispute* were addressing a community of interested citizens from a range of academic offices and disciplines. The jurists writing in Hobart in 1983 did not write as legists, in form or content, but used other practices – allegorical, evocative, jurisdictional – that similarly discharge the duties of office of the jurisprudent to protect place, and create a lawful place. We offer two examples here (and one further in the final section), drawn from the book, that show different forms of fulfilling the office of jurisprudent.[25]

Our first example is Sornarajah's own essay, 'International law and Dams case'.[26] We note that Sornarajah, as the only jurist of international law represented in either collection of writing about *Dams* in 1983, has particular duties in his address to the public (or at least the university community). This includes explaining international law as a distinct legal technique, and explaining how the nation state has a legal personality, and legal obligations, in an international context. We note as a matter of style his decision to treat 'legal personality' of Australia allegorically, as woman.[27] Rather than giving legal advice Sornarajah considers how to dress 'her' adequately for international life. The 'majority judgments', he notes, 'reflect the need for Australia to be clothed with sufficient legal powers to act effectively as an international person'.[28] It is, of course, thoroughly conventional for jurists (and others) to use images of women to bear 'symbolic burdens of virtues' (like prudentia and justitia).[29] While there is much more that can be said today about the dressing of the allegorical feminine forms of Australia,[30] Sonarajah's gesture as an jurist of

[24]Sawer (1983), p 199. Note to the emphasis he placed on dicta as telling a different kind of story of the power of judgments for future executive and legislative action: he did not limit himself only to the judgment, as to do so was 'such an old fashioned point of view': Sawer (1983), p 205.

[25]Note also the following contributions: Bates (1983), pp 1–22; Warner (1983), pp 132–144; and, Rutherford (1983), pp 145–151.

[26]Sornarajah (1983b), pp 23–36.

[27]Sornarajah (1983b), p 24 also notes how the 'founding fathers' when drafting *Commonwealth of Australia* Bill (1900) used the same allegorical gesture, which he takes up and adapts for 1983: '[T]heir hopes for Australia in the field of international relations were grandiose. They wanted to clothe the Federation with enough power so that it could merge as a power on the world stage'. Sornarajah uses 'she' and 'her' throughout the essay to describe Australia.

[28]Sornarajah (1983b), p 32.

[29]Castle and Pringle (1993), p 138.

[30]One concern, although not one found in the law journals of 1983, might be how a jurist might respond to such a gendered and sexualised gesture, of the men of law needing to clothe the female state. In some ways, this observation relates to our point at footnotes 59 and 60

international law in 1983 might be treated as a concern with what Peter Goodrich has called a 'visive power', the visible representation of authority.[31] We note that in this idiom, and from the viewpoint of the international lawyer, the comportment of Australia is a matter of honour and conduct between laws. Sornarajah argues that Australia's ability to adequately dress herself as a modern nation should not be 'hampered by narrow legalism' after *Dams*.[32] Instead, he suggests that every effort must be made by domestic courts and parliaments to draw the national and international into relation as matters of law. This includes making 'legislation based on human rights conventions'. So attired, Sornarajah points out that Australia would be able to take 'vigorous leadership', in the human rights and environmental fields', and to comport herself well on the regional, and world stage.[33]

Our second brief example relates to Tasmania as a place of law. By contrast with Australia as a legal person, Tasmania is treated as a prosaic place of law, albeit one of wild beauty. Ernest Braybrooke, for example, addresses two related jurisdictional disputes. One is about trespass: the movement of protestors across land that the Hydro-Electric Commission claimed was vested in them. The other is about whether a Stipendary Magistrate (SM) has adequate jurisdiction to hear the trespass dispute.[34] Braybrooke was a foundation and Emeritus Professor at La Trobe University, and in 1983 a temporary staff member at University of Tasmania. He joined in his work the practices of sociological jurisprudence and the practices of the common lawyer.[35] Braybrooke presents his account of the legal foregrounding of *Dams* as a morality tale about what happens when there is a failure to maintain adequate legal relations to land. He argues that the imposition of legislative forms in colonial Tasmania altered the civil wrong of trespass shaped by the common law: summary jurisdiction was lost in the consolidation of legislation of the *Trespass to Lands Act* 1862 (Tas.) into the *Police Act* 1935 (Tas.). One consequence, found in *Strickland v Killen,*[36] was to render the offence of trespass nugatory and the dispute between land holders and protesters non-justiciable. For Braybrooke, this is a story in which the poorly marked relations to land, and even more poorly articulated forms of authority in colonial legislation, lose the story of landownership and 'class legislation' that had been transplants of English law. It is also a tale that runs independently of the concerns of commonwealth and state's powers, and of international law.

We observe that the jurists represented in *The South West Dams Dispute* share duties of office that join them to an established tradition. Although practicing different idioms or genres to do so (international relations, or property law and political economy, in our examples) the writing of the Hobart jurists can be understood to address the conduct of law as part of the discipline of political jurisprudence. Their writing takes up forms of public law but addresses legal form as a matter of political arrangement, analysis and dispute rather constitutional doctrine.

---

[31]Goodrich (2008); Dorsett and McVeigh (2012), p 78.

[32]Sornarajah (1983b), p 34.

[33]Sornarajah (1983b), p 34: 'particularly in the Asian region'.

[34]Braybrooke (1983).

[35]Douglas (1989); Braybrooke (1973).

[36]*Strickland v Killen* (Full Court, Supreme Court of Tasmania, unreported, 12 April 1983); Braybrooke (1983), p 126.

As a matter of reporting, we also observe that while these duties are distinct to the advice giving practiced by the legists, all the jurisprudents who directly address *Dams* in 1983 share a concern with how law is conducted in Australia, but as yet no strong sensibility of what Australia might mean for law.

1983: Melbourne and Sydney

We move now from specific engagements on *Dams* in Canberra and Hobart, to report on the conduct of publishing life of Australian jurisprudents in 1983. We take up this story in Melbourne and Sydney. Reporting from different cities is important to jurisographic accounts. As already noted, place is integral to showing the practice and inheritance of legal, intellectual and jurisprudential traditions. Literary critic John Docker has observed in his now classic book *Australian Cultural Elites* (1974) that the intellectual life of Melbourne and Sydney Universities has been central to that story in Australia.[37] Important to our account is the establishment of law schools at the 'new' universities in these cities: Monash in 1964, UNSW in 1971, La Trobe University in 1972, and Macquarie University, also in 1972. Our concern here is not with the rivalries between Melbourne and Sydney intellectual traditions, as Docker might describe (although these are worthy of consideration in a different paper). Instead, we wish to report how the establishment of the new law schools in Melbourne and Sydney suggested duties in the conduct of the office of the university jurist that were distinct to those we reported from Canberra and Hobart; and that by 1983, some of these duties were observable in the writing for, and editing of, new law journals.

Our general observation is that in 1983, in established or professional journals (besides the *FLR*), commentary about *Dams* was limited.[38] Contemporaneous commentary on environmental law or international law was either connected to constitutional concerns (as in the *Law Institute Journal Victoria*), or appeared in professional or trade journals (such as *The Australian Foreign Affairs Record*).[39] This is not surprising, if we consider the institutional duties of the legists, or the local university scholar, in 1983, as described. What is surprising is that there is almost no consideration in Australian legal writing in 1983 of what *Dams* might offer as an example of 'law in action', or as a narrative of 'law and society'. We note this absence, or omission, as interesting, because by 1983 this 'alternative' viewpoint for Australian legal thinking and writing was well established.[40] The style and concerns of this jurisprudence was drawn in part from the traditions of American Realism, taught in Australian Law Schools through the writings of jurists such as Julius Stone (a very particular Sydney law story).[41] The 'new' law schools took those lessons

---

[37]Docker (1974).

[38]There were of course many more articles that appeared in subsequent years, when perhaps the implications of the decision could be more fully analysed, and assessed, and after Environmental Law established itself as a discipline. See for example: Tighe (1987); Bandler (1987).

[39]Derham (1984); Connolly (1983); Hawke and Evans (1983). It is interesting that in 1983, Shearer (1983) makes no mention of *Dams* at all.

[40]See for historical review: Appleby et al. (2013); and Bartie (2010).

[41]There are many reflections on the content and influence of Stone's teaching, for example Irving et al (2010); and as a particular Sydney story of law, see for example Kirby (2012).

seriously. Many Faculty at Monash and UNSW Law schools, from the 1970s, also established and worked in community institutions such as the Redfern Legal Centre, the Aboriginal Legal Service, Springvale and Fitzroy Legal Services. These new legal institutions were a response to the Whitlam Government's introduction of funding for legal aid in the early 1970s, and were embedded in community life.[42] We note that the experiences of working with clients in the lower socio-economic suburbs of Melbourne and Sydney suggested different ways for jurists to combine legal scholarship influenced by Stone (and others) with legal advice and direct political action.[43] What is interesting for us to observe is how the ideas and energy gained from public commitments to a range of law reform practices shaped jurisprudential duties, and how those duties were expressed in juristic writing.

This story is not linear, nor without rivalry. The early editions of *Monash University Law Review* (established in 1974), and the *University of New South Wales Law Journal* ('*UNSWLJ*', established in 1976, to coincide with the graduation of the first law class) give one account. These are journals in a true sense and tradition, in which observer participants directly record law's role in 'changing times'.[44] Yet the early articles in these journals did not necessarily challenge the form of juristic writing that might be suggested by Realism, including the core premise of Stone's teaching that understanding law in society required opening law as discipline to other disciplines.[45] We note that some scholars, by the early 1980s, began to consider that different scholarly styles and forms of writing should accompany this form of legal praxis. It was, it seems, not sufficient to enact 'law in society' as advocacy with observable consequences. Roman Tomasic, for example, argued in a 1982 *UNSWLJ* review essay of Stan Ross's *The Politics of Law Reform* (1982),[46] that it was unclear what would happen to the 'intellectual viability of a large sector of Australian legal academic endeavor' concerned with the 'socio-legal studies approach', when the legal realist ethos as praxis 'ran itself into the sand'.[47] His point was that the 'law reform school' were not inclined to cite, think with or reference theory or other disciplines when they wrote: their sources were legal, and empirical. We observe, too, that Ross's reply to Tomasic – also published in the *UNSWLJ* – indicates an initial rivalry and division between Australian left legal thinkers. Ross responded: '[o]bviously a book that that is meant for a wide audience will not impress academic "theoreticians" who reject references from newspapers as being unworthy sources of data and ideas'.[48]

In 1982 and 1983, coinciding with the *Dams* decision, two new journals were established that addressed the representative concerns expressed by Tomasic. These

---

[42]Basten et al (1983), p 170. CLCs were a direct consequence of the commitment by the Whitlam Government from 1972 to establish services for those traditionally 'without power' in the Australian community. This included establishing state funded inquiries into poverty, and the initiation of a Legal Aid Scheme.

[43]Goldring (1985); Basten et al (1983), p 166.

[44]Street (1975), p 2. For a prominent example, Enderby (1975) (Enderby was then Attorney-General, and responsible for the passage of the legislation).

[45]Stone (1950), pp 386–389.

[46]Tomasic (1982); Ross (1982b).

[47]Tomasic (1982), p 331. He is noting similarities between Australia and the United States, and is in part quoting Schlegel (1979), p 459.

[48]Ross (1982a), p 344.

journals were the *Australian Journal of Law and Society* ('*AJLS*') (at Macquarie University Law School, in 1982), and *Law in Context* (at Legal Studies, La Trobe University, in 1983). It is important to note that both of these law schools, in particular La Trobe which was part of the Humanities faculty at the time, had an institutional commitment to hire not only those with training in law, but with training in history, anthropology, and sociology.[49] The Editorial Board of *AJLS* (which included John Goldring, Gill Boehringer and Margaret Thornton) noted that Macquarie Law School aimed to produce lawyers with 'a wider and critical understanding of law and its integral place in the web of social relations'.[50] *AJLS,* when established, consciously decided 'to avoid duplication' of existing legal periodicals in Australia. The *AJLS* was declared 'new'[51] and the intended audience was wide.[52] Although the Editors recognised that the legacy of Realism formed part of the tradition of Australian jurisprudential writing, they argued that 'few break' from the dominant 'Anglo-Australian Legal tradition' of 'analsy[ing] cases and legislation in isolation'.[53] They were adamant that *AJLS* would provide an institutional forum to publish writing that 'ventur[ed] beyond closely defined disciplinary boundaries',[54] in order to challenge 'fundamental assumptions about the nature and function' of law'.[55] One of the significant characteristics of the *AJLS* that we observe was that opening law to other disciplines, traditions and readers was seen as necessary to speculate what law in Australia might mean as Australian law in 1983, and for whom. This was markedly different from other law journals as it invited university jurists to understand explicitly that their duties might involve the care of law in a place. While the *AJLS* hoped 'to focus on Australian studies', for example, it also 'wishe[d] to avoid both aggressive isolationist nationalism and the derivative approach of much Australian scholarship in the past'.[56] The Editors advocated that 'though the Journal is produced in Australia', Australian law should be investigated theoretically and technically in relation to other jurisdictions, for 'the Board accepts that...the contemporary legal order cannot be confined to any particular geographical area'.[57]

Law in Context, when it began in 1983, also articulated (perhaps less defensively) the need for a style and genre of jurisprudential writing that did not remain bound within the usual traditions of technical legal analysis. In the first edition, the Editors explained that their 'special commitment' or duty was to articulate an

[49]We note as a matter of accuracy the cross overs of individual personnel between these law schools. Our essay is not offered as a biography *per se*, nor is it an historical critique or narrative, but a report on the conduct of jurists in institutions, and the framing of shared institutional commitments. For a history, and critical engagement, with the enterprise and intellectual contribution of socio-legal studies in Australia, and in particular at Legal Studies at La Trobe University in the 1980s, see Tomlins (2013).

[50]'Editorial Comment' (1982), p 3.

[51]'Editorial Comment' (1982), p 3.

[52]'Editorial Comment' (1982), p 4.

[53]'Editorial Comment' (1982), p 3.

[54]'Editorial Comment' (1982), p 3.

[55]'Editorial Comment' (1982) p 4.

[56]'Editorial Comment' (1982) p 4.

[57]'Editorial Comment' (1982) p 5.

'interdisciplinary' jurisprudence that understood law as both 'too important to be left to lawyers', and a 'companion view' that 'legal matters can be more richly understood by placing them in their social context and subjecting them to study from range of disciplines'.[58] *Law in Context* contained contributions not only from Australian jurisprudents, but from international scholars with similar theoretical and methodological intent to the Editors' own.[59] This shows that some Australian jurisprudential writing in 1983 was consciously engaged with, and responding, to the more rapid emergence in the United Kingdom and the United States of what came to be known as the Critical Legal Studies Movement (*CLS*).[60] The CLS movement took shape in the late 1970s, although the major symposium of critical legal scholarship published by *Stanford Law Review* was, in many ways, its public academic statement. The early articles in *Law in Context* demonstrate that Critical jurists in Australia were not standing apart from international developments. In doing so, however, they were not resiling from applying those practices to writing about law in Australia, although we note that this was shaped by certain concerns, notably the theorisation of crime and punishment, the anthropology of law, and social histories of labour.[61]

We observe that this critical Australian juristic writing in 1982 and 1983, (like that produced in Hobart and Canberra), was almost exclusively the work of male jurists, or at least works of male jurisprudence (with the exception of the work and Editorial presence of Margaret Thornton). There was little attention in either *Law in Context* or *AJLS* to the conduct of office being reimagined in 1983 by feminist jurisprudents in their own journals, and their own jurisprudential writings.[62] This feminist re-imagination is not external to the projects of jurisprudence and law. It was simply not yet recognised in these journals as a form of work to be joined or understood as a part of the critical challenge to traditions of juristic writing.[63]

We also observe as part of report on the incident, and incidence, of Australian jurisprudence in 1983 that although there was no attention given to the *Dams* decision and thus no direct conclusion to be drawn about its influence, these new journals indicate a different direction, and reorientation, of the conduct of jurisprudents in universities. The praxis of the 1970s jurisprudents, and their duties to address law in

[58]'Editorial' (1983).

[59]For example, Hunt (1984). Note too that international scholars were publishing in the *Australian Journal of Law and Society* (hereafter *AJLS*): Fitzpatrick (1983).

[60]For an example of the broader field in 1983, see Unger (1983); Critical Legal Studies Symposium (1984).

[61]See for example, Chanock (1983); Bennett (1984); Hirst (1984). See in general Tomlins (2013) for the influences on the Australian Journals, and the nature and theoretical articulation of the scholarship published in this period.

[62]Bennett (1984) is one early exception in *Law in Context*. Margaret Thornton's early work appeared in either more traditional journals (a critical feminist activity), such as Thornton (1984), or in the 'new' journals as general critical scholarship by a feminist: Thornton (1985). Thornton's first major piece of feminist jurisprudence to appear in *AJLS,* in 1986, was also the first in that journal: Thornton (1986).

[63]For an overview of the forms and forums of feminist praxis and jurisprudence that were running in parallel in this period, including the other forums where Thornton's work appeared, see Genovese (2010).

society as lived, had become institutionalized within the University by 1983, and were joined in part to the duties of other disciplinary traditions, with other ways of recommending relationships between law, time, people and place. These Journals assumed there was a readership beyond the law school or the profession, and as a consequence, they offered an alternative way of addressing Australian law as the law that conducted the social, political and historical relations of Australians.

1983 after 1983

The activities and practices that we report of jurists in Hobart, Canberra, Melbourne and Sydney in 1983 were not yet related as rival accounts of Australian jurisprudence. They are discrete contributions, speak in different forums and to different audiences. In undertaking our report however we noted three pieces of writing that gesture towards how the duties of the jurist in Australia might be conducted after 1983 because of the events of 1983. These gestures concern the legal writing of place, race and nation.

First, we note the contribution by scholars working within the idioms and with the duties of the new schools of law (UNSW) and legal studies (La Trobe), who address traditional and doctrinal questions of constitutional law, through re-aligning the task of the legist. Anthony (Tony) Blackshield was educated and taught at the University Sydney. He was one of the founding members of the University of New South Wales (UNSW) Law School. In 1983 he was a Professor of Legal Studies at La Trobe University and a visitor to the University of Tasmania Law School. In 'Damadam to infinities! The tourneyold of the wattarfalls', Blackshield attempts to recast the office of the jurisprudent as caring for both law and place by reading *Dams* through James Joyce's *Finnegan's Wake*.[64]

Dams, much like the novel, Blackshield reminds us, begins and ends with a river, but in between is a torrent of words in the pursuit of the veiling and unveiling of a wrong. For Joyce, the 'words are the river' and the river collects the voices of all those involved in Finnegan's wake. The themes that follow the river are those of the cycles of western life: fall and the promise of resurrection, the cyclical structure of time and of law, as well as of the disputes of family, kin in love and war, and of the inhabiting and personification of land and landscape.[65] For Blackshield, the judgment, like *Finnegan's Wake*, is an endless return to the primordial concerns of statehood and power. In his narrative Blackshield joins two itineraries. In one mode he show us the gap between:

> [A]cceptable modes of constitutional exegesis, and the functional wish to use the process of legal argumentation as a vehicle for handing the causes and crises of social and political life; but this is no more than a … symbol of a deeper abyss by which the whole pattern of institutional procedures and traditions in the High Court is inevitably distanced from the world outside the precincts of the high court itself.[66]

---

[64]Blackshield (1983).

[65]Fargnoli and Gillespie (1996), p 78.

[66]Blackshield (1983), p 79.

In another mode, Blackshield's argument joins a range of scholarship in Australian and American social and legal studies that locates both the institutional and argumentative distance from life and language created by the Court. As he argues, '[b]etween "cultural products" and "external nature" – between "trade marks" and "cattle", law and life, a High Court and a Wilderness park – there is after all an unbridgeable gulf'.[67]

Alongside Joyce, Blackshield's route to restoring law to life (and life to law) is via the early eighteenth-century Neopolitan jurist Giambattista Vico. Vico provided a model for a secular jurisprudence that resisted both the pre-eminence of state authority and the rationalist claims of state jurisprudence. It offered a natural law of peoples, a science of institutions and a method or conduct of a humanist life directed towards the maintenance of the life of law and place.[68] Blackshield's closing comment follows Peter Dombrovskis' photographs in his book *Wild Rivers* (1983).[69] Blackshield writes that these photographs:

> [A]re one kind of response to the Western Tasmanian Wilderness National Parks; the High Court judgments in the Franklin Dam Case are another kind of response. Each response has its own kind of grandeur; but the former has a timelessness and a profundity to which the latter cannot aspire.[70]

There is no doubt that the re-telling of the decision of the High Court is also a prodigious and prestigious re-telling of the office of jurisprudent. Blackshield invokes not only a rival jurisprudence but also assigns new and old tasks for the jurisprudent to fulfil. His projection, then, is not of a world without law or lawyers, but of jurisprudents better attuned to place and the life of the river.

Second, we note the contribution of judges to the expression of conduct of an Australian jurisprudence that has not yet been written. Justice Lionel Murphy wrote the preface to the first edition of *AJLS* in 1982. In 1982, Justice Murphy was also part of the majority in *Koowarta v Bjelke-Petersen*.[71] In 1983, he formed part of the majority in *Dams*.[72] We do not make any direct comment on the relationship between his judgment and his extra curial writing, except to observe that Justice Murphy had an ongoing commitment to recalibrate the practice of jurisprudence in order for it to be relevant to the realities of Australian legal life in the 1980s.[73] 'The problem', according to Justice Murphy, writing in *AJLS* in 1982, 'was the tendency of both courts and profession to cling to 'colonial mentality' in their decision making, and their writing.[74] Justice Murphy, paraphrasing Frantz Fanon in *A Dying*

[67]Blackshield (1983), p 80.

[68]Blackshield (1983), p 38. Vico (1984); Bayer and Verene (2009).

[69]Blackshield (1983), p 80; Dombrovskis (1983).

[70]Blackshield (1983), p 80.

[71]*Koowarta v Bjelke-Petersen* (1982) 153 CLR 168 at 236–243.

[72]*Dams* (1983) 158 CLR 1 at 161–183 (Murphy J).

[73]See, for example, the considerations of Murphy's jurisprudence by scholars, politicians and jurists such as Michael Kirby, Mary Gaudron, Neville Wran, and Tony Blackshield in Scutt (1987).

[74]Murphy (1982), p 7.

Colonialism (1970),[75] argues that 'clinging to antiquated forms is indicative of the pathology of colonialism',[76] and that jurists (in the university and the court) had a special responsibility to recognise the ceremonial and professional limits of their legal inheritance. To refuse to do so was to neglect the fact that 'more and more or our law is dictated by our own parliaments and interpreted by or own appellate courts'.[77]

For Justice Murphy, the task of judges and jurists alike was to 'critically appraise [...] the social values that determine the gains and losses of the law',[78] and to situate these in an Australia that had undergone 'rapid social change' over the twentieth century.[79] That change included understanding Australia as a distinct nation, not a 'client state', and with relationships both to Britain, but also to the rest of the world. Murphy argues that the 'colonial mentality that manifested in the legal profession (which included those working in law schools) and the judiciary did not encourage those questions to be asked'.[80] His invitation to the scholars reading and contributing to the Journal, on the eve of *Dams,* was to address Australian law for what it was: as adaptive and responsive to the people and social values of its own time, place and history. Justice Murphy suggests that this includes coming to terms with colonialism as a legal experience, and, not unrelatedly, to come to terms with the forms of lawful conduct necessary to understand Australia's place in the world in a different, international form.

Third, we note the contributions of practitioners working with Indigenous peoples in the Australian community as beginning to join these concerns together. In the immediate aftermath of *Dams*, the only forum for considering how the 'colonial mentality' of Australian law might be challenged or incorporated as part of a jurisprudent's duties, we observed, was in the *Aboriginal Law Bulletin ('ALB')*. The *ALB* was specialist publication that commenced production in 1981 at the University of New South Wales, and was entirely devoted to the practical and on the ground matter of joining political struggles for land justice of Indigenous peoples to the practice of Australian law. In the August 1983 edition, John Terry, a solicitor involved with the Redfern Legal Centre and the Aboriginal Legal Service in NSW, wrote a case note, 'Damned Wilderness and Special Laws'.[81] He addressed the case not as a story about constitutional law and states' rights, but as a marker of how the High Court's interpretation of the race power had implications for Indigenous peoples. Terry writes:

---

[75]Murphy (1982), p 8. Fanon (1970).

[76]Murphy (1982), p 8.

[77]Murphy (1982), p 8. The *AJLS*, in Murphy's view, was part of that project, 'as there is a real need for a strong and sustained analysis of Australian laws and strong and sustained analysis of Australian law in the context of both Australian and international society': Murphy (1982), p 9.

[78]Murphy (1982), p 6.

[79]Murphy (1982), p 7.

[80]Although English law formed a tradition, and a 'rich source of principles which may be applicable to our legal problems', the question 'should *not* be whether we should *depart* from a particular English decision. It should be whether we *adopt* this English decision' [original emphasis]: Murphy (1982), p 8.

[81]Terry (1983), p 2.

> Since the referendum of 1967, [s51 (xxvi)] is a power of particular relevance to Aboriginal people. During the Fraser years, the Commonwealth steadfastly refused to intervene in the Queensland and West Australian Governments' dealings with Aborigines on the basis that it did not know if it had power to do so. *Dams* gives guidance in this regard.[82]

Terry carefully explains how the discovery of the Kutakina and Deena Reena Caves in the Franklin area, 'with evidence of human habitation from over 20,000 years ago' were open to be protected by the *World Heritage Properties Conservation Act* (1983); and formed the factual reason for the Commonwealth to argue that the Act was valid under the Commonwealth race power. Terry explains how the Minority Judges were of the opinion that the purpose of World Heritage protection was to protect sites of universal value, not to protect sites of specific significance to specific peoples. In addition, he explained that the Minority held that s 51 (xxvi) in this case would not uphold the legislation to prohibit the Dam, as it only enabled the Government to make particular laws for one particular race, that it could only support 'a special law'. Most significantly, Terry describes to his readers the Majority's rejection of that narrow view that just because an area is inseparably connected with one people does not infer that the area is not also of importance to humankind. In particular, he emphasizes Justice Murphy who found that 'such a law may not only strengthen the common understandings that make Aboriginal people conscious of their identity but may promote tolerance of their position among the general community. A law aimed at the preservation or uncovering of evidence about the history of Aboriginal people is therefore a special law'.[83] In this case note, Terry shows that constitutional arguments on the race power carried other histories and contentions, including about federalism and the Constitution, that most scholars were not prepared to address in 1983.

We observe that reporting and writing about the history of Aboriginal peoples as present day political and legal obligations, or at least not unrelated to tumultuous constitutional cases, was prescient, and important.

We have resisted treating the engagements of Blackshield, Murphy and Terry as direct forbears of a new Australian jurisprudence. The news of what would join these concerns together, at least for a while, appeared as small item in the 'news' section of the *ALB*, no 6, December 1982: the initiation of the Mabo litigation in the High Court of Australia.[84]

Concluding comment

In writing about how jurists and jurisprudents wrote in 1983, we chose the genre of report, rather than critical reflection or historical narrative. One reason for this choice was a matter of convenience: a report provides a way of engaging materials without attempting to encapsulate them in one reflective gesture. Another reason was more or less therapeutic: to pay attention to forms of jurisprudence that were

[82]Terry (1983), p 2.

[83]Terry (1983), p 2.

[84]'News' (1982), p 6.

being made available in 1983. Attending to how things are written, as much by whom they are written, and when, provides a way of addressing different accounts of living with law. While it is possible to phrase accounts of jurisprudence in terms of rival accounts of legalism, and social and critical response,[85] the brief survey presented here suggests not that such formulations of dispute were used, but that *Dams* was not treated in those terms, despite the deep political controversy it aroused.[86] In part, we have noted, this was because critical legal scholars and scholars of political jurisprudence were engaged with different kinds of debate, and in part because of the decision in-and around – *Dams* engaged constitutional scholars as legists offering advice on matters of legal form and consequence.

As an activity of jurisography, this report has also been concerned to comment on the styles, gestures, and themes that make the jurisprudence of 1983 available today. In taking a 'slice' of material from 1983, we have stepped aside from historicist claims about the trajectory of jurisprudence in terms of its development, schools, or jurisprudential practice. We have reported what it was in its own time. We note however that observing 1983 as a matter of 1983 does not end the question of jurisprudential inheritance or its investigation, including, of course, the choices of subject matter, method, and mode of address practiced in this essay. The activity of reporting on *Dams* and 1983 as a matter of conduct of office, and trying not to gloss, misremember, or give weight more than is due, is something made available through some of the engagements of 1983.

In many law schools today, for example, it is more clearly the case that the office of the jurist is occupied by more *personae* than the legists: although we note too that concerns of the legists in 2013 extend more to administration and policy than to advice giving and doctrine. We also observe that for many jurisprudents now, their training in conduct has been developed through transformed traditions of humanist jurisprudence;[87] yet at the same time, the tradition of political jurisprudence is a genre not so easily understood today as it was in 1983. Many issues that are treated as tangential to *Dams* in 1983 – place, the status of indigenous and non-indigenous law, and the specificity of law of Australia as Australian law – have now become central topics of doctrine, and represented in many genres of legal scholarship. As a

[85]For one contemporaneous example of dispute, see Kamenka (1983), and the reply by Hunt (1984). For a sustained critique experience and rivalries of schools of jurisprudence, and their relationship to administration of law schools and universities spanning this period, see Thornton (2011).

[86]There are many other accounts (contemporaneous, historical and reflective) that expressly describe the events of 1983 as political contest in the South West of Tasmania and political contest about the Franklin Dams in mainland Australia, and internationally. These are written by activists, journalists, film makers and novelists, and often in collaboration with photographers, including Peter Dombrovskis. These accounts also carry stories of how people lived with law in 1983. They are sources for an alternative jurisorgaphic account of 1983 (that one of us is currently writing); a companion to the report offered here on the conduct of the university jurists. See for example: Connolly (1981); McQueen (1983); Mosely and Messer (1984); Flanagan (1985); and, Hungerford (2013).

[87]We use the term loosely here to note that contemporary law and humanities and cultural studies scholarship joins a tradition. See for example Osler (1997); Leiboff (2012); McVeigh (2013a).

consequence the obligations and practices of the jurisprudent have changed significantly.

What seems clearer in 2013, and what seems to be mostly invisible in 1983, is that it might be a duty of office to consider the relationship between place, race and environment as central to an Australian jurisprudence.[88] We note however that the office of the common law jurisprudent continues to seek practices adequate to such duties. Paying attention as jurisographers to how we write in and about the repertoires and traditions of jurisprudence of this place is part of that task.

References

Primary Legal Sources

Commonwealth v Tasmania (1983) 158 CLR 1.
Koowarta v Bjelke-Petersen (1982) 153 CLR 168.
Strickland v Killen (Full Court, Supreme Court of Tasmania, unreported, 12 April 1983).

Secondary Sources

Gabrielle Appleby et al (2013) 'Critical Thinking in Legal Education: Our Journey' 23 *Legal Education Review* 345.

H Bandler (1987) 'Gordon Below Franklin Dam, Tasmania, Australia: Environmental Factors in a Decision of National Significance' 7 *Environmentalist* 43.

Susan Bartie (2010) 'A Full Day's Work: A Study of Australia's First Legal Scholarly Community' 29 *University of Queensland Law Journal* 67.

John Basten et al (1983) 'Legal Centres in Australia' 6 *University of NSW Law Journal* 163.

G M Bates (1983) 'The Aftermath of Lake Pedder' in M Sornarajah (ed) *The South West Dam Dispute: The Legal and Political Issues*, Sir Elliot Lewis Memorial Publication, University of Tasmania.

Thora Ilin Bayer and Donald Phillip Verene (eds) (2009) *Giambattista Vico: Keys to the New Science*, Cornell University Press.

Laura Bennett (1984) 'The Construction of Skill: Craft Unions, Women Workers and the Conciliation and Arbitration Court' 2 *Law in Context* 118.

Krim Benterrak et al (1984) *Reading the Country*, Freemantle Arts Centre Press.

Christine Black (2010) *The Land is the Sources of the Law: A Dialogic Encounter*, Routledge.

A R Blackshield (1983) 'Damadam to Infintities! The Tourneyold of the Wattarfalls!' in M Sornarajah (ed) *The South West Dams Dispute: The Legal and Political Issues*, Sir Elliot Lewis Memorial Publication, University of Tasmania.

Ernest K Braybrooke (1983) 'The Law of Trespass and Demonstrations in the South West Area' in M Sornarajah (ed) *The South West Dam Dispute: The Legal and Political Issues*, Sir Elliot Lewis Memorial Publication, University of Tasmania.

Ernest Braybrooke (1973) *Freedom, Law and Order*, La Trobe University.

Josie Castle and Helen Pringle (1993) 'Sovereignty and Sexual Identity in Political Cartoons' in Susan Magarey, Sue Rowley, and Susan Sheridan (eds) *Debutante Nation: Feminism Contests the 1890s*, Allen & Unwin.

Martin Chanock (1983) 'Signposts or Tombstones? Reflections on Recent Works on the Anthropology of Law' 1 *Law in Context* 107.

Bob Connolly (1981) *The Fight For The Franklin: The Story of Australia's Last Wild River,* Cassell.

[88]See Christine Black's elaboration of a modern Indigenous jurisprudence in Black (2010). In addition to its own accounts of Indigenous jurisprudence, this work comments on the Senior Law Men such as Neidjie (1989); Mowaljarli (1992); Marika and Isaacs (1995). See also Benterrak et al (1984).

Terry Connolly (1983) 'The Tasmanian Dam Case: Treaties and the Australian Constitution' 54 *Australian Foreign Affairs Record* 307.

Michael Coper (1983) *The Franklin Dam Case: Commentary and Full Text of the Decision in Commonwealth of Australia v State of Tasmania*, Butterworths.

Ross Cranston (1980) 'Lawyer in the Social Sciences – Geoffrey Sawer' 11 *Federal Law Review* 263.

Michael Crommelin (1983) 'Comment on the External Affairs Power' 14 *Federal Law Review* 208.

Critical Legal Studies Symposium (1984) 36 *Stanford Law Review*.

Richard Davis (1993) *100 Years: A Centenary History of the Faculty of Law, University of Tasmania 1893-1993*, University of Tasmania.

Sir David Derham (1984) 'Mere Surface Reflections (*Franklin Dam* Case)' 58 *Law Institute Journal* 771.

John Docker (1974) *Australian Cultural Elites: Intellectual Traditions in Sydney and Melbourne*, Angus and Robertson.

Peter Dombrovskis (1983) *Wild Rivers*.

Shaunnagh Dorsett and Shaun McVeigh (2012) *Jurisdiction*, Routledge.

Shaunnagh Dorsett and Shaun McVeigh (2014) 'Jurisprudences of Jurisdiction: Matters of Public Authority' *Griffith Law Review* [forthcoming].

Roger Douglas (1989) 'Obituary: Ernest Kingston Braybrooke: 1916-1989' 7 *Law in Context* 3.

'Editorial Comment' (1982) 1 *Australian Journal of Law & Society* 3.

'Editorial' (1983) 1 *Law in Context*.

Kep Enderby (1975) 'The Family Law Act Background to the Legislation' 1 *University of New South Wales Law Journal* 10.

Frantz Fanon (1970) *A Dying Colonialism,* Penguin.

Nicholas Fargnoli and Michael Patrick Gillespie (1996) *James Joyce A to Z: The Essential Reference to the Life and Work*, Oxford University Press.

Peter Fitzpatrick (1983) 'Marxism and Legal Pluralism' 1 *Australian Journal of Law and Society* 45.

Richard Flanagan (1985) *Terrible Beauty: History of the Gordon River Country,* Greenhouse.

S G Foster and Margaret M Varghese (1996) *The Making of the Australian National University*, Allen & Unwin.

Ann Genovese (2010) 'A Radical Prequel: Historicising the Concept of Gendered Law in Australia' in M Thornton (ed) *Sex Discrimination in Uncertain Times*, ANU e-press.

Ann Genovese (2013) 'Inheriting and Inhabiting the Pleasures and Duties of Our Own Existence: *The Second Sex* and Feminist Jurisprudence' 38 *Australian Feminist Law Journal* 41.

Ann Genovese (2014a) 'On Australian Feminist Tradition: Three Notes on Conduct, Inheritance, and the Relations of Historiography and Jurisprudence' 38 *Journal of Australian Studies* [forthcoming].

Ann Genovese (2014b) 'Critical Decision, 1982: Remembering *Koowarta v Bjelke Petersen*' 23 *Griffith Law Review* [forthcoming].

John Goldring (1985) 'Julius Stone and the Study of Law and Society in Australia' 2 *Australian Journal of Law and Society* 4.

Peter Goodrich (2004) 'Satirical Legal Studies: From the Legists to the *Lizard*' 103 *Michigan Law Review* 397.

Peter Goodrich (2008) 'Visive Powers: Colours, Trees and Genres of Jurisdiction' 2 *Law and Humanities* 213.

Jeffrey Goldsworthy (2006) 'Australia: Devotion to Legalism' in Jeffrey Goldworthy (ed) *Interpreting Constitutions: A Comparative Study*, Oxford University Press.

Pierre Hadot (2001) *The Inner Citadel: The Meditations of Marcus Aurelius* Michael Chase (trans.) Harvard University Press.

Pierre Hadot (2002) *What Is Ancient Philosophy?* Michael Chase (trans.) The Belknap Press.

Robert Hawke and Gareth Evans (1983) 'Statements' (Press Releases) 54 *Australian Foreign Affairs Record* 353–354.

Paul Hirst (1984) 'The Concept of Punishment' 2 *Law in Context* 73.

Alice Hungerford (2013) *UpRiver: Untold Stories of the Franklin River Activists*, UpRiver Mob.
Alan Hunt (1984) 'Contemporary Critical Legal Theory: A Reply to Eugene Kamenka' *2 Law in Context* 134.
Helen Irving et al (eds) (2010) *Julius Stone: A Study in Influence*, Federation Press.
Eugene Kamenka (1983) 'A Marxist Theory of Law?' 1 *Law in Context* 46.
Donald R Kelley (1970) *Foundations of Modern Historical Scholarship: Language, Law and History in the French Renaissance*, Columbia University Press.
Michael Kirby (2012) 'The Graduating Class of Sydney Law School 1962: Talented, Lucky, Unquestioning' 36 *Australian Bar Review* 189.
Marett Leiboff (2012) 'Ghosts of Law and Humanities (Past, Present, Future)' 36 *Australian Feminist Law Journal* 3.
Geoffrey Lindell (1983) 'The Corporations and Races Powers' 14 *Federal Law Review* 219.
Stuart Macintyre (2010) *The Poor Relation: A History of Social Sciences in Australia*, Melbourne University Press.
Wandjuk Marika and Jennifer Isaacs (1995) *Wandjuk Marika: Life Story*, University of Queensland Press.
James McQueen (1983) *The Franklin – Not Just A River,* Penguin Books.
Shaun McVeigh (2013a) 'Law and Postmodernism' in Reza Banakar and Max Travers (eds) *Law and Social Theory*, 2nd ed, Hart Publishers.
Shaun McVeigh (2013b) 'Office of Review', paper presented at the Symposium to launch the London Review of International Law, November.
Shaun McVeigh (2014) 'On Some Not Very Reflective Elements of Law' 4 *Irvine Law Review* 471.
J G Mosely and J Messer (eds) (1984) *Fighting For Wilderness: Papers from the Australian Conservation Foundation's Third National Wilderness Conference, 1983*, Australian Conservation Foundation/Fontana.
David Mowaljarli (1992) *Yorro Yorro: Evertything Standing Up Alive*, Magbala Books.
The Hon. Lionel Murphy (1982) 'Preface to the First Issue' 1 *Australian Journal of Law and Society* 6.
Bill Neidjie (author) and Keith Taylor (ed) (1989) *The Story About Feeling*, Keith Taylor (ed), Magbala Books.
'News' (1982) 6 *Aboriginal Law Bulletin* 6.
Douglas Osler (1997) 'The Myth of European Legal History' 16 *Rechtshistorisches Journal* 393.
Hadot Pierre (1995) *Philosophy as a Way of Life: Spiritual Exercises from Socrates to Foucault* Arnold I. Davidson (ed.), Michael Chase (trans.) Blackwell Publishing.
Dennis Rose (1983a) 'Comment on the Corporations Power and the Races Power' 14 *Federal Law Review* 253.
Dennis Rose (1983b) 'Comment on the External Affairs Power' 14 *Federal Law Review* 216.
Stan Ross (1982a) 'Reply to Tomasic' 5 *University of New South Wales Law Journal* 344.
Stan Ross (1982b) *The Politics of Law Reform*, Penguin Books.
R P Rutherford (1983) 'The Compensation Question' in M Sornarajah (ed) *The South West Dam Dispute: The Legal and Political Issues*, Sir Elliot Lewis Memorial Publication, University of Tasmania.
Geoffrey Sawer (1968) *The Australian and The Law*, Penguin.
Geoffrey Sawer (1983) 'The External Affairs Power' 14 *Federal Law Review* 199.
J H Schlegel (1979) 'American Legal Realism and Empirical Social Science: From the Yale Experience' 28 *Buffalo Law Review* 459.
Jocelynne A Scutt (ed) (1987) *Lionel Murphy: A Radical Judge*, McCulloch Publishing in association with Macmillan Australia.
Ivan A Shearer (1983) 'The Teaching of International Law in Australian Law Schools' 9 *Adelaide Law Review* 61.
Judith N Shklar (1964) *Legalism*, Harvard University Press.
Sir Laurence Whistler Street (1975) 'Foreword' 1 *University of New South Wales Law Journal* 1.

M Sornarajah (ed) (1983a) *The South West Dam Dispute: The Legal and Political Issues*, Sir Elliot Lewis Memorial Publication, University of Tasmania.

Muthucumaraswamy Sornarajah (1983b) 'International Law and the South West Dam Case' in M Sornarajah (ed) *The South West Dam Dispute: The Legal and Political Issues*, Sir Elliot Lewis Memorial Publication, University of Tasmania.

Julius Stone (first published 1946, 1950 ed) *The Province and Function of Law*, Maitland Publications.

John Terry (1983) 'Damned Wilderness & Special Laws' 8 *Aboriginal Law Bulletin* 2.

Margaret Thornton (1984) 'Loss of Consortium: Inequality Before the Law' 10 *Sydney Law Review* 259.

Margaret Thornton (1985) 'Affirmative Action, Merit and the Liberal State' 2 *Australian Journal of Law and Society* 25.

Margaret Thornton (2011) *Privatizing The Public University: The Case of Law*, Routledge.

Margaret Thornton (1986) 'Feminist Jurisprudence: Illusion or Reality?' 3 *Australian Journal of Law and Society* 3.

Philip Tighe (1987) 'Environmental Values, Legalism and Judicial Rationality: The Tasmanian Dam Case and its Broader Political Significance' 4 *Environmental and Planning Law Journal* 134.

Roman Tomasic (1982) 'Book Reviews: The Politics of Law Reform' 5 *University of New South Wales Law Journal* 331.

Christopher Tomlins (2013) 'Law "and", Law "in", Law "as": The Definition, Rejection and Recuperation of the Socio-Legal Enterprise' 29 *Law in Context* 137.

Roberto Unger (1983) *The Critical Legal Studies Movement*, Harvard University Press.

Giambattista Vico (1948, revised ed, 1984) *The New Science of Giambattista Vico* (revised translation of the third edition by Thomas Goddard Bergin and Max Harold Fisch, Cornell University Press) [trans of: *Scienza Nuova Seconda* (first published 1730/1744)].

Kate Warner (1983) 'The Dam Blockade: Some Issues Relating to Organised Protest and Bail' in M Sornarajah (ed) *The South West Dam Dispute: The Legal and Political Issues,* Sir Elliot Lewis Memorial Publication, University of Tasmania.

Max Weber (2004) *The Politics Lectures*, D Owen, T B Strong, and R Livingstone (eds) Hackett Publishing Company.

Tasmanian Dams and Australia's Relationship with International Law

Madelaine Chiam

Melbourne Law School, Australia

Tasmanian Dams remains a touchstone for the debate over Australia's relationship with international law because it entrenched an interplay between anxiety and promise at the heart of that relationship. This interplay arises from a tension between anxiety about the influence of international law in Australia, on the one hand, and the promises international law offers on the other. In this article, I show how the anxiety-promise dialectic has shaped Australia's relationship with international law since *Tasmanian Dams* in three contexts: treaty negotiations, the attitudes of State and federal parliamentarians to international law and the attitudes of international law academics to international law. I conclude that the dialectic has ultimately been unproductive for Australia's relationship with international law.

On 8 July 1983, in a letter to the editors of *The Australian* newspaper, Sir Charles Court, a former Premier of Western Australia, wrote that the High Court's decision in *Commonwealth v Tasmania*[1] (*Tasmanian Dams*) would:

> [place] increasing parts of Australia under the control of people from countries we hardly know and who have not the slightest understanding or concern for people in Australia, nor responsibility for our economic, social and political development.[2]

In a 1985 article in the *American Journal of International Law*, Hilary Charlesworth and Andrew Byrnes described the *Tasmanian Dams* decision as one that brought 'Australian jurisprudence … firmly into the modern age. … A state in a federation simply cannot isolate itself from international law'.[3]

These two contemporary reactions to the case – one fearful, the other celebratory – typified the contrasting responses to the aspects of the decision that affected Australia's relationship with international law. The High Court's interpretation of section 51(xxix) of the Constitution (the 'external affairs' power) invoked these reactions, even though its decision had been a relatively predictable outcome,

---

Madelaine Chiam, PhD Candidate, Melbourne Law School. My thanks to Ann Genovese for inviting me to be part of the *Turning Points* symposium and for her comments on earlier versions of this article.

[1] *Commonwealth v Tasmania* (1983) 158 CLR 1 (*Tasmanian Dams*).

[2] 'Decision strikes at the heart of Australia', *The Australian*, 8 July 1983, p 7. A version of this letter was also published as 'Australia's Black Day', *The Age*, 6 July 1983, p 13.

[3] Byrnes and Charlesworth (1985) 640.

following the decision in *Koowarta v Bjelke-Petersen* (*Koowarta*)[4] of the year before. At the time, leading constitutional lawyer Geoffrey Sawer characterised *Tasmanian Dams* as conceivably having 'added nothing to the judicial construction of the Commonwealth's external affairs powers'.[5] Yet, it is *Tasmanian Dams*, rather than the earlier cases of *Koowarta* or *R v Burgess* from 1936,[6] that, over 30 years later, is a continuing touchstone for the debate over the boundaries of Australia's interactions with international law. In this article, I suggest why this might be.

The place of *Tasmanian Dams* in Australia's relationship with international law arises from the key role that it played in entrenching an interplay between anxiety and promise that lies at the heart of Australia's relationship with international law. This interplay arises from a tension between anxiety about the influence of international law in Australia, on the one hand, and the promises international law offers on the other. These promises are often of a progressive or cosmopolitan politics, but they can also be promises of security or of prosperity, tied to the economics of the free market. The quotes that open this article are examples of this dialectic. Expressing anxiety, Sir Charles Court's concern was that international law was an all-encompassing foreign force that would overwhelm Australia's democratic laws and processes. Characterising promise, Charlesworth and Byrnes celebrated that *Tasmanian Dams* allowed Australia to be a fully participating member of the international community. *Tasmanian Dams* was crucial in establishing this interplay of anxiety and promise in Australia's relationship with international law.

I draw the ideas of anxiety and promise from a 2003 article entitled 'Deep Anxieties'.[7] In that article, I and three colleagues characterised Australia's view of international law as one that contained 'exaggerated and simplistic understandings about the international legal system' and in which 'international law is [seen as] an intrusion from "outside" into our self-contained and carefully bounded legal system'.[8] This combination, we argued, had generated an unwarranted level of anxiety about Australia's relationship with international law. With that article, and with subsequent publications, the four of us sought to demystify some persistent beliefs about the role of international law in Australia.[9] We particularly tried to demonstrate how flawed it was for many Australian politicians and others to insist that international law represented a threat to Australian sovereignty. Thus, while we did not use the term, we were arguing for a greater openness in Australia to the promises of international law, though we did not do so uncritically.[10] Many academics have made arguments based on the promise of international law. Indeed, to extend an argument that international law scholar David Kennedy has famously made, much international law scholarship can be described as *for* international law,

[4] *Koowarta v Bjelke-Petersen* (1982) 153 CLR 168 (*Koowarta*).

[5] Sawer (1983–84), p 199.

[6] *R v Burgess: Ex Parte Henry* (1936) 55 CLR 608 (*Burgess*). For different contemporary views on the significance of these cases see eg Byrnes (1985) and Rothwell (1987).

[7] Charlesworth et al (2003).

[8] Charlesworth et al (2003), pp 425 and 424.

[9] See eg Charlesworth et al (2006), Chiam (2003) and Hovell (2003).

[10] See eg Charlesworth et al (2003), pp 464–465, and Charlesworth et al (2006), pp 9–21.

in a way that scholarship on banking is not *for* banking.[11] The 'Deep Anxieties' article therefore identified the characteristic of anxiety in Australia's relationship with international law and argued for a judicious openness to its promise. I build on 'Deep Anxieties' to suggest that the place of anxiety and promise in Australia's relationship with international law extends at least as far back as *Tasmanian Dams*.[12] This then offers one explanation for its ongoing status as an iconic case in Australia's relationship with international law.

This article proceeds as follows. I first outline the doctrinal impact of *Tasmanian Dams* for the interpretation of the external affairs power and argue that the confirmation that there was no separate 'international concern' requirement was the key shift in enlivening the anxiety-promise interplay. I then present snapshots of the impact of *Tasmanian Dams* in three contexts: treaty negotiation, the attitudes of State and federal parliamentarians and the attitudes of international law academics. Each of these contexts represents an aspect of Australia's relationship with international law. In each example, the effect of *Tasmanian Dams* was to demonstrate or amplify the anxiety-promise dialectic in Australia's relationship with international law. I argue that anxiety and promise have continued to play against each other in the years since *Tasmanian Dams* by examining the situation in 1994/95, in the wake of the decisions in *Toonen* and *Teoh*.[13] Finally, I draw some conclusions about the longer-term impact of *Tasmanian Dams* on Australia's relationship with international law.

The relevant legal question

The constitutional question which made *Tasmanian Dams* a key case in Australia's relationship with international law was whether the federal government's power to implement treaties under the external affairs power was tempered by a requirement that the treaty in question had a separately determined 'international concern' status. In *Burgess* and *Koowarta*, the High Court had established that the federal government had the power to legislate to implement international treaty obligations, even where it did not have a corresponding constitutional power over the subject matter of the treaty. The open question for the Court in *Koowarta* was whether the federal government could legislate to implement all of Australia's international obligations under the external affairs power or whether the treaty or obligation in question needed to satisfy an additional requirement of 'international-ness', however defined. The Court in *Koowarta* split between three judges who decided that there was no such limitation,[14] and three who determined that a separate requirement of

[11] Kennedy (1994), p 335.

[12] It is not my argument that either anxiety or promise should or need to be parts of that relationship. In our earlier work we tried to demonstrate that the anxiety that has been expressed about international law in Australia is unfounded. There is also a formidable body of work in international law that challenges its promise of a progressive or cosmopolitan politics. See for example post-colonial scholarship in international law, especially Anghie (2005), Chimni (2007) and Pahuja (2011). See also critiques of particular fields, e.g. human rights: Kennedy (2005), Marks (2011); and international criminal law: Koskenniemi (2002), Simpson (2007).

[13] *Toonen v Australia* (No 488/192) 30 March 1994, UN Doc CCPR/C/50/D/488/1992; *Minister for Immigration and Ethnic Affairs v Teoh* (1995) 183 CLR 273.

[14] Mason, Murphy and Brennan JJ.

international character did apply.[15] Justice Stephen provided the 'lowest common denominator' position for the case, which was that to fall within the external affairs power a treaty must deal with a matter of 'international concern'.[16] After *Koowarta* therefore, it seemed at the very least that the external affairs power could be relied upon for legislation implementing a treaty where the subject matter was of 'international concern'.[17]

The court in *Tasmanian Dams* was confronted with the 'international concern' question. If the limitation applied, Australia would not be subject to international treaty law without an initial determination within Australia that the treaty was indeed 'international'. Such a limitation contributed to a sense that Australians – through parliament and the courts – retained some control over the adoption of international treaty obligations. Ultimately, the majority in *Tasmanian Dams* (Mason, Murphy, Brennan and Deane JJ) decided that no additional 'international concern' test was necessary. The federal government could legislate any and all of Australia's international obligations on the basis of the external affairs power alone. The minority in the case (Gibbs CJ, Wilson and Dawson JJ) adopted Justice Stephen's 'international concern' test from *Koowarta*, and all three held that building a dam that allowed a nation's own natural heritage to be damaged was not a matter of 'international concern'.[18]

In deciding this constitutional issue, the High Court helped to open Australia to the influence of international law by dismantling barriers that earlier Australian governments had constructed between Australia's legal system and the international legal system. In particular, the decision confirmed that the federal government could no longer disclaim its ability fully to implement international obligations on the basis of its federal constitutional system. The High Court also affirmed in *Tasmanian Dams* that federal governments could legislate in areas traditionally reserved for the States, if there was an international obligation underpinning that legislation. This gave federal governments potentially extensive powers in areas that had been the preserve of State governments. As a result of *Tasmanian Dams*, the High Court was seen to have removed the limits, the predictability and the sense of control that had existed in Australia's relationship with international law. This provided the foundations for approaches to Australia's relationship with international law that have since revolved around the interplay between anxiety and promise.

---

[15]Gibbs CJ, Aickin and Wilson JJ.

[16]*Tasmanian Dams* at 216 (per Stephen J). See also Williams, Brennan and Lynch (2014) at 911 and Sawer (1983) at 202–204. For a different view on Justice Stephen's position, see Charlesworth (2014).

[17]For a discussion of the impact of *Koowarta* on Australia's relationship with international law, see Charlesworth (2014).

[18]See *Tasmanian Dams* at 102 (per Gibbs CJ), 194 (per Wilson J) and 307 (per Dawson J). The volume of commentary on the external affairs aspects of *Tasmanian Dams* is too extensive to list here. For immediately contemporary accounts, see eg Coper (1983), Crock (1983), Lane (1983), Lumb (1983/4), Sawer (1983) and Sornarajah (1983). For a full doctrinal account of the place of *Tasmanian Dams* in the history of the external affairs power, see eg Williams, Brennan and Lynch (2014), pp 908–926, and especially the list of references on 929. For a short legal and political overview of the case, see Zines (2013).

Tasmanian Dams, the executive and Australian treaty negotiations

Tasmanian Dams enabled a change in Australia's treaty negotiation practice. The government of Bob Hawke had been elected in 1983 on a platform that included the implementation of Australia's international human rights obligations and stopping the construction of the Franklin Dam.[19] Both of these policies were based on the implementation of international obligations.[20] Attorney-General Gareth Evans in particular saw international law as providing the basis for new human rights protections in Australian law.[21] In combination with these and other policies of the Hawke government, *Tasmanian Dams* confirmed Australia's ability to adopt a new approach to international treaty negotiations.

Australia's federal system had slowed Australia's participation in international treaties in the years before 1983 because federal government practice had been to require consent of all the states before ratifying a treaty.[22] Government practice had also been to negotiate for the insertion of a 'federal clause' in multilateral treaties or to append a 'federal reservation' to a treaty if necessary. The effect of a federal clause was to oblige federal governments only to implement those treaty obligations that fell within their jurisdiction, and to allow federal governments to use their best efforts, but not be required, to comply with obligations that fell outside their jurisdiction.[23] These clauses were generally unpopular in international negotiations as they created an inequity of treaty obligations between unitary and federal states. These practices were considered a necessity in Australia, however, because the States expected consultation prior to ratification of the treaty in order to assure their cooperation in implementation of the treaty obligations.[24]

After it was elected, the Hawke government introduced policies that changed the way in which Australia participated in the international system. One of these was no longer to insist on the inclusion of federal clauses in treaty negotiations.[25] The Hawke government's policy not to seek federal clauses was assisted by the confirmation in *Tasmanian Dams* that there were no constitutional impediments to the federal government's ability to legislate to implement a treaty. The decision meant that the Australian federal government could no longer in good faith claim at international negotiations that a federal clause was necessary for Australia to comply with the treaty obligations. *Tasmanian Dams* was a blow to the Australian States, whose role in treaty implementation was stymied by the change in policy. To ease the

[19]See eg Australian Federal Election Speeches, 'Bob Hawke 1983'. http://electionspeeches.moadoph.gov.au/speeches/1983-bob-hawke

[20]See eg Byrnes (1985) at 314 and 'After the dam victory comes a Bill of Rights', *The Australian*, 2–3 July 1983, p 1.

[21]'After the dam victory comes a Bill of Rights', *The Australian*, 2–3 July 1983, p 1; Galligan (1983) at 103.

[22]Australian treaty practice up to 1985 is described in Byrnes (1985) at 302–316. See also, Burmester (1989) at 192.

[23]There are different kinds of federal clauses. For an overview, see Burmester (1985) and Byrnes (1985) at 302–338.

[24]For some examples of this process at work, see Byrnes (1985) at 306–314. See also Burmester (1978) and Opeskin and Rothwell (1995).

[25]Byrnes (1985) at 314–317.

States' anxieties both about the reach of federal government power and the impact of international law,[26] the Hawke government introduced a new practice. The government would issue a 'Federal Statement' in relation to multilateral treaties where the States had a role in implementation of treaty obligations.[27] In international law terms, this Statement amounted to a declaration accompanying Australia's ratification of a treaty. It meant a 'Federal Statement' was descriptive only and would not affect Australia's obligations under the relevant treaty. Three treaties ratified or acceded to in 1983/84, in the direct aftermath of *Tasmanian Dams*, had a 'Federal Statement' appended.[28] Also in 1984, a 'Federal Statement' replaced earlier reservations, including a federal reservation, to Australia's ratification of the *International Covenant on Civil and Political Rights*.[29]

The change in treaty negotiation practice by the Hawke government demonstrated the direct impact of *Tasmanian Dams* on Australia's treaty negotiation practice and on Australia's relationship with the international community. The Hawke government had signalled a commitment to the promises of international law – and in particular international human rights law. These necessitated changes in Australian treaty negotiation practice, some of which were designed to ease the anxieties of the States about their losses of influence in both treaty negotiation and implementation. The impact of *Tasmanian Dams* on Australia's treaty negotiation practice showed anxiety and promise playing out for the Australian state, both in its relationships with other nations and between the constituent parts of its federal structure.

***Tasmanian Dams*, legislators and the external affairs power**

Many State and federal politicians reacted passionately against *Tasmanian Dams*. These men expressed deep concern about how *Tasmanian Dams* would open Australia to the influence of international law. Their reactions illustrated an anxiety amongst State and federal legislators in particular that *Tasmanian Dams* had removed the limits, the predictability and the sense of control that had existed in Australia's relationship with international law.[30]

Two issues dominated the immediate public responses to *Tasmanian Dams*: the impact of the decision on the 'federal balance' under the constitution; and the impact

[26]See next section '*Tasmanian Dams*, Legislators and the External Affairs Power'.

[27]For the text of the 'Federal Statement', see 'Treaties' (1981–83) 10 *Australian Yearbook of International Law* 530.

[28]*Convention on the Elimination of All Forms of Discrimination Against Women* [1983] ATS 9; *International Convention On Standards Of Training, Certification And Watchkeeping For Seafarer 1978* [1984] ATS 7; *International Convention On Maritime Search And Rescue 1979* [1986] ATS 29.

[29]*International Covenant on Civil and Political Rights* [1980] ATS 23. See discussion in Charlesworth (1997) at 293–294.

[30]The examples I give here are from coverage of the case in five major metropolitan newspapers in the ten days after the decision: *The Age*, *Sydney Morning Herald*, *The Australian*, *The Mercury* ('Tasmania's newspaper') and *The Courier-Mail*. For a discussion of the political responses at the time see eg Galligan (1983).

on Tasmania – particularly economically.[31] The impact of *Tasmanian Dams* on Australia's relationship with international law also received media coverage across the newspapers. Prime Minister Bob Hawke and Attorney-General Gareth Evans were keen to assure the Australian people that they would use the power sparingly, only 'where the national interest demands action be taken'.[32] John Cain, then Victorian Premier, was reported as saying that the decision meant that the federal government 'had a duty to keep States informed about international treaties it signed'.[33] Terry White, the Minister for Welfare Services in Queensland, warned that signing an international agreement would give the federal government power 'regardless of ... the actual desires of the people'.[34] Peter White, also from Queensland, described international treaties as a 'stick' which the federal government could now use to 'beat the States into submission'.[35] The Tasmanian Premier Robin Gray invoked the spectre of over 1500 treaties to which Australia was a party that 'could now be invoked by Canberra to control the States'.[36]

Shadow Attorney-General Peter Durack, Tasmanian senator Brian Harradine, and former Western Australian premier Sir Charles Court were openly apprehensive about the impact that the legal exclusion of the States from Australia's decision-making about treaties would have on the 'federal balance'.[37] These men also had a deep concern about the *source* of the laws that would affect that federal balance: international law. Peter Durack was especially concerned about the imminent introduction of a Bill of Rights which would require courts to '"second guess" both federal and state State laws by reference to an international agreement'.[38] Brian Harradine relied on the number of treaties as a tactic, referring to the treaties to which Australia was a party as '1200 Pandora's Boxes'.[39] To address these fears, at different times, both Senator Harradine and Peter Durack attempted to introduce legislation that would have nullified the impact of *Tasmanian Dams*.[40]

With the exception of Bob Hawke and Gareth Evans, nearly all of these men portrayed international law as a foreign and uncontrollable force that did not, and indeed could not, comprehend the complexity of life in Australia. Their anxiety about the potential influence of international law was palpable. The outside-in view of international law that these men expressed created a dichotomous relationship

---

[31]See eg Blunden (1983), Cadzow (1983), White (1983), Goff (1983), Sturgess (1983). See also '500 mil?', *The Mercury*, 2 July 1983, p 1.

[32]'Canberra wins more power', *The Sydney Morning Herald*, 2 July 1983, p 1. See also 'PM Pledge: No rush on new powers', *The Courier-Mail*, 2 July 1983, p 1.

[33]'Gray accepts decision but disappointed', *The Age*, 2 July 1983, p 5. See also 'States will have to watch those treaties', *The Australian*, 2–3 July 1983, p 1.

[34]White (1983).

[35]'Hawke promises "to work with Tas"', *The Australian*, 2–3 July, p 8.

[36]'Tasmania looking to the nuclear alternative', *The Australian*, 8 July 1983, p 3.

[37]'Federal system is in peril: Durack', *The Age*, 2 July 1983, p 5; 'Durack sees peril in new federal power', *The Australian*, 8 July 1983, p 2; 'Decision strikes at the heart of Australia', *The Australian*, 8 July 1983, p 7; 'Bill will require both Houses to pass treaties', *The Australian*, 8 July 1983, p 3.

[38]'Durack calls for referendum on proposed bill of rights', *The Australian*, 8 July 1983, p 3.

[39]'Bill will require both Houses to pass treaties', *The Australian*, 8 July 1983, p 3.

[40]'Harradine plans bill on treaties', *The Mercury*, 7 July 1983, p 4. For a discussion of the Durack Bill, see Durack (1994).

between international and domestic law that failed to capture the complexity of that relationship. For Sir Charles Court, Brian Harradine, Peter Durack and the others, Australia needed to be protected from the external influence of international law. In their view, there was no promise of progress in international law, only a guarantee of lost Australian sovereignty. *Tasmanian Dams* was the progenitor of these legislators' anxieties about the influence of international law in Australia.

Tasmanian Dams, International lawyers and the external affairs power

International law academics parsed the consequences of *Tasmanian Dams* in two ways. Many were reserved in response – viewing the Court's interpretation of the external affairs power as having confirmed what had been established in *Koowarta* the year before. Three international law academics offered a more laudatory view of the impact of *Tasmanian Dams*. Andrew Byrnes, Hilary Charlesworth and M Sornarajah saw the case as much more than a doctrinal shift in Australian constitutional law. For them, *Tasmanian Dams* opened Australia to the promises of international law.

Most early published responses by international law academics to *Tasmanian Dams* were muted.[41] Noel D Campbell, for example, observed that, as a consequence of *Tasmanian Dams*, the federal Parliament could now 'pass laws giving effect to any treaty to which Australia is or becomes a party'.[42] Campbell absorbed without comment the impact of *Tasmanian Dams* and *Koowarta*. His sober approach is typical of the other contributions to a volume of essays on international law that discuss *Tasmanian Dams*.[43] For these writers, it was the combined effect of *Koowarta* and *Tasmanian Dams* that was significant, rather than *Tasmanian Dams* alone. The *Australian Yearbook of International Law* reflected the same view, publishing extracts of similar lengths of both cases in its practice section for 1981–83.[44] JG Starke, a leading Australia international lawyer, chose to focus on the way the judges in *Tasmanian Dams* had used *travaux preparatoires* and international law principles on the interpretation of treaties.[45] Starke did not ignore the doctrinal point about treaty-making, but rather left analysis of that aspect to the constitutional law scholar PH Lane.[46] For these international lawyers, *Tasmanian Dams* confirmed a change in Australian constitutional interpretation, but it was not a decision that warranted a vigorous response.

Andrew Byrnes, Hilary Charlesworth and M Sornarajah saw the consequences of *Tasmanian Dams* differently. For M Sornarajah, *Tasmanian Dams* acknowledged what he regarded as the reality of the shifts in the international legal order. In a piece from December 1983, Sornarajah, argued:

41Constitutional law academics responded much more vigorously. For a sample, see the references in footnote 18.

42Campbell, (1984) at 57.

43Ryan (1984), especially at 52, 53–70 and 71–135.

44'International Law in General' (1981–83).

45Starke (1983).

46Starke (1983) at 592. See also Lane (1983).

> In an increasingly interdependent world the distinction between internal and international events is vanishing fast. ... The World Heritage Convention must be looked at not in isolation, but as forming part of this movement for the creation of an international law for the protection of a value shared by the world community.[47]

Sornarajah thus celebrated the new influence that international law would have on Australian law. This influence was especially important in the areas of environmental and human rights law. In his view, the minority judges' determination that the construction of a dam on a World Heritage protected site was not an issue of international concern failed to comprehend 'trends and developments' within international law.[48] *Tasmanian Dams* allowed a space for these trends and developments to have an influence in the Australian legal system.

For Byrnes, Charlesworth and Sornarajah, *Tasmanian Dams* was about more than international environmental law – it was about how Australia managed its relationship with international law more generally. All of them emphasised that *Tasmanian Dams* allowed Australia to comply fully with its international obligations, without the hindrances raised by being a federation. Sornarajah argued on this point that:

> From an international lawyer's viewpoint the majority judgments are superior. ... Australia must give vigorous leadership particularly in the Asian region, in the human rights and environmental fields. Her claims to such leadership should not be hampered by narrow legalism.[49]

Sornarajah and Byrnes and Charlesworth embodied a particular idea about Australia's relationship with international law: that it was a positive (and overdue) move to lift Australia out of international isolation and enable it to function as a 'modern' state – one that would not just participate in but lead the broadening fields of international law. For these scholars, Australia's earlier resistance to international standards was short-sighted and futile. Australia had to find a way to come to terms with the new international environment and *Tasmanian Dams* was a key step in enabling Australia to do this. In the field of human rights in particular, *Tasmanian Dams* heralded the likely success of the Hawke Labor government's promised implementation of Australia's obligations under the *International Covenant on Civil and Political Rights.* Indeed, Sornarajah wrote that the next 'battle' for section 51(xxix) would be the Hawke government's Human Rights Bills.[50] For these international lawyers, Australia could finally enjoy the promises of international law because of *Tasmanian Dams*.

Anxiety and promise amplified after *Tasmanian Dams*

The interplay between anxiety and promise was at the core of the different responses to *Tasmanian Dams*. The interaction shaped the way the Hawke government implemented its changes to Australia's treaty negotiation practice,

[47]M Sornarajah is now a Professor at the National University of Singapore Law School, but was at the time a Senior Lecturer at the University of Tasmania. Sornarajah (1983) at 26.

[48]Sornarajah (1983) at 34.

[49]Sornarajah (1983) at 34.

[50]Sornarajah (1983) at 33.

tempering the promise it saw in international engagement with policies directed at easing State anxieties about their loss of influence. Different views of the role of international law in Australia generated the mixed responses of anxiety and promise from legislators and international law academics. The interplay of anxiety and promise has continued to shape the contours of Australia's relationship with international law. Since 1983, many of the flashpoints about the external affairs power have arisen in relation to either environmental or human rights issues.[51] A particularly divisive debate arose in 1994/95 in the wake of two decisions: the United Nations Human Rights Committee finding in *Toonen* and the High Court's decision in *Minister for Immigration and Ethnic Affairs v Teoh*.[52] The combined effect of *Tasmanian Dams*, *Toonen* and *Teoh* was a transformation in Australia's domestic processes for becoming party to international treaties in 1996. These changes, which remain in 2015, appeared substantive but do not affect the federal government's executive power to enter into treaties. They are an example of the anxiety-promise interplay in the way that they have addressed anxieties about the influence of international law in Australia without reducing Australia's capacity to engage with the international legal system.

Tasmanian Dams and the Events of 1994/95

The United Nations Human Rights Committee determination in *Toonen* that Tasmania's legislation criminalising homosexuality was a human rights violation saw the federal government force the decriminalisation of homosexuality in Tasmania by using legislation based on the external affairs power.[53] In *Teoh,* the High Court found that there was a legitimate expectation that an administrative decision-maker would act in a manner consistent with Australia's international obligations even where those obligations had not been implemented into domestic law.[54] *Teoh* was particularly divisive and was regarded as giving international law an unwarranted status in Australian law.[55] The cases – both of which raised human rights issues – combined to heighten the tensions between anxiety and promise that stemmed from *Tasmanian Dams.*

The Executive and Events of 1994/95 Teoh prompted an unprecedented response from the outgoing Keating and incoming Howard governments. Both governments issued their own 'Executive Statements' repudiating the outcome of the case and both introduced legislation to undo the impact of the case, although neither Bill was

[51]On environmental issues, for example, some Australian states continued to mount legal challenges continued to federal management and nomination of sites under the World Heritage Convention. See eg *Richardson v Forestry Commission (Tasmania)* (1988) 164 CLR 261; and *Queensland v Commonwealth* (1989) 167 CLR 232. For a discussion of Australia's approach to international human rights, see eg Charlesworth (1995) and (2002), and Joseph (2008).

[52]See Alston (1995) for an account of the events of 1994/95.

[53]*Human Rights (Sexual Conduct) Act 1994* (Cth). For a discussion of the *Toonen* case, see eg Morgan (1993) and Gelber (1999).

[54]For a discussion of the case, see Allars (1995) and (1997) and Lacey (2001).

[55]See eg the discussion in Charlesworth et al (2003) 437–8.

ultimately passed.[56] Both major political parties thus shared a concern that Australia would lose control over the influence of international law in Australia as a consequence of *Teoh*. Notwithstanding these anxieties, Australian federal governments retained the changes that had been introduced after *Tasmanian Dams* which gave them greater flexibility in international treaty negotiations. Subsequent Australian governments also continued the practice of not requesting federal clauses in multilateral treaties, although they adopted inconsistent practice on including a 'Federal Statement' in international treaty ratifications.[57] These 1994/95 responses showed both anxiety and promise at work in the attitude of executive governments to international law. Their particular anxiety about the influence of human rights law did not extend to a broader concern about international law and each executive government preserved its prerogatives in this area.

International Law Academics and the events of 1994/5 The 1994/95 events produced a considerable volume of writing by both international law academics and by other academics focussed on the international law dimensions. Two major edited collections and a special issue of the *Sydney Law Review* were published on Australia and international law between 1995 and 1997.[58] *Tasmanian Dams* was a touchstone for much of that writing. Brian Opeskin and Don Rothwell, for example, described *Tasmanian Dams* as having 'ignited' the debate on the impact of international law in Australia. The ramifications of *Tasmanian Dams* were also at the core of most of the contributions to the collection *Treaty-Making and Australia: Globalisation versus Sovereignty?*.[59] Judy Henderson, for example, identified *Tasmanian Dams* as providing the 'origins' of the 'current backlash' against international obligations, and expressed concern about Australia's 'outright obstructive behaviour' at international environmental negotiations.[60] Kenneth Wiltshire lamented the 'fear and ignorance' about international law that stemmed from *Tasmanian Dams* and urged acceptance of 'our interaction with other nations'.[61] This academic

[56]See the Joint Statement by the Minister for Foreign Affairs and the Attorney-General, 'International Treaties and the High Court Decision in Teoh' (10 May 1995); and the Joint Statement by the Minister for Foreign Affairs and the Attorney-General and Minister for Justice, 'The Effect of Treaties in Administrative Decision-Making', 25 February 1997. See also *Administrative Decisions (Effect of International Instruments) Bill 1995* and *Administrative Decisions (Effect of International Instruments) Bill 1997*

[57]The federal government position on federal clauses is described in the *Revised Principles and Procedures for Commonwealth-State Consultation on Treaties* (1996). Some treaties with implications for State action have not been ratified with an accompanying 'Federal Statement', see e.g. ILO Convention (No 142) concerning Vocational Guidance and Vocational Training in the Development of Human Resources [1986] ATS 2; Convention on the Rights of the Child [1991] ATS 2; and the Convention on the Rights of Persons with Disabilities [2008] ATS 12. The 'Federal Statement' appears to remain a part of the federal government's treaty negotiation armory: see the *Revised Principles and Procedures for Commonwealth-State Consultation on Treaties* (1996).

[58]Opeskin and Rothwell (1997); Volume 17 of the *Sydney Law Review*; and Alston and Chiam (1995). See also Barwick (1995).

[59]Opeskin and Rothwell (1997) p 13; Alston and Chiam (1995), especially the contributions of George Winterton, David Kinley, Michael Kirby, Ivan Shearer, Hilary Charlesworth, Martin Tsamenyi and Judy Henderson.

[60]Henderson (1995) at 236 and 238.

[61]Wiltshire (1995) at 76 and 79.

writing thus saw the anxiety produced by *Tasmanian Dams* as unhelpful, if not destructive, to maintaining an open and judicious approach to international law. For Henderson, Wiltshire and others, careful participation in the international legal system promised many more benefits than a restrictive approach.[62]

Legislators and the Events of 1994/5 Toonen and *Teoh* amplified a concern arising out of *Tasmanian Dams* about the 'democratic deficit' in the way the federal government become party to treaties. In 1995 when he was still opposition leader, for example, John Howard proposed a People's Convention to consider amendments that would address the 'illicit' use of the external affairs power since *Tasmanian Dams*.[63] Also in 1995, a Senate Legal and Constitutional References Committee inquiry into Australia's treaty-making power produced the report *Trick or Treaty? Commonwealth Power to Make and Implement Treaties*. The report recommended a series of changes to Australia's treaty-making process, most of which were introduced by the Howard government in 1996. Those reforms remain in place in 2015. They mean that with limited exceptions, all treaties are subject to Parliamentary scrutiny and public comment and the States have greater involvement in international treaty negotiation.[64] The reforms appeared to restore some of the predictability and control in Australia's relationship with international law that was lost after *Tasmanian Dams*. The actual impact of these reforms on federal government action has, however, been negligible. The government maintains its executive power to enter into international treaties and the Parliamentary process generally supports the government's position. The process introduced by the 1996 reforms provided a mechanism to manage anxiety about international law, even as it made little substantive change.[65]

Anxiety and promise after 1994/95

Tasmanian Dams made public the anxiety about international law that existed in parts of the Australian community and governments. The 1996 treaty reforms were designed to address this anxiety, while still allowing the executive to participate as a full member of the international community. The treaty reforms also, however, represented a gradual narrowing of a broad existential concern about the relationship between Australia and international law into a narrow procedural one about the implementation of treaties in Australia. Immediately post-*Tasmanian Dams*, there was a perception that Australia had been thrust into an openness to the promises of international law that was welcome for some and deeply disquieting for others. Rather than guide the debate into being one about the substance of the international obligations that Australia might adopt, Australia's political leaders preferred to dampen the broad existential crisis and create a concern for process. Proponents of

[62]See also Alston (1995) and Charlesworth (1995).

[63]'Treaty reform a thorny issue', *The Canberra Times*, 25 July 1995, p 11.

[64]For an overview of the reforms, see Twomey (2007), pp 89–95.

[65]For a critique of the way the reforms have worked, see Chiam (2004) and Charlesworth et al (2003).

the 1996 reforms seemed to believe that if the process through which Australia became party to treaties was fixed then the crisis would dissipate.[66]

But the anxiety about Australia's relationship with international law remains, it just finds different ways to manifest itself. The Howard government, despite introducing the 1996 treaty reforms early in its tenure, displayed a reluctance that came close to a wholesale rejection of the international human rights system.[67] It also consistently refused to ratify the Climate Change Convention and only secured Cabinet agreement to ratify the Rome Statute on the International Criminal Court on the condition that ratification was subject to a declaration confirming Australian sovereignty.[68] One of Kevin Rudd's first actions when he was elected Prime Minister in 2007 was to set his government apart from the Howard government's approach to international law by ratifying the Climate Change Convention.[69] The reluctance about international human rights standards nevertheless persisted through both the Rudd and Gillard Labor governments, particularly in relation to the treatment of refugees.[70] The Abbott government too has attacked the international human rights system, choosing, for example, to reject a report by the United Nations Special Rapporteur on Torture, rather than address the substance of its conclusions about Australia's violations. 'Australians are sick of being lectured to by the United Nations', claimed Tony Abbott in March 2015.[71]

Continued commitments to the promises of international law also remain. Australian governments have in different contexts supported international law in ways that belie their attitude to the international human rights system. Australian governments have, for example, embraced the promises of growth through the international trade system. The Howard government's preference for bilateral over multilateral free trade agreements has been carried on by the successor Rudd, Gillard and Abbott governments.[72] Foreign Minister Julie Bishop indicated in March 2015 that she was investigating ways in which Australia could secure a further term on the United Nations Security Council.[73] Commitment to international law is also apparent from the thriving community of international lawyers and academics working in Australian universities and government departments. A survey

---

[66] Alston (1995), p 1.

[67] For overview of Howard government's approach to international law see Charlesworth et al (2003) and (2006). See also Volume 27 of the *Australian Yearbook of International Law* which is devoted to an analysis of the Howard government's approach to international law, and in particular Joseph (2008) on the Howard government's record on human rights.

[68] See the Joint Media Release of the Minister for Foreign Affairs Alexander Downer and the Attorney-General Daryl Williams, 2 July 2002. For an account of events leading up to Australia's ratification of the Rome Statute, see Charlesworth et al (2006), pp 71–82.

[69] See eg 'Rudd's address to the UN conference', *The Australian*, 12 December 2007, http://www.theaustralian.com.au/archive/news/rudds-address-to-the-un-conference/story-e6frg6no-1111115095965?nk=02e1695a4eda6f00e78d0c01369856c2.

[70] For a review of the Rudd government's approach to international law, see Pert (2012).

[71] 'Tony Abbott: Australians "sick of being lectured to" by United Nations, after report finds anti-torture breach', *The Sydney Morning Herald*, 10 March 2015.

[72] A list of bilateral trade agreements in force and under negotiation is available at http://dfat.gov.au/fta/.

[73] 'Julie Bishop looks to get Australia back on UN Security Council' *The Sydney Morning Herald*, 26 March 2015.

from 1983 revealed that each of the ten university law schools in Australia offered international law courses, and 48 distinct international law options were available in total.[74] These offerings have increased significantly. In 2013 at Melbourne Law School, for example, there were 43 international law-related subjects on offer in either the JD or Masters programs. The 2014 annual meeting of the Australian and New Zealand Society of International Law was the largest ever held, with 25 panels and over 180 people in attendance.[75] Drawing again on David Kennedy's argument that to be an international lawyer is to be for international law,[76] these figures suggest there is a significant community of people in Australia who are committed to the promises of international law.

Conclusion

Even though its interpretation of the external affairs power largely confirmed the doctrinal view from earlier cases, *Tasmanian Dams* remains the decision to have 'ignited' the ongoing debate about Australia's relationship with international law. For some, this meant that *Tasmanian Dams* was the case that opened Australia to the promises of international law and allowed it to act as a 'modern' state in the international legal system. For others, *Tasmanian Dams* was the case which gave Australians reasons to be anxious about the unreasonable influence of international law. Key events in Australia's relationship with international law since 1983 show how the interplay between anxiety and promise entrenched by *Tasmanian Dams* remains.

This ongoing dialectic has not been productive for Australia's approach to international law. In 1995, Philip Alston called for the debate on Australia's relationship with international law to focus on the substance of international law rather than on the form of its regulation. Australians, he argued, needed to consider the 'large picture' in responding to international legal developments in order to promote the objectives of national interest and international cooperation.[77] In 'Deep Anxieties' (2003), my three colleagues and I made a similar argument, noting that international norms have 'no intrinsic superiority' to national norms and that what was needed was a system in which the substance of those norms was scrutinised.[78] In 2015, the same argument can still be made. The contours of anxiety and promise have produced conflicting responses to international law that have not allowed Australians to debate most international legal norms in a substantive way. Over a generation after the decision in *Tasmanian Dams* was made, it is time to move beyond both anxiety and promise.

---

[74]Crawford (1981–83) at 183–184. See also Shearer (1983).

[75]For the program, see anzsil.org.au/Resources/Conferences/2014%20Program_WEB.pdf The information on attendance numbers comes from a personal conversation with one of the conference organisers on 6 October 2014.

[76]Kennedy (1994) at 335.

[77]Alston (1995) at 25.

[78]Charlesworth et al (2003) at 425.

Primary Sources

Australian

Commonwealth v Tasmania (1983) 158 CLR 1
Koowarta v Bjelke-Petersen (1982) 153 CLR 168
Minister for Immigration and Ethnic Affairs v Teoh (1995) 183 CLR 273
Queensland v Commonwealth (1989) 167 CLR 232
R v Burgess: Ex Parte Henry (1936) 55 CLR 608
Richardson v Forestry Commission (Tasmania) (1988) 164 CLR 261;
Victoria v Commonwealth (1996) 187 CLR 416
Revised Principles and Procedures for Commonwealth-State Consultation on Treaties (1996), available at http://www.austlii.edu.au/au/other/dfat/reports/infokit.html#sect8.

International

Convention for the Protection of the World Cultural and Natural Heritage 1972 [1975 ATS 47.
Convention on the Elimination of All Forms of Discrimination Against Women [1983] ATS 9.
Convention on the Rights of the Child 1989 [1991] ATS 4.
Convention on the Rights of Persons with Disabilities 2006 [2008] ATS 12.
ILO Convention (No. 135) Concerning Protection And Facilities To Be Afforded To Workers' Representatives In The Undertaking [1994] ATS 3.
International Convention on Standards of Training, Certification and Watchkeeping For Seafarer 1978 [1984] ATS 7.
International Convention on Maritime Search And Rescue 1979 [1986] ATS 29.
International Covenant on Civil and Political Rights 1966 [1980] ATS 23.

Secondary Sources

Monographs and Edited Collections

Philip Alston and Madelaine Chiam(eds) (1995) *Treaty-Making and Australia: Globalisation versus Sovereignty?*, The Federation Press.
Antony Anghie (2005) *Imperialism, Sovereignty and the Making of International Law*, Cambridge University Press.
Donal K Anton et al (2005) *International Law Cases and Materials*, Oxford University Press.
Hilary Charlesworth (2002) *Writing in Rights: Australia and the Protection of Human Rights*, UNSW Press.
Hilary Charlesworth et al (2006) *No Country is an Island – Australia and International Law*, UNSW Press.
Brian Galligan (ed) (1989) *Australian Federalism*, Longman Cheshire.
David Kennedy (2005) *The Dark Sides of Virtue: Reassessing International Humanitarianism*, Princeton University Press.
HP Lee and George Winterton (eds) (2013) *Australian Constitutional Landmarks*, Cambridge University Press.
Brian R Opeskin and Donald R Rothwell (eds) (1997) *International Law and Australian Federalism*, Melbourne University Press.
Sundhya Pahuja (2011) *Decolonising International Law: Development, Economic Growth and the Politics of Universality*, Cambridge University Press.
Harry Reicher (ed) (1995) *Australian International Law: Cases and Materials*, LBC Casebooks.
KW Ryan (ed) (1984) *International Law in Australia*, 2nd edn, Law Book Company.
Gerry Simpson (2007) *Law, War and Crime: War Crimes Trials and the Reinvention of International Law* Polity.
M. Sornarajah (ed) (1983) *The South West Dam Dispute: The Legal and Political Issues*, University of Tasmania.
George Williams et al (2014) *Blackshield and Williams Australian Constitutional Law and Theory – Commentary and Materials*, 6th edn, The Federation Press.

Articles and Book Chapters

Margaret Allars (1995) 'One Small Step for Legal Doctrine, One Giant Leap Towards Integrity in Government: Teoh's Case' 17 *Sydney Law Review* 204.

Margaret Allars (1997) 'International Law and Administrative Discretion', in Opeskin and Rothwell (eds) *International Law and Australian Federalism*, Melbourne University Press 232.
Philip Alston (1995) 'Reform of Treaty-Making Processes: Form over Substance', in Alston and Chiam (eds) *Treaty-Making and Australia: Globalisation versus Sovereignty?* The Federation Press 1.
Garfield Barwick (1995) 'The External Affairs Power of the Commonwealth and the Protection of World Heritage' 25 *University of Western Australia Law Review* 233.
Henry Burmester (1978) 'The Australian States and Participation in the Foreign Policy Process' 9 *Federal Law Review* 257.
Henry Burmester (1985) 'Federal Clauses: An Australian Perspective' 34 *International and Comparative Law Quarterly* 522.
Henry Burmester (1989) 'Federalism, the States and International Affairs: A Legal Perspective', in Galligan (ed) *Australian Federalism*, Longman Cheshire 192.
Andrew Byrnes (1985) 'The Implementation of Treaties in Australia after the Tasmanian Dams Case: The External Affairs Power and the Influence of Federalism' 8 *Boston College International and Comparative Law Review* 275.
Andrew Byrnes and Hilary Charlesworth (1985) 'New International Law in National Systems: Federalism and the International Legal Order: Recent Developments in Australia' 79 *American Journal of International Law* 622.
IDF Callinan (2005) 'International Law and Australian Sovereignty', (July–August) *Quadrant* 9.
ND Cambell (1984) 'Australian Treaty Practice and Procedure', in Ryan (ed) *International Law in Australia*, 2nd edn, Law Book Company 53.
Hilary Charlesworth (1995) 'Australia's Split Personality: Implementation of Human Rights Treaty Obligations in Australia', in Alston and Chiam (eds) *Treaty-Making and Australia: Globalisation versus Sovereignty?*, The Federation Press 129.
Hilary Charlesworth (1997) 'International Human Rights Law', in Opeskin and Rothwell (eds) *International Law and Australian Federalism*, Melbourne University Press 280.
Hilary Charlesworth et al (2003) 'Deep Anxieties: Australia and the International Legal Order' 25 *Sydney Law Review* 424.
Madelaine Chiam (2003) 'Government Decision-Making and International Law: Australia and the Framework on Tobacco Control' 24(2) *Adelaide Law Review* 217.
Madelaine Chiam (2004) 'Evaluating Australia's Treaty-Making Processes' *Public Law Review* 265.
BS Chimni (2007) 'A Just World Under Law: A View from the South' 22(2) *American University Law Review* 1.
JR Crawford (1981–83) 'Teaching and Research in International Law in Australia' 10 *Australian Yearbook of International Law* 176.
Mary Crock (1983) 'Federalism and the External Affairs Power' 14 *Melbourne University Law Review* 238.
Peter Durack (1994) 'The External Affairs Power', *The Federalism Project Issues Paper No 1* Institute of Public Affairs.
Judy Henderson (1995) 'An Environmentalist Perspective', in Alston and Chiam *Treaty-Making and Australia: Globalisation versus Sovereignty?* The Federation Press 236.
Brian Galligan (1983) '*The Dams* Case: A Political Analysis', in Sornarajah (ed) *The South West Dam Dispute: The Legal and Political Issues*, University of Tasmania 102.
Katharine Gelber (1999), 'Treaties and Intergovernmental Relations in Australia: Political Implications of the Toonen Case' 45(3) *Australian Journal of Politics and History* 330–346.
Devika Hovell (2003) 'Lifting the Executive Veil: Australia's Accession to the First Optional Protocol to the *International Covenant on Civil and Political Rights*' 24(2) *Adelaide Law Review* 187.
Sarah Joseph (2008) 'The Howard Government's Record of Engagement with the International Human Rights System' 27 *Australian Yearbook of International Law* 45.
David Kennedy (1994) 'A New World Order: Yesterday, Today, and Tomorrow' [4] *Transnational Law and Contemporary Problems* 330.

Martti Koskenniemi (2002) 'Between Impunity and Show Trials' 6 *Max Planck Yearbook of United Nations Law* 1.
Wendy Lacey (2001) 'In the Wake of *Teoh*: Finding an Appropriate Government Response' 29 *Federal Law Review* 219.
PH Lane (1983) 'The Federal Parliament's External Affairs Power: The Tasmanian Dam Case' 57 *Australian Law Journal* 554.
RD Lumb (1983/84) 'The Franklin Dam Decision and the External Affairs Power: A Comment' 13 *University of Queensland Law Journal* 138.
Susan Marks (2011) 'Human Rights and Root Causes' 74(1) *Modern Law Review* 57.
Wayne Morgan (1993) 'Sexuality and Human Rights: The First Communication by an Australian to the Human Rights Committee under the Optional Protocol to the *International Covenant on Civil and Political Rights*' 14 *Australian Yearbook of International Law* 289.
Brian R Opeskin and Donald R Rothwell (1995) 'The Impact of Treaties on Australian Federalism' 27 *Case Western Reserve Journal of International Law* 1.
Alison Pert (2012) 'The Good International Citizenship of the Rudd Government' 30 *Australian Yearbook of International Law* 93.
Don Rothwell (1997) 'International Law and Legislative Power', in Opeskin and Rothwell (eds) *International Law and Australian Federalism*, Melbourne University Press 104.
Geoffrey Sawer (1983–84) 'The External Affairs Power' 14 *Federal Law Review* 199.
Ivan A Shearer (1983) 'The Teaching of International Law in Australian Law Schools' 9 *Adelaide Law Review* 61.
M. Sornarajah (1983) 'International Law and the South West Dam Case', in Sornarajah (ed) *The South West Dam Dispute: The Legal and Political Issues*, University of Tasmania 25.
JG Starke (1983) 'The High Court and Travaux Preparatoires in the Interpretation of Treaties' 57 *Australian Law Journal* 592.
Anne Twomey (2007 [1997]) 'International Law and the Executive', in Opeskin and Rothwell (eds) *International Law and Australian Federalism*, Melbourne University Press 69.
Kenneth Wiltshire (1995) 'The Federal Dimension', in Alston and Chiam (eds) *Treaty-Making and Australia: Globalisation versus Sovereignty?* The Federation Press 74.
Leslie Zines (2013) 'The *Tasmanian Dam* Case', in HP Lee and George Winterton (eds) *Australian Constitutional Landmarks*, Cambridge University Press 262.

Newspaper Articles

Verge Blunden (1983) 'What the High Court Justices Had to Say', *The Sydney Morning Herald,* 2 July 1983, p 7.
Wallace Brown (1983), 'Threat to Joh-mander', *The Courier Mail*, 9 July 1983, p 2.
Jane Cadzow (1983) 'The Most Centralist High Court since Federation', *The Australian*, 4 July 1983, p 7.
Bill Goff (1983) 'An Ideological Split: Violent Disagreement within High Court', *The Mercury*, 4 July 1983, p 5.
Gary Sturgess, 'Few Limits on What Canberra can do, Acting in Good Faith', *The Age*, 2 July 1983, p 4.
Terry White (1983) 'Have these Men Wrecked Our Federal System?', *The Courier-Mail*, 8 July 1983, p 4.

Making sense of indigeneity, aboriginality and identity: race as a Constitutional conundrum since 1983

Mark McMillan[1] and Martin Clark[2]
Melbourne Law School, Australia

This article is a conversation and encounter between an Indigenous and a non-Indigenous constitutional law scholar attempting to make sense of 'race' as it is written and interpreted in the Australian Constitution through a close re-reading of the Tasmanian Dams Case and the race power in s 51(xxvi). The conversation is intended to perform a conduct of jurisprudence in which the experience of law and the interpretation of law as a matter of doctrine are brought into relation. We first try to make sense of the significance of 1967 as a constitutional moment shifting the meaning of race in the Constitution, before turning to a close reading of the judgments in Tasmanian Dams on the race power. We argue that through analysis of these judgments it is possible to understand better the constrictions of Australian canons of constitutional interpretation as applied to race, with its focus on 'special' characteristics, heritage and culture. We also argue that a close reading of Tasmanian Dams offers a good starting place from which to question the possibilities of what meaning race might carry if the political and social experiences of Indigenous peoples with the Constitution are joined to more easily accepted interpretative conventions.

I. Introduction

When it comes to constitutional interpretations of the concept of 'race', the extent and reach of the 'race power' as considered by Australian judges, and the constitutional relationship between Indigenous peoples and the State, two cases decided by the High Court join in a way that constitutional scholars have spent little time investigating.[3] In the academy, the *Koowarta* and *Tasmanian Dams* decisions must be conjoined through the constitutional lens of 'race'. In 2012 and 2013, two symposia were convened to commemorate the thirtieth anniversaries of each case.[4]

---

[1]LLB; GDLP (ANU); LLM; SJD (Arizona), Senior Lecturer, Melbourne Law School.
[2]LLB(Hons)/BA(Hons) (Melb), MPhil Candidate and Research Fellow, Melbourne Law School. We thank the anonymous reviewers, Ann Genovese and Ed Mussawir for comments on an earlier draft. Email: mclark@unimelb.edu.au

[3]This may be beginning to shift with new scholarly interest in Australian constitutional culture: see Arcioni and Stone (2015).

[4]The symposia were convened by Associate Professor Ann Genovese at Melbourne Law School and were co-hosted by the Institute for International Law and the Humanities (IILAH), the Centre for Comparative Constitutional Studies (CCCS), and the Centre for Resources Energy and Environmental Law (CREEL): 'Turning Points: Remembering *Koowarta v Bjelke-Petersen* (1982) 153 CLR 16' held on Friday 11 May 2012 and 'Turning Points: Remembering *Commonwealth v Tasmania* (1983) 158 CLR 1' held on 28 June 2013.

Mark participated in both, and Martin in the *Tasmanian Dams* event only. As Ann Genovese notes in the introduction to the special edition of the *Griffith Law Review* commemorating *Koowarta*[5] the symposia aimed to create a meeting place where conversations could be had amongst academics, jurists and interested people. It was also a meeting place where jurisprudences could be exercised and new ways of knowing the cases could be created. The symposia were public considerations not only about how constitutional law operates, but also of how law is lived and experienced by people in Australia, in the 1980s and since. In particular, the symposia joined *Tasmanian Dams* and *Koowarta* together by emphasising how these cases can be understood as an account of the relationship between Indigenous peoples, the Constitution, and the State in the 1980s. Emphasising this historical and political fact about what *Tasmanian Dams* and *Koowarta* carried as a question for law, and as a lived experience of law, the symposia created space to think through the collective effect of the cases. It also produced space for conversations between Indigenous and non-Indigenous Australian public lawyers, about the possibilities of different relationships between laws for example: a meeting place of jurisdictions, equally esteemed. Above all, the events allowed participants to story-tell how past constitutional experiences exist in a relationship with the legal present.

In this paper, we draw out some of these concerns. What we offer is a conversation between Mark McMillan (a constitutional scholar and jurist of the Wiradjuri nation and Australian law) and Martin Clark (a non-indigenous Australian public and international law scholar) that we would like you to witness as a conduct of jurisprudence and as a meeting of our lived experiences and practice of law. Following the work of Shaunnagh Dorsett and Shaun McVeigh Mark has argued for the the assertion of indigenous jurisdiction or 'speaking the law' as an activity,[6] 'that must be practiced to be maintained'.[7] The form and tenor of the conversation, what each of us bring through our own learning, teaching, and acting with the Australian Constitution, is intended to demonstrate that constitutional jurisprudence is about more than doctrinal or analytical interpretation, conventionally practised or understood. We want to argue, in particular, that how Indigenous Australians understood, and politically experienced, s 51 (xxvi) in the 1967 referendum and since then, has supplied alternate possibilities for constitutional interpretation of race. By placing this ontological and historical constitutional experience into conversation with a more traditional Anglo-Australian interpretative convention (a close reading of the race power arguments in the judgments in *Tasmanian Dams*), we suggest that the lived effects of law carry possibilities and challenges to the usual limits of accepted thinking about what 'race' means for Indigenous and non-Indigenous Australians in our Constitution today. Our conversation, in other words, seeks to place lived experiences of Indigenous peoples back into *Tasmanian Dams*, and to demonstrate that the constitutional conception of 'race' has since 1967 become more than an issue about a 'subject' of the law and more than a mere head of legislative power for the Commonwealth.

[5]Genovese (2014).

[6]Dorsett and McVeigh (2012).

[7]McMillan (2014), p 118.

Our contribution to this issue of the *Griffith Law Review* in some ways takes up the questions raised by Sean Brennan and Megan Davis in the *GLR* special edition on the Koowarta Symposium.[8] Brennan and Davis are also concerned with how 'race' is a constitutional question that requires judicial attention despite and after *Koowarta*, and remains an important basis from which the constitutional relationship between Indigenous peoples and the State can be understood. They argue that the *Koowarta* decision is in one sense a 'lost opportunity'; that the High Court could have dealt with the form and content of section 51(xxvi) in ways that would make race a 'proper matter for constitutional law'.[9] Brennan and Davis sought to do this by arguing how that opportunity might have turned out differently, within the bounds of 'legitimate' constitutional arguments.[10]

We also understand that race remains a proper matter for constitutional law. Our focus, however, lies with how race is grappled with conceptually in *Tasmanian Dams* through a re-reading of the judgments. We emphasise 're'-reading not just because of the temporal distance between 2013 and 1983 that runs through the contributions to this symposium, but also because of the intervening silence around a constitutional concept of race heard in Australia's courts and law schools alike. Unlike *Koowarta*, the majority in *Tasmanian Dams* did conclude that the challenged provisions were supported by the races power. In doing so, however, both minority and majority judges did not necessarily, or satisfactorily, deal with race as a constitutional concept that carried renewed – or altered – meanings, after the public engagement of Indigenous and non Indigenous Australians about 'race' that were opened up by the referendum in 1967. Some judges refused to deal with race at all; for others they were limited, or were limited by the forms of questions asked by the litigants in *Tasmanian Dams*, to a consideration of race that bound its meaning and jurisprudence to an ossified understanding of heritage or culture. We use *Tasmanian Dams* to explore these complexities, and how the traditions of interpretation and argument before the High Court, in 1983 at least, could not yet allow 'race' to carry any real content without recourse to racialised generalisations or inappropriate group categorisations.

The method and intent of our conversation, then, is intended to interrupt the course of the existing conversation about race in Australian scholarly constitutional debates. Western trained Australian constitutional lawyers remain comfortable at the level of arguing over the scope of a head of power. They ask, in relation to s 51 (xxvi), for example: What is a 'special' law? How is it 'deemed necessary'? Does 'for' the people of any race include beneficial as well as detrimental laws? What characteristics can distinguish racial groups? Must the law apply to all members of a race, or can subgroups be included? Focusing solely on these questions of constitutional interpretation absolves Anglo-Australian lawyers of the need to ask questions that Indigenous peoples and Indigenous jurists might want answers to. For example, what exactly is 'a race' for the purposes of the Constitution? Is there a dominant race? And is it from that determination (of which there is no explicitly stated determination) that all other races may be constructed? Can there ever be a law passed for white people based solely on a racial classification? Does the

[8]Brennan and Davis (2014).

[9]Genovese (2014).

[10]Brennan and Davis (2014).

inscribing of racial superiority – of whiteness – into the Constitution make whiteness dominant for all time, due to the reasons for including the section in that form in 1901? What are the bases for determining the racial classification by which other races are constructed as being something that is particular to that racial group? And, importantly for this paper, does the experience of contesting the race power in 1967 change the conversation from race to indigeneity? A meeting of jurisprudences means all these questions are important for all participants. Rather than explore the parameters of 'legitimate' constitutional argument bounded by the first set of questions, we want to also explore what *Tasmanian Dams* both allows us to think – and prevents us from thinking – about possible constitutional concepts of race put into relation with Indigenous political experience in Australia. In this way, our conversation is intended to open up not only the limits and possibilities of what was said by the High Court in 1983, and in judgments since then, but to also show how this might matter to different audiences and participants of law.

In this spirit, Part I considers the role of 'race' as a concept before and after the 1967 Referendum, arguing that this change made race the 'everyday' for Aboriginal and Torres Strait Islander peoples in the exercise of their distinct jurisdictions with respect to 'race' and their relationship(s) with non-Indigenous people and institutions. Part II moves to try to make sense of race as a constitutional concept, bringing 1983 into conversation with today and suggesting that acknowledging race as a social construct means it no longer refers to anything that is either real or knowable – to society, to Parliament, and to the High Court. Part III moves to closely re-read the *Tasmanian Dam* decision. The difficulties of a constitutional concept of race quickly turn to an impossible task for legal interpretation, one which we hope the removal and replacement of s 51(xxvi) will mean no Australian Court will have to contemplate again in interpreting the fundamental law of the Anglo-Australia legal system.

II. Making sense of race as a constitutional concept by making sense of the 1967 referendum

There have been only a few attempts by judges to interpret the content of the constitutional concept of a race. Despite some such endeavours in *Tasmanian Dams* and in later cases such as the *Native Title Act Case*[11] and *Kartinyeri*[12] which clarified some questions and muddied others, we remain no closer to a judicial pronouncement of what a 'race' is for the purposes of the Constitution.

Brennan J in *Tasmanian Dams* may well offer the best content to a concept of race that could be hoped for. Later decisions in the *Native Title Act Case* and *Kartinyeri* simultaneously clarified some questions and muddied others about the construction of the race power. Yet we remain no closer to a judicial pronouncement of what a 'race' is for the purposes of the *Constitution*. Rather than urging such a pronouncement we try to clarify a concept of race that connects heritage and Indigenous identity to race. We then look to special distinctions attaching to races – both of which emerge in *Tasmanian Dams* and are taken up by some judges in

[11] *Western Australia v Commonwealth* (1995) 183 CLR 373 *(Native Title Act Case).*
[12] *Kartinyeri v Commonwealth* (1998) 195 CLR 337.

Kartinyeri[13] – and conclude that race is indeterminate as an ordinary and as a constitutional concept. The first point is not a new suggestion. We return to this idea as a conclusion. In what follows we explore how the strictures of constitutional interpretation prevent the Court from approaching race as anything besides an 'everyday' idea, which ultimately prevents it from really dealing with the significance of the 1967 Referendum as a constitutional moment that rearranged what race means within Australian public law.

What we take to be the most difficult conceptual question – what is a 'race' for the purposes of the *Constitution*? – does not receive a thorough answer from any judge in *Tasmanian Dams* for a myriad of reasons. The attention that it does receive is largely spent noting both the importance and difficulty of analysing it, without any real advance as to what it means. Race is acknowledged and assumed as a real category signifying some 'truth' that connects groups in Australian society, even as its demerits are noted alongside lamentations for Australia's brutal treatment of Indigenous people – as if the maintenance of race as a concept tracking something 'real' about 'inferior peoples' was not used to justify exactly that conduct.

Australian canons of constitutional interpretation make the Court's elision of any close consideration the notion of race seem understandable. Questions of constitutional interpretation are only to be tackled if necessary for resolving the dispute before the court. In neither case was the argument raised that 'Aboriginal Australians' did not constitute a race.[14] Moreover if that question did arise then, like the 'deemed necessary' aspect of the power, it might best be left to the resolution of the parliament (as Gibbs CJ arguably suggests in *Koowarta*).[15] While the many other intricacies of the wording of the power were relevant for resolving that issue, the dividing question in both cases was the specificity or generality of the laws purportedly for protection of a race. But attention to the complexities of race as a constitutional concept was ignored in favour of platitudes about the difficulty of its resolution. Where the judges in *Tasmanian Dams* do expand on what might connect a racial group, their common language is that of heritage: the shared spiritual and religious beliefs, history and culture, and the preservation of each of these things, and as applied here, special to the Aboriginal race. The variety of Indigenous nations is regarded as a constitutional race only through its placement into a landscape, as indistinct museum pieces enduring – and enduring together as a race rather than as individual nations or tribes – only through whatever artefacts or relics of their heritage remain. The link to heritage is more palatable than assessing characteristics

[13]See Gaudron J in *Kartinyeri v Commonwealth* (1998) 195 CLR 337, an approach discussed and endorsed in, eg, Malbon (1999).

[14]The argument that Tasmanian Aboriginals were extinct, and therefore no law could be passed for their benefit, was, however, raised by Mr Gleeson during argument in *Tasmanian Dams*: see *Commonwealth v Tasmania* [1983] HCATrans 24 (3 June 1986), p 361. See also the response of Tasmanian Aboriginal Centre disputing that suggestion: *Commonwealth v Tasmania* [1983] HCATrans 26 (8 June 1983) at 517–519.

[15]See *Koowarta* (1982) 153 CLR 168, p 187 (Gibbs CJ): 'may well be a law of the kind described in par (xxvi), if the definition of Aboriginal and Torres Strait Islander is not so wide as to include persons who are not of either race'. The comment might suggest that resolving a clear definition of a racial group is not an important question for the Court to resolve, and that in most instances it should defer to Parliament as the decider of what a racial group is.

or disadvantages based on race – questions and purported realities more familiar to the founders than Australians of the 1980s – but those characteristics still sit in the background of the heritage approach. What can be said, in the majority's mind, is that the Aboriginal race has a particular link to the kinds of practices and objects relevant to the commonalities of their race: rituals, spiritual and religious beliefs, artefacts, culture.[16] But these are linked to the Aboriginal race, rather than to indigeneity or cultural or racial identity. A focus on *the Aboriginal race* as a monolithic entity, rather than overlapping or shared patterns of identity retains the same interest in origins, genealogy, biology and fixedness – the suggestion that something about this purported race includes a need for particular objects – that keeps that idea of special disadvantage central, alive and doing crucial constitutional work.

The history of the 'race' power has been told (and experienced) differently by Aboriginal peoples, Australian historians and constitutional scholars. Bringing these into relation is part of having this conversation. Australian historians Bain Attwood and Andrew Markus have made clear in their work that one purpose of the 1967 referendum was to educate the populace about the impact of excluding Aboriginal people from the *Constitution*.[17] Those activists did this by demonstrating that Aboriginal people were not considered part of the constitutional meaning of race in 1901; that at that point race related to sinister 'outsider' qualities that had to be controlled. As Bain and Attwood suggest, the referendum campaign was responsible for educating the majority about the 'race' power and its effect or reach *for* and *to* Aboriginal people.[18] It is little wonder then that outsider views of 'race' were used to implement and sustain the 'white Australia' policy. Today when we think of 'race' in constitutional terms we subconsciously connect Aboriginal and 'race' together. This is because of the 1967 referendum. 1967 changed the nature of the conversation about the constitution, race and Aboriginal people. This was not always the case. We must be mindful that Aboriginal people were specifically and consciously excluded from the 'race' power. More importantly we must remember that Aboriginal people were excluded from any social understandings of 'race' or the social and legal developments of the conception itself.

In its pre-1967 wording, s 51(xxvi) authorised the Commonwealth parliament to make laws for the 'peace, order, and good government of the Commonwealth with respect to the people of any race, other than the aboriginal race in any State, for whom it is deemed necessary to make special laws'. The framers were entirely unconcerned about the status of Aboriginal people, their inclusion in the *Constitution*, or the need for federal parliament to legislate in relation to them.[19] It is argued that the framers' concerns were all about non-white immigrant workforces. Kirby J stated in *Kartinyeri*[20]

---

[16]See also *Onus v Alcoa of Australia Ltd* (1981) 149 CLR 27 on standing being based on a custodianship interest held by the Aboriginal plaintiffs in that case.

[17]Attwood and Markus (2007).

[18]Attwood and Markus (2007).

[19]See, eg, Sawer (1966).

[20]*Kartinyeri v Commonwealth* (1998) 195 CLR 337 as per Kirby J, p 403.

> The Convention Debates, particularly that of the Melbourne Convention of 1898, show that some delegates wanted to retain power for the States, and to permit the Federal Parliament, to enact laws far from beneficial for people of minority races (such as Chinese in factories and shops (282), "Asiatic or African....miner[s] and so on

The race power is said to relate to 'persons'[21] – not individual humans, but a collective legal person of a 'race' – referred to in the same breath as constitutional corporations and foreign sovereigns.[22] The only other reference in the text to 'aboriginal' appeared in s 127, which excluded 'aboriginal natives' from Commonwealth and State census counts. The 1967 Referendum reshaped s 51(xxvi) by removing 'other than the aboriginal race in any State', and repealed s 127 entirely. It is important to remind people of the severity of these clauses. We deal with them in reverse order.

Section 127 directly ensured that Indigenous Australians were irrelevant to the mechanics of Anglo-Australian law-making in the federal parliament, so the State rules, laws and processes developed to keep them less than human could not be challenged constitutionally. Making us human at Federation would have effectively acknowledged that the acquisition of the territory that is now Australia was incorrect at law; both international and common. The doctrine of *terra nullius* is implicated in the *Constitution*, not because of its lack of attention to it, but because allowing Aboriginal and Torres Islander people to exist within the *Constitution* itself would be legal recognition that the mode of acquisition was – in *fact* and *law* – incorrect. Excluding the Commonwealth from the State legislatures' desire to 'smooth the pillow of the dying breed' – or said another way, genocide – was more than just the States wanting control of the land on which Aboriginal peoples were confined, and then policed (though this was certainly the purpose of s 51(xxvi)).[23] Section 127 is a reminder of how sinister the legal system was (and remains, despite its removal) in ensuring that its own legal shortcomings would not and could not be addressed, thereby perpetuating the justification that Australia was indeed *terra nullius.* Not counting Aboriginal and Torres Strait Islander peoples in the census for the purpose of democratic ideals and the advancement of the rule of law was more about the shaky foundations of the acquisition itself than it was about racial superiority.

Similarly, s 51(xxvi) had a severe and sinister purpose of leaving Aboriginal and Torres Strait Islander peoples to the States to control, police, quarantine and eliminate. State responsibility for governing Aboriginal peoples stemmed from each State's interest in retaining control over powers of land management and policing. Indigenous people remain part of the landscape as wildlife or property to be managed – albeit capable of crime – soon to disappear; by dying out, being bred out, or being socialised out of Australia forever. The reference to 'aboriginal race' for the purpose of s 51(xxvi) forbade the humanising of Aboriginal people. But to what 'other' races – other than the 'white' race or the 'aboriginal' race – was s 51(xxvi) intended to apply? The conventional narrative (noted above) holds that immigrant

---

[21]Sawer (1966) at p 20.

[22]As in, eg, *Strickland v Rocla Concrete Pipes Ltd* (1971) 124 CLR 468, p 507 (Menzies J).

[23]'Genocide' was used in the draft report in the *Bringing them Home* inquiry, headed by Sir Ronald Wilson. It was removed as too harsh for the white audience. See Tatz (1999).

worker races were the major subjects of s 51(xxvi) and that Indigenous people were presumed by the drafters and white Australia alike to be a small, dwindling and soon to be dead race, whose passing could be managed adequately by the States.[24] The drafters' discussions were close to silent on Aboriginal peoples in general, and entirely silent on their interests in the new nation. This new nation, whilst denying them individual legal personality, recognised their existence in the text as a collective 'the aboriginal race'; but only for the purpose of excluding them as a collective concern for white Australia. The silence of 1901 is partly about federal–State relations. But the neglect also reflects an inability to conceive of how the new federal government could or would have any capability or interest in dealing with Indigenous peoples. Understanding the significance of 1967 is also partly about federal–State relations, but with the sentiments of 1901 somewhat reversed. In removing the words 'other than the aboriginal race in any State' from s 51(xxvi) and deleting s 127, the 1967 Referendum gave the Commonwealth power to legislate for Aboriginal peoples and solidified a constitutional status of formal equality and concern matching that granted to white Australia. But that status was not equal but instead 'special'. Changing the original words of s 51(xxvi) placed the Commonwealth's capacity in the language of problems: 'special', 'deemed necessary' – also meaning 'deficient', 'less than', 'other' from the white race – with Indigenous peoples now the only race left to legislate for.

For Aboriginal lawyers attempting to live with and do justice to the legacy of 1967 – because 1967 changed the expectations and demands of our families, communities and nations' lives – is the permanent reminder of the efforts (including demands and expectations) of Indigenous activists that represented our families and communities that led to the referendum, and entrusted the *Constitution* itself to remind all Australians of the place and role of Aboriginal peoples as a distinct group worthy of a national relationship that is distinct from any other segment of Australian society – that is what the acquisition of the land mass demands in Western legal systems and international law.

To return to our interest in race as a constitutional concept, 1967 is not just a removal of the 'aboriginal race' from State responsibility, but also involves a profound change in the constitutional concept of race. The way in which the *Constitution* of 1901 dealt with race and Aboriginality is acknowledged as a reprehensible failure; and the overwhelming majority of the nation voted for a move towards inclusion and the recognition of us as having our own 'law and customs' that must exist within the constitutional framework. The High Court in *Tasmanian Dams* moves too – yet in its construction of the power it remains unable to deal with the significance of 1967 or the complexities of a constitutional concept of race.

The High Court has also struggled with the social – or humanising – impacts of the constitutional referendum when deploying constitutional interpretation rules. Constitutional interpretation – both then and now – requires a focus on text and structure. This leaves the High Court ill-equipped to make any real assessment of the significance of social movements or changes in political worldviews that might affect

[24]See, eg, Williams and Bradsen (1997), pp 105–113; French (2010), pp 181–185; Castles (1982).

how we understand our *Constitution. Koowarta* and the *Tasmanian Dam Case* show that, however, we might understand that significance, it is not something that slips easily into canons of constitutional interpretation. Even after sensitivity to historical texts and context is acknowledged as important for constitutional interpretation,[25] the problem remains the same. In the later case of *Kartinyeri v Commonwealth*[26], in which the justices employ a range of approaches to constitutional construction, only Kirby J made a significant attempt to embed into s 51 (xxvi) the unspoken requirements to see the 1967 referendum as being about people (Aborigines) not just 'law'.[27] The other judgments exemplify that the Court in 1998 still seems no better placed to grapple with that significance, other than to focus on how the text itself was changed in 1967.[28] Gaudron J, for example, characterises the 1967 amendment as 'minimalist':

> As a matter of language and syntax, it did no more than remove the then existing exception or limitation on Commonwealth power with respect to the people of the Aboriginal race. And unless something other than language and syntax is to be taken into account, it operated to place them in precisely the same constitutional position as the people of other races.[29]

In holding that 1967 changed only the limits and not the nature of the power in s 51(xxvi), Gaudron J avoids the need to inquire into the significance and aims of 1967. The issue of the intention of the electors could be put to one side, because at stake is the scope of the power, whether it permits beneficial laws only – and not whether 1967 changed the meaning of 'race': '[w]hatever the international standards and community values in 1967 and whatever the intention of those voting in the 1967 referendum, the bare deletion of an exception or limitation on power is not, in my view, capable of effecting a curtailment of power'.[30] This might seem dismissive of the efforts of 1967, but we read it as simply acknowledging that there is no judicial language with which the High Court can evaluate social movements and their impact on texts.

Legal education is also part of the inability to work through some of the difficult issues about race that arose in *Koowarta* and *Tasmanian Dams*. Western legal education is premised on two things: first, that there is *only* one legal system and that system recognises only those jurisdictions that exist independently and outside it; and second, that the *only* role of a lawyer is to perpetuate that legal system. Ann Genovese and Maureen Tehan teach a subject at the Melbourne Law School called *Encounters*. Its aim and purpose is to train students away from thinking about laws as passive and outside of the reach of people. They propose that the legal system and people are in a different relationship to Aboriginal systems of law and ways of knowing. The course takes its cues from, and bases its reading list around the work

[25] *Cole v Whitfield* (1988) 165 CLR 360.

[26] *Kartinyeri v Commonwealth* (1998) 195 CLR 337 as per Kirby J, pp 386–422.

[27] *Kartinyeri v Commonwealth* (1998) 195 CLR 337 as per Kirby J.

[28] We raise this point briefly. An interesting and thorough reading of *Kartinyeri* that takes a perspective from Gadamer's hermeneutics can be found in Reilly (1999).

[29] *Kartinyeri* (1998) 195 CLR 337, at 361.

[30] *Kartinyeri v Commonwealth* (1998) 195 CLR 337, at 363.

of, Indigenous jurisprudents, to see what we can learn about how to conduct western jurisprudence in a different way that takes responsibility for its own traditions, and remains open to a lawful encounter with Indigenous peoples. Their point, also shared by many others,[31] is that Western legal education itself creates an ontology – a way of being and knowing – but that this is unacknowledged or obscured by the system of law itself. Legal training can transform or even sever an individual's relation to social change. Too often private institutions lead them to think about law's contribution to social change as principally contained in and explained by 'landmark' cases which become the actual historical event.[32] In understanding law's involvement in social change, the focus remains on the 'landmark' rather than the social upheavals that predate it. Those questions do not interest judges and lawyers within their institutional roles; and the more sophisticated response is that they cannot be of interest for the determination of legal questions because it is said they must stay irrelevant to those determinations. This is not the only possible ontology, and a crucial purpose of these symposia has been to challenge this singularity.[33] As a Wiradjuri jurist and Western trained lawyer, I do not have that same ontology. The conversation between the current authors is a meeting place of the ontologies, a place of hope; that complex issues raised in the cases can be engaged with differently. This meeting of ontologies seeks to provide other constitutional lawyers with the willingness and ability to see these two cases differently; when it comes to Indigenous peoples and our relationship to the 'people' this can – and in our view *must* – be characterised differently. Otherwise for other constitutional lawyers and scholars the issues of the Indigenous space in the cases will be one of a wasted constitutional opportunity. Judges sometimes lament academic opinions on 'wasted opportunities', but judicial refusal or inability to think through race as a constitutional concept is itself revealing about the links and silences lying between Australian constitutional law and Indigenous peoples.

Re-thinking and re-characterising the race power and the Indigenous–State relationship likely starts with a new constitutional attitude towards 1967. How might we re-think the 1967 referendum as a social movement taken up by law? The referendum required and demanded that the relationship between Indigenous peoples and the Commonwealth be characterised in the language of 'benefits' that may come from nationally mandated laws, policies and practices aimed at ameliorating the interruptions to our very lives – as individuals, and as distinct governing bodies. 1967 was the social mandating of a particular relationship between Aboriginal and Torres Strait Islander peoples and nations. The effect must be that constitutional arrangements *must* be capable of recognising that Aboriginal and Torres Strait Islander peoples as exercising their own jurisdictions independent of the Western legal system. The 1967 referendum was the constitutional requirement to pay attention to society's demand that the Commonwealth – through legislative power (that is, the 'people') – have a unique and distinctive legal relationship with Aboriginal and Torres Strait Islander peoples and nations. The 1967 referendum was not merely a grant of legislative power to the

[31]See eg Curthoys, Genovese and Reilly (2008); Dorsett and McVeigh (2007); Black (2011).

[32]See Rajagopal (2003), p 233.

[33]See for example Bauman and Glick (2012), Genovese (2015) and Genovese (2014).

Commonwealth. Articulating it as simply allowing the Commonwealth a head of power denigrates the role and place of the 'people' in the *Constitution*. Further, such characterisation of the legal effects of the 1967 referendum diminishes Aboriginal and Torres Strait Islander legal and jurisdictional capacity within the constitutional framework, placing them *within* the legal framework and *subjected* to the Commonwealth's legislative whim. That was *not* the purpose of the referendum and it certainly was not the understanding of Aboriginal and Torres Strait Islander peoples' expectations when they were encouraging the 'people' to amend their *Constitution*.[34]

Such explanations of the legal effect of the decisions by the High Court in both *Koowarta* and *Tasmanian Dams* misunderstands and diminishes the expectation and demands of Aboriginal and Torres Strait Islander peoples' relationship with the 'people' in Australia's constitutional form. Legal scholars that participate in the perpetuation of legal orthodoxy around Indigeneity and 'race' and the role of the constitutional demand of the 'people' in amending s 51(xxvi) in 1967 are actively perpetuating the misunderstanding of the Court about the legal demands and expectations of Aboriginal and Torres Strait Islander peoples since 1788 and the constitutional relationship that was demanded of the 'people' since 1967. It is frustrating as an Indigenous constitutional lawyer that such connections and conceptions of the relationship between the 'people' and Aboriginal and Torres Strait Islander peoples must be explained in such nuanced terms. For Aboriginal and Torres Strait Islander peoples that have had to experience the *Constitution* in intimate (and often conflicting ways) this *is* the way *we* understand the 1967 referendum. This is the *only* way that I understand s 51(xxvi) as a Wiradjuri jurist and academic and a Western legally trained constitutional and public law scholar. And why? Because this is the way Indigenous people *experience* the race power. It is not merely a change that is observed to give the Commonwealth a head of legislative power. It is the place where I have a constitutional relationship with the 'people'. The referendum created the space in which the Western legal system *must* accept Aboriginal and Torres Strait peoples' distinct legal rights to retain and maintain our distinct place within the Australian governing framework and that any laws passed with respect to us are for our relationship *with* the state and that such laws are fair and do not harm us as Aboriginal and Torres Strait Islander peoples: as all laws should aim to do for all people.

III. *Tasmanian Dams*: heritage, special distinctions and the concept of race

Both *Koowarta* and *Tasmanian Dams* had at their core a fundamental disconnection between Aboriginal peoples (as human beings) and the laws that sought to 'protect' them,[35] supported by the race power. To make any sense of the complexity of this one issue alone (and there were many other legal issues before the Court in both cases) was a monumental judicial undertaking. Each judge in *Tasmanian Dams* reveals a different set of uncertainties and peculiarities about what race actually

[34] *Kartinyeri v Commonwealth* (1998) 195 CLR 337 as per Kirby J.

[35] The *Racial Discrimination Act 1975* (Cth) and the *World Heritage Properties Conservation Act 1983* (Cth), respectively.

means in constitutional interpretation. These problems were raised briefly in *Koowarta* and further developed in *Tasmanian Dams*, but what passes as answers to them ultimately remain divergent and unclear. The lack of clarity in both cases may well be explicable through several factors: the strictures of constitutional jurisprudence; the time within the century that such matters came before the Court; the legal and policy environment in which the cases were being litigated; and the public discourse more generally about rights and their placement within the structure of constitutional arrangements.

In the *Tasmanian Dam Case*, four judges held that ss 8 and 11 of the *World Heritage Properties Conservation Act* were supported by the race power. The general conclusion among the majority – though supported by different reasoning – was that a law protecting cultural heritage is a special law for the purposes of the power because the Aboriginal race has a special need for the protection of its cultural property. For the majority, the fact that the cultural and archaeological sites were of significance to the whole of humankind as well as to the Aboriginal race did not prevent the race power from supporting the law. For the minority, the sites were of significance to all Australia, not just Indigenous peoples, and therefore were not 'special' to the latter. In *Tasmanian Dams* we see further exploration of the difficulties of the race power and now an explicit and close link between race and heritage. Certainly the case did focus on a law protecting heritage, so a close discussion of heritage is to be expected. But ideas of heritage now become a central part of the way a constitutional concept of race is articulated (as nascent as that concept was). The language of heritage as an attribute of the 'Aboriginal' race worth 'protecting' operates to dehumanise us as living humans and limits the possibility of a constitutional exploration of the race power that is not grounded in the intention of the power as enlivened and modified by the 'people' with the 1967 referendum. Each of the judgments, to which we turn now, insofar as they consider race at all, examine it through heritage and, in more sophisticated analyses, culture and identity. We deal with them in order of the attention and consideration they devote to race.

3.1 The majority

The majority in Tasmanian Dams laid the foundation for the conceptions of race that we use today in constitutional interpretation. It may be easy to forget that *at the time* the judges were advancing and grappling with a constitutional conundrum – not of their making – about the silence of 'race' in the courts and in the constitution for 82 years. They were working within the limitations and strictures of judicial decision-making: the issues and arguments as presented to them by the parties, and within the rules of interpretation. Instead of dealing with what is missing in the judgments in comparison with today's understandings, we seek to demonstrate the conundrums that each judge struggled with.

We deal with Mason J first because his judgment does not engage with race as a concept, but instead connects race, culture and heritage through a language of protection, which we suggest is problematic. Rejecting Tasmania's narrow construction that suggested a law supported by s 51(xxvi) must focus on rights between or within racial groups, Mason J took an expansive view of the power, stating that it could support laws '(a) to regulate and control the people of any race in the event that they constitute a threat or problem to the general community, and (b) to protect the people of a race in the event that there is a need to protect them'.[36] The power is about threats, problems or protection connected to a racial group. Mason J accepted that a distinction between injury to individual members of a race and broader injuries to cultural heritage can be drawn, but rejects any need to draw it for a power so broadly expressed. Rather than separating race and heritage, Mason J draws a close association between them, so much so that for the purposes of the law at issue in *Tasmanian Dams*, race becomes effectively synonymous with heritage:

> [T]he cultural heritage of a people is so much of a characteristic or property of the people to whom it belongs that it is inseparably connected with them, so that a legislative power with respect to the people of a race, which confers power to make laws to protect them, necessarily extends to the making of laws protecting their cultural heritage.[37]

The 'inseparable connection' between culture and race extends the reach of the power, articulated as protection. Mason J then moves from the general to the specific: 'A law which protects the cultural heritage of the people of the Aboriginal race constitutes a special law for the purpose of par (xxvi) because the protection of that cultural heritage meets a special need of that people'.[38] Applied here, people of the Aboriginal race have a special need for the protection of cultural heritage. Relics of significance to humankind as a whole may have 'a special and deeper significance' to a particular race: 'Thus an Aboriginal archaeological site which is part of the cultural heritage of people of the Aboriginal race has a special and deeper significance for Aboriginal people than it has for mankind generally'.[39] Besides making this close connection between race, culture and heritage, Mason J avoids any inquiry into the concept of race itself, and ends his analysis there. What is glossed over in this approach is that sites have particular significance for particular groups of Indigenous Australians, as markers of the place and ontology of a particular group. Certainly, the overall heritage of Indigenous Australia is important for people of all Indigenous nations (or really any person), and as Mason J rightly notes, special and deeper significance should not detract from general significance. But connecting particular sites to the 'Aboriginal race' across Australia ignores the diversity of Indigenous nations as political bodies with individual histories and membership. It posits race as the first connection where an Indigenous national one should lie.

Unlike Mason J, the judgments of Murphy J, Deane J and Brennan J each consider the meaning of race itself, albeit in stilted ways. We deal with them in order of increasing attention to the complexities of race as a constitutional concept: Murphy J offers brief reflections, Deane J some consideration, and Brennan J the most consideration that foregrounds race's centrality as a concept though in an ultimately unsatisfactory way.

Murphy J does so briefly, with a simplistic gesture towards the complexity of the idea that draws explicitly on the 1967 Referendum:

[36] *Commonwealth v Tasmania* (1983) 158 CLR 1, at 158.
[37] *Commonwealth v Tasmania* (1983) 158 CLR 1, at 159.
[38] *Commonwealth v Tasmania* (1983) 158 CLR 1, at 159.
[39] *Commonwealth v Tasmania* (1983) 158 CLR 1, at 159.

> Whatever technical meaning 'race' might be given in other contexts, in the *Australian Constitution* it includes the Aboriginal and Torres Strait Islanders and every subdivision of those peoples. To hold otherwise would be to make a mockery of the decision by the people to delete from s 51(xxvi) the words 'other than the aboriginal race in any State' which was manifestly done so that the Parliament could legislate for the maintenance, protection and advancement of the Aboriginal people.[40]

Murphy J likewise looks to the protection of history and culture as a special circumstance. After canvassing a similar dispossession story to that told by Deane J, Murphy J states that

> Because of the attempted genocide of the Aboriginal race in Tasmania, which extended to their customs, tribal structures and culture, a law aimed at the preservation, or the uncovering, of evidence about their history is a special law with respect to the people of this race.[41]

In Murphy J's formulation, the preservation of heritage is not just connected to Aboriginal racial identity, but also a means of redressing past injustices and attempted genocide. An imputed special characteristic of Indigenous people is that they are a race that has suffered wrongs, which may be partly redressed by laws protecting their culture that thereby ensure it – and hence them as a race – is not destroyed.

After briefly considering the Constitution's relationship with Indigenous peoples in Australia and the 1967 Referendum,[42] and placing the movement towards 1967 in the idea that 'Australia, as a nation, must be diminished until acceptable laws be enacted to mitigate the effects of past barbarism' to be achieved by a federal power to pass laws beneficial to the Aboriginal race, Deane J states that it is 'unnecessary, for the purposes of the present case' to consider the meaning of 'people of any race':

> Plainly, the words have a wide and non-technical meaning. The phrase is, in my view, apposite to refer to all Australian Aboriginals collectively … By 'Australian Aboriginal' I mean, in accordance with what I understand to be the conventional meaning of that term, a person of Aboriginal descent, albeit mixed, who identifies himself as such and who is recognized by the Aboriginal community as an Aboriginal.[43]

Deane J expanded have a wide and non-technical meaning. The phrase is, in my view, apposite to refer to all Ae Executive branch since the late 1970s. This case was the first opportunity for the High Court to delve into this test judicially, but it appears here as an aside. It was not central to the resolution of the question in *Tasmanian Dams*, but it is taken up and developed in later cases that do not address s 51(xxvi) but rather statutory references to Aboriginality.[44] The three-part test is

---

[40] *Commonwealth v Tasmania* (1983) 158 CLR 1, at 180. Indeed, the only reference to 1967 in *Koowarta* is an anodyne one by Gibbs CJ: *Koowarta* (1982) 153 CLR 168, p 186.

[41] *Commonwealth v Tasmania* (1983) 158 CLR 1, at 181.

[42] *Commonwealth v Tasmania* (1983) 158 CLR 1, at 272–273.

[43] *Commonwealth v Tasmania* (1983) 158 CLR 1, at 273–274. Citing, like Brennan J, *King-Ansell v Police* [1979] 2 NZLR 531 and *Mandla v Dowell Lee* [1983] QB 1.

[44] See, eg, *Queensland v Wyvill* (1989) 90 ALR 611, p 515 (Drummond J); *Attorney-General (Cth) v Queensland* (1990) 25 FCR 79, p 127 (Jenkinson J); p 132 (Spender J); pp 140, 146

placed on us all today: I [Mark] have a certificate that outlines my fulfilment of this criterion. This test does not make someone a Wiradjuri, Yorta Yorta, Barkindji (or whichever nation that you are born into). The test allows the Western legal system to place you as an Aborigine or Torres Strait Islander. Aboriginal and Torres Strait Islander jurisprudences were still clear and being exercised out of the view of the Western legal system. The test is also a reminder that these jurisdictions and jurisprudences are not predicated or exercisable because of the Western legal system. Turning to race and heritage, Deane J acknowledges the importance of connection to land for 'traditional' Aboriginal culture and life, before stating that, following dispossession and brutal treatment and the establishment of the Australian nation,

> Aboriginal sites which once would have been of particular significance only to the members of a particular tribe are now regarded, by those Australian Aboriginals who have moved, or been born, away from ancient tribal grounds, as part of a general heritage of their own race.[45]

A constitutional rethink of connection to place would have been of particular significance. Lawful connections to place give us our very identity. Indigenous people have long been excluded from Western concepts of ownership. That is not dispossession of our status as Aborigines either. From that we can never (nor must we) navigate away. To suffer dispossession suggests that those connections could have been lawfully taken, and concedes that Indigenous peoples might only be repossessed of those connections at the bequest of the Western legal system. Indigenous people could, nor can, ever be dispossessed of those connections. It is a shortcoming of the Western legal construct to think it could. And yet here, all Indigenous sites, regardless of actual connection to country, are imputed to have significance for all Indigenous people as an 'aboriginal race'.[46] According to Deane J the protection requirement is a dual one: a site must be both of outstanding universal value as well as particular value to people of the Aboriginal race – it is then a law both 'for all Australians' as well as a special law for Aboriginal Australians.[47] Again, a close connection is made between heritage and race as a concept: 'people of any race' covers 'all that goes to make up the personality and identity of the race: spirit, belief, knowledge, tradition and cultural and spiritual heritage'.[48]

While Brennan J makes a significant step forward in locating 'race' as conceptually fundamental for interpreting the race power – indeed, he is the only judge in *Tasmanian Dams* to explicitly deal with race as a concept – his analysis remains ultimately unsatisfactory because it falls back to heritage and culture as a

(French J); *Gibbs v Capewell* (1995) 54 FCR 503, p 506ff; and recently in *Eatock v Bolt* (2011) 197 FCR 261, p 302 (Bromberg J).

[45]*Commonwealth v Tasmania* (1983) 158 CLR 1, p 275.

[46]This can be contrasted with the discussion of 'custodian' connections to relics in *Onus v Alcoa of Australia Ltd* (1981) 149 CLR 27 at 37.

[47]This 'dual' approach, had it been raised in *Koowarta*, might arguably support the *Racial Discrimination Act* as a law both for all Australians as well as having special significance to racial minorities which the law aims to protect; as a 'special law' aimed at races that, by virtue of their race, suffer an additional disadvantage of being subject to racial abuse than white Australians.

[48]*Commonwealth v Tasmania* (1983) 158 CLR 1, p 276.

marker of race. After a brief discussion of the original meaning of the race power, the 1967 amendment is interpreted as 'an affirmation of the will of the Australian people that the odious policies of oppression and neglect of Aboriginal citizens were to be at an end'.[49] Rejecting the narrow focus on changes to 'legal rights, powers or privileges' afforded as a discriminatory benefit to a racial group, Brennan J takes up and extends Stephen J's point in *Koowarta* that special qualities might lie in 'facts dehors the legislation' and also in the concept of race:

> Is it sufficient that the discriminatory benefit is found in the special importance or significance which the people of a race attach to the rights, powers or privileges generally conferred? ... The concept of 'race' suggests the answer.[50]

That concept is 'not a term of art; it is not a precise concept'.[51] Relying on English, New Zealand and international law, Brennan J held that while race had a biological element contained in genetic history and commonality, racial membership extended to common identity found in history, beliefs and culture:

> Membership of a race imports a biological history or origin which is common to other members of the race, but Richardson J is surely right in denying the possibility of proving ultimate genetic ancestry ... I do not think his Honour was propounding his 'real test' of common regard as being conclusive or exhaustive ... Physical similarities, and a common history, a common religion or spiritual beliefs and a common culture are factors that tend to create a sense of identity among members of a race and to which others have regard in identifying people as members of a race ... [these commonalities indicate] the scope and purpose of the power granted by par (xxvi). The kinds of benefits [are ones] which tend to protect or foster their common intangible heritage or their common sense of identity.[52]

Commonalities underpinning racial identity inform the scope and purpose of the power. Brennan J appears to take up Stephen J's suggestion in *Koowarta* that the focus should be on effect not form: the law need not be special in its terms, but may simply be special in operation.[53] The Act protects sites that are of 'particular significance', which, though incapable of precise definition, means those that are of 'neither minimal nor ephemeral' importance.[54] Applied to Aboriginal and Torres Strait Islanders, the significance of the site may be 'found by the Aboriginal people in their history, in their religion or spiritual beliefs, or in their culture'.[55] The relevant special group then, is 'a group of whatever size who, having a common Aboriginal biological history, find the site to be of that significance', and to conclude otherwise

[49] *Commonwealth v Tasmania* (1983) 158 CLR 1, at 242.

[50] *Commonwealth v Tasmania* (1983) 158 CLR 1, at 242–243. See *Koowarta* (1982) 153 CLR 168, 211 (Stephen J).

[51] *Commonwealth v Tasmania* (1983) 158 CLR 1, at 243.

[52] *Commonwealth v Tasmania* (1983) 158 CLR 1, at 244. Referring to *King-Ansell v Police* [1979] 2 NZLR 531, at 542ff (Richardson J).

[53] *Commonwealth v Tasmania* (1983) 158 CLR 1, at 245. See *Koowarta* (1982) 153 CLR 168, 211 (Stephen J).

[54] *Commonwealth v Tasmania* (1983) 158 CLR 1, at 245.

[55] *Commonwealth v Tasmania* (1983) 158 CLR 1, at 245.

would be inconsistent with 'the high purpose which the Australian people intended' in 1967.[56] Here there is certainly an advance on Mason J's formulation; the significance of a site need not attach to the 'Aboriginal race' as a whole, but only to a specific group holding a connection to a particular place. But the invocation of 1967 here is hollow. We read it as acting only as a 'brake' on less favourable interpretations; its significance beyond simply broadening protection – and in particular as changing the concept of race itself that Brennan J acknowledges is important for the races power – is not explored.[57] Brennan J's concept of a constitutional race, then, is a group with biological commonalities that share culture, beliefs, history. Section 51(xxvi) supports laws that 'protect or foster' that identity or heritage of such a group. Identity and heritage form the core of Brennan J's concept of a constitutional race. Again, while this formulation of the concept is articulated in the context of heritage laws at issue in *Tasmanian Dams* and a strong link between race and heritage is understandable, it remains problematic for the reasons outlined above regarding Mason J's connection between race, culture and heritage. More fundamentally, articulating the constitutional concept of race as partly subsumed under heritage seems unthinkable when applied to other races, and particularly the white race: for what could be considered 'white culture' and what measures would serve to protect it? Aboriginality, Indigeneity and identity are not heritage, and do not derive their enduring power from the past alone. They have agency and reality today, evidenced by Indigenous peoples in their thousands, citizens of hundreds of distinct nations. Brennan J grapples with these problems far better than the other judges – and in its most favourable light his concept joins heritage with identity – but nonetheless we still find the presence of heritage in a constitutional concept of race, that is to be forward looking and apply equally beyond the posited 'Aboriginal race' to be a problematic conclusion. Finally, the majority judges do not contemplate the possibility of Indigenous laws, existing, operating, and connected to place. Nor should they have. At that time, the judges do not have the modern concept of race nor Indigenous jurisdictions and jurisprudence. Law is not among the several aspects of racial identify raised by the majority. The significance of these sites is drawn from the past; their importance does not extend into the future, even though new custodians and responsibilities are created within Indigenous jurisdictions. This case – and witnessing the struggles of the judges – allowed us to form new understandings and opportunities of, and for, understanding Indigenous laws and jurisdictions. Current judges should be able to take the difficulties expressed by the judges in the case and now contemplate such Indigenous laws and their relationship to the Anglo-Australian legal system.

3.2 The minority

The Minority Judges each ignore race as a concept, and resolve the s 51(xxvi) issue on the 'special' law requirement of the paragraph by subsuming 'particular' significance for Indigenous people under general significance for Australian heritage as a whole. Like the majority, the minority judges link race and heritage. In denying

[56] *Commonwealth v Tasmania* (1983) 158 CLR 1, at 245.

[57] *Commonwealth v Tasmania* (1983) 158 CLR 1, at 245–246.

'specialness', however, they also appropriate Indigenous culture and heritage into Australia as a whole, eliding any significance to particular Indigenous nations. A nation founded without national concern for Indigenous peoples or culture, becomes the wider beneficiary of the culture it sought to destroy, on behalf of the people it sought to destroy. Further still, Indigenous culture in the minority judges' treatment seems to hold the glint of museum pieces: these things belong to us all because their cultural significance is fixed and generated from the past, rather than as part of an enduring, living culture contributed to and continued by today's Indigenous peoples. For Gibbs CJ, universal heritage trumped local importance:

> Although the protection or conservation of a site to which s 11 applies must be of particular significance to the people of the Aboriginal race, the site itself must be of outstanding universal value, since otherwise it cannot form part of the cultural heritage or natural heritage. A site which may be of very great significance to the people of the Aboriginal race will not be within the section if it is not of outstanding universal value.[58]

Site protection attaches to this universal significance, and 'not to the preservation of any particular feature of the site which may give it significance to members of the Aboriginal race'.[59] Most importantly for Gibbs CJ, special significance is not connected to the regulations because Aboriginal people gain no special rights, privileges or obligations in relation to a site, and hold no better rights of access or special immunity from s 11 than any other person.[60] The narrow, legalistic need for a connection between special rights and racial characteristics precludes any wider appreciation of significance for particular people: 'Artefacts and relics of such antiquity are of significance to all mankind; a law for their protection is not a special law for the people of any one race'.[61] Wilson J, like Gibbs CJ, focused on the generality of the law and subsumed specific significance under universal significance:

> ... the law serves the interest of the Aboriginal people in the sites in question and any artefacts or relics on them by protecting them against damage or destruction. But in so doing it is serving, at the same time and by the same law, the interest of a much wider constituency, the whole of mankind.[62]

Special laws must be aimed at 'a problem that is peculiar to the people of a particular race'. Dawson J similarly distinguished between 'special application' in the sense of a law having greater significance or importance for one racial group and 'special application in a legal sense' in creating a distinction between 'those people and others in the rights which [the law] confers or the obligations which it imposes'.[63] Protected Aboriginal sites 'are, by definition, part of the cultural or natural heritage of the nation ... There may be, and probably are, Aboriginal sites or artefacts or relics which are far more significant to the people of the Aboriginal race,

---

[58] *Commonwealth v Tasmania* (1983) 158 CLR 1, at 110.
[59] *Commonwealth v Tasmania* (1983) 158 CLR 1, at 110.
[60] *Commonwealth v Tasmania* (1983) 158 CLR 1, at 110.
[61] *Commonwealth v Tasmania* (1983) 158 CLR 1, at 111.
[62] *Commonwealth v Tasmania* (1983) 158 CLR 1, at 203.
[63] *Commonwealth v Tasmania* (1983) 158 CLR 1, at 320.

but the Act has nothing to say about them'.[64] What is common to the minority judges is a strict emphasis on legalism, playing out in various ways: the universal excludes the particular, connections must be made between rights and obligations and racial characteristics, the Act must treat these explicitly as having special operation in a legal sense. Race is just another word.

IV. Conclusions

Writing extra-curially of the chimerical nature of the race power, Chief Justice French noted in 2010 that it reflects 'both the nineteenth-century social Darwinism which gave it birth in 1901 and the inclusive worldview that led to its amendment in 1967'.[65] While social Darwinism is not endorsed in the judgments in *Koowarta* or *Tasmanian Dams*, and the purportedly 'scientific' gloss associated with theories of race is explicitly disapproved in some of the judgments,[66] the assumptions central to that worldview – that races exist, that they have shared characteristics, some of which are disadvantages – remain. Those assumptions are then linked to the possibility that races might have 'special' characteristics, disadvantages, threats or problems that legislation may address. Certainly some acknowledgement of non-racial factual bases for these characteristics is made – particularly by Stephen J in *Koowarta* and Brennan J in *Tasmanian Dams* – but there is still an assumption that specialness might inhere in a race as a whole. For all the recognition of 'an outdated, false and harmful taxonomy of humanity' made with undoubted sincerity,[67] the operation of this power, as capable of supporting *any* law at all, still requires taking up and giving effect to an assumption that race is capable of disclosing truths about special disadvantages, threats, problems, fears, protection.

If we take seriously the reality of socially constructed racial groups, then the race power construed through special characteristics must be seen as incoherent and incapable of supporting any law because we can no longer speak of characteristics tracking anything meaningful in a race. Race – as either an ordinary or constitutional concept – is indeterminate. Such an approach would not require the Court to substitute its own evaluation for the Parliament's as to what is necessary or special.[68] Instead it would acknowledge that s 51(xxvi) no longer refers to anything known to our society or the members of it who sit in Parliament. The legacy of 1967 might be finally realised. A best result would be the repeal of the race power and its replacement with a power specifically aimed at advancing the interests of Aboriginal and Torres Strait Islander peoples.[69] This repeal is warranted because the question of the meaning of the term 'race', however the text is formulated, cannot be competently addressed by any court or any parliament with the definiteness that constitutional interpretation demands. Any attempt to give it content falls back to the legacies of centuries we thought were left behind. But in the absence of that

[64]*Commonwealth v Tasmania* (1983) 158 CLR 1, at 321.

[65]French (2010) 180.

[66]See, eg, *Commonwealth v Tasmania* (1983) 158 CLR 1, p 243ff (Brennan J).

[67]See, eg, French (2010), p 181.

[68]See *Kartinyeri v Commonwealth* (1998) 195 CLR 337.

[69]Expert Panel (2012) ch 5.

repeal, acknowledging the indeterminacy of race is the only development we might expect. None of this is how Aboriginal and Torres Strait Islanders view your jurisprudence and bear witness to your lawfulness. This is what we expect of your constitutional interpretation of 'race' and 'Aboriginality'.

Reference List

Books, Articles, Reports

Elisa Arcioni and Adrienne Stone (2015) 'Australian Constitutional Culture and the Social Role of the Constitution' *International Journal of Constitutional Law* (forthcoming).

Bain Attwood and Andrew Markus (2007) *The 1967 Referendum: Race, Power and the Australian Constitution*, 2nd edn, Aboriginal Studies Press.

Toni Bauman and Lydia Glick (eds) (2012) *The Limits of Change: Mabo and Native Title 20 Years On*, Australian Institute of Aboriginal and Torres Strait Islander Studies, Canberra.

C F Black (2011) *The Land is the Source of the Law: A Dialogic Encounter with Indigenous Jurisprudence*, Routledge-Cavendish.

Sean Brennan and Megan Davis (2014) *Koowarta*: Constitutional Landmark, Transition Point or Missed Opportunity 23(1) *Griffith Law Review* 79.

Alex C Castles (1982) *An Australian Legal History*, Law Book Co.

Shaunnagh Dorsett and Shaun McVeigh (2012) *Jurisdiction,* Routledge.

Expert Panel on Constitutional Recognition of Indigenous Australians (2012) 'Recognising Aboriginal and Torres Strait Islander Peoples in the Constitution'.

Robert French (2010) 'The Race Power: A Constitutional Chimera' in HP Lee and George Winterton (eds), *Australian Constitutional Landmarks*, Cambridge University Press, 180.

Ann Curthoys, Ann Genovese and Alexander Riley (2008) *Rights and Redemption: History, Law and Indigenous People*, Sydney, University of New South Wales Press.

Ann Genovese (2014) 'Critical Decision, 1982: Remembering *Koowarta v Bjelke-Petersen*' 23 (1) *Griffith Law Review* 1.

Ann Genovese (2015) 'Critical Decision 1983: Remembering *Commonwealth v Tasmania*' 24(1) *Griffith Law Review* 1–15.

Justin Malbon (1999) 'The Race Power under the Australian Constitution: Altered Meanings' 21 *Sydney Law Review* 80.

Mark McMillan (2014) 'Koowarta and the Rival Indigenous International: Our place as Indigenous Peoples in the International' 23(1) *Griffith Law Review* 110–126.

Shaun McVeigh and Shaunnagh Dorsett (2007) 'Questions of Jurisdiction' in Shaun McVeigh (ed), *Jurisprudence of Jurisdiction*, Routledge-Cavendish, 3.

Balakrishnan Rajagopal (2003) *International Law from Below: Development, Social Movements and Third World Resistance*, Cambridge University Press.

Alexander Reilly (1999) 'Reading the Race Power: A Hermeneutic Analysis' 23 *Melbourne University Law Review* 476.

Geoffrey Sawer (1966) 'The Australian Constitution and the Australian Aborigine' 2 *Federal Law Review* 17.

Colin Tatz (1999) 'Genocide in Australia', Research Discussion Paper No 8, Australian Institute of Aboriginal and Torres Strait Islander Studies.

John Williams and John Bradsen (1997) 'The Perils of Inclusion: The Constitution and the Race Power' 19 *Adelaide Law Review* 95.

Case Law

Attorney-General (Cth) v Queensland (1990) 25 FCR 79

Cole v Whitfield (1988) 165 CLR 360

Commonwealth v Tasmania (1983) 158 CLR 1

Eatock v Bolt (2011) 197 FCR 261

Gibbs v Capewell (1995) 54 FCR 503

Kartinyeri v Commonwealth (1998) 195 CLR 337

King-Ansell v Police [1979] 2 NZLR 531
Koowarta v Bjelke-Petersen (1982) 153 CLR 168
Western Australia v Commonwealth (1995) 183 CLR 373 (*Native Title Act Case*)
Mandla v Dowell Lee [1983] QB 1
Queensland v Wyvill (1989) 90 ALR 611
Strickland v Rocla Concrete Pipes Ltd (1971) 124 CLR 468.

Legislation, Conventions and Transcripts
Commonwealth v Tasmania [1983] HCATrans 24 (3 June 1986)
Commonwealth v Tasmania [1983] HCATrans 26 (8 June 1983)

Law and the practices of 'damming': *Tasmanian Dams Case* as a turning point

Lee Godden

Melbourne Law School, The University of Melbourne

Synopsis

By contrast to many analyses of *Commonwealth v Tasmania (Tasmanian Dam case)*, this article focuses on what the case reveals about the damming of rivers and the role of law in constituting institutions, technologies and practices for that purpose. Australia was colonised by a civilisation that had embedded a technical utilisation of rivers within its laws. Damming rivers, as a reified practice was fostered by modern, technical knowledge. That knowledge displaced other knowledges; including Aboriginal traditional knowledge of land and waters. In 1983, law held the promise of instantiating a new dynamic for human interaction with rivers, as the *Tasmanian Dam's case* juxtaposed the international principles of environmental protection with the centralised control over water by large, bureaucratic state agencies that had developed in Australia over the twentieth century. The judgments of Chief Justice Gibbs and Justice Brennan are remarkable for the contrasting visions of dams that they reveal. Yet the dam, and even the river itself, have largely been occluded form legal memory; although the legacy of the case as a platform for later environmental legislation has been significant.

Introduction

The people who colonised Australia from the well-watered lands of the United Kingdom and Europe were to become water-dreamers.[1] The civilisation and law that they brought with them presupposed an abundant water supply.[2] In Australia, by contrast, the search for adequate water to support a transplanted civilisation would shape early exploration and contribute to the dispossession of Aboriginal peoples.[3] As visions of vast inland seas and mighty continental rivers receded, the dreaming took a more prosaic and technical turn by the mid to late nineteenth century. Water dreaming turned to making the desert bloom by harnessing technical, engineering and bureaucratic expertise necessary to dam building and the associated water distribution infrastructure. Dam building became not simply a means of transgressing harsh environmental limits, but so integral to how European civilisation settled itself within Australia as to become virtually invisible – water dreaming became reified through the physical manifestation of building dams on rivers.

[1]Cathcart (2009), p 4.

[2]Fisher (2000), pp 4–5 and 65–66. See also, *Gartner v Kidman* (1962) 108 CLR 12, 23. The very concept of a watercourse is challenged by Australia's physiography.

[3]Giblett (2007), p 41, Morgan (2006), p 138.

From the turn of the twentieth century, few questioned the state control of water to allow an expanding program of damming, and the public funds expended to support commercial agriculture, industry and growing populations.[4] The inheritance of modern thinking about the natural world that came with European civilisation was mobilised in the relationships created with the rivers, billabongs, creeks, swamps and groundwater of inland Australia, many of which were progressively converted into resources for development.[5] Over time, the building and imagining of dams, and the conversion of rivers for these purposes, effected a 'structural coupling' between socio-economic systems and rivers within Australia.[6] Law supported that linkage with the introduction of major statutory regimes governing water allocation and use from the late nineteenth century.[7] The potential to break open the highly reified construct of 'the dam', and to refashion the character of the relationships between people and rivers within Australia, surfaced in the public arena with the proposal to dam the Gordon below Franklin River in Tasmania in the early 1980s.

The campaign mounted in opposition to the proposed hydroelectricity dam in Tasmania culminated in the High Court's decision in *Commonwealth v Tasmania*[8] *(Tasmanian Dam case)*. The archiving of the case in legal memory marks it with signifiers of constitutional law;[9] of a disputed federalism;[10] Australia's international obligations;[11] and, less prominently, with a national environmental law.[12] While cognisant of the significance of the case in those registers, this article focuses on what the case reveals about the actuality of damming rivers and the role of law in constituting institutions, technologies and practices for that purpose.

Modern practices of damming are predicated upon a technical knowledge of rivers that emphasises the spheres of human action and purpose, as separate from the natural world.[13] The turning point precipitating the *Tasmanian Dam case* was the emergence of an environmental conservation ethic in Australian society that crystallised the reification of long-accepted practices of damming rivers.[14] The emergence of environmental consciousness made transparent the human actions and purpose that shaped and ordered the natural world, and which juxtaposed the practices of damming with the possibility of alternative framings for relationships with rivers. In this alternative view, dams are revealed, not as a necessity, but as a

---

[4]For example, see *Irrigation Act 1886* Victoria, and the establishment of the State Rivers and Water Supply Commission in 1905.

[5]Weir (2009), p 3.

[6]Structural coupling within systems' theory suggests that bio-physical and social elements exist in a dynamic relationship of interconnection; see for example, Ison (2010).

[7]McKay (2008), p 47.

[8]*Commonwealth v Tasmania* (1983) 158 CLR 1.

[9]Coper (1983), pp 1–2.

[10]Grinlinton (1990), p 74.

[11]Boer (1992).

[12]Peel and Godden (2005), p 668.

[13]Weir (2009), p 3.

[14]Environmental groups challenged major project developments from the mid 1970s. See for example, *Australian Conservation Foundation Inc v Commonwealth* (1980) 146 CLR 493.

contingent technological, social and legal artefact.[15] In 1983, law held the promise of instantiating a new dynamic for human interaction with rivers – a dynamic captured by reference to the outstanding universal heritage values articulated in the *World Heritage Convention.*[16] Examination of the dam proposed for the Gordon below Franklin River, and indeed of the river itself, receives relatively minimal attention in the judgments.

The reification of damming as an accepted means of shaping human interactions with rivers transcends the *Tasmanian Dam's* dispute. The modality of 'damming', as a set of normative practices, exists in relatively stable form in many societies.[17] Water law, and its instantiation of damming in 'hydraulic civilisations' is discussed below as a historical phenomenon, before considering how these ideas informed the focus upon nation-building that was associated with the damming of rivers in Australia prior to the *Tasmanian Dam case*. The case, and its reinforcement of Commonwealth legislative power, strongly influenced the subsequent development of Australian water law and energy policy. It provided the framework for later challenges to dam projects that were initiated under the judicial review provisions of the *Environment Protection and Biodiversity Conservation Act* 1999 – the successor to the legislation challenged in the *Tasmanian Dam case*. The 'anti-dams' sentiment is now waning, as indicated by the adoption of policies to promote dams as a major plank in the development of Northern Australia.

The co-evolution of damming and 'hydraulic civilisations'

From the perspective of an evolutionary model of history, techniques of damming rivers are seen as having co-evolved with societies, commencing from 'primitive' forms and progressing to 'modern' western, scientific knowledge.[18] All forms of damming fundamentally influence the relationship that communities have with rivers. Accordingly, legal rules governing how water is used and appropriated, in concert with technologies for the storage and diversion of water, enable water to be available for agricultural production, energy and myriad industrial and subsistence uses. The lens of evolutionary progress has been highly persuasive in shaping hierarchical constructs of civilisations by prioritising modern scientific knowledge and its instrumental understanding of rivers.

Thus, the technology of storing and diverting water for irrigation and power supply is regarded as a central modality of 'civilisation'. According to this perspective, societies utilise rationality and associated technologies of damming and irrigation systems – often formalised by legal rules – to allow the fixity of a settled system of production in order to support increasingly complex social and economic forms. By contrast, Mitchell critiques the view of a dam as the outcome of a singular application of human reason. Ideas and technology do not precede the

---

[15]For a discussion of dams as artefacts, see D'Souza (2006), p 5.

[16]*Convention for the Protection of the World Cultural and Natural Heritage*, opened for signature 16 November 1972, 1037 UNTS 151 (entered into force 17 December 1975) (*World Heritage Convention*). Australia ratified the Convention on 22 August 1974.

[17]For discussion of how practices constitute a 'modality', see Humberto Maturana Romesin (2002).

[18]Weir (2009), p 21.

damming of rivers, 'as pure systems of thought brought to bear on the messy world of reality';[19] rather, pure science is embedded within the social fabric and its implicit values. However, the putatively instrumental approach to rivers has prevailed.

Similarly, it is a moot point in legal scholarship whether water law was a determining factor in the development of western societies, or whether water law forms part of the 'superstructure' that emerged from the exploitation of water.[20] Getzler, in his study of the derivation of the common law governing water, argues that law was 'central to England's precocious economic development' in the thirteenth to sixteenth centuries,[21] as the medieval economy was heavily dependent on water power. In a later period of commercialisation and industrialisation, 'property rights' based in the riparian doctrine, as it was established by the English courts and legislature, reformed the law in ambivalent synchrony with economic development.[22]

Conflicts over water use in rivers in the United Kingdom exemplify how practices around damming became formalised as, 'medieval doctrines were adapted and simplified as judges sought legal solutions to economic problems.'[23] The riparian doctrine focussed on local resolution of conflicts. The governing rules were oriented towards resolving the respective rights of upstream and downstream users of rivers, in the context of the increasing upstream diversion of water from the rivers, driven by an expanding technology of mills, dams, weirs and channels.[24] The doctrine mediated the rights of respective landowners along a water course, rather than managing water diversions within a wider river catchment.

An assumed convergence between the damming of rivers and the emergence of civilisations spawned the hydraulic civilisations' thesis. It was propounded by Marx and Engels at a time when European industrialisation was leaving behind its dependency on water power. The thesis proposed that 'pre-modern' Asiatic societies were 'despotic and slave owning', due to the need to build and maintain irrigation technologies. In turn, these technologies required centralised bureaucratic and legal institutions to institute those measures.[25] More recent scholarship situates water governance and 'associated' social and economic forms in a more contested space. As Sultana and Loftus suggest, 'struggles over water have, undertaken different forms, reworking spaces, scales and peoples in complex ways, underscoring that discursive and material struggles over water are bound up with questions of power and governance'.[26] Analysis of the practices of damming in societies therefore must engage with 'major transformations in the regimes for control and use of water, and the consequent conflicts over water that they entail, [which in turn] need to be located in wider generative structures.'[27] These views temper an evolutionary model

---

[19]Mitchell (2002), p 52.

[20]Rose (1990), p 261.

[21]Getzler (2004), p 1.

[22]Getzler (2004), p 5.

[23]Getzler (2004), p 6.

[24]For a general discussion on common law riparian principles, see Gardner et al (2009), chp 2.

[25]See discussion in Getzler (2004), p 9.

[26]Sultana and Loftus (2012), p 5.

[27]D'Souza (2006), p 27.

of history that benchmarks the indicia of the technical 'progress' of western civilisations.[28] A one-dimensional equation of damming practices with civilisation therefore should be avoided, but it is possible to discern 'hydraulic civilisations' – both 'pre-modern' and 'modern' – where complex bureaucratic and normative orders to support engineering technologies for damming rivers are an integral component of the laws in those societies.[29] Arguably, Australia is a society that is still characterised by large bureaucratic structures for water management.[30]

Modern western societies and dams in river basins

Damming rivers to enhance productivity across a large river basin became a robust twentieth-century development ideal that transcended earlier localised controls on rivers. At one level, the river basin presents itself as a neutral concept, apparently uncontroversial as the physical delineation of a watershed; the 'natural' unit for planning and managing water resources by societies.[31] Molle, however, traces the emergence of a river basin – as opposed to a single river or watercourse – in western knowledge, to the period of colonial expansion, commencing in the eighteenth century. Premised upon the advent of empirical science and geographical exploration, its emergence underpinned western European expansion into territories (and rivers) occupied and used by indigenous communities.[32] Over time, the river basin became a key organising construct for managing rivers and their environs.[33]

In the mid nineteenth century, the concept also became progressively aligned with managed hydrological regimes for rivers as 'the river basin gradually became a tenet of productivism.'[34] Explicit ideals of controlling nature were embodied in these goals of managed river basins,[35] as '[t]he epistemology of technology makes it possible for the physical and human worlds to coexist as independent categories that can be manipulated … into desired nature-society relationships.'[36] The consequent objectification of water as a resource[37] contributed to the primacy of technical knowledge of rivers, while rendering other knowledges invisible.[38] Hence the reification of dams, and the practices of damming neutralised structural and localised conflicts over water.[39] Knowledge of rivers was not seen as embedded within cultural and social narratives,[40]

[28] *Case Concerning the Gabčikovo-Nagymaros Project* (1997) ICJ Reports 7, pp 88–119 (Vice President Weeramantry).
[29] De Silva (2005), p 40.
[30] The most recent iteration being the Murray-Darling Basin Authority initiated under the *Water Act 2007* (Cth).
[31] Molle (2009), p 484.
[32] Molle (2009), p 484.
[33] For a discussion of 'hard law' and 'soft law' in governing river basins, see Johns et al (2012).
[34] Molle (2009), p 486.
[35] Weir (2009), p 8.
[36] D'Souza (2006), p 47.
[37] Weir (2004), p 14.
[38] Giblett (2007).
[39] D'Souza (2006), p 30.
[40] Ison (2010), chp 1.

but rather as part of the institutional arrangements by which a society informs itself about the 'natural world' of rivers.[41] Large dams, as complex infrastructure projects, shape landscapes, harness environmental resources, and significantly modify the socio-cultural environment.[42]

Therefore, while the practices of damming are embedded in complex systems, it is technology that has enabled dam projects on an enormous scale. Modern binary-thinking which is central to technology, is pivotal to dam building.[43] In the post-war period, the dam became the quintessential project for securing national development ambitions.[44] The Aswan Dam is an archetype where 'modern thinking informed the rationale of the project ...but the reality was a complex engagement of many actors.'[45] The mixing of water, nature, culture, and human agency ultimately produced the artefact of the dam.[46]

Similarly, the dam gathered significant momentum as a 'development project' in post-colonial India.[47] Dams were integral to policies that sought to realise social visions – India 'created an artefact first, and then hoped the artefact would induce social change'.[48] The failure of many major dam projects to effectively realise social change and economic independence, led to acute critique of the massive-scale engineering projects initiated by international organisations such as the World Bank.[49] Internationally, large dam projects have continued to be controversial, especially when their construction transcends country borders.

A perceptive understanding of how law should govern disputes over dams informs the Separate Opinion of Vice-President Weeramantry in the International Court of Justice's decision in *Hungary v Slovakia* (*Gabčíkovo-Nagymaros Dam Project*).[50] The *Gabčíkovo-Nagymaros Dam* dispute echoes the conflict in the *Tasmanian Dam case* in juxtaposing environmental concerns about the impacts of a dam on the Danube River, with the need to develop water resources for power supply to enhance economic productivity. The dispute arose almost contemporaneously with that in the *Tasmanian Dam case*.

Briefly, the dispute concerned the construction of a series of barrages and a dam project on the Danube River that had been agreed in a bilateral treaty between Hungary and Czechoslovakia (later Slovakia); engineering work had commenced on the barrages. In 1988, following considerable public pressure, the Hungarian parliament resolved that ecological concerns should take priority, and ultimately Hungary suspended works. Slovakia unilaterally diverted water from the Danube River as the dispute heightened. As its defence for not proceeding, and in its submissions before the Court, Hungary raised an ecological necessity argument

---

[41]Cheney et al (2007).

[42]Slinger et al (2011).

[43]Mitchell (2002), p 9.

[44]D'Souza (2006), chp 15.

[45]Mitchell (2002), p 10.

[46]For a discussion of the artefact concept, see Maturana and Poerksen (2004); Giddens (1984).

[47]D'Souza (2006), chp 2.

[48]D'Souza (2006), p 7.

[49]D'Souza (2006), p 31.

[50]*Case Concerning the Gabčíkovo-Nagymaros Project* (1997) ICJ Reports 7, p 88.

about irreparable damage to its downstream aquatic environment that it argued would be caused by the dam. Slovakia argued that the project was necessary to the welfare of its people, bringing benefits of flood control, and electricity production.

Justice Weeramantry proposed sustainable development as a set of governing principles to resolve the dispute,[51] drawing the principles, in part from Sri Lanka's early history, which centred dam building in a Buddhist philosophy of environmental care. Thus, the central tenet of a 'necessarily despotic' hydraulic civilisation was rejected.[52] His Opinion concludes that 'reference to the practice and philosophy of a major irrigation civilisation of the pre-modern world illustrates that when technology on this scale was attempted it was accompanied by a due concern for the environment'.[53]

The Opinion stands as a landmark in bringing together analysis of the past and present practices of the damming of rivers, and in constituting sustainable development as a guiding principle for managing rivers and river basins, in contrast to the prevailing instrumental views. More generally, the principle of a defence of ecological necessity, as raised by Hungary, was accepted by the Court; although, it was held not to be substantiated on the facts, as no grave or imminent peril was identified that could serve as a defence for Hungary's action.[54] Ultimately, the Court found both parties in breach of treaty obligations.[55] As the dispute over the damming of the Danube was re-shaping international environmental law principles, concurrently Australia was experiencing similar changes, which were strongly influenced by this evolving body of international environmental law.

The practices of damming within Australia

In Australia, the practices of damming also have a long history, and can be traced back at least 5000 years; for example, to the fish traps of western Victoria, built by Aboriginal communities.[56] Damming of several watercourses by the Gunditjmara peoples produced large eel ponds, requiring a sophisticated utilisation of the contours of the physical landscape, and technical requirements for rock wall building:

> Dating back thousands of years, the area shows evidence of a large, settled Aboriginal community systematically farming eels for food and trade in what is considered to be one Australia's earliest and largest aquaculture ventures. This complex enterprise took place in a landscape carved by natural forces and full of meaning for the Aboriginals who lived there.[57]

In 2007, the determination of native title over this area of south-western Victoria drew heavily upon the evidence of aquaculture, and dam-building, as a critical

---

[51] *Case Concerning the Gabčikovo-Nagymaros Project* (1997) ICJ Reports 7, p 89.

[52] *Case Concerning the Gabčikovo-Nagymaros Project* (1997) ICJ Reports 7, p 103.

[53] *Case Concerning the Gabčikovo-Nagymaros Project* (1997) ICJ Reports 7, p 104.

[54] *Case Concerning the Gabčikovo-Nagymaros Project* (1997) ICJ Reports 7, pp 39–46.

[55] For further discussion, see Sands and Peel (2012), p 305.

[56] Head (1989), p 10; *Lovett on behalf of the Gunditjmara People v State of Victoria* [2007] FCA 474 at 3.

[57] *Lovett on behalf of the Gunditjmara People v State of Victoria* [2007] FCA 474 at 2.

component in proving that Aboriginal people had a connection with traditional country that pre-dated colonisation.[58]

Prior to British colonisation, Aboriginal water management occurred across Australia, drawing upon sophisticated knowledge of water availability and its sustainable utilisation.[59] Supported by modern water management, the practices and institutions of damming have only recently – and very inconsistently – begun to incorporate Aboriginal peoples' views about their relationships with rivers.[60]

Australian water law largely remains predicated upon the efficient utilisation of rivers.[61] Yet perversely, the imagining and building of dams has rested upon a mythology, where communities seek to deny the realities of Australia's arid and highly variable ecological systems.[62] Australians continue to contest that reality into the future by persisting in an overwhelming reliance upon dams and large-scale infrastructure projects for water supply and power generation.[63]

Damming as a technical intervention is designed to manage the intense variability of rainfall across the continent that produces periods of 'drought and flooding rains'.[64] That variability is one of the most extreme in the world, and contributes to a situation where dams, proportionally, need to have very large storage capacity.[65] A substantial component of in-stream water use occurs for hydroelectricity generation in Tasmania.[66]

Interventions in river systems have been so extensive in parts of Australia, particularly in the south-east corner, that the concept of a 'natural' river is problematic. The Murray-Darling River is an example of such a highly regulated system with its series of weirs, dams and reservoirs. The Murray-Darling Basin Authority which 'runs' the river, controls the river flows in seasonal contrast to any 'natural cycle.'[67] This reversal of flows serves the needs of irrigated agricultural production, and reflects the legacy of the state-sponsored dam building schemes that proliferated from the early twentieth century.[68]

As noted by Musgrave, 'having vested control of water, created the necessary bureaucratic agencies, and having the necessary political will to proceed the [(Murray-Darling] basin states were ready to construct the storages and infrastructure to enable the establishment of substantial areas of government-sponsored irrigation farming.'[69] Large, state-sponsored dam projects were not confined to irrigated agriculture. The Commonwealth government was the major driver of the

---

[58]*Lovett on behalf of the Gunditjmara People v State of Victoria* [2007] FCA 474 at 5.

[59]Morgan et al (2006).

[60]Jackson and Langton (2012).

[61]Crase (2008), p 2.

[62]Musgrave (2008), p 38.

[63]Crase (2008), p 7.

[64]Slinger et al (2011).

[65]Australian Bureau of Statistics (2011). Over 500 'large' dams in Australia have a combined capacity of 83,853 gl as at June 2005.

[66]Duncan and Kellow (2008), p 109.

[67]Weir (2009), chp 2.

[68]Musgrave (2008), p 35.

[69]Musgrave (2008), p 35.

Snowy Mountains' scheme; Australia's largest hydroelectricity generation project. Commenced under Commonwealth war-time emergency powers, the scheme was seen as a monument to Australian nation-building, but proved to be a more controversial development with the passage of time.[70]

The rationale for state-sponsored dams was 'the achievement of specific hydraulic and engineering objectives ... vigorously executed with high levels of technical expertise and utility – there was no legislated obligation to consider external consequences.'[71] While some doubts were raised about the economic viability of irrigation schemes, the creation of water storages continued apace until the late 1960s. From the early 1970s, trenchant economic critique of irrigated agriculture and the building of dams began to appear.[72] In concert, there were emerging concerns about environmental consequences.[73] The legitimacy of the legal and institutional structures built around the artefacts of controlled river basins and large-scale dams began to rupture. Water law reforms, which commenced in the 1980s, gained strong momentum. Eventually, the package emerged as the Council of Australian Government's structural adjustment package – the 2004 *National Water Initiative*.[74]

By the early 1980s, the critique of damming within Australia led to a virtual cessation of large-scale dam projects on the mainland,[75] coinciding with a global river conservation movement, as the Danube River dispute illustrates.[76] Nonetheless, Australian public agencies have continued to invest heavily in water and natural resource management; more recently, to ensure environmental sustainability.[77]

In Tasmania, the island state, the picture was somewhat different. With a more mountainous landscape and a temperate climate, Tasmania did not invest as heavily in irrigated agriculture and associated water storages. Nonetheless, its economy remained heavily dependent upon natural resource exploitation. Hydroelectricity generation was the central reason for large-scale dam construction. With over 50 dams and 24 power stations currently in the system, Tasmania maintains the highest water usage for hydroelectricity generation of any Australian state.[78] Duncan and Kellow note that 'development of water power became a de facto state development policy, for much of the development of hydro potential in Tasmania occurred with the express purpose of developing not just water power, but the state's natural resources'.[79]

---

[70]Musgrave (2008), p 38. See also, Duncan and Kellow (2008), p 117.

[71]Ward (2000), p 27.

[72]The seminal work is Davidson (1969).

[73]Musgrave (2008), p 39.

[74]Council of Australian Governments, *Intergovernmental Agreement on Addressing Water Over-allocation and Achieving Environmental Objectives in the Murray Darling Basin* (2004); Council of Australian Governments, *Intergovernmental Agreement on a National Water Initiative* (2004).

[75]Musgrave (2008), p 38.

[76]Slinger et al (2011), p 35.

[77]The Commonwealth Environmental Water Holder (a statutory authority) is now the major 'owner' of water entitlements in Australia. See Part 6 of the *Water Act 2007* (Cth).

[78]Duncan and Kellow (2008), p 109.

[79]Duncan and Kellow (2008), p 111.

The Hydro-Electricity Commission – forerunner to the current Hydro Tasmania – was a major state utility that, like the water agencies in the irrigation sector, operated within a modern knowledge framework dominated by engineering and technical expertise. Public funding of the extensive infrastructure to produce power was largely unquestioned, until the conflict over the damming of the Gordon below Franklin River. More recently, Hydro Tasmania has transformed itself from dam-builder to renewable energy company.[80] At the time of the Tasmanian Dam dispute, the Hydro Electricity Commission clearly saw itself as a dam-builder with a mandate to develop the water resource potential of the Gordon below Franklin in the public interest.

Dams as conflict points within Australia

The *Tasmanian Dam's* dispute was one of many conflicts that arose in the 1980s, where the respective powers of state governments to develop natural resources, was tested against the extent of Commonwealth legislative competence for environmental protection.[81] The lack of an express Commonwealth environmental legislative power, together with the history of control exercised by states,[82] suggested that respective states had central responsibility for water management – and thereby dam construction. Conservation approaches, on the other hand, drawing upon a growing ecological knowledge suggested that a national, and even an international, approach to environmental protection was warranted.[83] Conflicts arose as community groups asserted the need to protect 'wild rivers'.

Lake Pedder and Tasmanian Dams case

For more than half a century, Tasmania has figured prominently in conflicts around natural resource use. Early Tasmanian disputes were an important rallying point for the nascent environmental movement in Australia.[84] In the late 1960s, the state, its administration, and statutory utilities were dominated by a view that dams were integral to the future prosperity of Tasmania, based on cheap hydroelectricity. In 1967, the Tasmanian Hydroelectricity Commission instigated a proposal for a new power scheme that would flood Lake Pedder.[85] A campaign to save the lake

---

[80]Duncan and Kellow (2008), p 114.

[81]The only provision of the *Commonwealth of Australian Constitution Act 1900* ('the Constitution') to deal expressly with natural resource issues is section 100, which prohibits the Commonwealth 'by any law or regulation of trade or commerce' abridging 'the right of a State or of the residents therein to the reasonable use of the waters of rivers for conservation or irrigation.'

[82]Crawford (1991), p 13. See also, Grinlinton (1990), p 77.

[83]Internationally, countries attending the Stockholm Conference on the Human Environment in June 1972 agreed that '[t]he protection and improvement of the human environment is a major issue which affects the well-being of peoples and economic development throughout the world; it is the urgent desire of the peoples of the whole world and the duty of all Governments': *Declaration of the United Nations Conference on the Human Environment* (1972) 11 ILM 1416, 1416; (1973) UN Doc A/Conf.48/14/Rev. 1.

[84]Hutton and Connors (1999), p 118.

[85]Hutton and Connors (1999), p 119.

ultimately failed. Like other water and power authority counterparts within Australia at that time, the Commission was largely unaccountable for its decisions in relation to rivers, and water use in general.[86] Even today, the Hydro authority retains considerable control over state water resources.[87]

Despite the defeat around Lake Pedder, a national conservation movement was growing. It was highly influential in opposing the next Hydro Electricity Commission proposal to build a large hydro-electric dam in a world heritage listed area.[88] Formed in the mid 1970s, the Tasmanian Wilderness Society was integral to the campaign challenging the dam.[89] As the conflict escalated, the 'No dams' symbol adopted by the campaign, garnered national support.[90] The Franklin River was portrayed as a wild and untrammelled river, with the iconic photograph of Rock Island Bend appearing on thousands of election posters in the first national environmental media campaign. The blockade of the river was one of the largest civic protests within Australian history. These movements signalled a major shift in how the Australian community configured its relationship with rivers. The strength of the movement to protect the Franklin River represented a surprising radicalism for a traditionally conservative Australian public that had rarely challenged the nation-building ethos of governments and statutory authorities.

With an electoral mandate,[91] the Hawke Labor government enacted the *World Heritage Properties Conservation Act 1983* (Cth) to domestically implement the *World Heritage Convention*.[92] The World Heritage nomination for the South-west wilderness, in which the Franklin River is located, was based upon outstanding universal natural heritage and cultural heritage values. The legislation, based principally on the Commonwealth's external affairs' and corporations' powers,[93] expressly prohibited the various works necessary to construct the dam without approval from the Commonwealth Environment Minister.[94] In turn, Tasmania, together with other states, challenged the Commonwealth legislation before the High Court. Thus, the question of whether to dam a Tasmanian river became a conflict about the scope of national legislative power.

The conflict over the dam assumed significance well beyond its mere physical impacts. Where once, the symbol of the dam promised unity and common purpose

---

[86]Duncan and Kellow (2008), p 116.

[87]Hydro Tasmania still retains priority access to a large component of Tasmania's water. See Duncan and Kellow (2008), p 117.

[88]See Boer (1992), p 247.

[89]Hutton and Connors (1999).

[90]Hutton and Connors (1999).

[91]Hutton and Connors (1999), p 163.

[92]Boer (1992), p 136. Boer notes that this Act was the only statute enacted by a party to the Convention to ensure its domestic implementation.

[93]Boer (1992), p 136. The Commonwealth government also sought to rely on the 'race' power to support provisions of the *World Heritage Properties Conservation Act 1983* given that 'much of Australia's distinctive heritage of universal value consists of relics of Aboriginal culture': Commonwealth, *Parliamentary Debates*, House of Representatives (21 April 1983), pp 46–52 (Mr Cohen, Minister for Home Affairs and the Environment).

[94]*World Heritage Properties Conservation Act 1983* (Cth), ss 9 and 10. This Act was repealed with enactment of the *Environment Protection and Biodiversity Act 1999* (Cth).

as a nation of water dreamers, it now threatened conflict and fragmentation. This fragmentation of views was reflected in the majority judgments in the High Court, with a 4-3 decision in favour of the validity of the Commonwealth legislation.[95] By majority, the decision confirmed that Australia's obligations under an international treaty entered into in good faith,[96] enlivened the exercise of the external affairs power.[97] Justice Murphy held that:

> [t]he co-operation of Australia with other nation States to preserve the world cultural and natural heritage falls easily within the external affairs power ... It is also part of Australia's external affairs to co-operate with others, each nation doing what it can to preserve the sites within its area, as part of a web of international regulation and supervision of such sites.[98]

Overall though, the Court sought to distance itself from national political implications. At the outset of the judgments, the Court proclaimed:

> The questions concern the validity of certain Commonwealth Acts, regulations and proclamations which have been brought into being for the immediate purpose of preventing the construction of the Gordon below Franklin Dam. They are strictly legal questions. The Court is in no way concerned with the question whether it is desirable or undesirable, either on the whole or from any particular point of view, that the construction of the dam should proceed.[99]

Although the Court based its decision upon 'strictly legal grounds', in articulating the matters for decision, it highlighted particular insights into competing representations of damming. Chief Justice Gibbs, who ultimately held the Commonwealth law invalid, and the Tasmanian Hydroelectricity laws as valid, set out the facts about the dam:

> The construction of the dam, and of associated works, including a power station, is authorized by the *Gordon River Hydro-Electric Power Development Act 1982* (Tas.), a law of Tasmania which came into force on 12th July 1982. The construction work commenced on 14th July 1982. The dam ... will dam the waters of the Gordon River to a maximum depth, at the toe of the dam, of approximately 84 metres, will raise the levels of the Franklin River and other tributaries and will have a storage capacity of about 2,700 million cubic metres. The power station will add about 180 megawatts on average to the capacity of the Tasmanian electricity generating system ...[100]

The statement of relevant facts emphasises the physical properties of the dam, and its productive capacity, followed by a brief statement of the characteristic of the area to be flooded.

---

[95]Fisher (2010).

[96]*Commonwealth v Tasmania* (1983) 158 CLR 1 at 121–122 (Mason J); p 129 (Brennan J).

[97]*Commonwealth v Tasmania* (1983) 158 CLR 1 at 121 (Mason J); pp 171–172 (Murphy J).

[98]*Commonwealth v Tasmania* (1983) 158 CLR 1 at 174.

[99]*Commonwealth v Tasmania* (1983) 158 CLR 1 at 58.

[100]*Commonwealth v Tasmania* (1983) 158 CLR 1 at 59–60.

> [T]he government of Tasmania wishes to proceed with the Gordon below Franklin Scheme ... since it considers that the ability to generate electricity at low cost by this means is necessary to enable the State to achieve economic growth and to increase the opportunities for employment. However, the government of the Commonwealth wishes to stop the construction of the dam, which it considers will inundate significant Aboriginal archaeological sites, and will cause damage to a wilderness area ... which satisfies the criteria for listing on the World Heritage List ...[101]

Thus what is remarkable, in the extract from the judgment, is the apparent fascination with the technicality and engineering complexities of the dam, with matters such as the depth of the waters being raised, whereas discussion of the wilderness area and river are much less detailed. By contrast, Justice Brennan, who decided the legal issues differently, begins his judgment with the wilderness areas:

> Three separate areas of land known respectively as the Cradle Mountain Lake St. Clair National Park, the Franklin Lower Gordon Wild Rivers National Park and the Southwest National Park in the south western part of Tasmania were proclaimed or were deemed to be proclaimed to be State reserves ... The three parks are known collectively as the Western Tasmania Wilderness National Parks ... Within the boundaries of the Franklin Lower Gordon Wild Rivers National Park (hereafter the Wild Rivers Park) lies the junction of the Franklin River with the Gordon River. A short distance below the confluence of the two rivers there is a site on the Gordon River suitable for the construction of a dam.[102]

Justice Brennan carefully names the wilderness areas, situates the Gordon below Franklin River within them, and only then, identifies the site for the proposed dam. The disjunction between the different views of the dam in the two judgments arguably reflects wider perceptions, which contrast the 'engineering' knowledge of rivers and the technical achievements of damming, against an emerging environmental consciousness that situated a dam as an object, as an artefact – almost 'out of place' within the unique natural heritage areas.

The dam, and even the river itself, is largely obscured in the other judgments in the *Tasmanian Dam case*, which focus attention on the scope of international obligations under the *World Heritage Convention*, and the validity of the Commonwealth law in implementing those obligations. Justice Mason, for example, simply refers to an area of 14,125 hectares that 'comprises the site of the dam and associated works and the major part of the water storage area behind the dam'.[103] He notes that the dam site is a small part only of the World Heritage area. The practices of damming are masked by a focus on the legitimacy of the respective regimes of control (federal or state) to be exercised over these lands and waters.[104]

---

[101] *Commonwealth v Tasmania* (1983) 158 CLR 1 at 60.

[102] *Commonwealth v Tasmania* (1983) 158 CLR 1 at 205.

[103] *Commonwealth v Tasmania* (1983) 158 CLR 1 at 137 (Mason J).

[104] See for example, *Commonwealth v Tasmania* (1983) 158 CLR 1 at 143. Mason J discusses whether the Commonwealth 'regime of control' will impact upon Tasmania's capacity to control development.

Damming after the Tasmanian Dam Case

In confirming the validity of the Commonwealth's legislative powers, the *Tasmanian Dam case* was a political shear in Australia's federal fabric.[105] Most legal commentary regards these matters as the pivotal turning point of the decision. Much less remarked upon is the legal impetus given to a social movement that challenged the bureaucratic control of rivers. The *Tasmanian Dam case* marked a point of departure from a predominantly state-centric model for water management and energy production.[106] The disputes around the dam fractured accepted practices that had allowed large public agencies to centralise control over water, and also highlighted the growing ambivalence toward modern river-basin management, which was opening up within Australian society. The *Tasmanian Dam case* marked a period when relatively fewer dams were built. Attention turned to promoting sustainability and the efficient use of water resources, rather than a continued focus upon building more dams to expand water supply.

Ironically, while the *Tasmanian Dam case* affirmed the Commonwealth's constitutional power to legislate for environmental protection, natural resource disputes continued, driven by states' rights arguments, which proved tenacious.[107] Later decisions, including the *Lemonthyme Forestry* case,[108] and the *Wet Tropics case*,[109] reaffirmed the Commonwealth's legislative power to override state-based natural resource management and project development. The *Tasmanian Dam* case provided the platform for the enactment of a range of Commonwealth environmental legislation.[110]

After a period of considerable tension, Commonwealth–state conflict receded with the rise of a policy of 'cooperative federalism'.[111] This policy culminated in the Commonwealth's agreement to limit its involvement in environmental protection to 'matters of national environmental significance'.[112] The narrowed basis for Commonwealth involvement took practical shape in the omnibus environmental legislation, the *Environment Protection and Biodiversity Conservation Act 1999* (Cth) ('EPBC Act'), as the successor legislation to the *World Heritage Properties Conservation Act 1983* (Cth).

Challenges after the Tasmanian Dam Case

Following the Tasmanian dam conflict and the emergence of national environmental legislation, projects likely to have a significant impact on a matter of national environmental significance are subject to mandated environmental impact

[105] *Commonwealth v Tasmania* (1983) 158 CLR 1 at 131 (Mason J); p 172 (Murphy J); p 232 (Brennan J) and p 259 (Deane J). See also, *Richardson v Forestry Commission* (1988) 164 CLR 261 at 289 (Mason CJ and Brennan J).

[106] Dryzek (2005), p 75.

[107] Crawford (1991), p 11.

[108] *Richardson v Forestry Commission* (1988) 164 CLR 261.

[109] *Queensland v Commonwealth* (1989) 167 CLR 232.

[110] See Lindell (1999).

[111] The cooperative approach to environmental management was formalised by Commonwealth, State and local governments in the *Inter-Governmental Agreement on the Environment*, 1 May 1992 (IGAE).

[112] See the *Heads of Agreement on Commonwealth/State Roles and Responsibilities for the Environment* (HoA) concluded at the Council of Australian Governments (CoAG) meeting in December 1997, [3].

assessment and approval at a Commonwealth level.[113] More recently, there has been devolution of decision-making for major projects to state governments through the adoption of 'approval' bilateral agreements between the Commonwealth and State Governments.[114]

Dam projects have continued to be politically and legally controversial. Another high profile case, *Nathan Dams*, reached the Full Federal Court in 2003.[115] A proposal for a large dam on the Dawson River in Central Queensland, which promised a significant boost to economic growth, was referred to the Commonwealth Environment Minister for decision as to whether it was a controlled action under the EPBC Act.[116] Environmental groups had raised the possibility of adverse environmental effects of the proposed dam upon the Great Barrier Reef, a listed property under the *World Heritage Convention*. Ultimately, the Full Federal Court held that the cumulative impacts of the downstream effects of the dam on the Great Barrier Reef should be considered in assessing the environmental impacts of the proposed dam.[117]

State governments have adopted a relatively conservative approach, with few dam projects being proposed, even as the effects of the millennium drought created problems in maintaining water supply to urban areas.[118] In 2006, the proposed Traveston Crossing dam on the Mary River, which aimed to boost urban water supply to Brisbane, was one of a handful of projects not approved by the Commonwealth government under the EPBC Act. The grounds for refusal were the significant impact on listed threatened species, including the endangered lung fish that has its habitat in the Mary River.[119] Community groups have continued to agitate against the possibility of a dam on the Mary River in Queensland.[120] Desalination plants have been a more favoured policy option in the context of severe water shortages.[121] However, in the last few years, there has been a resurgence of dam building. Major Commonwealth policy papers and inquiries into the future of water supply and energy production in Northern Australia have been undertaken.[122] The numbers of

---

[113]See, for example, *Environment Protection and Biodiversity Conservation Act 1999* (Cth) ss 12–24.

[114]See *Environment Protection and Biodiversity Conservation Act 1999* (Cth) ss 44–65A.

[115]See *Minister for the Environment & Heritage v Queensland Conservation Council* (2004) 139 FCR 24 (Full Federal Court). The Full Federal Court upheld the decision of Justice Kiefel in the earlier case of *Queensland Conservation Council Inc v Minister for the Environment & Heritage* [2003] FCA 1463. The Full Federal Court decision was not appealed by the Commonwealth Environment Minister to the High Court.

[116]*Environment Protection and Biodiversity Conservation Act 1999* (Cth) s 75.

[117]Godden and Peel (2010), p 674.

[118]For discussion of the range of adaptation to water scarcity that emerged, see Poh-Ling Tan (2010).

[119]Australian Government, Department of Environment, Heritage, Water and the Arts, Refusal of Approval Traveston Crossing Dam, http://www.environment.gov.au/epbc/notices/assessments/2006/3150/refusal-approval.pdf.

[120]See the Save the Mary River website at http://www.savethemaryriver.com/drpl/, accessed 1 May 2015.

[121]See Barnett and O'Neill (2010), pp 211–213.

[122]Department of Industry, Parliament of Australia, *Energy White Paper: Green Paper* (2014) http://ewp.industry.gov.au/files/egp/energy_green_paper.pdf; Joint Select Committee on Northern Australia, Parliament of Australia, *Pivot North: Inquiry into the Development of*

large-scale dams being approved may escalate if the controversial policy of 'Northern Development' is implemented.[123] The policy of northern development is being pursued vigorously by the Commonwealth government, in concert with the Western Australian, Queensland and Northern Territory governments – with an eye to the relatively 'under-utilised' water resources of northern rivers.[124]

The ramifications of the *Tasmanian Dam case* have been significant for other areas of water law, river basin management, and environmental protection. Confirmation of the Commonwealth's powers to legislate in respect of international obligations for environmental protection were a significant component of the foundation for the Commonwealth *Water Act* in 2007 – arguably the most significant shift in Australian water law in a century of predominantly state-based water governance.[125]

Conclusion: a global reassessment of dams?

Despite the legacy of the *Tasmanian Dam case*, and some forty years of experience with environmental legislation in Australia, many of the same tensions around the damming of rivers, that gave rise to the Franklin River dispute, remain. A core community critique is that assessment is an administrative hurdle to the realisation of dam projects, rather than an engagement with possible alternatives to damming rivers. Public participation is regarded as tokenistic, rather than meaningful.[126] For many Australians, and particularly Aboriginal people, the existential meaning of a river itself is still buried beneath a concern with projects, planning and risk management that obscures a deeper ontological commitment to rivers.[127] As Weir comments in her study of Aboriginal people's relationship to the intensely controlled Murray River:

> Traditional owners offer a deep understanding of ethical relationships with rivers, the ecological life along rivers and river country. Often referred to as 'being connected' the traditional owners appreciate the rivers as being embedded within networks of relationships. This is in stark contrast to modern water management that interprets river water as a mute resource – undifferentiated and unconnected.[128]

Despite the murmurings of other ways of knowing rivers and water, river basin management maintains its orientation towards the deployment of scientific expertise.

Northern Australia - Final Report (2014) http://www.aph.gov.au/Parliamentary_Business/Committees/Joint/Northern_Australia/Inquiry_into_the_Development_of_Northern_Australia/Tabled_Reports.

[123]See for example, 'Green groups react angrily to Abbott government's development plans for northern Australia', *Sydney Morning Herald*, http://www.smh.com.au/federal-politics/political-news/green-groups-react-angrily-to-abbott-governments-development-plans-for-northern-australia-20140610-39vdq.html, 14 June 2014.

[124]See Office for Northern Australia and the Commonwealth's forthcoming White Paper on Developing northern Australia, http://northernaustralia.dpmc.gov.au/

[125]For a discussion of these changes and their federal impact, see Gardner (2012).

[126]Holley and Sinclair (2013), p 52.

[127]Weir (2009), p 46.

[128]Weir (2009), p 47.

The institutions and the legal frameworks that govern rivers still struggle to encompass the social and cultural values of rivers.[129] Legal ruptures, such as the *Tasmanian Dam case*, reinforce the notion that dams are more than just a physical 'intervention' controlling rivers and managing river catchments for utilitarian ends. Dams are part of a complex legal, organisational, socio-economic, and a cultural performative that stabilises as a set of 'damming practices'.[130]

Dams as 'artefact' mediate in significant ways, the relationship between people and rivers within Australia, and perpetuate our water dreaming. Damming practices have produced agencies to control rivers with wide legal and economic powers for the co-option of water. The water 'controlling' institutions, and indeed water law, draw heavily upon modern knowledge that privileges technical understanding of rivers. The linking of that knowledge with legal rules on water use has distinguished many societies over time.

The capacity to manage environmental risks, and to hedge against the 'drought and flooding rains' of the Australian continent, have been major motivating mythologies in the nation building narratives that have supported dam construction in much of Australia's post-colonisation history. At turning points, these reified practices become more transparent, illuminating dams as a source of social, political and legal conflict. The Franklin dam conflict was the platform for challenging the necessity of damming rivers, offering a countervailing imagining of rivers, that continues to be asserted – even if only partially, and at times, ineffectually – in law, through the *Environment Protection and Biodiversity Act 1999*.

Ironically, even in the *Tasmanian Dam case*, the conflict about damming rivers plays a relatively small role in the legal analysis; although, the judgments of Chief Justice Gibbs and Justice Brennan are remarkable in the contrasting vision of dams that each of them presents. Over time, the legal memory of the case has virtually occluded the iconography of the river and the Tasmanian wilderness through which it flows. The facts of the proposal to build a dam on the Gordon below Franklin River are rehearsed as the preliminary to consideration of more significant issues of constitutional law, and Australia's international obligations under the *World Heritage Convention*.

Yet the international dimensions of the Tasmanian dam's conflict are not only matters of constitutional import, but illustrative of the influence of a worldwide environmental movement of such cogency that it re-ordered trans-jurisdictional water governance and infrastructure projects in countries as far flung as Australia and Hungary; and, coalesced the knowledge of sustainability principles from past and present civilisations. The UNESCO *World Heritage Convention* itself owes its genesis, in part, to the damming of the Nile River.[131] The practices of the damming of rivers have shaped law more profoundly than is often acknowledged. In remembering *Commonwealth v Tasmania*, the resonance of the case as one involving a conflict over the damming of a river should not be forgotten.

---

[129]Mackinnon (2007).

[130]Law and Urry (2004).

[131]A major impetus for the Convention was the need to remove cultural heritage items due to the flooding of the Nile Valley by the Aswan High Dam.

Acknowledgements

The author gratefully acknowledges the contribution made to this article by a number of people. First, many ideas were initially discussed in collaborative work with Professor Ray Ison and Dr Phil Wallis, Monash Sustainability Centre. Second, much of the over-arching inspiration for the article was provided by Dr Ann Genovese in developing the turning points theme for the *Commonwealth v Tasmania* symposium and the Special Issue of the GLR. The Melbourne Law School Research Service, in particular Robin Gardner and Cate Read, was wonderful in the research and editorial support that was offered. Finally the GLR editors were very patient about extended time frames. I thank them all for allowing me the opportunity to develop the article.

References

Secondary Sources

Australian Bureau of Statistics (2011) 'Water Account, Australia, 2009-10' http://www.abs.gov.au/AUSSTATS/abs@.nsf/DetailsPage/4610.02009-10?OpenDocument

Jon Barnett and Saffron O'Neill (2010) 'Maladaptation' 20 *Global Environmental Change* 211.

Ben Boer (1992) 'World Heritage Disputes in Australia' 7 *Journal of Environmental Law and Litigation* 247.

Michael Cathcart (2009) *The Water Dreamers: The Remarkable History of our Dry Continent*, Text.

Helen Cheney et al (2007) 'Weirs and Flows in the Hawkesbury-Nepean' in Emily Potter et al (eds) *Fresh Water: New Perspectives on Water in Australia*, Melbourne University Press.

Michael Coper (1983) *The Franklin Dam Case: Commentary and Full Text of the Decision in* Commonwealth of Australia v State of Tasmania, Butterworths.

Lin Crase (2008) 'An Introduction to Australian Water Policy' in Lin Crase (ed) *Water Policy in Australia: The Impact of Change and Uncertainty*, Resources for the Future.

James Crawford (1991) 'The Constitution and the Environment' 13 *Sydney Law Review* 11.

Bruce Davidson (1969) *Australia, Wet or Dry? The Physical and Economic Limits to the Expansion of Irrigation*, Melbourne University Press.

Robyn Duncan and Aynsley Kellow (2008) 'Hydroelectricity' in Lin Crase (ed) *Water Policy in Australia: The Impact of Change and Uncertainty*, Resources for the Future.

John Dryzek (2005) *The Politics of the Earth: Environmental Discourses*, Oxford University Press.

K M de Silva (revised ed, 2005) *A History of Sri Lanka*, Vijitha Yapa Publications.

Radha D'Souza (2006) *Interstate Disputes over Krishna Waters: Law, Science and Imperialism*, Orient Longman.

Douglas E Fisher (2000) *Water Law*, LBC Information Services.

Douglas E Fisher (2007) 'Delivering the National Water Initiative: The Emergence of Innovative Legal Doctrine' in Karen Hussey and Stephen Dovers (eds) *Managing Water for Australia: The Social and Institutional Challenges*, CSIRO Publishing.

Douglas Fisher (2010) *Australian Environmental Law: Norms, Principles and Rules*, Lawbook Co.

Anita Foerster (2012) 'Emerging Environmental Water Governance in Australia' 22(2–3) *Journal of Water Law* 58.

Alex Gardner et al (2009) *Water Resources Law*, LexisNexis Butterworths.

Alex Gardner (2012) 'Water Reform and the Federal System' in Paul Kildea et al (eds) *Tomorrow's Federation: Reforming Australian Government*, Federation Press.

Joshua Getzler (2004) *A History of Water Rights at Common Law*, Oxford University Press.

Rod Giblett (2007) 'Black and White Water' in Emily Potter et al (eds) *Fresh Water: New Perspectives on Water in Australia*, Melbourne University Press.

Anthony Giddens (1984) *The Constitution of Society: Outline of the Theory of Structuration*, University of California Press.

Marion Glaser et al (2008) 'Human/Nature Interaction in the Anthropocene: Potential of Social-ecological Systems Analysis' http://www.dg-humanoekologie.de/pdf/DGH-Mitteilungen/GAIA200801_77_80.pdf.

Lee Godden and Mahala Gunther (2010) 'Realising Capacity: Indigenous Involvement in Water Law and Policy Reform in South-Eastern Australia' 20 *Journal of Water Law* 243.

Lee Godden and Jacqueline Peel (2010) *Environmental Law: Scientific, Policy and Regulatory Dimensions*, Oxford University Press.

David Grinlinton (1990) 'The "Environmental Era" and the Emergence of "Environmental Law" in Australia – A Survey of Environmental Legislation and Litigation 1967-1987' 7 *Environmental Planning & Law Journal* 74.

Lesley Head (1989) 'Using Palaeoecology to Date Aboriginal Fishtraps at Lake Condah, Victoria' 24 *Archaeology in Oceania* 110.

Cameron Holley and Darren Sinclair (2013) 'Deliberative Participation, Environmental Law and Collaborative Governance: Insights from Surface and Groundwater Studies' 30 *Environmental and Planning Law Journal* 32.

Drew Hutton and Libby Connors (1999) *A History of the Australian Environment Movement*, Cambridge University Press.

Ray Ison (2010) *Systems Practice: How to Act in a Climate Change World*, Springer.

Sue Jackson and Marcia Langton (2012) 'Trends in the Recognition of Indigenous Water Needs in Australian Water Reform: The Limitations of "Cultural" Entitlements in Achieving Water Equity' 22 *Journal of Water Law* 109.

Fleur Johns, B Saul, P Hirsch, T Stephens and B Boer (2010) 'Law and the Mekong River Basin: A Socio-legal Research Agenda on the Role of Hard and Soft Law in Regulating Transboundary Water Resources' 11(1) *Melbourne Journal of International Law* 154.

John Law and John Urry (2004) 'Enacting the Social' 33 *Economy and Society* 390.

Geoff Lindell (1999) 'Scope of the Commonwealth's Environmental Powers and Responsibilities' in Paul Leadbeter et al (eds) *Environmental Outlook No.3 : Law and Policy*, Federation Press.

Humberto Maturana Romesin (2002) 'Autopoiesis, Structural Coupling and Cognition: A History of These and Other Notions in the Biology of Cognition' 9(3–4) *Cybernetics and Human Knowing* 5.

Humberto Maturana and Bernhard Poerksen (2004) *From Being to Doing: The Origins of the Biology of Cognition*, Carl Auer Verlag.

Alison Mackinnon (2007) 'River Memory: Narratives of Generation, Hope and Amnesia' in Emily Potter et al (eds) *Fresh Water: New Perspectives on Water in Australia*, Melbourne University Press.

Jennifer McKay (2008) 'The Legal Frameworks of Australian Water: Progression from Common Law to Sustainable Shares' in Lin Crase (ed) *Water Policy in Australia: The Impact of Change and Uncertainty.*

Timothy Mitchell (2002) *Rule of Experts: Egypt, Techno-politics, Modernity*, University of California Press.

François Molle (2009) 'River-basin Planning and Management: The Social Life of a Concept' 40 *Geoforum* 484.

Monica Morgan et al (2006) 'Authority, Knowledge and Values: Indigenous Nations Engagement in the Management of Natural Resources in the Murray-Darling Basin' in Marcia Langton et al (eds) *Settling with Indigenous People: Modern Treaty and Agreement-making*, Federation Press.

Warren Musgrave (2008) 'Historical Development of Water Resources in Australia' in Lin Crase (ed) *Water Policy in Australia: The Impact of Change and Uncertainty*, Resources For The Future.

Jacqueline Peel and Lee Godden (2005) 'Australian Environmental Management: A "Dams" Story' 28(3) *University of New South Wales Law Journal* 668.

Carol M Rose (1990) 'Energy and Efficiency in the Realignment of Common-Law Water Rights' 19 *Journal of Legal Studies* 261.

Phillipe Sands and Jacqueline Peel (2012) 'Freshwater Resources' in *Principles of International Environmental Law*, Cambridge University Press.

Jill Slinger et al (2011) 'The Governance of Large Dams: A New Research Area' in Michael R van der Valk and Penelope Keenan (eds) *Principles of Good Governance at Different Water Governance Levels* http://www.unesco.nl/sites/default/files/dossier/water_governance.pdg_.pdf.

Farhana Sultana and Alex Loftus (2012) *The Right to Water: Politics, Governance and Social Struggles*, Earthscan.

Poh-Ling Tan (2010) 'Adaptation Measures for Water Security in a Changing Climate: Policy, Planning and Law' in Tim Bonyhady et al (eds) *Adaptation to Climate Change: Law and Policy*, Federation Press.

James Emerson Tennent (2nd edn, 1859) *Ceylon: An Account of the Island: Physical, Historical and Topographical: With Notices of its Natural History, Antiquities and Productions* (Volume 2), Longman, Green, Longman and Roberts.

John Ward (2002) 'The Evolution of Water Management in Australia' in John Tisdell et al (eds) *The Development of Water Reform in Australia*, CRC For Catchment Hydrology.

Jessica Weir (2009) *Murray River Country: An Ecological Dialogue with Traditional Owners*, Aboriginal Studies Press.

Primary Legal Sources

International Agreements

Convention Concerning the Protection of the World Cultural and Natural Heritage, opened for signature 16 November 1972, 1037 UNTS 151 (entered into force 17 December 1975). *Declaration of the United Nations Conference on the Human Environment* (1972) 11 ILM 1416; (1973) UN Doc A/Conf.48/14/Rev. 1.

Government Documents

Australia, *Intergovernmental Agreement on the Environment* (1992).

Australia. Department of the Environment and Heritage & Council of Australian Governments, *Heads of Agreement on Commonwealth and State Roles and Responsibilities for the Environment* (1997).

Council of Australian Governments, *Intergovernmental Agreement on Addressing Water Overallocation and Achieving Environmental Objectives in the Murray Darling Basin* (2004).

Council of Australian Governments, *Intergovernmental Agreement on a National Water Initiative* (2004).

Cases

Case Concerning the Gabcikovo-Nagymaros Project (1997) ICJ Reports 7.

Commonwealth v Tasmania (1983) 158 CLR 1.

Gartner v Kidman (1962) 108 CLR 12.

Koowarta v Bjelke-Petersen (1982) 153 CLR 168.

Lovett on behalf of the Gunditjmara People v State of Victoria [2007] FCA 474.

Minister for the Environment and Heritage v Queensland Conservation Council Inc (2004)139 FCR 24.

Queensland v Commonwealth (1989) 167 CLR 232.

Queensland Conservation Council Inc v Minister for the Environment and Heritage [2003] FCA 1463.

Richardson v Forestry Commission (1988) 164 CLR 261.

Legislation

Commonwealth of Australian Constitution Act 1900 (The Constitution).

Environment Protection and Biodiversity Conservation Act 1999 (Cth).

Water Act 2007 (Cth).

World Heritage Properties Conservation Act 1983 (Cth).

Index

Note: Page numbers followed by 'n' refer to notes

For Product Safety Concerns and Information please contact our EU
representative GPSR@taylorandfrancis.com
Taylor & Francis Verlag GmbH, Kaufingerstraße 24, 80331 München, Germany

www.ingramcontent.com/pod-product-compliance
Ingram Content Group UK Ltd.
Pitfield, Milton Keynes, MK11 3LW, UK
UKHW050054200926
475702UK00019B/2823

9780367077068